Modern Motherhood

Modern Motherhood

An American History

JODI VANDENBERG-DAVES

RUTGERS UNIVERSITY PRESS
NEW BRUNSWICK, NEW JERSEY, AND LONDON

Library of Congress Cataloging-in-Publication Data

Vandenberg-Daves, Jodi.
  Modern motherhood : an American history / Jodi Vandenberg-Daves.
      pages cm
  Includes bibliographical references and index.
  ISBN 978–0–8135–6379–4 (hardcover : alk. paper)—ISBN 978–0–8135–6378–7 (pbk. : alk. paper)—ISBN 978–0–8135–6380–0 (e-book)
  1. Families—United States—History. 2. Motherhood—United States—History. 3. Mothers—United States—History. I. Title.
  HQ535.V36 2014
  306.874'3—dc23   2013027195

A British Cataloging-in-Publication record for this book is available from the British Library.

Visit our website: http://rutgerspress.rutgers.edu

Manufactured in the United States of America

To my children, Allison, Sylvia, and Brad Vandenberg-Daves

And to all mothers, past, present, and future

Contents

PART III

Mothers of Invention: World War II to the Present

Acknowledgments

Years go by while a person labors over a book like this, about six years in this case, a significant chapter in a lifetime. I am extremely grateful to those who supported me along the way, contributed ideas, and made the often solitary journey less lonely. This project has been generously supported by the University of Wisconsin–La Crosse, the College of Liberal Studies (CLS) and my home department, Women's, Gender, and Sexuality Studies. A CLS Sabbatical Grant, a UW–La Crosse Faculty Research Grant, a UW–La Crosse Faculty Development Grant, a CLS Small Grant, crucial release time from teaching, and an atmosphere of constant encouragement in my department made this book possible. I want to especially thank Dean Ruth-ann Benson and my department chair, Deb Hoskins. At an institution with a heavy teaching load, it is a rare faculty member whose department chair asks her, "What do you really need to get this book done?" and then works with the dean to make it happen. Deb's leadership and dedication to genuinely supporting the work of her colleagues are incomparable.

I also appreciate the support of Rima Apple, whose work I have admired for many years and whose perceptive critiques, suggestions, and kind encouragement of this project came at critical junctures. Special thanks, too, to Andrea O'Reilly and the Motherhood Initiative for Research and Community Involvement (MIRCI). Andrea's leadership of MIRCI and her personal collegiality have nurtured my thinking about mothering and motherhood for more than a decade. Dr. Apple's and Dr. O'Reilly's works inform this book, as do the works of several generations of scholars whose names are scattered throughout my endnotes. This book is a tribute to the collective work of great historical and feminist minds, and I hope I have done them some justice in these pages. Among these scholars, a special note of thanks to Sara M. Evans, my Ph.D. adviser, who originally gave me a model of accessible historical writing, and to Norman Rosenberg, Peter Rachleff, James Stewart, and Emily Rosenberg, who first taught me how to think historically. Thanks also for the expertise of Leslie Mitchner, my editor at Rutgers University Press, who saw the potential of this book immediately and supported its development along the way.

Special thank yous, as well, to Adi Hovav and Lisa Jerry, both of whom lent their significant talents as professional editors to the manuscript, improving it in many substantial ways.

It is especially humbling to sit down and thank the many people in my life who have carefully and generously read chapters and offered thoughtful and immensely helpful suggestions. Friend and colleague readers include Beth Cherne, Jaralee Richter, Louise Edwards-Simpson, Mahurq Khan, Elise Denlinger, Deb Hoskins, Christina Haynes, Terry Lilley, Sanna Yoder, as well as a number of members of the History Author Working Group (HAWG.) Over several years, HAWG provided me an encouraging and intellectually challenging space to workshop chapters as they evolved. Special thanks goes to HAWG member James Longhurst, whose keen editorial eye shaped this manuscript in many places, to Marti Lybeck, whose sense of the historical big picture is unparalleled, to Víctor Macías-González, who directed me to numerous resources and provided editorial advice and encouragement, and to Jennifer Trost, who kindly helped me with additional grant-seeking for the project.

Thanks, too, to kind departmental colleagues Andrea Hansen, Terry Langteau, James R. Parker, and Nizam Arain, to long-term career mentor, Sandi Krajewski, and to the many people across the UW–La Crosse campus who encouraged me in the process. I am very appreciative of the work of librarian Jenifer Holman, whose expertise proved invaluable throughout the research process, and to Saundra Solum for technical assistance. I am also grateful for the talents of Kelly Nussbaum, historical research assistant par excellence, and Taylor Goodine, whose skills with the English language made this a much better book. And thanks to all my hundreds of students of women's history and the history of motherhood. Without their energy, ideas, and questions, this book would be much less rich and interesting. I also want to especially thank Elise Denlinger for sharing her family history with me and with the book's readers and, while I'm at it, for years of friendship and support for all my endeavors. And thanks to my many friends at Jule's Coffee House, where the vast majority of this book was written and edited, and to owner, Chris Kahlow, who let me occupy a booth for hours on end for the small price of the world's greatest tea and scones.

For great meals, distraction, and fun along the way, special thanks to Kitty Howells, Sanna Yoder, Jaralee Richter, Beth Cherne, and their families, to Keely Rees, Christine Hippert, Karyn Quinn, Sharon Jessee, Shu Li and Stefan Smith, to Melissa Wallace, Kay Dailey, Janice Hansen and Heather Christiansen, part of my book group/life support group, to Karen Dame, Sue Kuncio, Kim Ruth, and Mary Zimmermann, the original "moms" in my maternal circle from the early 1990s and still so close to my heart, and to my dear friend from graduate school days, Louise Edwards-Simpson, a razor-sharp historical mind. Thanks also to my mother-in-law, Paula Daves, for many great conversations about motherhood, and of course to my own mother and father, Charlene and Leslie Vandenberg, who originally taught me what is most important about parenting, family, and the need for social justice. In addition to new conversations with my parents while writing the book, it has been a joy to connect my own mother to history. I especially thought of her as I wrote the chapter on resilience and adaptation because she is my model for both, and she has encouraged me with all her heart in my many endeavors. Thanks, too, to my supportive brothers, Chuck and Todd Vandenberg, their families, and to my wonderful Daves in-laws.

Besides professional editors, only one person read the book manuscript cover to cover. I could not have asked for a better research assistant and in-house editor than my daughter, Allison Vandenberg-Daves. Working with the person who first turned me into a mother, who also happens to be a gifted, incisive editor and historical thinker, was about as much fun as I had writing this book. It has also been a joy to share many thoughtful conversations about mothering and gender with my ever compassionate and questioning daughter, Sylvia, and my deep-thinking son, Brad, who teach me so much about the world as they grow up. Allison, Sylvia, and Brad Vandenberg-Daves grounded me, freed my mind from its ponderous writing mode, and, like they always do, made life worth living and motherhood worth writing about. In all this, they had help from their father, John Vandenberg-Daves. I owe so much to John's support. His unflagging generosity, encouragement, patience, kindness and compassion, along with his sense of humor and keen intellect, have all informed the book and my career as a whole and have also been the foundation and fabric of my adult life.

Modern Motherhood

Introduction

Reading cultural pronouncements on mothers from the late eighteenth and early nineteenth centuries, we might think that no force on earth was more noble or more powerful than the mother. In 1795, *New York Magazine* told American mothers that, quite simply, "the reformation of the world is in your power." Several decades later, the Reverend William Abbott flattered American mothers that their influence outweighed that of "all earthly causes." We know, of course, that women could not vote at the time and therefore had limited direct impact on the larger public world. Still, Sarah Josepha Hale insisted, "If the future citizens of our republic are to be worthy of their rich inheritance, they must be made so principally through the virtue and intelligence of their mothers." Hale edited an early American women's magazine, *Godey's Lady's Book*, for forty years, and her views on the role of mothers in shaping society were significant.[1]

The idea here was that mothers had a unique and singular influence on their children. Their child-rearing mattered not only in the development of their children's individual character but also in the preservation and advancement of what was good and noble in the young nation's civic and religious life. The bond between mothers and children was sacred. Gentle and pure mothers guided innocent children, who were malleable to feminine guidance and inspiration. "Why does an infant love its mother better than any other friend?" asked an anonymous mother who wrote to *The Mother's Magazine*, which answered: "Because her voice is gentlest, her eye beams with fondest affection; she soothes his little sorrows, and bears with his irritability with the tenderest and untiring patience. These silken threads are harder to burst than the iron chains of authority." In early nineteenth-century women's magazines as well as in messages from the pulpit and from other cultural commentators, a new middle-class family ideal emerged. Mothers would nurture, as their feminine nature suited them, and they would be appropriately confined to the domestic "sphere" of the home. Fathers, venturing into "the bustling affairs of life," would earn a living while their wives formed the moral fiber and good habits of their children.[2]

These idealized concepts were invented by white, middle-class Americans on the East Coast at a time when most of the American population could not afford such a neat division of labor and approach to mothering. Most people lived in families that required everyone's labor for family survival, and flexibility of roles was necessary. Nonetheless, the new ideals of civic and moral motherhood were the first steps in creating middle-class mothers' modern identities, and these ideals would eventually impact a much broader segment of society. Modern mothers would be self-consciously gifted with—and burdened by—the idea that they had a unique influence on their children. At least initially, their influence was thought to depend upon their virtue, their watchfulness, their confinement to the home, and their constant availability.

As we fast forward into modern times, we see women's lives undergoing vast changes, as they increasingly pursued higher education, worked outside the home for longer phases of their lives, and gained the right to vote and access to contraception and abortion. Still, throughout American history, motherhood—with its lofty ideals and its complex and sometimes gritty realities, has lurked behind nearly every debate about women's place in society, women's psyches, and even the future of the nation's moral rectitude.

In our new millennium, alarm bells continuously ring about mothers and motherhood: Can they "do it all" and still raise good kids? What do we make of the raging ambivalence mothers often express today, the feeling of being torn between being a mother and being a self? And can we actually trust women with mothering, especially with reproductive decisions? Meanwhile, the media serves up continuous stories of "bad mothers," defined in a plethora of ways: mothers who neglect their children, breastfeed them too long, consume them with their own needs, use drugs during their pregnancies, or fail to supervise adolescents who turn out to be budding criminals.

These seemingly disparate debates and judgments about maternal behavior and roles are connected by some core tensions between mothers and society as a whole. We continue to expect mothers' influence to trump all others. Yet, over time, as women both expanded their roles into the public and gained new rights within the family American society grew more ambivalent about female power, both private and civic. It was one thing to talk in flowery terms about mothers at home shaping little minds in the early years of an exclusively male-governed American nation. It has been quite another matter to integrate into civic life female voters, officeholders, professionals, and empowered public decision makers who now make up roughly half the American workforce and who are also, in most cases, mothers.

At the same time, women have been expected to accomplish the task of rearing each new generation, even as public policy has given them few new resources. The conditions in which women have raised children are vastly shaped by social inequality, especially around race, gender, and class. It is easier to point to extremes of maternal behavior than it is to address the structures that make mothering so difficult to accomplish in our society, especially for those with less privilege.

Mothers' adaptations and sacrifices are supposed to make up for the shortfalls of our social safety net and structures that have not caught up to women's modern lives: inflexible workplaces, schools with decreased funding, inadequate access to health care, and exponentially expanding income inequality, to name a few.

Added to all this is a more modern dilemma, one that was not acknowledged by Americans living in the late eighteenth and early nineteenth centuries: In part because of the conditions of modern life, mothers often find themselves wrenched between the demands of caregiving, on the one hand, and the requirements of self and society, on the other, a recipe for the chronic ambivalence that shapes contemporary maternal identities. We are continually told that no job is more important than motherhood and that all women are essentially maternal. Yet there seem to be a million ways to fail at this crucial job and an abundance of complex claims on women's time.

All these tensions reflect the complex history of the evolution of modern motherhood, the subject of this book. Beginning with the development of a unique role for mothers in children's development, as suggested in the high-minded prose of early American commentators, the modernization of motherhood added new layers over time. The forces of modernization—industrialization, scientific expertise, and an expanding government—complicated motherhood ideals without ever fully dislodging the notion of an irreplaceable maternal effect on children. As motherhood modernized, it intertwined deeply with the idea of a private nuclear family. By the late nineteenth and early twentieth centuries, motherhood was caught up with science and medicine as well. Mothers' job descriptions became medicalized: the good mother would learn how to deal with and defer to an ever-expanding and often contradictory field of advice from medical experts.

An expanded government also became involved in mothers' lives. Public policy initiatives have ranged from prohibiting birth control information to promoting the sterilization of "unfit" mothers to providing small provisions for worthy impoverished mothers without male support. As the job description of mother became more complex, discussions of modern motherhood also distinguished between good mothers and bad mothers by reinforcing and sometimes exacerbating class, race, and other inequalities among women.

Again and again, Americans have infused motherhood with cultural and political significance. Early American political and social theorists considered mothers crucial to maintaining the integrity of the American experiment in self-government, and religious leaders have instructed mothers about their moral place in society. Organized women, whether or not they were actual mothers, have also used the mantle of motherhood in support of movements for abolition, suffrage, peace, environmental regulation, abortion rights and restrictions, among many others. With each new generation, social reformers have used the idea of mothers' special interest in children and presumably selfless nature to influence public debates and sometimes public policy. For example, female health reformers expanded women's reproductive and health choices by claiming the nation needed healthy mothers. Suffrage activists claimed mothers needed the vote to clean up American society and expanded government services and regulation to protect vulnerable women and children.

As feminist writer Adrienne Rich pointed out in the 1970s, motherhood has long been an institution, a fundamental one to American society. Motherhood has provided both a critical reference point for social, political, and religious agendas of all sorts and a field on which Americans have wrestled with their ambivalence about female power, social justice, the needs of families, and even the social order. As an institution, motherhood includes not only the laws that define and constrain a society's definition of legitimate forms of maternity and that control access to reproductive rights and to resources generally, but also the ideologies that define "good" and "bad" mothers in relation to cultural values.

In tandem with motherhood as an institution, a history of mothering has also contributed significantly to social change. Mothering includes the practices of caregiving and educating, the integration of maternal labors with other necessary and desired pursuits, and the instilling of values in children from generation to generation. Mothering has necessarily been shaped by motherhood, but mothering also has a life of its own. When we look at the patterns of social history, we see how mothers' lives have departed from the ideals of institutional motherhood. Mothers have adapted, resisted, and moved in their own ways, within and sometimes under the radar of the limits imposed by society, thereby forcing gradual changes in society and values. For example, over time, mothers have more or less continuously increased their participation in the labor force, changing the face of labor itself and pushing against a cultural ideal of the mother at home. And women's exercise of reproductive options gradually redefined female identities.[3]

Who were the agents of transformation in developing modern motherhood? And how much power did women exercise in all these causes and debates? In some respects, mothers themselves modernized by joining the workforce, limiting their family size, and demanding new resources for maternal and child health and education, to name a few examples. In other ways policy makers, physicians, religious leaders, advice columnists, and moral crusaders shaped modern motherhood. (And sometimes, of course, these categories overlapped.) As medical professions consolidated and enlarged their reach, those claiming specialized medical or psychological expertise had an increasing impact on the way women mothered. With the expansion of magazines, newspapers, and eventually radio, television, and the Internet, popular culture and consumerism did much to shape the ideals to which mothers were supposed to aspire and the morality lessons they were supposed to learn. Meanwhile, millions of conversations about mothering and millions of day-to-day decisions existed within this tableau. Interactions between mothers and fathers, mothers and grandmothers, neighbors, other relatives, and community members all provide part of the powerful but often invisible historical patterns of mothering.

Method and Approach of This Book

This book explores the development of modern motherhood ideals as they connected to how women actually did the work of mothering and thought about their identities as mothers. I use questions about modern motherhood to focus what is really a larger exploration of how motherhood and mothering have changed over the course of American history. I have borrowed and given a new forum to stories others have collected. Although I have gathered and interpreted selected primary sources, the principal contributions I make in this book are to put into conversation, synthesize, and provide a narrative framework and analysis for the disparate strands of maternal history. Social historians have been working on close studies of specific times, places, and themes related to motherhood for several generations now. This book pulls together the knowledge, insights, and perspectives of literally hundreds of specific studies as well as a number of larger surveys of women's history, children's history, and histories of American families. It is the product of my review of more than a quarter century of women's history scholarship focused on or somehow connected to motherhood.

The range of sources that informed this book is vast, though it was not possible to make it comprehensive. Even as I write, new and exciting work is emerging in this field. Still, this book represents a significant representation of "what we know" about the history of mothering and motherhood, especially from the nineteenth century until the present. Readers will certainly notice gaps: there are long and frustrating silences in history. Histories' stories have seldom been written from the perspectives of busy mothers, who often did not have time to write about their experiences and whose work was quite often taken for granted and not considered worthy of story or study. Especially for the earlier periods covered in this book, we often know more about the ideals of motherhood than about the realities of ordinary mothers' lives.

This dearth of firsthand information also reflects women's differences: who had the privilege of literacy, and who did not? Who had the leisure to write, and who was encouraged to do so? Whose aspirations for motherhood were catered to in popular advice literature? And whose stories have so far been written by historians? The history of white middle-class women has been well documented in the scholarly literature. This group left behind more records than other populations and received more commentary in the dominant culture, whether from the pulpit, in the magazines, or on television. African American women's stories are the next most researched. Thankfully, the multicultural story broadens out much more near the beginning of the twentieth century, a time of expanding access to literacy, and more sources emerge to detail the lives of immigrant women, Asian American, Hispanic, American Indian, and working-class and poor women in general.

Some areas remain understudied, even for the twentieth century. Much more work is needed, for example, on diverse Native American mothering practices. Historians must also consider more detailed work on the role of religions other than Protestant Christianity in American mothering. Similarly understudied are historical patterns in same-sex parenting and the multifaceted roles of grandmothers and stepmothers as caregivers. To the extent that these topics are still underresearched, I hope the framework I develop to think about culture, race, and class in mothering and motherhood can lead my readers, including historians working on new material, to ask new questions. In that way the next survey of the history of American motherhood will be richer and more complete. In providing richer detail on the topic of motherhood, stories of fatherhood and parenthood generally can also be better researched.[4] For now, I invite readers to learn from what decades of historical research on mothers and motherhood has been able to uncover, while asking their own questions about what else we need to explore.

ORGANIZATION AND THEMES

This book is organized roughly by chronology and also by theme. It begins by examining the emergence of republican moral motherhood as early American middle-class ideals. Part one addresses these origins from the American Revolution roughly through the nineteenth century, as Americans invented a special role for mothers in moral development, in contrast to their colonial forebears. Nineteenth-century Americans also became fascinated with scientific ideas, especially related to maternal health, and these ideas began to compete with earlier religious worldviews. The first steps toward modern motherhood were entwined with middle-class identity, and, given the long duration of slavery, these American motherhood ideals were deeply racialized. Over time, dominant culture ideals, including a sentimentalized, nonbreadwinning mother, would increasingly impact most American mothers, whether or not the ideals made sense for their life circumstances.

In part two of the book, I address the promises and pitfalls of modern motherhood in what the commentators of the day were calling modern times, roughly 1890 to 1940. Mothers in this period experienced the gifts of modern science through better maternal and infant health, increasing both mothers' and children's chances for survival. Yet mothers also endured the charge that their "maternal instincts" were no longer capable of guiding them in their mothering roles. A growing cadre of experts in medicine, psychology, and social work reached out to women while offering advice, reassurance, and sometimes chastisement. These experts fostered new psychological expectations for motherhood and encouraged women to measure their mothering against ever-changing notions of what was "normal" for themselves and their children. Here, as throughout American history, race and class shaped women's access to the benefits of modern life and helped define their positions vis-à-vis the ideals of modern motherhood.

As American mothers developed new experiences with scientific expertise, their family lives were also transformed. Rapid industrialization, urbanization, and immigration created new roles, new vulnerabilities, and new opportunities in this modernizing period. By the early twentieth century, the legal rights of fathers to control the labor, behavior, and resources of their children and their wives had greatly diminished, and the state showed a greater willingness to intervene in family life by usurping some traditional prerogatives of fathers. Women were demanding new public roles and freedoms, such as the rights to vote and to access birth control. It was an era full of social and cultural confusion, rapid economic change, and the hope of scientific progress.

In part three, I examine the power of gender ideology, from the rigidly defined gender roles that shaped motherhood after World War II to the challenges posed to mother-care traditions by Second Wave feminism. Simultaneously, this section of the book explores the impact of major changes in women's working and reproductive lives since the Second World War. I argue that ultimately women have been able to wrest some control over the conditions in which they mother, in part by taking modern ideals to their logical conclusions: good mothers limit the number of children they have by exercising reproductive and relationship choices, and good mothers take care of their families both morally and materially by pursuing education and participating in the labor force. Finally, after a long unequal relationship with the mostly male experts who advised mothers, some mothering knowledge has again become diffuse and decentered from expert points of view. Especially since the birth of the Internet, the experts compete with a vast arena of information and perspectives, even as scientific, expertise continues to influence many areas of mothering. We see a proliferation of possibilities for maternal identities in an era that has questioned scientific and expert certainty and created an information (and opinion) revolution.

History is about continuity as well as change, and nothing has been more continuous than the fact that women—mothers or not—are still significantly underrepresented in the centers of political and economic power. The underrepresentation of women's voices has meant that mothers have been burdened with an inadequate social policy structure and little power to shape the conditions in which they mother their children. This structure not only hinders their work as mothers but also limits their access to the public achievements that have been historically defined as male preserves. This is particularly true when it comes to women's participation in the labor force. Most mothers now work outside the home, but the lack of paid maternity leave and other care-giver-friendly policies makes the task of raising children while working extremely difficult. Despite expanded roles for fathers in child care, the incomplete revolution in gender roles has combined with a continued emphasis on mothers as the primarily available and present parent, which leaves modern mothers overscheduled and often overwrought. Meanwhile, women's access to a hard-fought right, to control when and whether they become mothers, is being painfully rehashed in both political discourse and attempts to mandate new forms of surveillance of the maternal body.

Nevertheless, the historian's long view cautions me against jumping to conclusions about the impact of recent changes in modern motherhood and how these will or will not reshape old patterns. So much has changed so quickly that most of us can plainly see the difference between our own lives and those of our mothers. In terms of mothers' increased labor force participation alone, these changes have been revolutionary. Very few mothers are confined to the sealed domestic sphere imagined by nineteenth-century moralists. Even those who stay home with children are often connected to the broader world via technology. Throughout history, both individually and collectively, mothers have been nothing if not resourceful. The ideals of motherhood have moved women and men to action in the name of a more just society on many occasions. I hope that through the voices and perspectives of mothers in history, this book will inspire the social imagination of those who value the contributions of mothers, caregivers, and women generally to our society and our future.

PART I

Roots of Modern Motherhood

EARLY AMERICA AND THE NINETEENTH CENTURY

CHAPTER 1

Inventing a New Role for Mothers

To understand the historical significance of modern motherhood, it helps to take a brief look backward to the essentially premodern world of mothers in the English colonies. Ideas about mothers as unique moral guardians only emerged at the time of the American Revolution. Before that, the nation's Puritan ancestors, who left us the most voluminous records about seventeenth- and early eighteenth-century family life, held starkly different views. For them, mothers had no special place in the moral and spiritual education of their children. Fathers were considered the morally stronger of the two parents. According to one Puritan minister, "Persons are often more apt to despise a Mother, (the weaker vessel, and frequently, most indulgent)." Because a mother was sometimes "overmoved by her tender & motherly affections," to quote another colonial commentator, she was not as capable as a father of exercising the stern authority Puritan children were thought to require.[1]

A Look Backward: Colonial Mothers under English Patriarchy

"There is in all children . . . a stubbornness and stoutness of mind, arising from natural pride, which must in the first place be broken and beaten down," noted one Puritan minister. The stated goal of "breaking the child's will" appears in a great deal of colonial sources about family life. For example, Susanna Wesley, an English woman, wrote to her grown son on the eve of his departure to Georgia in 1732, insisting that "in order to form the minds of children, the first thing to be done is to conquer their will and bring them to an obedient temper." Such conquest was, in her view, "the only strong and rational foundation of a religious education without which both precept and example will be ineffectual." Parents, especially fathers, commonly used whipping or caning as the physical discipline necessary to prepare a child for subservience within a patriarchal social order. Children were considered miniature adults, as is evident from seventeenth-century paintings that depict an adult face—and head/body proportion—on young children. Even babies were set forth on the path to early self-control: Puritans swaddled their babies with wooden rods and encouraged walking at an early age.[2]

Colonial parents loved and treasured their children, as is amply evidenced. One of the very few women writers of the period, Anne Bradstreet, frequently makes that point in her poetry. For example, she lamented the limits on a mother's power to keep her beloved children safe from harm:

> Great was my pain when I you bred,
> Great was my care, when I you fed,
> Long did I keep you soft and warm,
> And with my wings kept off all harm,
> My cares are more, and fears than ever,
> My throbs such now, as 'fore were never:
> Alas my birds, you wisdom want,
> Of perils you are ignorant.

Puritan minister Cotton Mather, who saw eight of his fifteen children die before reaching adulthood, poignantly acknowledged parents' pain in losing children at a time of very high infant and child mortality. "We have our children taken from us . . . the Desire of our Eyes taken away with a stroke."[3]

Still, there is no denying that children were considered economic assets in the colonial world. In the English colonies this was most obviously true for enslaved African children, most of whom began field labor around age ten.[4] It was also true for the thousands of poor English children shipped overseas to work in the cash-crop colonies of Maryland, Virginia, and points farther south. Even in the Northeast, where more children lived in intact families and family labor prevailed, children's labor was sorely needed. Because of this economic reality, people did not talk about innocent children, but rather about children whose wills needed to be broken.

At the same time, Puritan religious thought found even babies tainted with original sin. For all these reasons, socializing children into a religious worldview and teaching them to work for the family were tasks assigned to the father, at least in theory. By English and colonial law, fathers ruled their families, including their wives, their children, and their servants. The English common-law tradition of coverture meant that married women were legally "covered" by their husbands. Without legal identity of their own, wives were simultaneously defined as economically dependent. Married women had no rights to either the property they brought into the marriage or any money they earned while married, and they had no legal rights to their children. They could not sign contracts in their own names and could not make their own wills unless and until they were widowed. Widows were customarily entitled to only one-third of a husband's estate. The will of New England "goodwife" Judith Coffin's husband instructed one of their sons to "take spesshal care" of Judith and "provid for har in all Respectes." The other sons were instructed to also pay a yearly maintenance sum for their mother's upkeep. But in practice, many widows struggled to survive on the good graces of sons to whom most of the family's wealth had been bequeathed.[5]

Fathers' rights in the family were especially strong in New England. Here, a healthful climate made possible a strong patriarchal family structure in which a father would be likely to live long enough to exercise his rightful authority. Puritan fathers led their households, including children and servants, in learning both religious education and the "good lawes of the Colony." They also guided their sons in finding vocations, and their consent to their children's marriages was a legal right. At a time when land was the basis of the next generation's livelihood, fathers' control of property gave them a powerful voice in the occupational plans of their sons and the timing and selection of their daughters' husbands.[6] Fathers, especially those who had the most wealth and status to protect and control for the next generation, were ideologically invested with civic responsibility as well as moral and familial leadership.

In colonial New England, the town fathers policed the behavior of children through their laws and established themselves as the ultimate disciplinarians in cases where a son was "Stubborn and Rebellious, and will not obey [his parents'] voice and chastisement." In Massachusetts, town fathers assigned themselves the tasks of overseeing particular families to ensure that community norms were enforced. In actuality, women informally policed a great deal of community behavior. But when informal mechanisms failed, the hand of the law was clearly male, patriarchal, and not particularly concerned with what more modern Americans would consider a sphere of familial privacy.[7]

In practice, too, the socialization of children was a widely shared task, certainly not reserved exclusively for, or even assigned primarily to, mothers. Because home and work were not separated for most colonial families, fathers and mothers were often present in children's day-to-day life. In families that could either afford servants or own slaves, these nonfamily members also shared in child care. These servants or enslaved persons, therefore, had limited opportunities to spend time with their own children. Children were kept busy in all cultures, from fieldwork to tending to babies. Children often spent much of their childhood in apprenticeships, farm labor, or household service. Thus, many people beyond parents participated in socializing children.

To the extent that women had a special role in rearing the next generation, they were to bear children and help them survive their early years in the harsh disease climate of colonial North America. Women's fertility was essential to community survival. Ministers told women that pregnancy was the "first privilege of the Sex." Colonial headstones emphasized not women's social or religious influence on children, but the fact that they were, as Judith Coffin's stone read in 1704, "Brave, sober, faithful, and fruitfull of vine." Coffin's progeny at the time of her death numbered 177 children and grandchildren combined. Her fecundity was typical of New England white women, who spent on average twenty to twenty-five years pregnant or nursing babies.[8]

Premodern cultures conceived of fertility broadly, from pregnancy through the end of the nursing period. The birthing process was an especially dangerous ordeal.

Bradstreet, for example, emphasized her role in her children's survival at least as much as in their socialization. In one poem, she asked her children to remember that

> You had a Dam that lov'd you well,
> That did what could be done for young,
> And nurst you up till you were strong,
> And 'fore she once would let you fly,
> She shew'd you joy and misery;
> Taught what was good and what was ill,
> What would save life, and what would kill.

In another poem, Bradstreet suggested that the "travail" of birthing a child was a sacrifice for which children owed a mother special gratitude and respect. In Bradstreet's day, New England women bore an average of seven to nine children and stood a one in eight chance of dying in childbirth. Bradstreet also wrote of the physical burden and special sacrifice of nursing children in another poem, written from her imagined perspective of a child:

> With tears into the world I did arrive,
> My mother still did waste as I did thrive,
> Who yet with love and all alacrity,
> Spending, was willing to be spent for me.
> With wayward cryes I did disturb her rest,
> Who sought to appease me with her breast:
> With weary arms she danc'd and By By sung
> When wretched I ingrate had done the wrong.[9]

For colonial women breastfeeding was not only a physical sacrifice but also a spiritual gift. Providing the only sustenance that allowed infants to live, women who nursed their children sustained life in ways that sometimes inspired religious metaphors among the Puritan clergy. "Grace goes directly to Christ, as a childe new borne goes to the mothers breast, and never leaves crying till it be laid there." Ministers referred to themselves as "breasts of God" and invited good Christians to church services to "suck the breast while it is open." Breast milk could be also found in medicinal recipes, and many a sick adult was said to have been "cured by sucking a Woman's Breast," as a publication for midwives reported in 1660. It was used in salves and employed to treat eye problems, earaches, and any number of other ailments, as well as in childbirth. Many believed that drinking another mother's milk might speed up a woman's labor or relieve her pain. Women's fertility, including their fertile, breastfeeding function, was highly valued by premodern cultures throughout the world. For example, in the West African societies from which enslaved women were forcibly removed, the announcement of an upcoming marriage prompted the friends of the bride-to-be to ritually prepare her for pregnancy.[10]

In practice, colonial women were also valued for their contributions to the material survival of their families. Throughout most of human history, the vast

majority of women have had to combine "productive labor," the work of producing goods and services that provided food, shelter, and other material goods, with
"reproductive labor," the labor of bearing and rearing children, caring for the sick,
and generally maintaining family life. Colonial women in all the major cultural
groups of North America were no exception. Indeed, both kinds of labor were so
extensive that colonial mothers had little time to focus on tending to each individual child's spiritual and emotional development. New England housewives worked
from dawn to dusk: they planted and maintained kitchen gardens, spent hours each
day building and tending to fires to heat homes and cook, baked bread and other
foods, made cider and beer, traded and bartered for sugar, wine, spices, and other
goods produced beyond the farm, spun and carded wool, and sewed and ironed
clothing. Women's work was seasonal, from processing milk and making butter in
the spring to butchering livestock and preserving meat and vegetables in the fall.
In Native agricultural tribes, women were the farmers, who also provided most of
the subsistence necessary for family and community survival: they baked bread;
gathered wild plants for food, medicine, and dyes; harvested, processed, stored,
and prepared other foods; ground grain for bread; cured meat; made utensils and
clothing; and wove mats and carpets.[11]

Most of the labor of enslaved women belonged to their masters. Most enslaved
African women in the southern English seaboard colonies worked in the fields.
By working very long hours from approximately age ten to age fifty, these women
produced wealth for the English planters of rice, tobacco, and indigo. Some also
worked more intimately for Europeans in domestic service. Charles Pinckney
and Thomas Jefferson received a great deal of their physical nurture as children
from enslaved women. Pinckney said that he had "gained strength at the breasts of
domestic slaves." When possible, African women and men tried to provide extra
sustenance for their own children through planting small garden plots, hunting,
and fishing.[12]

But the English had long placed less cultural value on women's contributions
to the material well-being of families than did Native or African societies. Indeed,
English women were considered simply the "helpmeets" of their husbands. In 1704
Judith Coffin's husband's headstone emphasized not his ability to produce children, but his economic role: "On earth he purchased a good degree," read the first
line. In both the Old World and the New World, European women were denied
access to apprenticeships to become skilled tradespersons, and once the Industrial
Revolution created more wage-earners, women's economic second-class citizenship would be everywhere apparent in their measly wages, when compared to men.
For example, women's wages averaged less than half those of men between 1800
and 1850.[13]

The English view of women's labor would prevail and be elevated by the good
fortune of New Englanders. The Puritans liked to think of themselves as enjoying
God's favor as they gradually gained control of the northeastern seaboard. In reality, historical accident was a critical factor: the British crown protected the settlers,
while Old World diseases killed enormous swathes of the Native population. New

World diseases also wiped out scores of Europeans farther south, which meant that family formation for the first century of colonization in the southern colonies was extremely difficult. The traditions of Africans, American Indians, and many other cultural groups continued in spite of many obstacles. But ultimately it was the good fortune of the English to be the lawmakers of what became the United States; British laws and cultural values would have a lasting and disproportionate impact on the family lives of all Americans.[14]

The English came from an Old World society that valued private property. Marriage determined how property would be passed from generation to generation, and marriage laws reinforced social inequality. In English law and custom, marriage was the only legitimate avenue to social acceptance for mothers and children. "Bastard" children lacked the legal right to support from their fathers, and woe to the woman who conceived out of wedlock and could not convince the baby's father to marry her. Indentured servants who became pregnant out of wedlock could face fines, whippings, and extra years of service for lost labor. Courts could also take children away from these mothers and indenture the child as a servant to another family. A free woman who became pregnant out of wedlock might receive help from her family in persuading the future father to marry her. She was far more likely to succeed if the father-to-be was from an established family of means, but, if this effort failed, she might be publicly tried for fornication and face poverty and social ostracism. Even economically privileged married women's place as mothers was shaped by their legal and economic dependence on men. Long after mothers gained a special status as children's moral guides, they continued to be shackled by the coverture laws that kept them without a legal identity outside the context of marriage.[15]

Prohibitions on interracial marriage and the placement of an economic value on African women's reproductive capacities were also important legacies of colonial America. In 1644 and 1662, respectively, Marylanders and Virginians legislated "legitimate" families and furthered the system of race-based chattel slavery. Maryland outlawed interracial unions between "freeborne Englishwomen forgetful of their free Condition" who "to the disgrace of our Nation doe intermarry with Negro slaves." This first "anti-miscegenation" law—a law to prohibit interracial sex or marriage— was followed by many more state laws. Not until 1967 did the U.S. Supreme Court strike down these state laws, which also had an impact on American Indians and Asian Americans. In Virginia, English colonists defied the mother country's legal tradition of offspring receiving their social status from their fathers. Enslaved women who became pregnant—no matter who made them pregnant—instead passed their enslaved conditions onto their children.[16] In this way, the child of an enslaved woman was automatically defined as a slave for life; therefore, the rape of enslaved women by white men, endemic to the system of slavery, often resulted in economic gain in the form of interracial children defined as slaves.

Another important legacy of the premodern world was what historians Margaret Marsh and Wanda Ronner have called the "motherhood mandate," the idea that all women must be mothers. If colonial Americans did not uphold a special cultural role for mothers beyond children's infancy, they nevertheless placed very little value on women's gifts to society other than maternity. Colonial women who were unable to biologically conceive children could function as mothers to the children of others, and couples could adopt children informally and with relative ease. The bodies of women who did not produce children, however, were suspect; in the Puritan view they were marked with the Lord's disfavor. As Marsh explains, "Men were never considered to be incapable of procreation unless they were impotent; only women could be 'barren.'" Far beyond the colonial era, arguably even up to the present, cultural ideas about womanliness would remain strongly linked to the social compulsion and what has been thought to be the innate desire of women to bear children. The booming industry in infertility treatments today speaks to the powerful continuation of the idea that motherhood is women's biological, as well as social, destiny.[17]

Women's Revolutionary Prize: Mothers instead of Citizens

In the latter half of the eighteenth century, across the Atlantic world, Enlightenment ideas of human progress and perfectibility encouraged youthful rebellion and the casting off of old ideas of hierarchy, both familial and political. The best examples of these enlightened ideas are, of course, well known: the political revolutions of the English colonies inspired creation of the United States; in France, the old nobility was dethroned, even beheaded, and replaced by popular sovreignty; and in Haiti, enslaved people took over the island and created their own government. Self-government was the right of rebellious sons, it seemed.

But some believed that rebellion against arbitrary authority was a broader human right for all people. The possibilities briefly seized upon by women, enslaved persons, and youth were downright dangerous to the patriarchal rule of white, propertied men for several decades of the late eighteenth century. Abigail Adams famously questioned her husband John on the matter of the new nation's complicity in keeping women under the rule of their husbands. "Remember the Ladies," she admonished, "And be more generous and favourable to them than your ancestors. Do not put such unlimited power into the hands of the Husbands. Remember all Men would be tyrants if they could." And she was not alone. Writing under a pseudonym, one woman publicly called on members of her sex to "consider yourselves as intitled to a Suffrage, and possessed of Influence, in the Administration of the great Family of the Publick."[18] But such anti-patriarchal questioning of authority, with all its familial metaphors, only went so far. The founding fathers had a more private patriarchal family in mind, and their legislative acts sought to ensure women's continual confinement in what would come to be envisioned as a "separate sphere" of family privacy.

By the end of the American Revolution, the new nation offered women something other than citizenship, something historian Linda Kerber aptly termed "republican motherhood," a kind of compromised maternal citizenship. Mothers, through their virtue, would sustain the nascent republic, but not as voters or office holders; instead, they would raise virtuous sons who could continue to handle effectively the experiment of youthful self-government that was the new nation's light to shine in the world. Abigail Adams expressed this notion well in her stern advice to her grown son: "Justice, humanity, and benevolence are the duties you owe to society in general. To your country the same duties are incumbent upon you, with the additional obligation of sacrificing ease, pleasure, wealth, and life itself for its defence and security. . . . To become what you ought to be, and what a fond mother wishes to see you, attend to some precepts and instructions from the pen of one, who can have no motive but your welfare and happiness."[19] Adams kept her place in this writing, confining herself to selfless maternal advice, while simultaneously expressing her own patriotism.

And yet the American Revolution dovetailed with social, demographic, and religious changes that were beginning to erode the rule of the father in families. Propertied men were having greater difficulty controlling their progeny. As the northern land base shrank, fathers' authority weakened. Without land to inherit, young people left home as teens and young adults, seeking new positions outside agriculture in the growing towns and cities that were the product of the trans-Atlantic trade networks. Young people married earlier, not always with parental permission. Rates of early marriage and premarital pregnancy rose over the course of the eighteenth century.[20]

Meanwhile, women were finding new voices and cultural influence within Protestant religions. Even as early as the 1690s, church membership was 70 percent female, and historians have argued that a "feminization of New England religion" was beginning. Theologically, eighteenth-century Americans began emphasizing a humble, sacrificing, and more feminine-seeming Christ. These changes corresponded with greater religious activism on the part of what was called the "gentler sex." By the early decades of the new nation, American women were beginning to create voluntary associations within their churches, and they were vocal and influential participants in the evangelical fervor that swept the Northeast.[21]

The evangelical movements of the early nineteenth century also contributed to the revaluing of motherhood. In the Second Great Awakening of Protestant revivalism, especially prominent in New York, three of every five new converts were female. Women converts contributed to an important change in religious ideology and cultural ideals. To put it bluntly, the "weaker vessel" of colonial times now became the morally superior sex. Morally speaking, it was men who needed a feminine influence, not the other way around. By the 1830s, it was not uncommon to find men writing about women as "created . . . in a superior though more fragile and delicate mold, endowed with purer and better feelings, stronger and more exalted affection."[22]

Combined with the novel ideas of a more egalitarian social contract, one that questioned the divine right of kings and fathers, these changes pointed in a potentially radical direction. The rule of the fathers could be challenged not just between colonists and kings, but between individual men and the subordinate members of their households. Propertied men, who actually wrote the Constitution and subsequently made the laws, limited the egalitarian possibilities of all these new ideas by keeping both coverture and slavery in place. The new motherhood ideals allowed for some female cultural authority but no formal political power.

Many people worried that in an increasingly commercial society, men would lose their moral bearings in the rough-and-tumble world of money. Thus, maintaining the virtue of the republic was to be accomplished in part by pious women, who kept the home fires burning without sullying themselves with business or politics. These views justified the fact that only propertied men became enfranchised. Women, property-less men, and of course enslaved persons were left out of the seemingly all-encompassing notions of human rights to "life, liberty, and pursuit of happiness." Culturally, too, Americans in the new nation began to emphasize complementary roles for mothers and fathers in the family, but these ideas still preserved the idea of father rule. "The man bears rule over his wife's person and conduct. She bears rule over his inclinations. He governs by law; she by persuasion. . . . The empire of the woman is an empire of softness . . . her commands are caresses, her menaces are tears."[23]

Despite its limitations, republican motherhood elevated the cultural role of women—and of mothering—in important ways. Revolutionary-era Americans exalted "reason" and denigrated "passion." Passion had actually long been associated with the female sex, but now republican mothers taught reason as well as piety. A larger excerpt from New York Magazine's 1795 exhortation makes the point:

> Let us then figure to ourselves the accomplished woman, surrounded by a sprightly band, from the babe that imbibes the nutritive fluid, to the generous youth. . . . Let us contemplate the mother distributing the mental nourishment to the fond smiling circle . . . watching the gradual openings of their minds . . . see, under her cultivating hand, reason assuming the reins of government, and knowledge increasing gradually to her beloved pupils. . . . While you keep our country virtuous, you maintain its independence.

In fact, many argued that women needed more educational opportunities so that they could better nurture young minds and thus "keep our country virtuous." Benjamin Rush, a Philadelphia physician and a patriot who signed the Declaration of Independence, insisted that to secure the American experiment in republican government, mothers must be educated. "Our ladies should be qualified to a certain degree, by a peculiar and suitable education, to concur in instructing their sons in the principles of liberty and government."[24]

By 1800, maternal ideology came to emphasize piety and goodness over reason; republican motherhood shaded into religiously infused moral motherhood. But the nineteenth-century ideals retained the concept of the mother as the watchful and righteous guardian of the young. Women used republican and moral motherhood ideas both individually and collectively to fulfill the obligations of proper womanhood and eventually to expand their influence well beyond the home. Over time, the idea of women's moral superiority encouraged women to claim that society and government needed the special perspectives of motherly women.

WOMEN'S CLAIMS ON MORAL MOTHERHOOD IN
THE EARLY NINETEENTH CENTURY

At a time when writing and public speaking were considered male activities, many nineteenth-century women nevertheless felt empowered to take up the pen in praise of mothers and their vast influence. Mrs. Elizabeth Hall, for example, told mothers "the destiny of a redeemed world is put in your hands; and it is for you to say, whether your children shall be . . . prepared for a glorious immortality." After all, a mother had "'in her own hands' the *perfect formation* [of her children's] *entire character.*" What she did or did not do would stay with her children "eternally." Her emotional closeness to the child, in this view, almost merged the identities of mother and child. As one writer in *The Mother's Magazine* explained, "'the mother must dwell in the heart of the child and be, as it were, the soul of its every action—enter into all its joys—feel its every sorrow."[25]

Though nineteenth-century commentators did not usually wax quite so poetic and religious about breastfeeding as their colonial forebears, they did connect it to moral motherhood. Mary Palmer Tyler, who authored a widely read book on child care, took pity on mothers who could not nurse their babies. But like many of her contemporaries, she judged harshly those women who selfishly refused this important maternal obligation. Tyler insisted that those women "who neglect this sweet endearing office are more fit objects of censure than pity." A male author of a marriage manual similarly noted, "It is well known that when children are committed to the care of mercenary nurses, maternal love and tenderness diminish." All aspects of the physical care of infants, says the historian Mary P. Ryan, were "now invested with moral as well as material meaning." According to one popular book of the time, the housewife who took care of her family was not only "ministering to the wants of a few bodies, considered merely as bodies, but through these bodies to the wants of immortal souls."[26]

As a result, mothers needed to be irreproachable. They were warned not "to permit the anxieties of your mind to mantle your countenance with forbidding gravity or gloom." They should be affectionate and gentle. They should not raise their voices. As one advisor put it, "every irritable feeling should . . . be restrained." Lydia Maria Child, a leading writer on child care, social reformer, and abolitionist, wrote, "The simple fact that your child never saw you angry, that your voice is always gentle, and the expression of your face always kind, is worth a thousand times more than all the rules you can give him about not beating his dog, pinching his brother, &c. It is in vain to load the understanding with rules, if the affections are not pure." According to the venerable nineteenth-century domestic advice writer Catharine Beecher, "It is certainly very unlady-like, and in very bad taste, to *scold.*"[27]

It almost went without saying that self-sacrifice was pivotal here. Ideal mothers would live through their children and even, as historian Jan Lewis points out, atone for their child's sins. Sons left home and gave into temptation, but, through remembering their mothers, the sons (and their mothers) were redeemed. "Blessed are they, in the earth, who possess the inestimable dowry of a pious mother's grave!

I had almost said, the example and counsel of a living mother could hardly equal in power, upon the filial heart, the silent but thrilling preaching of a departed one," claimed a writer in *The Mother's Magazine*. Mothers, still economically dependent and politically disfranchised, would nonetheless be saving the world through self-abnegation and virtue, one child at a time. As one writer on the theme of family government and national prosperity observed, "While, therefore, the father is engaged in the bustling affairs of active life, the mother, with almost irresistible sway, is forming the characters of the future defenders of our faith, the administrators of our laws, and the guardians of our civil liberties and lives." Mothers should do so even when fathers were intemperate or uncooperative.[28]

For many reasons these ideals seemed possible in the emerging white middle class at this time. With the expansion of industrialization, the productive work of middle-class urban women was declining. The production of goods was increasingly moving into factories and out of the home, and the work of middle-class professional men took them outside the home. Middle-class women, however, still had much work to do within the home. Middle-class families were also less likely to pass along property and status than their ancestors had been, and they had to invest in the lengthy training and education of smaller broods of children to preserve or advance their place in the American class structure. To do so, families had to rely on child-rearing methods that taught children self-control, a signature value of a middle class that touted work, temperance, and honesty as pathways to successful living. Women's socialization of children was thus as necessary, and as important, as their many material contributions to their family's success.

At the same time, women's magazines helped popularize a cult of feminine domesticity by furnishing increasingly complex ideas about cooking, home care, and consumption of goods for the family, all "women's work." Domestic management and child care, now amplified in importance in the popular literature, were very much defined as women's domain. Widely read authors such as Catharine Beecher leveraged the power of "the home" to elevate women's work as housekeepers. Good housekeeping, for Beecher, reflected a woman's morals. American women's willingness to engage in domestic labor and to teach their daughters to do so was important to sustaining American democracy. In her book *A Treatise on Domestic Economy*, Beecher argued that "domestic economy" was too often neglected in girls' education. Moreover, she opposed what she saw as a pervasive assumption "that women's business and cares are contracted and trivial; and that the proper discharge of her duties demands far less expansion of mind and vigor of intellect, than the pursuits of the other sex." As with revalued child care, greater cultural value on housework also meant elevated standards of meticulousness. Careful attention to a myriad of detailed household duties meant that the home kept women too busy to engage deeply in activities beyond its boundaries.[29]

Women in the nineteenth-century middle class in particular did devote their energies to fewer numbers of children than did their grandmothers. The growing emphasis on a child-focused nuclear family corresponded with a declining need for child laborers as the nation began to industrialize. The birth rate fell remarkably during the nineteenth century, a phenomenon discussed at length in chapter 3. Elite and middle-class families were particularly successful at reducing the number of children, which allowed them to invest more in the education and training of each child.

Innocent Children Who Needed Their Mothers

Moral motherhood necessarily coexisted with new notions of childhood. Only a different kind of child than the innately depraved one envisioned in Puritan social thought would respond to such teaching by feminine example. Nineteenth-century Americans began to romanticize childhood; they imagined children as innocent, even vehicles of redemption for adults. Unlike the inherently sinful youth depicted by colonial era thinkers, the nineteenth-century ideal child was someone who could be influenced simply by the mother's "loveliness"—her example, rather than rules or rods. The child was a malleable being, emerging in American ideals as a result of Enlightenment thinking about progress and the possibilities of human perfection.

John Locke explored these notions in the late seventeenth century, and the French theorist Jean-Jacques Rousseau elaborated upon them a century later, at a time of political revolutions replete with rhetoric hostile to heavy-handed patriarchal authority. Locke's and Rousseau's influential ideas represented a middle ground that arced toward discipline through gentle influence and the establishment of internal controls.[30] These ideas contributed to an important step toward modern motherhood: the notion of the child-centered family gently guided by the moral mother.

The nineteenth century saw an even grander elaboration of childhood innocence. Enlightenment-era ideas about human perfectibility were amplified by Romantic nineteenth-century cultural values of emotion and expressiveness. Commentators insisted that children should have opportunities for play and education and be sheltered from excessive labor as well as from exposure to death and sexuality. More middle-class households began to contain toys. Middle-class children began to be dressed in looser, more comfortable clothing. Novels for the middle class included charming examples of baby talk in the dialogue.[31]

In Puritan times, children who died in infancy were thought to be ineligible for entrance to heaven, owing to their innate depravity. In the nineteenth century, Christian doctrine changed. Babies were pure and free of sin, an idea that proved of great comfort to parents who lost their infants. By the middle of the nineteenth century, Protestant denominations were also legitimating childhood conversion, endowing children with new religious significance. In the words of Lydia Maria Child, children "come to us from heaven with their souls full of innocence and peace . . . under the influence of angels." Some even suggested, as did the writer Harriet Beecher Stowe, that innocent babies inspired moralism and selflessness in mothers. The baby would "awaken a mother from worldliness and egotism to a world of new and higher feeling!"[32] Children's innocence and receptivity and the "plastic hand of maternal affection" gently used by the morally superior of the two genders complemented each other in this ideology.

It is important to realize, however, that these ideas were not universally agreed upon, even among the white middle class, to which they most clearly applied. Catharine Beecher suggested a "medium path" of discipline and reminded her readers that "*submission of the will*" was a critical first step in child-rearing. Heman Humphrey, president of Amherst College for more than two decades, wrote in his book *Domestic Education*, "Children are brought into existence and placed in families not to follow their own wayward inclinations, but to look up to their parents for guidance; not to teach, but to be taught; not to govern but to be governed." His view of children corresponded with his staunch (and, in 1840, rather defensive) idealism of the patriarchal family:

> Every family is a little state, or empire within itself, bound together by the most endearing attractions, and governed by its patriarchal head, with whose prerogative no power on earth has a right to interfere. Nations may change their forms of government at pleasure, and may enjoy a high degree of prosperity under different constitutions. . . . But in the family organization there is but one model, for all times and all places. It is just the same now, as it was in the beginning, and it is impossible to alter it, without marring its beauty, and directly contravening the wisdom and benevolence of the Creator.

In various ways these ideas revived themselves in American child-rearing literature, but they never again overwhelmed the emphasis on gently persuasive moral mother care, which Lewis has aptly described as "part of our national civil religion."[33]

Ideals of childhood innocence began to be reflected in lasting shifts in American law. Children achieved the right to some autonomy in their youth and early adulthood. In the 1840s and 1850s several states created adoption laws that fit with the emerging modern family defined by love, affection, and care of children. Massachusetts's law involved a judge's determination of the ability of prospective parents "to bring up the child . . . and furnish suitable nurture and education." Such laws displaced older ideas of parents' inherent rights to children. Over the course of the nineteenth century, courts began to consider the "best interests of the child" in custody cases, and they increasingly awarded children to the mother rather than the father. They also began to strike down laws that had required young people to get their parents' consent to marry. These changes lessened the rule of the father and diminished the right to use children's labor. Families were now more obligated to provide the kind of tender care that was presumably best expressed by the "gentler sex."[34]

In some ways, children were more freed from patriarchal authority in domestic arrangements than were their mothers. Women's nineteenth-century gains in this regard were nominal, although women in numerous states achieved rights to marital property and earnings in the middle of the century; these gains paled in comparison to all the ways in which married women lacked both access to legal or political identities separate from men and means of economic support without men. Stephanie Coontz has persuasively argued, "Women gained new contract rights as wives and mothers, including expanded inheritance and divorce possibilities, but these rights identified them more completely by their domestic roles. Married women's property acts merely protected property that women brought with them into marriage, not what they earned during marriage. Women could win a divorce only if they could prove that they embodied domestic virtues; their custody rights were expanded only insofar as they became primarily identified as nurturers and men as breadwinners."[35]

As for the trend toward awarding children to mothers in the relatively rare custody disputes of the nineteenth century, it was not coincidental that this shift paralleled the declining function of children as economic assets in the home. Emotionally defined relationships to children (as opposed to economic rights to children) favored the mother, and, as a result, she was often left economically burdened. With severely limited access to jobs that paid good wages, poorer women especially bore the brunt of this problem, and it is impossible to estimate the number of women who remained in problematic marriages because they knew they had no other way to support their children.

The ideology of moral motherhood was clearly a shift toward valuing mothers' relationships with their children, but, without the economic support of a husband, a mother rarely had the means to put food on the table while performing her duties of character development. Meanwhile, the developing ideal of a private, intimate nuclear family, morally presided over by a woman untainted by the world of economics, fueled the cultural modernization of motherhood. With its stress on innocent, malleable children negotiating with gentle mothers, moral motherhood ideology facilitated child-centered mothering, best accomplished with fewer children in a private setting defined by nuclear family roles.

BECOMING MORAL MOTHERS: PRACTICES AND IDEALS
AMONG WHITE, MIDDLE-CLASS WOMEN

Many women found their literary and public voices through the elaboration of the ideology of moral motherhood. But how did the rise of this ideology influence the way women actually reared their children and experienced motherhood? The existing private sources, such as diaries and letters, mostly come to us from white, middle-class women because they had the greatest access to literacy and were the primary target of the parental advice literature. These sources reveal a great emotional investment in the role of motherhood and the acceptance of the notion that they had a unique influence on their children.

When Fanny Longfellow privately expressed her fear of the "awful responsibility" of motherhood as she contemplated her relationship with her newborn, she gave voice to a heightened self-consciousness among white middle-class women about their roles as mothers in the first half of the nineteenth century. Similarly, Abigail Alcott wrote to her brother in 1833, "It seems to me at times as if the weight of responsibility connected with these mortal beings would prove too much for me—am I doing what is right? Am I doing enough? Am I not doing too much? Is my earnest inquiry."[36] Historian Sylvia Hoffert found that considerable anxiety was connected to the changing motherhood ideals of the era. Some of the mothers' worries concerned the ever-present specter of infant death. Teething was considered a time of special vulnerability to new diseases for babies. But Hoffert also observed that "when a woman weaned her child, and particularly if she did so within the first year, she assumed in a rather dramatic way responsibility for the moral training of her baby." Diarists and letter writers expressed regret about depriving their babies of "so much comfort," about having to be "cruel" to their babies by "weaning the poor little botherations," as Martha Coffin Wright wrote in a letter to her friend Lucretia Mott. Another mother wrote of her worry about her daughter's emotional development because of "my leaving her all day when I weaned her," which she regretted.[37]

Although mothers continued to carry great responsibilities for physical nurture, the weight of their moral responsibilities also shaped middle- and upper-class maternal identities in powerful ways. As a step toward the making of modern motherhood, moral motherhood ideas both heightened women's authority in the family and increased their susceptibility to guilt and regret. Their children's health, development, and spiritual destiny were measured by their own individual actions, as opposed to the broader actions of many family and community members or those of the patriarchal father.

We see this new cultural emphasis on the mother-child bond in middle-class mothers' expressions of feelings about their babies. "What a wilderness would this world be without my children. I should have none to love, nor anybody to take of me," lamented Lavinia Johnson, a middle-class woman of Utica, New York. And Mary Rodman Fisher Fox wrote, "In my baby I possess a source of pleasure unalloyed even by the anxiety which ever attends anything so much beloved." A mother had to remember, when an estimated one in four babies died before their first birthday in this region at this time, that children could easily be lost. Anna Colton Clayton wrote in a letter to her husband, "I don't forget—she is not wholly ours." Some mothers even feared their intense attachments to their children. One mother expressed her anxiety that it was "astonishing impiety" to love her child so much: "I feel that child possesses *all* my love, that child has weaned my heart from God. . . . Too dearly do I love him. Alas I tremble lest my God who will not accept a divided heart should snatch from me this little object of my love."[38]

These fears were especially magnified because many mothers had already lost infants as they began to care for new ones. Even before her own child died, Fanny Longfellow wrote of a friend who had lost a child, "Such a blow must soon sever, I should think, the mother's slender hold upon life." When Fanny Longfellow and her famous husband, Henry Wadsworth Longfellow, lost their seventeen-month-old daughter, they both expressed their deep and long-standing mourning in heartbreaking ways, even wondering how to love their remaining children. Fanny wrote that she would sometimes "devour my children's faces as if looking my last upon them."[39]

Many mothers found great satisfaction and joy from their children. The generational continuity of experience between middle-class mothers and their daughters contributed to what might strike us today as a lack of ambivalence about the actual rearing of children beyond infancy. "Awful" responsibility though it may have been, middle-class women settled into it quickly. Their lives—and usually their mothers' lives—revolved almost exclusively around domesticity. Mothers prepared daughters for lives much like their own, and what historian Carroll Smith-Rosenberg has called "the female world of love and ritual" was closely knit. Growing numbers of daughters attended some schooling away from home by the mid-nineteenth century, but for most coming of age simply meant moving from their fathers' homes to their husbands' homes.[40]

Within this tight "sphere" of the home, daughters learned what their futures would be like by watching their mothers in what Smith-Rosenberg has termed an "apprenticeship system." Mothers taught their daughters both household management and child care. Popular advice literature encouraged mothers to enlist their daughters as confidantes and friends: "When your daughter is old enough to be your companion and friend allow her to participate in your cares and duties. It is the affectionate daughter and kind sister who will make the self-denying wife, and devoted mother." Women taught one another culturally sanctioned selflessness, which was supposed to find its greatest expression in the roles of wife and mother. They also shared experiences of domestic life, including frequent pregnancies. Smith-Rosenberg observed,

> An intimate mother-daughter relationship lay at the heart of this female world. The diaries and letters of both mothers and daughters attest to their closeness and mutual emotional dependency. Daughters routinely discussed their mother's health and activities with their own friends, expressed anxiety in cases of their mother's ill health and concern for her cares. Expressions of hostility . . . seem to have been uncommon indeed.

One mother wrote to her recently married daughter, "You do not know how much I miss you, not only when I . . . no longer pour into your sympathizing ear my senile gossip, but all the day I muse away, since the sound of your voice no longer rouses me to sympathy with your joys or sorrows. . . . You cannot know how much I miss your affectionate demonstrations." In Utica, New York, two out of three women in the mid-nineteenth century still lived with their children after age sixty, a reminder that such ties between mothers and daughters were often lifelong.[41]

Sons, however, were socialized toward different worlds than the ones their mothers inhabited. Ideally, sons would occupy the breadwinner half of the gendered division of labor. Still mothers' success in emotionally binding their children to them is further evidenced by the letters exchanged between mothers and sons. During the Civil War, for example, sons were more likely to address mothers in their letters than fathers.[42] In those letters, mothers urged their sons to "keep out of temptation, avoid bad company, try and do good," as Mrs. Mary Perry wrote to her son. "My dear Win," she continued, "once more be a good boy, don't forget your Mother who thinks of you when the rest of the folks are asleep." Perry's son wrote back frequently. He addressed his mother as "dear homely mother," and "Dear Ma." Mary Ryan points out that letters between fathers and sons were "more stilted and instrumental," including, for example, requests for funds.[43] This evidence speaks to the ways that middle-class mothers often embraced moral motherhood and incorporated its ideals into their relationships with their children.

MATERNAL AUTHORITY AND ITS LIMITS

In 1811, Mary Palmer Tyler, a mother with no formal training, anonymously published a child-care manual, *The Maternal Physician*. In her book, she claimed authority over children's physical health by virtue of her experience as a mother. At a time when physicians were not yet an organized professional group and actually claimed to know little about children's health, Tyler's readers probably agreed with her when she admonished physicians: "These gentlemen must pardon me if I think, after all, that a mother is her child's best physician, in all ordinary cases." Though perhaps afraid of public censure for publishing anything as a woman (hence the anonymity of her authorship), Tyler was not shy about staking a singular maternal claim to her children's character training. Her book gives detailed examples of how to guide young children. Discipline, Tyler's examples suggested, taught a child to see reason and justice in the form of maternal authority. If the child had a "just sense of right and wrong," she claimed, then he would, in good republican fashion, resist "arbitrary government." In practice, Tyler lived and espoused republican motherhood principles in child rearing, as Marilyn S. Blackwell's analysis of her life and work shows.[44] Tyler's successors in the field of child-care advice, including Lydia Maria Child, emphasized affection and selflessness more than reason, thereby making motherhood an even more ideally feminine occupation. Essentially, as moral motherhood ideas began to gain prominence, motherhood in general was more closely intertwined with ideals of womanhood.

Tyler also considered herself a moral leader in the family, and she acted on that notion. The fact that Tyler's husband was frequently absent from the home on business probably contributed to the latitude she exercised in "governing" her family of nine children. When her children were young, Tyler expanded her influence in the home through the idea of the republican mother with moral duties, but, when her children grew older, her economic vulnerability shaped her relationships with them. After a fall in family fortunes and the deterioration of her husband's health, Tyler, like generations before her, became economically dependent on her sons. Her insecurities about their moral training became more marked when they left home, even as she continued to depend upon them. To one son, she wrote, "be assured my son that the tender love I bear you is the reward of your goodness and whenever you forfeit your right to it, although it may break in the separation, you will tear yourself from my heart—and then farewell happiness this side of the grave—!" Fortunately for Tyler, this son continued to support his parents, even buying them a house before he married, taking in two of his younger brothers as apprentices, and helping with education for the other sons. Nevertheless, in her widowhood Tyler continued to write to her sons asking for money and time away from their studies to help her with physical labor. "While you work in the garden I will work for you," she suggested to one son and promised to make him new shirts in exchange for his help.[45]

In Tyler's story, we see how republican and moral motherhood might empower a woman in her home and provide her with a significant sense of purpose and effectiveness, yet her relationships with her older children reveal the limits of these cultural ideals. When it came to real economic needs, for themselves or for their children, mothers had little power. For many cultural commentators, this was entirely as it should be. To involve women in the competitive world of economic gain would be to "unsex" them, to use the nineteenth-century parlance. Catharine Beecher claimed that women's economic and political dependence on men was a positive good, even a fundamental piece of the fabric of the new democratic American civilization. After all, luckily for the American woman, "No woman is forced to obey any husband but the one she chooses herself." And free women were not "compelled to perform the rough labor of the fields." Beecher lauded American civilization for its careful delineation of women into a domestic sphere. To secure their "privileges," it was appropriate that a woman "in the domestic relation . . . take a subordinate station, and that, in civil and political concerns, her interests be intrusted [sic] to the other sex, without her taking any part in voting, or in making and administering laws."[46]

Beecher was not only a very influential writer, but she also founded one of the new female academies of the early nineteenth century. Beecher never married and, like Lydia Maria Child, did not have children of her own. Such was the power of maternal ideology, or, seen another way, such were the restrictions on the topics about which educated women could passionately write. Despite her own public presence and her interest in the cause of abolishing slavery, Beecher insisted that women use indirect moral persuasion rather than direct political influence to sway powerful men toward a more just society: "Let every woman become so cultivated and refined in intellect that her taste and judgment will be respected; so benevolent in feeling and action, that her motives will be reverenced; so unassuming and unambitious, that collision and competition will be banished; so 'gentle and easy to be entreated,' that every heart will repose in her presence; then, the fathers, the husbands, and the sons, will find an influence thrown around them, to which they will yield not only willingly but proudly."[47]

Like many of her contemporaries, Beecher argued for greater education for mothers as well, but insisted that this education focus on domestic enlightenment. Beecher resisted publicly the demands made in her era by feminists such as Elizabeth Cady Stanton, Susan B. Anthony, Frederick Douglass, and many others, that women needed the public rights of citizenship, including the right to vote.

The New Motherhood and the Private Middle-Class Family

The moral mother operated within the home, a space exalted by nineteenth-century moralists that increasingly reflected an ideal of nuclear family privacy. Geographically and demographically, the northern white middle class was retreating into a new and more modern form of familial privacy. As the Industrial Revolution advanced over the course of the nineteenth century, the home became a separate space, a place of moral training of children, leisure for men, and a refuge from the competitive world of economic striving. Residentially, urban middle-class Americans increasingly segregated themselves from factory laborers, new immigrants, casual laborers, and the growing population of the urban poor. Servants, once considered part of the moral responsibility of the father as master, receded into the background in cultural portraits of "the home." New legal precedents defined the nuclear family as the norm, exempting northern family patriarchs from the right to punish their servants or require them to live with them. Middle-class mothers were encouraged to keep the problems of the "lower orders" at arm's length. Within the home, *The Mothers' Magazine* told its readers, mothers could protect children from the "contamination of the streets." Even middle-class men were chided for frequenting taverns and political meetings instead of going home.[48] By midcentury, some religious groups were advocating private prayer, and among evangelicals one reverend even decried the long meetings of his church because they took Christians away from "the duties of the family."[49]

The middle-class home was actually only a partially private place. Servants and, before 1865, slaves provided essential labor in making "the home" functional. "Between 1800 and 1850, the proportion of servants to white households doubled, to about nine to one," historian Stephanie Coontz has noted.[50] Neither the female nor the male advocates of the new ideology of moral motherhood, however, acknowledged the roles of servants as significantly reducing the workload of the ladies of the house. Colonial-era domestic servants in the North had often been apprentices of similar class and ethnic background as their mistresses. By the mid-nineteenth century, ethnic, race, and class differences stunted the sociability of women in the home and created the middle-class home as a place of hierarchy. Of course, this situation had long been the case in the South, where enslaved women more often did domestic work. Now, in the North, middle-class women thought of their servants, often new immigrants or women of color, not as apprentices but as social inferiors, even as they entrusted some essential functions of child care to these less privileged women.

Upper- and middle-class families frequently hired wet nurses as servants, commodifying one of the most intimate areas of mothers' lives. In colonial times, northern children were sent to neighbors or to board in the country to be suckled by other women more capable and/or less wealthy. Between the American Revolution and the Civil War, wealthier women began to bring wet nurses into their homes instead of boarding children with families; in this way, they could still keep a watchful eye on their babies and begin their moral training. For example, Harriet Beecher Stowe, the mother of five children born within the first seven years of her marriage, employed an Irish wet nurse who lived in her home for three months.[51] The shift in wet-nursing employment highlights the increasing privatization of class-privileged families.

Older married women, while still nursing their own babies, had served as wet nurses in colonial times, but the nineteenth-century situation was rife with exploitation. In the North, most wet nurses were poor immigrants, often the mothers of babies conceived out of wedlock. Directors of maternity hospitals in the Northeast sent former patients to the homes of upper- and middle-class women. In an era that saw an upswing in infant mortality, owing to urban disease environments and concentrated poverty, more wet nurses were available for hire because their own infants had died. Women of living babies sometimes brought their infants to live in the homes of their employers, but this was unusual. Mothers who employed wet nurses rarely made allowances for their employees' maternal roles. Consequently, many single or widowed mothers desperate for an income turned their own infants over to orphan asylums or other charitable institutions so that they could nurse middle- and upper-class babies for pay.[52]

This small example speaks to the paradoxes of familial privacy and the middle-class assumptions built into the new motherhood ideals. The idea of bringing a woman to live with one's family and nurse one's children hardly suggests an emphasis on privacy, yet the control involved in selecting and monitoring the behavior of a person perceived to be one's social inferior actually fit with the role of the moral mother. Moreover, the invisibility of the work of servants in the popular literature of the period reminds us that so much of this ideology was a fiction, even for the class for whom it was intended. Mothers may have been the moral directors of their households, but in valuing their own labors they made invisible the labor of other women, some, like the wet nurses, who were unfortunate mothers themselves.

This conflict was particularly true among well-to-do southern women, most of whom were part of slave-owning families. Diaries and letters suggest that elite southern women saw mothers' care of infants as a vital role, about which they were particularly self-conscious in the pre–Civil War decades that saw the rise of moral mother ideology: "It is a woman's place to raise her children herself," remarked one southern woman in a letter to her brother, "and though to do this faithfully she must make some sacrifices and many a time deny herself amusements and pleasures, I am grateful I have given up everything else for those duties, they were sometimes irksome, but as far as my children are concerned, I am paid back with interest." This woman's difficulty letting go of the topic of her children's irksomeness suggests self-consciousness and introspection about what were probably heightened expectations placed on privileged southern white mothers during this time. Historians' documentation of enslaved women's lives tells a different story. The actual child-care burdens of privileged white women were greatly lightened by the enslaved population whose presence and labor also belied the emerging national idea of the private, mother-centered family.[53] The exploitation of enslaved mothers, the starkest contrast to the idealized notion of the moral mother, was one among many contradictions that invigorated debates about moral motherhood and society.

CONCLUSION

The ideology of moral motherhood had a widespread impact on literate white women who were in or struggling to be in the middle and upper classes. The ideas of republican motherhood and moral motherhood, respectively, were born from the Enlightenment, Protestant religious developments, and the early Industrial Revolution's separation of home and work for the growing northern middle class. These ideas spread far and wide in the nation's first mass media: wide-circulation popular magazines and domestic advice books catered to an increasingly literate female audience. Moral motherhood ideals were evident in the South as well as the North, and white women on the expanding western frontier sometimes espoused similar domestic idealization in their writings, though the conditions of their lives also mitigated against the realization of the Victorian home.[54]

The ideology of moral motherhood represented a vast cultural shift toward elevating the psychological, spiritual, and even civic contributions of women in the home. It created a new sense of self-consciousness, introspection, and arguably empowerment for middle-class women who tried to understand and more deliberately shape the development of their children. At the same time, moral motherhood also exacerbated gender distinctions and legitimated women's economic and political dependence.

Moral motherhood also espoused a sheltered familial ideal available only to those with economic privilege. The conditions of most women's lives in the mid-nineteenth century were far removed from these new mother ideals. Until 1865, most African Americans were ensnared in the system of slavery, and an ever-growing population of economically marginal immigrants, displaced craftsmen, and landless poor struggled to survive through family strategies at odds with moral motherhood.

CHAPTER 2

Contradictions of Moral Motherhood

SLAVERY, RACE, AND REFORM

By the time the enslaved Harriet Jacobs reached the age of sixteen, she had been trying to ignore her master's sexual overtures for years. She later became involved with another white man, whom she hoped would purchase her from her master, Dr. Flint. But Flint threatened Jacobs and vowed never to sell her. Jacobs did not have the right to her own person, and, when she eventually became a mother, her slim claims to her children haunted her throughout her life. When her first child was born "sickly," Flint "did not fail to remind me that my child was an addition to his stock of slaves," she recalled. As her child's health improved, Jacobs's love for her son was mixed with sorrow:

> The little vine was taking deep root in my existence, though its clinging fondness excited a mixture of love and pain. When I was most sorely oppressed I found a solace in his smiles. I loved to watch his infant slumbers; but always there was a dark cloud over my enjoyment. I could never forget that he was a slave. Sometimes I wished that he might die in infancy. God tried me. My darling became very ill. . . . Alas, what mockery it is for a slave mother to try to pray back her dying child to life! Death is better than slavery.[1]

Jacobs bore another child and hatched a complicated plan to avoid seeing the children made into field laborers. She believed she could not escape with her two children, but she refused to leave them and tried everything in her power to exercise some control over their future. Still negotiating with the children's white father, Mr. Sands, Jacobs hid in her grandmother's attic for seven years. She saw her children sold to an agent representing Mr. Sands and fervently hoped for their freedom at Sands's hands. Sands did not treat Jacobs's children as slaves, but neither did he free them. After sending them north to live with one of his relatives, he promised them an education. Jacobs managed to follow her daughter north and spent a brief time reunited with her son. But she lived in constant fear of being sold or having her children sold back into slavery. This was always a possibility after Congress passed the federal Fugitive Slave Act of 1850, which empowered southerners to capture escaped slaves in the North.

Jacobs wrote her story with religious zeal for a growing abolitionist audience. Like many other abolitionist writers, she spoke passionately of the evils the slave system visited on the mother-child tie. In fact, many of the sources we have to examine the situation of enslaved mothers come from abolitionist writers, who, whether African American or white, usually emphasized the moral sin of slavery and the abject victimization of everyone in its grip—most especially the enslaved, but also the immortal souls of those who profited from the system.

Enslaved persons were not allowed to learn to read or write, and, although some were secretly literate, firsthand documentation like the kind Jacobs provided is very limited. Another important set of sources comes from interviews with formerly enslaved persons, often many years after the end of slavery. Less directed at an immediate social cause than the abolitionist literature, these sources often differ in tone and frequently include some version of dialect rendered by the interviewer. It is easy to find here, too, the traumatic reality of lost family ties. For example, a woman who endured a life of slavery and was sold three times recalled the situation vividly: "Babies was snatched from dere mother's breas' an' sold to speculators. Chilluns was separated from sisters an' brothers an' never saw each other ag'in. Course dey cry; you think dey not cry when dey was sold lak cattle. . . . It's bad to belong to folks dat own you soul an' body." As the formerly enslaved abolitionist Frederick Douglass pointed out, "The domestic hearth, with its holy lessons and precious endearments is abolished in the case of a slave mother and her children."[2]

The dominant culture painted a portrait of the economically dependent mother, defined in relationship to a child who was innocent and malleable, and a father whose primary responsibility was economic support. Meanwhile, millions of enslaved women labored night and day to create wealth they could not access and brought into the world babies whom they could not claim as their own. By the nineteenth century, enslaved women were bearing large numbers of children compared to their colonial ancestors, while their odds of being separated from their children were greater than before. With the end of the international slave trade in 1808, slavery continued to expand south and west through the sale of people already in the United States. This expansion rested on the breakup of families: 875,000 enslaved people were moved from the upper South to the lower South between 1820 and 1860.[3]

The coexistence of slavery with the ideology of moral motherhood reveals divisions of race and class that endure today. It is also notable that a vocal segment of the very class that touted moral motherhood recognized something of the exploitation and suffering inherent in the plight of the enslaved mother. Indeed, initial steps toward the making of modern motherhood included the cultural construction of a unique place for an idealized mother figure within the American family. For some women, it became important to confront situations in which this ideal mother role was impossible to attain, and slavery represented just such a situation.

It is a testament to the power of maternal ideology that it did so much to animate the abolitionist cause.

By the 1820s and 1830s, a motivated group of northern middle-class women, both white and African American, as well as a few brave southerners, seized on the horror of slavery as an affront to moral motherhood. This idea had a profound impact on abolitionist advocacy in the form of literature, most notably in the novel *Uncle Tom's Cabin* and a range of political speech. In the particular racial crucible in which moral motherhood emerged, important patterns developed that continue throughout American history. Less privileged mothers coped with situations in which they had little control over their lives but intense responsibility for their family's survival. Meanwhile, the contradictions inherent in the moral motherhood ideal actually empowered some women to speak on public issues. In the nineteenth century, both evangelical religious zeal and a concept of shared maternal feelings created passionate pleas for the rights of mothers to be heard on public issues. Maternal outrage over slavery was the most politically charged complaint, but pointed maternal critiques ranged broadly from men's alcohol consumption to sexual slavery, and eventually to the problem of poverty in a capitalist society.

African American Mothering and Nineteenth-Century Slavery

In the most basic ways, enslaved African American women were denied the right to care for and nurture their children. The system of slavery circumscribed every aspect of the possibility of ideal womanhood. As Harriet Jacobs's story illustrates, one of the most fundamental realities of the system was that African Americans were the legal owners of neither their own bodies nor the children they bore. Enslaved women very frequently faced unwanted sexual advances and assaults that often resulted in pregnancy outside marriage. Mary Chestnut Boykin, whose family owned slaves, confessed in her diary what was common knowledge but still a taboo subject among white southerners: "Like the patriarchs of old," she said, "our men live all in one house with their wives and concubines; and the mulattoes one sees in every family partly resemble the white children. Any lady is ready to tell you who is the father of all the mulatto children in everybody's household but her own. Those, she seems to think, drop from the sky." Fom the perspective of an African American mother, vulnerable to losing her children through sale, Jacobs made a similar point: "Southern women often marry a man knowing that he is the father of many little slaves," Jacobs wrote. "They do not trouble themselves about it. They regard such children as property, as marketable as the pigs on the plantation; and it is seldom that they do not make them aware of this by passing them into the slave-trader's hands as soon as possible, and thus getting them out of their sight."[4]

Enslaved African American women's relationships to men of either race were not legally recognized, although within enslaved communities marriage was valued. When masters did openly acknowledge their relationships with enslaved women, the situation was an emotional powder keg in which the African American mother was the most vulnerable party. Formerly enslaved Solomon Northrup, for example, recounted the story of a woman named Eliza, "the slave of Elisha Berry, a rich man." After a falling out with his wife, Mr. Berry left his wife and daughter in one house and built a new house on his estate. "Into the house he brought Eliza; and, on condition of her living with him, she and her children were to be emancipated." Not surprisingly, Eliza and her daughter Emily became "the object of Mrs. Berry's and her daughter's hatred and dislike." When Berry came into hard times, Eliza was told that she and her daughter would get their free papers; instead, they were sent "into the pen" to be sold. This woman, once "arrayed in silk, with rings upon her fingers . . . above the common level of a slave," and her daughter, "seven or eight years old," were separated at sale. Slave traders complained frequently that heartbroken mothers carried on so much about the sale of their children that the marketplace lowered their value. Eliza, after being struck by the man who had just bought her daughter, begged her own new owner: "Please, master, buy Emily. I can never work any if she is taken from me; I will die." Though Eliza's purchaser eventually conceded, the slave trader refused to sell Emily. "There were heaps and piles of money to be made of her, he said, when she was a few years older. There were men enough in New Orleans who would give five thousand dollars for such an extra, handsome, fancy piece as Emily would be."[5]

Sale and other separations of children, husbands, and other kin were critical pieces of the emotional brutality of slavery. Indeed, women were more likely than men to be sold and sold more than once.[6] In situations like Eliza's, the jealousy of a mistress heightened the risk. When enslaved women were able to rear their children, husbands' help was often lacking because in the tradition of "abroad" marriages many husbands lived on other plantations. Because African lineage and intergenerational ties were severed by slavery, African traditions of extended-family child care had to be reinvented in the context of slavery as far back as the seventeenth century. As the population of enslaved persons in the United States stabilized, African Americans created new intergenerational ties, but their vulnerability to family disruptions continued.

African American women created mother-child ties that demonstrated motherly love while emphasizing survival skills, protection from physical harm, preservation of cultural and family bonds, and an awareness of the middle line between self-affirming resistance and dangerous rebellion. They worked with every tool and resource at their disposal. Though Frederick Douglas remembered rarely seeing his mother by the light of day, she visited him in the evening after traveling from her plantation to another at the end of her long day's work. Enslaved mothers, pleading with slave owners not to sell their children, exercised any power they could in such situations, including hiding their children and even, on occasion, threatening to kill them to intimidate their masters. Enslaved mothers also tried to protect their daughters from the endemic problem of sexual abuse and to shield their children from beatings. When Jacob Stroyer's mother tried to stop her son from being whipped by a horse trainer, she was whipped herself. Another man, the son of a slave-owner and an enslaved woman, recounted to the abolitionist Angelina Grimke his mother's efforts to protect her sons: "When she remonstrated at their unjust treatment she was thrown into a loathsome cell and kept there for six days eating nothing during her stay there."[7]

African American parents and elders had complex tasks as disciplinarians. One African American husband, working in the gold fields of California, wrote to his wife that she should "Learn them to be Smart and decent, allow them to Sauce no person." The balance between submission and personal dignity, something parents struggled to find in their own lives, was a constant tension in the socialization of children. Jacobs recalled poignantly the loyalty conflict for African American children between one's kin and one's mistress, a revelation of African American parents' general lack of power to exert authority with their children.

> My brother was a spirited boy; and being brought up under such influences, he early detested the name of master and mistress. One day, when his father and mistress both happened to call him at the same, he hesitated between the two; being perplexed to know which had the stronger claim on his obedience. He finally concluded to go to his mistress. When my father reproved him for it, he said, "You both called me, and I didn't know which I ought to go to first." "You are *my* child," replied our father, "and when I call you, you should come immediately, if you have to pass through fire and water." Poor Willie! He was now to learn his first lesson of obedience to a master.[8]

A more dramatic story comes from a woman born into slavery: "My mother certainly had her faults as a slave," she remembered. "Ma fussed, fought, and kicked all the time.... With all her ability for work, she did not make a good slave.... The one doctrine of my mother's teaching which was branded upon my senses was that I should never let anyone abuse me. 'I'll kill you, gal, if you don't stand up for yourself,' she would say. 'Fight, and if you can't fight, kick; if you can't kick, then bite.'" The "almost daily talks" her mother gave her "on the cruelty of slavery" stuck with the daughter and were made especially vivid on several occasions: Her mother resisted so strongly to being whipped by her mistress that her mother attacked her mistress, tearing off her clothes. When she then resisted a renewed whipping by men called in from beyond the plantation, the master told her she would have to leave the plantation and abandon her baby and her older children. At the moment she was pushed to abandon the baby, the mother "took the baby by its feet, a foot in each hand, and with the baby's head swinging downward, she vowed to smash its brains out before she'd leave it. Tears were streaming down her face. It was seldom that ma cried, and everyone knew that she meant every word. Ma took her baby with her." But her daughter and the other children had to live without their parents' care for another year. Knowing of her impending separation from both parents, the daughter "cried until my eyes looked like balls of fire. I felt for the first time in my life that I had been abused."[9]

Personal power was a hard lesson to teach to enslaved children. Few accounts of slavery contain such stories like the one recounted here, in which an individual mother overcame all the legal and police authority that backed up the system of slavery. In this case, she did so simply through her own claims as a family member and her ability to leverage established relationships with white power. Most enslaved mothers could do very little to protect their children from this cruel system of extrafamilial authority, with "justice" meted out by masters, mistresses, overseers, and the law.

Enslaved mothers also suffered the humiliation of having their children and their husbands, often powerless to protect or be protected, see them physically abused. One man remembered a child's point of view on a mother's limited power in this way: "Many's de time I edges up to the whip," Jacob Branch said, to "take some dem licks off my mammy."[10] Another son remembered helping his mother spin and card her quota of wool in the evening to help her avoid fifty lashes the next day for failing to complete her task.[11] Many men risked their lives intervening to protect women they loved, but the system sanctioned violent retribution for any defiance of white authority.

Family bonds endured anyway. Enslaved mothers' ties to their children were apparent in their intense grief over lost children. A formerly enslaved woman remembered after the death of her child, "I like to went crazy for a long time atta dat." Stories abound of enslaved mothers who grieved forever, often while being sold from place to place, for children torn away from them. Like Harriet Jacobs, most enslaved mothers stuck with their children whenever possible. Men had, and were more likely to take, greater opportunities to escape slavery because of traditions that allowed them visiting privileges to wives on other plantations and because women were more likely to attempt to take children with them when trying to flee.[12]

Enslaved women and men also worked to provide for their children, despite not owning the fruits of their labor. Adding this labor to the work they were compelled to do was no small feat. Amelia Walker remembered that she saw her mother plowing with three horses and "thought women was 'sposed to work 'long with the men." With the rise of the cotton economy in the nineteenth century, picking 150 to 200 pounds of cotton each day in the harvest season drained the energy of enslaved adults of both sexes. Still, the work of enslaved parents included supplementing their children's meager diet by hunting, fishing, and maintaining small gardens. With the permission of their owners, a few also hired themselves out or took in extra work to help purchase food or shoes, which were rarely provided to enslaved children. One child of an enslaved mother recounted that instead of taking her four days of holiday leave after Christmas, as most adults did, her mother "used the four days to weave and wash for white people who lived in the area, and with the meager pay was able to provide materially for her children beyond what their owner provided."[13]

In the infrequent situations when masters allowed enslaved parents to earn wages, some worked for many, many years to purchase their children's freedom. A formerly enslaved person recalled a mother who secured a job as a cook in a large tavern, worked in a garrison, and then developed her own business selling pies and coffee to marines in exchange for some of their rations. Mrs. Jackson, a woman from Kentucky "bought herself by washing and ironing of nights after her mistress' work was done. During seven long years . . . her sleep was little naps over the ironing board. . . . She had a son and daughter nearly grown, and to purchase their freedoms she was now bending her day and night energies." When her master planned to sell one of her children in payment of a debt, Jackson could come up with only $400 of her child's $900 price tag. She went door to door, mortgaging the value of her own person to find the money. A Baptist deacon finally purchased her daughter, and then Jackson herself purchased her daughter.[14]

African American women's resourcefulness in providing for their children meant that their identities as providers necessarily contradicted the moral mother ideology. By working for someone else and providing subsistence and care in the stolen hours after they had completed their work requirements, African Americans set a precedent that more and more women would follow as industrialization separated family labor from making a living. Of course, women who were not enslaved performed the work for others in exchange for pay and had far more rights to their own persons after those working hours. African American women were breadwinners both during slavery and, for the vast majority, after slavery. Like other nineteenth-century women who combined "productive" and "reproductive" labor out of necessity, they created traditions of shared care that contradicted the privatized maternal ideals of the middle class.

An often-hidden tradition among women with few resources, especially women of color, was what Patricia Hill Collins has called "othermothering," the practice of caring for children who were not biologically one's own. Enslaved women devised, or were enmeshed in, these systems by necessity. Siblings often cared for babies, and on larger plantations elderly women and men served as othermothers for children who may have had no biological relationship to them. In part because slave-owners considered elderly enslaved people less productive in the fields, they assigned them the task of caring for young children while insisting that women of reproductive age continue to work in the fields or the master's house. These arrangements no doubt contributed to the intergenerational and cross kin bonds that led to the use of "fictive kin" terms among African Americans. Naming nonblood relatives as kin (aunties or uncles, for example) was part of how people adapted to the disruptions of family life endemic to the system of slavery. That being said, not all enslaved women could rely on shared care arrangements for their children, especially if they worked in smaller environments. One woman recalled hanging her baby in a basket with a mixture of flour and boiled water for food so she could go to the fields. She said, "It cry all day an' I cry all day, an' he died, 'cause he cry so."[15]

Although most African American women were enslaved before the end of the slave system in 1865, by 1830 more than three hundred thousand free African Americans inhabited both the South and the North. Sharing some religious sensibilities with Protestant whites and enjoying greater access to literacy, they left behind more sources revealing how they incorporated and modified the growing cultural emphasis on mother care. Like their white counterparts, those who were most outspoken about abolishing slavery drew on notions of moral motherhood as rhetorical persuasion. Maria Stewart, a domestic servant in the Northeast, was the first woman to speak publicly against slavery to mixed audiences in Boston. She called upon her fellow African American women to use their maternal virtues toward the purification of society: "Who can find a virtuous woman? for her price is far above rubies. Blessed is the man who shall call her his wife; yea, happy is the child who shall call her mother."[16]

The sharing of moral motherhood ideals between a small cadre of middle-class African American and white women was more evident by the end of the nineteenth century. Even then, as we will see, African American women retained from the patterns of slavery and legally sanctioned discrimination an economic realism about motherhood and a view of child rearing that was more collective than individualistic. Traditions of othermothering, which buffered but also decentered the nuclear family, continued throughout African American history. Many formally educated African American women seem to have embraced the notion of their unique and moral influence on children, but most African American mothers also persisted in seeing their duties as a combination of materially providing for and emotionally nurturing children, while working with kin and community to do so. Their approach to mothering represented one of many real-world counterexamples to the ideal of a privatized nuclear family.

Throughout the nineteenth-century United States, the middle-class motherhood model was unavailable to the vast majority of the American population. True, the middle class grew, indeed came of age, in the early nineteenth century. But that group always remained a minority of the population, even in the nation's industrial urban areas. Estimates of the percentage of employed middle- and upper-class men (those whom census takers could measure) range from approximately 23 to 40 percent of the population, depending on the measure of occupational status and the decade.[17] Because they were financially tied to less privileged men, most nineteenth-century mothers toiled in homes with few accoutrements, in the homes of others as domestic servants, or in fields or factories. Often, too, the women brought in income through a patchwork of strategies, ranging from selling agricultural produce to taking in laundry and sewing projects. In other words, a "domestic hearth" isolated from the economic world was a fiction for most of the population.

The Continuing Significance of Race

Meanwhile, in the aftermath of slavery, African Americans tried to wrench their labor away from the owning class and did everything in their power to direct that labor toward their families. An enslaved woman during the Civil War represented the plight of millions when she wrote her husband of the harsh treatment she endured. She lamented, "Our child cries for you." But she added hopefully, "Do not fret too much for me for it wont [sic] be long before I will be free and then all we make will be ours." Even after the abolition of slavery, however, most African Americans would have no choice but to continue working on large plantations as sharecroppers. African Americans would try to change the arrangements of their working lives by the withdrawal of wives and mothers from full-time field labor under white supervision. Former slave-owners complained bitterly about their reduced authority over women laborers and took out their frustrations in spasms of violent retribution. Freedwomen's efforts to claim their family labor was part of a broader effort of ordinary mothers to define their own work needs with respect to mothering and other family duties. Maud Lee Bryant later recalled her years working in cotton, wheat, and tobacco fields after slavery: "My object of working was wanting the children to have a better way of living, that the world might be just a little better because the Lord had me here for something, and I tried to make good out of it, that was my aim."[18]

This taking ownership of labor for one's own family was the hope African Americans tried to realize, despite the fact that, as a group, their economic dependence on the slave-owning class was virtually guaranteed after the war. The federal government created a Freedmen's Bureau in an attempt to negotiate slightly altered relationships between formerly enslaved persons and their old employers. But without access to land, few African Americans were able to break out of debt peonage through the sharecropping system. Most worked as field laborers for cash crops, often on the estates of their former owners. Most were told by those owners that after paying their "share" of the costs of seeds, tools, and rent on the land, they were still in debt to those owners year after year. Freed people were regularly defrauded of the fruits of their agricultural labor. Reconstruction, the northern commitment to assisting with the transition in the southern labor system and guaranteeing the vote to African American men, ended abruptly in 1877.

The vast majority of white southerners also became more economically vulnerable after the Civil War; more than ever before many former slaveholders themselves became debt-ridden sharecroppers. But southern politicians "redeemed" the South with a new system of white supremacy from which even the poorest whites benefited. By the end of the nineteenth century they had created an "American apartheid" through which they legally disenfranchised and segregated African Americans while enforcing the arrangement through violence, as exemplified by the Ku Klux Klan. Thus, while some white women had access to textile labor, clerical work, or teaching, African American women remained largely confined to sharecropping and domestic work. Under the new laws, disproportionate poverty and lack of access to both the justice system and the ballot box were institutionalized on the basis of race.[19]

In 1870, more than 90 percent of southern African Americans lived overwhelmingly in poverty in rural areas, and most were unable to read or write. Most mothers bore six to seven children, and those children rarely had an opportunity to attend school; instead, they began work in the homes or fields of whites before they hit puberty. Of families in the Cotton Belt, black and white, 80 percent were two-parent families, but African American families, poorer than their white neighbors, were far more likely to need to work outside their homes and to send their children to work. White southerners were remarkably united in their refusal to sell property or extend credit even to African Americans who could afford it. As late as 1910, 90 percent of southern African Americans in farming were tenants, sharecroppers, or contract laborers.[20]

Economic necessity forced most African American women to continue in some field labor and to scrape together a combination of seasonal work, picking or hoeing various crops, or doing laundry work and other domestic labor for pay. The cost of reproducing the labor force that sustained the southern economy was now shifted fully to African American families, who had to become self-sustaining economic units in spite of all the obstacles arrayed against them. African Americans often had to make use of their own and their children's labor directly in the fields in order to acquire their "shares" in the continuing southern agricultural system. They traded full-time field labor under white supervision for bare economic survival, but also gained some familial control.

Despite all these constraints, African American mothers strove to define the meaning of freedom. Rosaline Rogers, the mother of fourteen, for example, said she chose to stay on her former master's plantation rather than break up her family by moving and having her children "apprenticed" as workers in other people's homes or fields. Women frequently took in laundry to avoid full-time field work and instead stay at home with their children. Mothers defied the system in spite of the threat of violence. Eliza James, a mother brought before the Freedmen's Bureau for "impudently" refusing to follow a white man's orders that she punish her son, "said she would not whip her child for no poor white folks." Such action reminded her too much of slavery. Others petitioned the Freedmen's Bureau in disputes over wages and sometimes also took advantage of this new institutional resource to lodge complaints against abusive husbands. Few markers of freedom existed for these women beyond the ownership of oneself and the relative freedom to make decisions, in concert with their husbands, about family life. But, as historian Jacqueline Jones aptly observed, "Freedwomen derived emotional fulfillment and a newfound sense of pride from their roles as wives and mothers. Only at home could they exercise a measure of control over their own lives and those of their husbands and children and impose a semblance of order on the physical world."[21]

The small minority of African American women living in cities was also especially active in improving children's lives by developing educational and religious services and doing charity work. Part of the meaning of freedom for them was the opportunity to create their own institutions, including churches, mutual aid societies, clubs, health services, and charities. By the end of the nineteenth century, the collective concerns of some of the more privileged African American women for the future of "the race" resulted in the creation of the first national African American women's organization, the National Association of Colored Women (NACW). These organizations built bridges between the small population of northern African American women and their more circumscribed southern sisters. The NACW women protested lynching, which escalated dramatically in the late nineteenth and early twentieth centuries. They also opposed bans on interracial marriage and spoke out about the continued sexual abuse suffered by women working in the homes of southern white people, which persisted long after slavery. As activist Mamie Fields noted of her early twentieth-century club's work with homeless African American girls, "We all could see that we had a responsibility for those girls: they were the daughters of our community coming up."[22]

While the voices of African American women activists had a very limited audience in the larger society during the half-century after the abolition of slavery, white Americans collectively fell in love with a mythological distortion of African American motherhood: the "mammy" icon. "Mammy" represented the faithful slave and later servant in white American memory, the woman whose love for white children anchored her to white families. The film *Gone with the Wind* immortalized this stock character in the 1930s, but the idea had been around since the time of slavery. After the Civil War, it gained great traction in a whole school of southern writing that immortalized the South's "Lost Cause" and romanticized slavery. By the 1910s, white women impersonators of "mammy" were drawing on many decades of minstrel show caricatures to amuse white audiences with "Stories of the Old South, the Crooning Lullaby's of the Old Negro Mammies with Many Amusing Anecdotes of a Later Generation of Negroes." Mildred Lewis Rutherford, "historian general" of the United Daughters of the Confederacy (UDC) in the early 1910s, collected obituaries of presumably faithful former slaves. A UDC scrapbook contained stories such as "Black Mammy and Her White Baby." In this story, an African American "mammy," learning of the new freedom at the end of the Civil War, reassures her young white charge that she would never leave her. "Leave that chile? Nebber. Nebber. No freedom for dis ole nigger if I have to give up my white baby."[23]

After more than two centuries of slavery robbed generations of African American women of rights to their children, this mythology of the mammy wildly distorted the nation's collective memory of slavery and made invisible African Americans' love for their own children. As historian Micki McElya has shown, the mammy imagery and stories also used the idea of African American women's devotion to white children to absolve the South—and even the nation—of collective guilt over the actual, coerced relationships that constituted slavery and, to a considerable extent, postslavery race relations.

The juxtaposition of real racial violence and highly idealized notions of the black mother as primarily devoted to white children was bizarrely displayed in a series of events in Washington, DC, in the early 1920s. Lynching, the brutal murder of African Americans, mostly male, had reached epic proportions by this time. "Between 1882 and 1930, cotton-state lynch mobs murdered 1,663 black people," Jones notes, "and state officials executed 1,299 more through the 'legitimate' judicial process." African Americans, especially in the South, lived under a reign of terror, yet the U.S. Senate caved to a southern filibuster in late 1922 and failed to pass what would have been the nation's first and only federal law preventing lynching. (Lynching was primarily justified as a retribution for African American men's alleged sexual violation of white women, a crime that no sane African American man would commit under the southern "justice system." Southern congressman Finnis Garret of Tennessee declared to great applause on the House floor, "Mr. Speaker, this bill ought to be amended in its title so as to read: 'a bill to encourage rape.'"[24])

Just a few months after the filibuster, the U.S. Congress gleefully advanced leg-islation supporting the creation of a monument to "the black mammy," a cause advocated by the United Daughters of the Confederacy for more than two decades. Because this occurred at a historical moment in which many thousands of African Americans were migrating to the North, using their votes there, and publicly cham-pioning civil rights in spite of white retribution in the form of race riots, African American reaction was swift and pointed. The Baltimore newspaper *Afro-American* ran a cartoon that showed an African American woman with a sign saying, "Use that monument fund to pass a law that will *stop* the lynching of my children!!" The African American–owned *Chicago Defender* printed another political cartoon that depicted an African American man hanging from a tree while a white southerner looked up at him and pointed to a paper that read "Plans for Black Mammy Statue." The *Defender* even proposed the erection of a monument to the "White Daddy." The cartoon version of this monument, says McElya, "presents a leering white man assaulting a young black woman who struggles to fend him off but appears to be overpowered."[25] A crying child is behind her, witnessing her struggle.

African American activists were outraged, by both the crassly self-serving nature of the political turn of events and the ways in which the mammy monument cru-sade obscured the real struggles of African American mothers. The cartoons were part of a broader attempt to reclaim African American maternity. Many years ear-lier, Harriet Jacobs herself had sought to expose the sacrifices African American mothers had to make under slavery, through not only the sale of their children and the free gifts of their field labor but also the coerced care of white children above their own. Jacobs noted that her mother's mistress was the "foster sister of my mother; they were both nourished at my grandmother's breast. In fact, my mother had been weaned at three months old so that the babe of the mistress might obtain sufficient food." In the midst of the mammy monument controversy, the president of the NACW, Mary Church Terrell, pointedly observed that "no colored woman could look upon a statue of a black mammy with a dry eye when she remembered how often the slave woman's heart was torn with anguish, because the children, either of her master or the slave father, were ruthlessly torn from her in infancy or in youth to be sold 'down the country,' where, in all human probability, she would never see them again." Racial justice activist James Weldon Johnson declared, "It would be more worthy to erect a monument to the black mother, who, through sacrifice, hard work and heroism, battled to raise her own children and has thus far so well succeeded." In the context of a battle of images over the meaning of Afri-can American motherhood, the African American artist Sargent Johnson created the sculpture *Forever Free* in 1933. It depicts an African American mother standing erectly and proudly with two African American children by her side.[26] The outcry of the African American press contributed to the eventual defeat of the proposed federally funded "mammy" monument.

Meanwhile, the willingness of white southern women to resist the prototype of the white mother as her child's whole universe of nurture and moral tutelage is curious in and of itself. Rhetorically, white southern mothers foreswore the glory of do-it-yourself child rearing for the status of aristocratic employer of a maternal servant class. For white middle- and upper-class mothers, these regional differences would eventually recede, but the national mythology of "mammy" persisted and stretched to include other women of color.[27]

MORAL REFORM AND MATERNAL POWER BEYOND THE HOME

In the nineteenth century, antislavery was one of many reform causes embraced by those who extended the ideals of motherhood beyond the middle-class hearth. When the founding fathers denied women citizenship rights and encouraged them instead to raise virtuous sons, they probably did not have in mind Sara Josepha Hale's idea of just how influential women's virtue might be. "WOMAN," wrote Hale in *Godey's Lady's Book*, was quite simply "God's appointed agent of morality." Women's work in the world and even education to perform that work were necessary because men, with all their power, had failed. They needed mothers, and mothers needed to influence the world while preserving the virtue they modeled and taught in the nursery. In a tract titled "Maternal Instruction," *Godey's* readers were told, "It takes a long time for the world to grow wise. Men have been busying themselves these six thousand years nearly to improve society. They have framed systems of philosophy and government, and conferred on their own sex all the advantages which power, wealth, and knowledge could bestow . . . and, after all, the mass of mankind are very ignorant and very wicked." The reason? "Because the *mother*, whom God constituted the first teacher of every human being, has been degraded by men from her high office . . . denied those privileges of education which only can enable her to discharge her duty to her children with discretion and effect."[28]

A central contradiction of moral motherhood was that it was too grand a notion to confine to the domestic sphere. By the middle decades of the nineteenth century, the moral qualities associated with middle-class motherhood had public resonance. Evangelical Protestant zeal underlay the causes women supported as God's "appointed agent of morality." Women reformers significantly expanded their public influence by setting out to mother the world. Female reformers financed orphanages, asylums for "lying-in" (birthing) women, and charity support organizations for poor widows. Some took up the causes of prison reform, care of the mentally disabled, abolition of slavery, and an end to the sale of alcohol and prostitution. Others took up missionary work in the West, where their objective was often the remaking of marriage and motherhood among Native Americans and Asian immigrants to fit middle-class norms.[29] Reformers' ranks included women who were mothers and those who were not, but most were the very women for whom the moral mother ideology was intended, which is to say Protestant, white, northern middle-class women. Although men also took up moral reform work, women claimed a special moral—and maternal—sensibility.

In the 1830s and 1840s, a sizeable contingent of female antislavery activists and writers pushed the righteousness of moral motherhood into the era's most pressing social justice cause. The famous southern antislavery sisters, Sarah and Angelina

Grimke used this idea, as did the African American racial justice advocate, Maria Stewart, whose energies were also focused on discrimination against free African Americans: "Methinks I hear [the question] 'Who shall go forward, and take off the reproach that is cast upon the people of color? Shall it be a woman?'" Stewart asked. "And my heart made this reply—'If it is thy will, be it even so, Lord Jesus!'" Women abolitionists heard the testimony of formerly enslaved women and men. According to one account, Sojourner Truth spoke to a woman's rights convention in 1851 with the pain of a woman who had lost her children. After citing her extensive experience doing heavy agricultural work considered inappropriate for white women, Truth added, "I have borne thirteen children, and seen 'em most all sold off to slavery, and when I cried out with my mother's grief, none but Jesus heard me! And ar'n't I a woman?"[30]

Female antislavery rhetoric drew on the most positive dimensions of moral motherhood as political common cause: slavery was an immoral institution because it disrupted the mother-child bond that had reached genuinely sacred proportions in the popular culture of the day. Harriet Jacobs, in her memoir, employed moral motherhood rhetoric in appealing to free mothers by creating empathy with the enslaved mother. Harriet Beecher Stowe, perhaps the most famous cultural radical on the issue of slavery, penned the famous abolitionist novel *Uncle Tom's Cabin*, which was saturated with Christian maternal imagery:

> And you, mothers of America,—you who have learned, by the cradles of your own children, to love and feel for all mankind,—by the sacred love you bear your child; by your joy in his beautiful, spotless in-fancy; by the motherly pity and tenderness with which you guide his growing years . . . I beseech you, pity the mother who has all your affections, and not one legal right to protect, guide, or educate, the child of her bosom![31]

In *Uncle Tom's Cabin*, Stowe evoked "a mother's agonies" by reminding her female readers of their shared pain in the all-too-common experience of an infant's death. She wanted to elicit compassion for enslaved women who lost their children not through death, but through the cruel system of slavery. Mothers, she insisted, needed to find a voice on this public issue: "By the sick hour of your child; by those dying eyes, which you can never forget; by those last cries, that wrung your heart when you could neither help nor save; by the desolation of that empty cradle, that silent nursery,—I beseech you, pity those mothers that are constantly made childless by the American slave-trade! And say, mothers of America, is this a thing to be defended, sympathized with, passed over in silence?"[32]

Abolitionists were often cultural radicals and, as such, were not broadly representative of northern white opinion. Still their extension of the ideals of moral motherhood to enslaved African American women made visible the struggle of enslaved African American women for a growing segment of the northern white public in the decades before the end of slavery. At the same time, white abolitionist writers such as Stowe also drew on unthreatening and universalist notions of selfless mothers and often condescending portraits of African Americans.

Women's involvement in the antislavery cause became the catalyst for the first women's rights convention. The spark for the meeting had been the second-class treatment received by women abolitionists at an international antislavery convention. The women and men who convened in Seneca Falls, New York, in 1848 demanded property rights for married women, educational opportunities, and, most radically of all, suffrage. They posed powerful challenges to their era's gender ideals. But most female reformers did not envision a world in which women participated in public life on equal terms with men. Women's activism in reform movements was certainly not always a springboard to feminism.[33]

Instead of challenging a social order in which women's roles as mothers and wives were considered sacrosanct, most mid-nineteenth-century reformers lauded women's moral example and indirect influence over the direct, but often corrupt, influence of electoral politics. "Woman's" modeling of piety, just like the mother's example in the home, would move slave-owners to abandon their cruel system of human bondage and move men to foreswear alcohol consumption and involvement with prostitution. Within their communities radical moral reformers sometimes used confrontational tactics, as when they gathered outside saloons and tried to discourage patrons from entering. In these circumstances women could be radically forthright and public only because their interests were presumably selfless and maternal. Even women's rights activists, notes historian Sara Evans, "never, despite the fears of their opponents, seriously questioned women's primary responsibility for the home and for children."[34]

By the time the Women's Christian Temperance Union (WCTU) formed in 1874, moral motherhood was poised to become more fully engaged with the political system, not simply as supplicant mothers pleading with errant slave and liquor store owners but as potential citizens. Women moral reformers expanded the maternal sphere with large, efficient organizations and sometimes overt political claims. In the decades after the Civil War, the WCTU became an especially powerful national organization and cultural phenomenon, attracting a cross class female membership and highlighting the social problem of economically dependent mothers. The organization's wide appeal spoke to the vulnerability of married women because men, who controlled money, could also drink away paychecks. Temperance crusades had been active in the country since the 1830s, but the earlier activists had tended to demand moral solutions; the WCTU increasingly leaned toward political action.

In the late nineteenth century, the WCTU was still using highly sentimental, mother-inspired language as persuasive fodder. Abolitionist Julia Ward Howe said, "The neglected child, wandering about the streets to learn the lessons of meanness and of crime. . . . At the sight of him, oh! Women, let your woman's hearts be touched. Let your blessed motherhood put itself at interest, multiply itself so as to embrace him, the homeless, the friendless."[35] Such language actually revealed some of the class prejudice that drove more privileged women into reform work. At a time when mere survival among an increasingly immigrant working-class in the northern cities was precarious, women charity workers frequently contrasted the "squalor" of tenements and the street living of unsupervised children with the order of the middle-class home.

Working-class and poor children were in fact frequently out in the streets, where they sold newspapers or scavenged for their families because their parents' wages were usually inadequate for family support. Children were also providing critical funds to their families by working in factories. But middle-class reformers were often unable or unwilling to see the structural causes of poverty that shaped different familial norms. Indeed, the venerably domestic maternal advice-giver Lydia Maria Child, who edited Harriet Jacobs's story of slavery and helped share it with the world, conveyed a less sympathetic message about impoverished northern white children. She remarked that the worst part of the situation of the "squalid little wretches" in New York's streets was that they were not orphans. Clearly, the redeeming agents for these children were not their own mothers. Class—as well as race—limited the possibilities of a sisterhood of mothers. Such prejudices even justified large-scale projects such as the Children's Aid Society program, which removed New York City children from their parents, often without consent, and sent them to farm families with "proper" homes or to live-in training programs for domestic service or seamstress work.[36]

Meanwhile, the WCTU's emphasis on private morality obscured its growing public role. The WCTU was closely affiliated with a range of women's reform organizations and even, by the end of the century, the Populist movement, which attracted many activists from the temperance ranks. In areas ranging from "social purity" to providing free medical care or education for the working class, the WCTU took the lead by softening the idea of women's actual public influence through the flowery language of maternal sentimentality. The WCTU was quite successful in its lobbying of state legislatures to raise the "age of consent" for girls in sexual encounters. In a national petition drive, the WCTU advanced the maternally tinged causes of protecting both children and women when they argued that "the age at which a girl can legally consent to her own ruin [should] be raised to at least eighteen years." (This was in opposition to a state statute that legislated the age of consent at ten.) Such political victories were potent reminders of the links between social policy and the moral and domestic causes with which women had been publicly concerning themselves for many decades.[37]

Temperance also sometimes overlapped with and informed feminism, especially when activists criticized the conditions that made it difficult for women to fulfill their maternal duties. For example, Elizabeth Cady Stanton argued in 1852 that a woman should not be forced to remain married to a confirmed "drunkard." She advocated, "Let no drunkard be the father of her children." To allow women the opportunity to properly care for their children, she urged, "Let us petition our state governments so to modify the laws affecting marriage, and the custody of children, that the drunkard shall have no claims on either wife or child."[38]

For decades, the WCTU embodied the tensions of endowing middle-class mothers with high moral claims while denying them formal political power, but it was becoming clear to many that women needed the ballot to reform laws surrounding alcohol, sexuality, and the working conditions of girls and women. By the 1880s, WCTU leader Frances Willard called for a "Home Protection Ballot," a limited suffrage that would allow "the mothers and daughters of America" to participate in decisions about whether "the door of the rum shop is opened or shut beside their homes." Such visions of female reformers amounted to what Sara Evans has called the late-nineteenth-century "maternal commonwealth" idea, where the "private" values of the middle-class home could redeem the public world.[39]

Conclusion

Over the course of the nineteenth century, middle-class women in particular drew on the ideas of moral motherhood to expand their sphere of influence. They participated in the early modernization of motherhood by elevating maternity into a kind of high-minded civic discourse. Along with male spokesmen, many of whom also considered women's influence civilizing and essential, the women solidified a place for the moral mother in both the social order and the national identity of the United States. These tensions and these possibilities became even more salient over time. Mothers, especially class-privileged mothers, considered it their duty to perform the "social housekeeping" involved with taming American excess, from the moral evils of slavery to what they saw as the social chaos of a rapidly industrializing, urban, and multicultural America.

The vastly different experiences of motherhood, based on economic resources, race, and class, profoundly limited the potential for improving the lives of the nation's most vulnerable mothers. The ideal mother was self-consciously morally superior, which made her a good mother. In reality, middle-class mothers were often unself-consciously privileged as they sought to shape others in their image. Meanwhile, the conditions of slavery, sharecropping, and industrial life severely circumscribed the claims to mothering for women with few resources. Enslaved mothers had virtually no rights to protect and nurture their children; they were even unable to put their own extensive labor toward the material needs of their families. After slavery African American mothers continued to struggle with new forms of institutionalized racism, across economic, legal, and cultural channels. As twentieth-century examples show, the survival and child-rearing strategies of millions of other less-privileged women were also shaped by a need to combine mothering with breadwinning and to rely on a broad network of kin and community to rear children.

In the nineteenth century, the making of modern motherhood was an ideological project of the middle class. The contradictions of the emerging motherhood ideal embodied both the strengths and limits of culturally sanctioned maternal moral power. Moral motherhood, invited women to expand their "sphere" of influence into a world beset with evils only pure mothers could right. At the same time, self-righteousness led many to a less sympathetic view of those mothers whose poverty could be blamed, not on a brutal system of slavery, but a less clearly recognized system of industrial capitalism in the North and race-based labor systems in the South. Class and race divisions continued to hinder the grander ideals of moral motherhood, even as the hope for shared opportunities for mothers would lead to new efforts to renew American civilization through the hearts of mothers.

CHAPTER 3

Medicalizing the Maternal Body

"I was not surprised," Peggy Nicholas wrote to her daughter in 1828, "nor would I have been grieved, to hear that you were again in the family way; but I must acknowledge [that] to hear that your confinement [birth] was to take place next Month, dashed me not a litle [*sic*]." She confessed, "I had hoped that you had got into a confirmed habit of an interval of two years, that there was no doubt of your continuance in this, and that [there] might be some reasonable guide in calculating your number." Despite these concerns, Peggy's daughter Jane bore thirteen children over the course of twenty-four years, a pattern very similar to Peggy's own twelve births. Similarly, Abigail Adams expressed her sadness about her daughter Nabby's repeated pregnancies and thought her sister "foolish" to have more children in middle age. She even seemed relieved to hear of the miscarriage of a young relative because "it is sad slavery to have children as fast as she has."[1]

As far as historians can tell, these attitudes toward smaller families and limiting fertility only began in the late eighteenth century. Emerging in the Revolutionary era and advancing with the Industrial Revolution, these views evolved with moral motherhood ideals and the development of the middle class. Peggy Nicholas's admonition of her daughter, with its slightly scientific ring, shown through the calculation of births at intervals, reflected broader realities of the era. The birth rate among white women declined in truly remarkable fashion between 1800 and 1900, from 7.04 to 3.56 births per woman. Historians have also found a decline in the birthrate of African American women as slavery was gradually abolished in the North and later abolished completely after the Civil War. The sharp decline in fertility aptly reflected women's changed attitudes toward reproduction. A similar "demographic transition" occurred in European countries as well, although the United States and France were the first nations to start reducing their birth rates.[2] As women participated in this process, they set in motion long-term changes in ideas about ideal family size and raised expectations about women's health and their purpose as mothers. Essentially, they participated in modernizing cultural ideas about maternal female bodies. As Americans began embracing smaller families, they simultaneously engaged in highly charged, even alarmist debates about who should control women's fertility. Medical expertise and science increasingly influenced ideas about modern maternal bodies in areas that included not only reproductive rights, but also childbirth, gynecological medicine, and interventions in fertility problems. As physicians developed a professional identity, formalizing their training and expanding their cultural authority, they competed with traditional female knowledge of the body while generally excluding women from the ranks of their profession. The reach of the new medical profession extended from slave quarters to urban hospitals, where especially vulnerable women bore the brunt of the obstetric and gynecological medical experimentation, to the private rooms of middle-class and elite women giving birth with the assistance of the new "male midwives." Modernizing the maternal body meant bringing medical science to bear on female health and life experiences that had once been the province of midwives and other traditional healers. Modern medical science promised women both safer childbirth and the possibility of curing problems with conception, while also claiming unprecedented authority to regulate women's reproduction. In short, medicalizing the maternal body was a key part of modernizing American motherhood.

Even though women's access to contraception and abortion continues to be emotionally debated today, it is hard to imagine modern motherhood, indeed modern women's lives, without the possibility of limiting reproduction. We also know that throughout human history, societies have organized themselves to reduce birthrates when circumstances required. Methods have included extending the period of breastfeeding for some natural contraceptive effects, prescribing ritual abstinence through religion or social custom, encouraging later marriage ages, and experimenting with contraception, abortion, and, in extreme cases, infanticide. From records dating back to ancient Egypt, there is evidence that women of all cultures sought to prevent or end pregnancies, or simply "restore menses," in the early stages of pregnancy. They used herbs, potions, and oils, simple barrier methods, instruments, and assistance from midwives. By the time of the colonial era in North America, women desperate to end pregnancies sometimes tried external methods such as "lifting heavy objects, climbing trees, taking hot baths, jumping from high places, shaking," and a few engaged physicians to provide abortions.[3] Such methods were medically risky, but so too were pregnancy and childbirth.

What makes the situation in the late eighteenth and early nineteenth centuries unique is the potent combination of new family and health ideals, the professionalization of medicine, and heightened fears about women's autonomy. New efforts to regulate women's reproduction were critical in the making of modern motherhood—a motherhood that allowed for rational and scientific control of a process formerly deemed primarily the will of God. Physicians would be especially influential on the question of controlling reproduction by successfully advocating for legal changes to limit women's reproductive choice. So too women and their male partners exercised their own options and contributed to the possibility of reproductive freedom.

WOMEN AND FERTILITY: FEAR AND FREEDOM

In 1786, Ann Warder wrote of her frustration that "our worthy and much-to-be-pitied sister" had a "husband who exceed [sic] the description of my Pen for Insensibility— Her Children are presented Yearly which, keep her in constant Ill health." Some women and men in this era began thinking in terms of a set number of children as an appropriate human intervention in nature. Historian Susan Klepp found in the private writings of the middle and upper-middle classes references to two, four, or six children as ideal family sizes in this era, advancing the idea that couples should prudently manage their family size, not just let nature take its course.[4]

Before the late eighteenth century, there was widespread agreement not only that fertility was the fate and blessing of women but also that large families were signs of status. Elite families especially welcomed the birth of boys as extensions of their lineage. The colonists used agricultural metaphors to talk about women's fertility and described pregnant women as akin to nature's generosity itself, "flourishing," "breeding," "teeming," and especially "fruitful." But beginning in the Revolutionary era, such language changed markedly toward what Klepp calls "a language of reason, foresight, constraint, and sensibility." By the nineteenth century, "breeding" became associated mostly with enslaved women. For middle- and upper-class women, references to pregnant bodies discreetly disappeared; these women were awaiting the "little stranger," "the beloved object," or "the first pledge of matrimonial love." They were not "teeming" but rather, more prudently, "in the way to become a mother."[5]

Married women struck out in the direction of embracing fewer pregnancies in advance of their husbands. New Englanders were among the first to reduce family size. Americans in the mid-Atlantic states, then the South, and then the West followed suit. Reducing fertility took on special significance for an emerging middle class and had resonance for both sexes and eventually across regions. The language of family size became a language of class. At a time of increasing stratification, some spoke of the poor "like vegetables" that "shoot up wherever nourishment is most copious."[6] The growing urbanization and industrialization of the United States encouraged middle-class Americans to invest their resources in smaller numbers of children. The children of this emergent bourgeoisie would need education for new positions. Children generally were becoming economic liabilities rather than remaining the economic assets they might have been as laborers on the farm or in the family business.

The upper class, however, clung to the idea of lineage longer than did the less well-off, in part because they could afford to do so. Meanwhile, derogatory notions of the poor as continuing to reproduce without regulation or forethought continued over the course of the nineteenth century and indeed into the twenty-first. The diversification of the American population through nineteenth-century immigration and territorial expansion furthered these ideas and set the stage for deliberate efforts to regulate the "breeding" of populations deemed threatening to American-born, white, middle-class Americans.

By the early nineteenth century, concerns about middle- and upper-class women's health lent more credence to the idea that fewer children were better. Eighteenth-century Virginia gentry, for example, had been matter-of-fact about the inevitable dangers of childbirth. As one woman wrote to another in 1794, "The necessary time of retirement may God of his mercy grant you a favorable time." Another Virginia woman wrote of her own impeding delivery, "My present poppet is such a source of hope and comfort to me that I do not allow myself to repine at the thought of another, although I should certainly have preferred to defer the arrival of the little sister another year."[7]

But privileged women increasingly referred to childbirth as "'this dreadful event' a 'trial,' 'an affliction,' 'one of the evils of this life.'" Though some husbands shared these fears, women expressed them more strongly and were also more likely than men to refer to the economic pressures that might result from additional children. Both upper-class women and men began to discuss childbirth, say historians Jan Lewis and Kenneth Lockridge, "as something unnatural, a disruption of a woman's health." This shift is also evident in the diaries of nineteenth-century northern middle-class women. Mary Poor, for example, wrote to her mother in the 1830s, the day before her daughter's birth, "I have everything to cheer me and try not to dread the future. Pain is the lot of man and we ought not to shrink from our individual share of it." We know from Janet Farrell Brodie's careful study of Poor's diary that after she'd borne that daughter and another one at age thirty-nine, "Mary's letters and diary leave no doubt. She wanted no more children and became obsessively alert to the slightest possibility of pregnancy." Like so many mothers of all classes, Poor was deeply worried about not only dying in childbirth and leaving motherless children but also maintaining her ability to care for the children she already had.[8]

Mothers had reason to fear. Because of their vulnerability to death in or after childbirth, women of childbearing age were much more likely to die than men of the same age. They also suffered from long-term health complications from frequent pregnancies, and families with more children experienced higher infant mortality. Even women who had not yet become mothers feared for their health and that of their future children. A late nineteenth-century diarist worried, toward the end of her pregnancy, "It is *possible* I may not live. I wonder if I should die, and leave a little daughter *behind* me, they would name her 'Clara.' I should like to have them." In a subsequent entry, "If I shouldn't live I wonder what they will do with the baby." When she was out of danger, her husband wrote in his wife's diary of his relief at her safety: "Everything is all right, but at what cost. My poor wife, how you have suffered, and you have been so brave . . . I have seen the greatest suffering this day that I have ever known or imagined."[9] Such suffering, in the view of some, could be avoided by human action. Women, and often their husbands, began to adopt more modern views of the maternal body by taking increasing control over both the number and timing of their pregnancies and their experiences of childbirth.

The Radical Potential of Early Nineteenth-Century Maternal Health

When the nineteenth century began, physicians were by no means established authorities in maternal health. Women, with their "domestic medicine" of home-made remedies and reliance on specialized healers and midwives, were the primary health-care providers in their families and communities. There was significant overlap between medicinal recipes compiled by laywomen and those sanctioned by physicians. And by the second quarter of the century, a popular health move-ment expanded many women's knowledge about and sense of ownership over their reproductive health. Interest in sectarian or "irregular" medicine was sweeping the country, offering treatments and preventatives ranging from the very popu-lar "water cure" to homeopathy and botanicals. Information on reproductive con-trol and women's health increased thanks to itinerate lecturers, including women, traveling throughout the North and West. Growing numbers of publications on contraception and reproductive health also appeared, and health activists devel-oped the American Physiological Society in 1837, whose membership was nearly one-third female. As Brodie has observed, because of new information on contra-ceptives, "discussions that had been mostly private now became more public, more structured, and more accessible."[10]

Emphasizing exercise, air quality, and diet, health reformers offered what must have felt like empowering advice and information. "I wish to teach mothers how to cure their own diseases and those of their children," wrote the famous health reformer Mary Gove Nichols, "and to increase health, purity, and happiness in the family and the home." Nichols used the language of the purity of women and the home to advance a passionate commitment to women's sexual and reproductive rights. She traveled throughout the Northeast speaking on "the laws of life and health" and "the physical and emotional problems resulting from 'indissoluble marriage.'" After her first husband finally granted her a long-sought divorce, she wrote and lectured with her second husband, who advocated Mary's position in his published work: "If a woman has any right in this world it is the right to herself; and if there is anything in this world she has a right to decide, it is who shall be the father of her children . . . she has an equal right to decide whether she will have children and to choose the time for having them."[11]

By the middle of the century, many health reformers and feminists claimed that men's sexual passions needed to be controlled by the more "naturally" restrained pattern of women. With women in charge of sexuality, society could limit women's exposure to the life- and health-threatening risks of continuous pregnancy and even help produce healthier babies. Some asked, when "will men and women show a rational, conscientious, loving forethought, in giving existence to their children as they do in commerce, politics, and religion?" Children should not be the result, they said, "of chance, of mere reckless, selfish passion." Male feminist and aboli-tionist Henry C. Wright even declared that the "great object" of sexual intercourse was ideally the *perpetuation and perfection of the race*."[12] Men, whose "passions" were reckless and selfish, could not be trusted to regulate sexuality in such a way so as to produce this improved race.

The reformers who led the crusade to improve female health did so in the name of motherhood, and, like other promoters of the ideology of moral motherhood, credited wives and mothers with being "second only to the Deity in the influence she exerts on the physical, the intellectual, and moral interests of the human race."[13] For this reason, women needed to be educated about their health. Some also believed they needed the right to refuse sex with their husbands in the name of an enlightened maternity. Moral mothers should be the leaders, from the bedroom to the nursery and, for some, beyond. Indeed, from moral mothers' choices about the timing of children, a more rational and healthy society could emerge. Human regulation of nature should be in female hands.

As Henry Wright's words remind us, not only women advocated this point of view. Controversial but widely circulated books by somewhat radical male health reformers offered women very specific advice about contraception and abortion. These writings were informed by an acute awareness of the risks of pregnancy and "puerperal fever," a wound infection following birth that caused many maternal deaths. Robert Dale Owen's book *Moral Physiology*, published around 1831, argued for fertility control in the interest of women and the nation. Owen, a utopian socialist, primarily advocated coitus interruptus, an ancient method that involved withdrawal before ejaculation, but he also peppered his fairly knowledgeable advice with feminist arguments. Noting how single women were punished with the disgrace of out-of-wedlock sex and childbirth while men were not, Owen appears to have been the only nineteenth-century health writer who actually argued for reproductive rights for unmarried women. At least thirteen editions of his work circulated throughout the United States for more than three decades.[14]

Similarly, Charles Knowlton's *Fruits of Philosophy* in 1832 offered much specific advice on potential spermicides. Knowlton, a trained physician, argued that "checks" on reproduction made for better families, managed by prudent mothers. He advocated withdrawal, vaginal sponges, condoms, and spermicidal douching. He was not opposed to abortion; he argued that "the fetus, because it was attached to a woman's body, had no more rights than any other extremity." In this, as we will see, Knowlton would be superseded in medical opinion within a few decades with a quite opposite professional view. Also, unlike his colleagues a few decades later, Knowlton saw moral motherhood and reproductive control as entirely compatible with, even essential to, one another. As Brodie summarized, "a knowledge of checks would allow couples to marry young without fear of excessively large families and would reduce men's use of prostitutes. Knowlton advised women to manage their household affairs in a thrifty, prudent, and rational manner, to avoid parties, servants, and fashion, and to assume the fundamental responsibility of keeping the family size small. If a young wife were careful and prevented a too-large family, then her husband could accumulate money and their marriage would succeed."[15] In other words, women's efforts to reduce the size of families became part of the building middle-class virtues and solid middle-class families.

As medical opinion coalesced in the middle of the century, however, most physicians disagreed with Knowlton. Modern "regular," or allopathic, medicine began to consolidate with the founding of the American Medical Association (AMA) in 1846. The consequences of this, concerning how women thought about and experienced their bodies and maternal health, would be enormous.

CREATING MEDICALIZED AND RACIALIZED MATERNAL BODIES

For the newly professionalizing medical men of the nineteenth century, women's maternal functions could be assisted by modern science. Like the sectarian health reformers, they believed that a new age was dawning in which humans could improve the outcomes of reproduction with better maternal health and ultimately better health for the population as a whole. But they parted company with health reformers like Mary Gove Nichols in important ways. The physicians saw women's health as fundamentally linked to their reproductive purpose and their reproductive organs, and they cast the bodies of middle-class and elite mothers—their primary clientele in the urban North—as frail and often ill, consistently in need of medical intervention. Physicians also advanced a new view of conception and abortion in which women could not be trusted to regulate their own reproduction.

In seeking to both establish their own authority and create a client base for their services, physicians echoed and refined popular notions of "true womanhood." Widely believed to be pious, pure, domestic, and maternal, white women also were cast as passive and weak in medical language. Seventeenth- and early eighteenth-century Americans had spoken of "travail," or the work, of giving birth. Nineteenth-century Americans referred to women's "confinement," "sickness," or "illness" as euphemisms for birthing.[16] Women's fears about childbirth contributed to this redefinition. Medical literature and practice helped to further solidify the idea of female passivity and weakness, at least for middle-class white women.

Medical ideas about the female reproductive body also developed from the encounters between physicians and much more vulnerable populations of women. In the years before the Civil War, physicians learned a great deal about gynecology and obstetrics from their work with enslaved African American women. Slaveowners employed physicians in the hopes that they could increase fertility among enslaved women and therefore increase the supply of human chattel. But to most white Americans—physicians and nonphysicians—African American women's bodies did not allow for frailty. If they had, how could the onerous workloads of enslaved women be justified? Indeed, since early colonial encounters, Europeans had claimed that African women not only gave birth more easily than Europeans but could also more easily handle the strains of childbearing and nursing while continuing to perform hard physical labor. Nineteenth-century physicians made similar claims and also argued that African American women were more fecund and menstruated earlier than white women.[17]

As medical knowledge and opinion evolved in the decades before the Civil War, old prejudices had a new context. With the end of the international slave trade in

1808, slave-owners had an intense interest in increasing the fertility of enslaved women because they would now have more difficulty buying new slaves. Alice Douglass remembered her experience in slavery: "You better have them whitefolks some babies iffen you didn't wanta be sold." Elite white southern families often did not trust physicians for the reproductive care of their own women, in part because reproductive medicine in the antebellum period was so experimental,[18] but they were willing to allow physicians to try out medical procedures on enslaved women. Therefore, in situations when consent was deemed utterly unnecessary, enslaved African American women played a pivotal role in the advancement of medicine through gynecological surgeries, fertility treatments, and often extreme obstetric measures taken in the throes of complicated birthing situations.

The Alabama physician J. Marion Sims, for example, operated without anesthesia on enslaved women suffering from vaginal fistulas, an opening between the vagina and another organ, such as the bladder or colon (a condition that today is treated surgically). Sims practiced this way because not only was anesthesia scarce and considered of questionable safety but also because he did not hold African American women's bodies in high regard. Some women may have wanted to try surgery because fistulas were awful conditions to endure, but we have no way of really knowing. One enslaved woman, Anarcha, endured thirty gynecological surgeries at Sims's hands; it is hard to imagine that she did so voluntarily.[19]

Physicians basically knew and agreed upon the idea that women's bodies were anatomically the same regardless of race. This was evidenced by their assumptions that what they learned from practice on African American women could be readily applied to obstetric and gynecological treatments for white women. Treatment and care of the patients, however, differed greatly. While class-privileged white patients were accorded privacy, African American women were subject not only to medical examinations without their consent but also to dangerous, excruciating gynecological surgeries in front of onlookers. Medical colleagues were invited to witness scientific progress by physicians like Sims, who only used anesthesia when he began practicing on white women. (It is interesting that Sims later downplayed his experimental work with enslaved women, in part because of the disapproval he received from physicians outside the American South. Such disapprobation does not seem to have forestalled his fame; he eventually served as president of the AMA and the American Gynecological Association and is still widely credited as the "father" of modern gynecology.) Sims and other physicians seem to have felt justified in what, to the modern reader, sounds like medical torture; he claimed that African American women tolerated pain more easily than white women.[20]

Physicians in the South also knew for whom they worked: slave-owners. Some dared to express the view that enslaved women's problems conceiving and carrying babies probably had to do with their workload and the onerous conditions of slavery. Dr. John H. Morgan of Tennessee, for example, told his medical colleagues in 1860 that if enslaved women "were kindly treated, and proper regard paid to the catamenial [menstrual] periods, we should hear of but few cases of abortion among them." Physicians often observed enslaved women with pelvises deformed by rickets from malnutrition, for example, and gynecological problems resulting from sexual trauma or physical abuse. They also knew that the incidence of complications and death in childbirth were greater among enslaved women than among white women. Slave-owners, however, generally did not want to hear these views, and physicians knew that. Some even crassly served the slave-owners with explanations for fertility problems such as "intemperate sexual indulgence" or "an unnatural tendency in the African American female to destroy her offspring." Consequently, as historian Marie Jenkins Schwartz astutely observed, "Instead of writing treatises on the effects of hard labor on pregnancy, physicians accepted the material conditions of slavery and the social relations of power that imposed them."[21]

These racialized views of maternal bodies continued to inform medical practice long after the end of slavery and exerted a powerful impact on the willingness of African American women to extend their trust to physicians. Indeed, after the Civil War, most former slave-owners were no longer willing to pay for medical care. Former slaves sought help from the Freedmen's Bureau in trying to acquire general medical care, but very rarely did African American women seek assistance for reproductive care from physicians. Some physicians tried to encourage planters to provide for medical care for the now freed people who worked on their plantations, but these efforts usually failed. Over time, given the reduction of both physicians' financial incentives for treating African Americans and most freed people's inability to pay physicians, medical care became a rare luxury. Southern African American mothers went from a class of women subject to medical experimentation to a class of women who received precious little medical care of any kind. The medical profession's academic attention to their health issues declined as well.[22]

Poor women in the North also endured gynecological experimentation in hospitals and almshouses in an era—a very long era, in retrospect—when standard medical practice did not require consent. Nineteenth-century middle- and upper-class Americans generally did not yet see hospitals as a viable place for health care. Hospital care was less safe than health care at home, especially because of the rapid spread of disease, and physicians did a great deal of home care, including surgeries, for those who could afford it. The New York City hospital that Marion Sims founded after leaving the South had a patient clientele of mostly Irish immigrants. The disproportionately poor Irish faced intense discrimination in the North. Although not subject to the harsh racial generalizations made about African American women, Irish women also endured some degree of medical experimentation as physicians learned about the female reproductive body through gynecological surgeries and dramatic interventions in birth. By historian Judith Walzer Leavitt's estimate, only about 5 percent of women gave birth in hospitals, and these were—usually only the most desperate women, often homeless and resourceless. The medical care poor women received as the nation's pioneers of institutionalized maternity and gynecology ranged from cutting-edge, where some of the country's most distinguished obstetricians supervised the delivery-room training of medical students, to abysmal, as in the 1860 case reported by *Harper's Weekly* where a woman gave birth totally unattended in Bellevue Hospital, after which her baby was attacked by rats. Like enslaved women, hospitalized women who underwent gynecological surgeries received little follow-up care.[23] In short, medicalized views and treatment of women's bodies tended to reinforce social hierarchies of gender, race, and class, even as medicine promised new hope for very old reproductive dilemmas, from childbirth to control of fertility.

CONTRACEPTION AND ABORTION: MEDICINE, MORALITY, AND MOTHERHOOD

One of the most important roles played by physicians in the nineteenth-century was in redefining pregnancy and becoming vocal advocates for criminalizing abortion. The early nineteenth-century window that opened for women, in which they could find diverse information about contraception and varied perspectives on health care, started to close when physicians increased their professional credibility. They began to redefine traditional forms of preventing or terminating pregnancy and to gain increasing authority on matters of women's health. To understand this transition, we need to understand the traditions that physicians sought to displace.

Traditional views of pregnancy focused on the idea of "quickening" as the definitive marker of a pregnancy. This was the point in a pregnancy when a woman could feel the fetus move in her body, usually occurring at about four and a half months of gestation. Even the Catholic Church held the view that human life was not decisively present until quickening. The term "abortion" was generally used only in reference to the termination of a pregnancy (intentional or unintentional) after quickening. Although there had long been some cultural ambivalence about terminating a pregnancy, in colonial America people's concerns focused primarily on women's risk through medically induced termination. English law since 1623 had forbidden termination of pregnancy only after quickening, and even later-term abortions were very rarely prosecuted in the English colonies. Many associated abortion with unsavory physicians and marketers of abortificant concoctions who endangered the lives of desperate women. Given the notion of quickening, concern that early term abortion was terminating a life was not widespread. "The use of the term 'life's porch,' for the birth canal," says historian Susan Klepp, "was another indication of the ambiguous status of the fetus prior to birth, especially given the high rate of stillbirths and neonatal deaths." The term *fetus* itself came from the Old English for womb, suggesting that a baby was not a distinct being until it came across the "porch."[24]

Traditionally, a woman might fret about the "blocking" or "obstruction" of her menses or want to "regulate" her flow. This language was typical for what was likely, but not certainly, early pregnancy, and it persisted even into the twentieth century. In an age before immunization and antibiotics, not to mention ultrasound or even urine tests, a woman had no way of knowing whether she was pregnant or if her blocked menses was the result of one of many mysterious health problems. In fact, no one could make a definitive judgment about whether a woman was pregnant; therefore, the very definition of the beginning of human life lay with a woman's assertion that a baby had moved inside her. Before the mid-nineteenth century, physicians as well as laypeople acknowledged that various health conditions could mimic the symptoms of pregnancy. Dr. Samuel K. Jennings wrote in 1808, for example, "An entire suppression of the menses attends almost every case of pregnancy. But as suppressions may be brought about by other causes this cannot be an infallible mark."[25]

Adding to the obscurity of women's actual practices around termination of pregnancy was the fact that people used contraceptive and abortifacient herbs for such a variety of purposes. Emmenagogic herbs were widely believed to promote regular menstruation, but they were also suggested by women healers, pharmacists, and physicians for conditions like "congestion, swelling, infestation, and anxiety." To "restore menses," colonial-era European, American Indian, and African women used widely available noncommercial herbs, such as savin, juniper, rue, aloe, pennyroyal, madder, Seneca snakeroot, and wild ginger, and healers treated women who were not menstruating for possible conditions such as "mental despondency" and hysteria.[26]

Not until the late eighteenth century is there mention of the use of barrier methods, such as crude condoms, for limiting the fertility of married couples. These early references correspond to Americans' emerging acceptance of the idea of limiting fertility. By the time of the American Revolution, people could join herbal remedies with new barrier methods and douching. Over time, more people knew about sexual techniques such as coitus interruptus. Interest in contraceptive or abortive techniques grew as well, as women voiced their concerns about avoiding death in childbirth. Before the mid-nineteenth century, this experimentation took place without a significant distinction between preventing pregnancy and terminating pregnancy.

As information about contraceptive methods became more widespread, women increased their use of diverse contraceptive methods. Women who could afford to do so took advantage of new published information, the sale of sponges, early forms of the diaphragm (also known as "womb veils" or pessaries), intrauterine devices, and condoms. The vulcanization of rubber in the 1860s improved condoms, and upgrades in diaphragms and malleable IUDs probably increased effectiveness. Women and men also discussed coitus interruptus more openly, and they used the nineteenth-century version of the rhythm method, based on the idea that women could not conceive during a certain phase of the menstrual cycle. Unfortunately, nineteenth-century advisers were dead wrong on the actual timing of women's most fertile portion of the menstrual cycle. Most suggested refraining from sex until eight to twelve days after the end of a woman's period, the portion of a woman's cycle in which, as we now know, she is most fertile.[27]

Though denied access to literacy and funds for new contraceptive measures, some enslaved women managed a degree of reproductive control. Many sources tell us of their use of cotton root, sage tea, and dogwood or dog-fennel root to regulate menstrual flow or "bring the women right." Formerly enslaved Dave L. Byrd remembered that women "would slip out at night and get them a lot of cotton roots and bury them under their quarters." Local studies suggest that enslaved women spaced their children further apart than white women in the same region, though it appears that, between 1800 and 1860, slave-owners efforts to foster increased fertility actually increased the intervals between the births for enslaved women.[28]

At the same time, what we would today define as abortion appears also to have been increasing, though the historical record will probably always be very incomplete in helping us understand the extent of abortion and women's attitudes toward it. Poor women, especially unwed women, had long had desperate need to avoid bearing babies they could neither afford nor acknowledge without social ostracism. Now middle-class married women had greater motivation as well. A careful analysis by historian James Mohr also suggests that abortion "became highly visible, much more frequently practiced, and quite common as a means of family limitation among white, Protestant, native-born wives of middle- and upper-class standing." References to termination of pregnancy were often matter-of-fact. One schoolteacher's letter to her parents in 1859, for example, spoke of an acquaintance who had probably terminated a visible pregnancy: "her poor health was caused by getting rid of a child as I suppose . . . you must not say anything as I have only guessed it. She was very large when she came here and in a short time she shrank to her normal size." Acknowledging the extreme challenge of estimating, Mohr nevertheless speculates that abortion rates might well have gone from one abortion per twenty-five live births to one in every five or six, between the beginning of the nineteenth century and the 1860s.[29]

The commercialization of "regulator" products probably increased women's sense of their options, even if these products were unproven and often unreliable. Women continued to use ancient methods to discontinue pregnancies, including herbal concoctions such as tansy tea, ergot, and cotton root, and to induce abortion with instruments in more desperate situations. But from about the mid-nineteenth century, there were more abortificant products on the market. Women could use pills, fluids, and oils marketed with names like "Female Regulator," or "Woman's Friend," or "Dr. Caton's Tansy Regulator," all understood by urban acculturated women (perhaps not by new immigrants) as products that would "restore" menstruation or remove an "obstruction."[30] Again, women experimenting with these products probably did not distinguish between preventing and terminating a pregnancy.

Women's contraceptive use and recourse to abortion continued throughout most of the nineteenth century, but not without serious attempts to disrupt such behaviors by physicians and a growing cadre of moral crusader allies. Academic and medical journal writings of the almost entirely male medical and scientific professions also shaped how women's access to reproductive control developed. In the middle of the nineteenth century, the medical profession as a whole began to oppose termination at all stages of pregnancy. This mattered a great deal because "regular" allopathic physicians were beginning to consolidate medical authority, pushing out sectarian approaches to health care that gave voice and authority to women, through preventive care and midwifery.[31]

Mid-nineteenth-century physicians' views of abortion and contraception were shaped by views of female bodies that were both medical and sentimental. Most saw female bodies as essentially determined by and designed for reproduction. As one physician noted in 1870 of the female body, it was "as if the Almighty, in creating the female sex, had taken the uterus and built up a woman around it." Or, in the words of gynecologist Charles D. Meigs, woman is "a moral, a sexual, a germiniferous, gestative and parturient creature."[32]

Scientific and evolutionary thought depicted women as more nurturing and less competitive as a result of their biology. Charles Darwin, for example, could have been writing for a women's magazine rather than for his scientific colleagues when he opined in 1871, "Woman seems to differ from man in her greater tenderness and less selfishness. Woman owing to her maternal instincts, displays these qualities toward her infants in an eminent degree; therefore it is likely that she would often extend them toward her fellow-creatures." The famous social philosopher Herbert Spencer, who translated Darwin's evolutionary theory into human society quite liberally, advocated the notion that women's supreme function was reproduction. And taxonomist Carolus Linnaeus actually identified "an entire class of animals—Mammalia—by the odd milk-secreting glands that develop in only half the members of the class." He did so, says anthropologist and primatologist Sarah Hrdy, "to highlight the importance of lactation," a preoccupation shared by physicians and evolutionary theorists alike. Physicians such as William Buchan claimed that women who chose not to nurse their babies themselves were wanting in "conjugal love, fidelity, modesty, chastity, or any other virtue." In other words, nursing babies was one of the duties of moral motherhood.[33]

Men of science, physicians in particular, took their evolving view of women as upright uteruses and began the nation's first sustained campaign against women's reproductive rights. In the antebellum South, physicians tried to placate the worries of slave-owners about whether enslaved women "knew a secret" to prevent reproduction. In the North, physicians sought new authority in defining when life began and contributed to cultural anxiety about changes in women's roles, including their reproductive options. Becoming the first, and often the only, documenters of what they saw as an alarming trend, physicians began decrying women's use of abortion around the middle of the nineteenth century. Seizing upon the language of moral motherhood, physicians argued that proper motherhood was incompatible with abortion. Dr. Thomas Blatchford lamented that abortion had been "*rare* and *secret*" and had become "*frequent* and *bold*." As a result, "the moral sense of community wants correcting."[34]

Many physicians lambasted "abortionists," including midwives and "irregular" doctors, in part as a way of legitimizing their own authority and driving out the competition. But many also castigated women in no uncertain terms. Some turned the idea of pure moral mothers on its head with the image of a woman who would shirk her maternal duties. Consider this opinion of the AMA's Committee on Criminal Abortion in 1871:

> She becomes unmindful of the course marked out for her by Providence, she
> overlooks the duties imposed upon her by the marriage contract. She yields to

the pleasures—but shrinks from the pains and responsibilities of maternity; and, destitute of all delicacy and refinement, resigns herself, body and soul, into the hands of unscrupulous and wicked men. Let not the husband of such a wife flatter himself that he possesses her affection. Nor can she in turn ever merit even the respect of a virtuous husband. She sinks into old age like a withered tree, stripped of its foliage; with the stain of blood upon her soul, she dies without the hand of affection to smooth her pillow.

The reason the AMA had a committee on "Criminal Abortion" in 1871 was because, by the 1870s, their campaign had seen astounding success through the enactment of state laws criminalizing abortion. The AMA launched investigations of the practice of abortion and even offered a prize for the best popular antiabortion writing. Their influence on public opinion was undeniable. By 1871, the *New York Times* was referring to abortion as "The Evil of the Age."[35] Thanks in no small part to physicians' activism, by 1900 all but one state imposed a criminal ban on abortion.

Using scientific language and exacerbating cultural anxieties, physicians gradually contributed to the transformation of cultural attitudes from ambivalence, especially about surgical abortions, to outright condemnation. One physician described this development: "Many indeed, argue, that the practice is not, in fact criminal, because, they argue, that the child is not viable until the seventh month of gestation.... The truly professional man's morals, however, are not of that easy caste, because he sees in the germ the probable embryo, in the embryo the rudimentary foetus, and in that, the seven months viable child and the prospective living, moving, breathing man or woman."[36] As a "truly professional man" with "morals," this physician claimed both the scientific authority to determine when life began and the sense of moral rectitude that accompanied the making of such claims.

From moral reformers beyond the medical ranks came advocacy for legislation against contraceptive devices of all kinds. By 1873, under the Comstock Law, the federal government prohibited the very circulation of information on contraception. Postmaster General and evangelical Christian Anthony Comstock expanded his authority to successfully push for federal legislation that made it a crime to distribute "obscene" materials through the U.S. postal service. A combination of the federal law and "Little Comstock" laws passed by the states made it a felony to distribute through the mail any information about contraception and abortion, which were considered obscene topics. Some states even made it illegal either to have private conversations about contraception and abortion or to possess instructions for preventing conception. Some allowed for search and seizure of contraceptive information. These laws went hand-in-hand with abortion restrictions that proliferated in state legislatures in the 1870s and 1880s. Moral crusaders efforts' enhanced the physician-led campaign to limit women's reproductive rights in the name of decency.

Despite the new laws and the stern pronouncements of some medical men, cultural attitudes and people's behaviors were generally slow to change. Even within the medical profession, many physicians continued to oppose their colleagues' stance against reproductive rights. Some argued that physicians had no business taking on the role of moralists. As one New York doctor wrote in 1886, "Woman's equality in all the relations of life implies her absolute supremacy in the sexual relation . . . it is her absolute and indefeasible right to determine when she will and when she will not be exposed to pregnancy."[37] Others expressed deep concern about limiting women's access to a procedure that could save their lives or their health.

Women's attitudes were similarly complex. Some incorporated medical views into their own thinking about the issue, comparable to the way that the idea of pregnancy as "illness" was adopted by—or perhaps partially invented by—women themselves. The male feminist Henry C. Wright published letters from numerous women who wrote to him about abortion in the middle of the century. The tone of the letters suggests that some women were struggling with a growing concern about the appropriateness and necessity of reproductive control. "My only trouble," wrote one woman who had obtained more than one abortion, "with God's view of the case, I could not get rid of the feeling that it was an outrage on my body and soul, and on my unconscious babe." While her physician told her that "[her] child, at five months . . . had no life," she was uncertain. "Though I determined to do the deed, or get the 'family physician' to do it, my womanly instincts, my reason, my conscience, my self-respect, my entire nature, revolted against my decision. My Womanhood rose up in withering condemnation."[38]

That this pregnancy was probably further along than the traditional demarking moment of "quickening" probably contributed to this woman's anxiety. Still, the negative juxtaposition of terminating a pregnancy and the idea of "womanhood" reflected deeply conflicted feelings which seemed to have been experienced by many other women. Moral motherhood prescribed a profound selflessness, even self-abnegation. This made many women uncomfortable with the medically influenced idea that they might not just be restoring menses but committing an "outrage" against something that might be life in the making. The new medical language—with its religious and cultural overtones—created great anxiety for women who feared not only death in childbirth but also the moral consequences of intervening in a pregnancy. With both contraception and abortion, religious and moral zeal amplified what had started as a project of physicians. By the end of the nineteenth century, as condemnation of abortion reached the pulpit and the newspapers, many women had to begin thinking differently about intervening in their own pregnancies.

Even many women's rights activists were ambivalent about reproductive control. The Seneca Falls Convention in 1848, the first official gathering to advocate for women's rights, produced the nation's first formal set of demands for women's rights, which included demands for marital property rights, education, and female suffrage. Beyond Seneca Falls, popular feminist ideas incorporated into the sectarian health movement included the idea that women should control their reproductive destinies within marriage by regulating the frequency of sexual intercourse with their husbands. Feminists were advocating "voluntary motherhood," meaning women's right to refuse sex to their husbands, and decrying their lack of power in succumbing to what suffragist Paulina Wright Davis called "compulsory

maternity," throughout the middle decades of the nineteenth century and especially after the Civil War.[39]

Elizabeth Cady Stanton, an organizer of the Seneca Falls Convention, pushed
the envelope of cultural notions of femininity in her emphasis on women's rights
to their own health through reproductive control. When asked by a magazine what
it meant for women to own their bodies, she responded, "Womanhood is the pri-
mal fact, wifehood and motherhood its incidents. Must the heyday of her existence
be wholly devoted to the one animal function of bearing children?" And, in language that spoke to the concerns of millions of women, she continued, "Shall there
be no limits to this but woman's capacity to endure the fearful strain on her life?"[40]

Demanding access to contraception or abortion, however, was another matter.
Many feminists saw contraception devices as unnatural. Most preferred to argue
for more freedoms from and within marriage for women, including exercising control over the frequency and timing of sexual intercourse. Advocating contraceptives
might have associated them with prostitutes, and they feared that contraceptive
access would free men, not women, to pursue extramarital sex. Nineteenth-century
sexual reformers generally, argues Linda Gordon, "did not seek to make an infinite
number of sterile sexual encounters possible. They wanted to make it possible for
women to avoid pregnancy if they badly needed to do so for physical or psychological reasons, but they did not believe that it was essential for such women to engage
freely in sexual intercourse."[41]

This was partly because of squeamishness surrounding female sexuality. Any
suggestion that women themselves had sexual "passions" was radical even for feminists. Many of them shared broader cultural ideas that men had sexual instincts
while women had maternal ones. Indeed, popular ideas about the maternal body
reinforced a distinction between sexual and maternal functions, for example, in the
idea that sexual arousal could contaminate a woman's breast milk. For feminists
to hint at female interest in sexuality was to risk impugning women's maternal
instinct and with it the social respectability of their causes concerning education,
marital property rights, and suffrage. Even the most outspoken advocates of wom-
en's sexual rights, such as Victoria Woodhull, hoped that women's education and
enfranchisement would so empower women that the need to terminate pregnancies would no longer exist.[42] Ambivalence, even among feminists, helps explain why
historians have found relatively little evidence of concerted public resistance to the
gradual erosion of access to contraception information and to abortion.

Examples of resistance in other forms do exist, though. Long-standing woman-
centered definitions of pregnancy and the beginning of life could not be so easily
dislodged. On a practical level, the federal government gave the zealous Mr. Comstock few resources to enforce the letter of the law. He and his deputies frequently
resorted to entrapment of marketers of contraceptives: for example, Mr. Comstock
himself used a pseudonym to meet with distributor Sarah Chase, ostensibly asking
for a douching syringe for his wife. Once Ms. Chase sold him the device, he arrested
her and confiscated additional "obscene" devices. Alas for Mr. Comstock, Ms. Chase
was not convicted; like many others, she even went back to selling contraceptives,

in part, because American juries regularly refused to adopt the view that contraception was criminal. Some 38 percent of people arrested in violation of the Comstock laws in New York City in the late nineteenth century went free, and sentences were light for those who were indicted. Some even challenged Comstock directly, as did Chase, who sued him for false arrest, and the socialist Ezra Heywood, who referred to him as a "religio-monomaniac" and taunted him by advertising a "Comstock syringe for preventing Conception." Heywood then successfully defended himself in court by asserting that the syringe had hygienic, not just contraceptive purposes.[43] Indeed, the therapeutic possibilities of most devices used for contraception meant that people could and did advertise them with references to their medical value alongside euphemistic references to their contraceptive potential.

Similarly, public attitudes about abortion were slow to change. In the early years of criminalization, the courts often refused to convict abortion providers if quickening had not occurred. Most states also made exceptions for abortions performed to save women's lives, a situation that, in the legal loopholes defined by the state law, had to be determined by a physician, not by the woman herself. In 1895, physicians like Dr. Joseph Taber Johnson still felt the need to try to persuade a reluctant public to believe that terminating a pregnancy before quickening constituted a crime. In his view it was "the moral and Christian duty of our profession" to correct such ideas.[44]

Certainly, the laws contributed to fear and anxiety for pregnant or potentially pregnant women, their male partners, and the midwives and dissenting physicians who continued to assist women in terminating pregnancies. Physicians or midwives could face second-degree homicide or manslaughter charges. Women seeking abortions could be criminally prosecuted, although this happened very rarely before the mid-twentieth century. Many women continued either to self-induce or attempt to self-induce their abortions. We will probably never know even an approximate number because abortion cases rarely came to light unless there was a death involved. Mohr estimates that the abortion rate probably declined between 1840 and 1880 in response to criminalization. To the extent that access to medically assisted abortions occurred, women with the least financial means were the most vulnerable. Meanwhile contraceptive product information became harder to access, and sexual advice literature declined in volume and quality.[45]

Still, resistance to the new laws can also be seen in the fact that the birth rate continued to decline. Women used the resources they had, both new and traditional. Susan Klepp estimates that emmenagogues and contraceptives were effective between 70 and 85 percent of the time,[46] but women's access to these products was uneven. Because herb gardens and folk knowledge of contraceptive and abortificant herbs declined, many people resorted to those products available on the commercial market. As a result, women immigrants, rural women, and others who had limited access to the products labeled with code words for contraception and abortion had more difficulty controlling reproduction, a situation that continued well into the twentieth century.

At the same time, the declining birth rate among white, middle-class women was beginning to create a sense of national distress. Dr. Horatio Storer, active in the antiabortion campaign, claimed that it was the duty of white women, through their reproduction, to prevent population surges in the West from Mexicans, Chinese, and other "lesser" races. By this time, the United States had expanded westward all the way to the Pacific, evidence of the belief that it was the "manifest destiny" of white Americans to claim the continent from coast to coast. "Upon [women's] loins depends the future destiny of the nation," Storer claimed.

Racial and class anxieties were also amplified by the growth in women's educational access. Elite women's colleges emerged between the 1860s and 1890s, and state colleges and universities increasingly offered coeducational opportunities. White, middle- and upper-class women had the greatest access to higher education, especially in the East and the Midwest. By 1880 women made up 33 percent of all enrolled students in higher education.[47] And these early generations of educated women were less likely to marry than those without education.

Around this time the medical fraternity put forth the notion that nothing could weaken a woman's reproductive capacity and increase the frailty already endemic to women like advanced education. As historians Carroll Smith-Rosenberg and Charles Rosenberg summarized, "A girl who curtailed brain work during puberty could devote her body's full energy to the optimum development of its reproductive capacities. A young woman, however, who consumed her vital force in intellectual activities was necessarily diverting these energies from the achievement of true womanhood. She would become weak and nervous, perhaps sterile, or more commonly, and in a sense more dangerously for society, capable of bearing only sickly and neurotic children."

While medical writers considered boys' development to be fairly steady, not toppled and tossed about by puberty, they suggested that the female body could not "do two things at one time." That is, young women could not simultaneously develop reproductive systems and engage in intensive study, an opinion that today's multitasking female adolescents and women would no doubt find especially laughable. Dr. Edward Clarke published a book called *Sex and Education* in 1873, in which he argued that intellectual pursuits diverted women's physical energy from the reproductive organs to the brain, with dangerous results for motherhood.[48]

Once again, physicians tapped into, as well as contributed to, fears about the disruption of gender roles that seemed inherent in women's pursuits beyond the domestic realm and their now sanctified and scientifically legitimized maternal roles. Paralleling the physicians' complaints were university policies that insisted on a lighter course-load for women based on notions of their maternally focused biology. In 1877 the University of Wisconsin Board of Regents declared, "Every physiologist is well aware that at stated times, nature makes a great demand upon the energies of early womanhood and that at these times great caution must be exercised lest injury be done." In fact, they continued, it was "better that the future matrons of the state should be without a University training than that it should be produced at the fearful expense of ruined health; better that the future mothers of the state should be robust, hearty, healthy women, than that, by over study, they entail upon their descendants the germs of disease." Feminists argued that it was not study that constricted women's bodies. Corsets were a more likely deterrent to health than education, claimed the female physician Alice Stockman.[49] But her views were in the minority. As with the mid-nineteenth-century abortion controversy, medical opinion served as a channel for conservative and negative views of the maternal or potentially maternal body. The debate around women's reproductive rights was a tug of war over what progress meant in an age of science and what role women would play in preventing conception, terminating pregnancies, and choosing to pursue even a small measure of public opportunities, such as formal education, available to men.

With limited opposition from an ambivalent public and even ambivalent feminists, physicians and other "moral reformers" such as Anthony Comstock succeeded in complicating but not really preventing what would eventually became a hallmark of modern motherhood: reproductive choice leading in the direction of smaller families. This meant, at the very least, access to contraceptive devices, and eventually broader claims to reproductive rights.

<h2 style="text-align:center">MEDICALIZING CHILDBIRTH AND INFERTILITY:
REPRODUCTIVE CONTROL EXPANDED</h2>

"Male midwives," as they were initially called, began making inroads into birthing situations as early as the late eighteenth century. Over the course of the nineteenth century, the specialties of obstetrics and gynecology developed, and doctors began to cultivate some clinical experience in midwifery. With the knowledge they gained through gynecological and obstetric experimentation, physicians began to transform women's experiences with childbirth and infertility. In these areas, too, modernizing the maternal body meant controlling and medicalizing what God or nature had seen fit to direct before.

Northern middle-class women were important participants in the transformation of childbirth. From this generally willing group of patients who left records of their experiences, we can learn a great deal about why physician-assisted birth eventually gained such broad credibility that it became the gold standard experience for safe childbirth. Physicians promised to relieve fear and pain and facilitate better outcomes. They often did so with more bravado and theory than actual experience. In the second half of the century, "demonstrative midwifery" became more common in medical schools, but as late as 1904 one female graduate described her obstetrical training as consisting of "reading my textbooks, listening to lectures dealing chiefly with abnormalities, delivery of a manikin put into presumably abnormal positions, and the witnessing from the amphitheater of the delivery of a few cases." Still, physicians' formal training and education contributed to their acceptance by middle-class women.[50] In the urban North, what began as an occasional summoning of doctors to women's homes in anticipation of complicated deliveries evolved by midcentury into more routine use of physician-assisted birth for middle- and upper-class women.

For the northern middle-class, being attended in one's home by a physician seems to have gradually become a sign of status. One health reformer derided husbands who would "employ gentlemen to attend their wives, not because they think it necessary, but because their neighbors will consider them unfashionable [otherwise] . . . and perhaps call their wives countrified and homespun, because they can have children without a scientific operator." Part of the emerging modern, scientific worldview was the decline in the idea that women endured the pain and danger of childbirth as God's punishment for Eve's sin. It would have been self-defeating for physicians offering pain medication to promote this old-fashioned notion. Related, too, was the notion that "civilization" made middle- and upper-class women weak and unprepared for childbirth because of their "luxurious living, their modes of dress, their neglect of exercise, and erroneous mental and moral culture," to quote physician Henry Miller. This was in contrast to more "primitive" cultures in which women appeared to birth with greater ease. Though seldom observed by physicians, the health risks of poorer women were significantly higher, in part because they had more children and therefore had more opportunities to experience the risks of childbirth.[51]

As middle-class women increasingly expressed fear and concern about childbirth, physicians were able to cultivate hope in the form of medicine. Some women were willing to experiment with physicians' new techniques, such as forceps, for difficult deliveries, or with new forms of anesthesia, such as opium, laudanum, chloroform, and "ether," to control pain. To speed labor the physicians used a muscle-contracting fungus called ergot (a substance also used to induce abortions), and they also used new techniques to stimulate contractions, dilate the cervix, and break waters to move labor forward.[52]

The medical profession at this time thrived on concerted action, including "heroic" techniques such as bleeding and otherwise shocking the body. At the same time, because normal deliveries were an unsuitable environment for the use and display of new medical knowledge, physicians sometimes needed to prove their value. As one physician put it, a doctor attending a laboring woman "must do something. He cannot remain a spectator merely, where there are many witnesses, and where interest in what is going on is too deep to allow of his inaction." Some even claimed that "the very presence of a medical practitioner will often afford relief."[53]

One physician spoke for many when he said that a laboring woman should be passive and was "not entitled to be her own directress." The home environment was, however, still the norm in the nineteenth century, and here physicians had limited control. Laboring women sometimes took the advice of their midwives, nurses, relatives, and their own understandings of the situation, thereby challenging the authority of doctors. Early on, standards of propriety often confined doctors to conducting vaginal exams "indirectly through a female attendant," and one physician lamented that he had "many times been kept out of [his] house all night attending a woman supposedly in labor who refused to allow the examination." He found her "unreasonable backwardness" to be "exceedingly vexatious." One physician, who felt it appropriate to bleed a patient until she fainted, had to persuade other female attendants in the birthing chamber.[54]

Physicians struggled with these problems in their work with enslaved women in the South as well. "Granny midwives," often present in the slave quarters, provided care through most of the labor. Some even received training from physicians, while others irritated physicians who saw the midwives as threats to their authority.[55] Generally, throughout the first half of the century, doctors accepted and acknowledged the utility or inevitability of female attendants in the birthing chamber, despite the loss of control and sometimes unwanted advice inherent in this arrangement.

There was still a great deal of fear among women about the drastic measures to which physicians might resort, including the commonly used forceps. But middle-class women expressed hopefulness about the potential of saving their babies' lives and their own by calling in a physician. The first American woman to experiment with physician-administered ether as a pain reliever, Fanny Longfellow, wrote to her sister in 1847: "Two other ladies, I know, have since followed my example successfully, and I feel proud to be a pioneer to less suffering for poor, weak womankind. This is certainly the greatest blessing of this age, and I am glad to have lived at the time of its coming and in the country which gives it to the world." Judith Walzer Leavitt has even argued that "women, in fact, initially were more eager than physicians to use anesthesia."[56]

White women like Fanny Longfellow saw themselves as pioneers on the frontier of pain relief in childbirth. But overall, women who used physicians were gradually accepting an increasingly passive, medically managed, and, by the late nineteenth century, usually privatized experience of childbirth. This shift occurred despite the limited actual benefits of "male midwifery." Certainly there were cases in which the use of forceps saved lives, but, when such instruments were not properly used, the results were often lacerations and injuries to the baby. Historians have found that women suffered a growing incidence of birth-related injuries from the new equipment and instruments. Nineteenth-century physicians do not appear to have improved women's outcomes with childbirth, in terms of either maternal or infant survival rates.[57]

Physicians' experiments with women, from the privileged to the highly coerced, were important in establishing new patterns and new authority, but change was slow in the nineteenth century. By the end of the century, most women never experienced physician-assisted birth, either at home or in a hospital. Normalization of hospital birth, in which physicians exercised far greater control, was a thing of the future. As late as 1900, women delivered 95 percent of the nation's babies at home. And by 1910, Molly Ladd-Taylor points out, "long after childbirth had been medicalized for middle-class whites, midwives attended at least half of all births in the United States." Use of midwives varied greatly by class and ethnicity in the early twentieth century. To cite a few examples from a study done in the 1910s, "midwives delivered 61 percent of Polish babies in a Wisconsin county, but only 16 percent of Anglo-Americans. In rural Mississippi, 88 percent of African American mothers used midwives, while 79 percent of white mothers were delivered by doctors."[58]

Other aspects of medicalization of the female body in the nineteenth century moved forward, eventually redefining the relationship between medicine and women's reproductive health. The maternal body was symbolic of the potential of humans to control the frightening vagaries of conception and birth and emblematic of a modernizing family. Discussions around infertility also reflected these patterns. Margaret Marsh has demonstrated that middle-class women wrote about this problem with an increasing sense of agony and urgency in the middle of the nineteenth century, and, as with reproduction control and childbirth, they increasingly expressed the idea that the fate of childlessness was not simply "God's will." Perhaps, instead, it was a medical problem, with potential solutions. Earlier in the century, guides to roots and herbs, like the proliferation of printed information on contraception, informed increasingly health-conscious readers hopeful to conceive. Self-administered remedies could help with "obstructions" to menstruation (a term also used with reference to unwanted pregnancies) because people believed that irregular or painful periods generally caused women's problems with conceiving. As the century progressed, however, privileged women hoping to conceive could and did turn to physicians.[59]

Most people saw problems with conception as entirely the responsibility of women, just as in the colonial period, when women, not men, were referred to as "barren." Despite the medical evidence available as early as the 1860s on male sterility, physicians rarely acted on this information. Physicians remained sensitive to men's concerns about a perceived connection between infertility and sexual performance well into the twentieth century, and men often avoided examining their potential role in a couple's problems with conception.[60]

Just as women tend to be more distraught by infertility problems today and tend to assume the burden of attempting solutions, in the nineteenth century women similarly castigated themselves for infertility. Southern diarist Mary Chestnut Boykin referred to herself as a "childless wretch" in discussing the pain of her mother-in-law's frequent references to her lack of children. She lamented, "God help me, no good have I done—to myself or anyone else." A belief that motherhood was a woman's chief reason for being, in which all women faced what Marsh has called "the motherhood mandate," surely informed the self-perception of Boykin, as well as other women who wrote sadly of their infertility. The famous child-rearing advisor, antislavery journalist, and novelist Lydia Maria Child is another example. "I never felt so forcibly as within the last year, that to a childless wife 'life is almost untenanted,'" Child wrote in a letter congratulating friends on the impending arrival of a child.[61]

And so, over the course of the century, another area of mutual, if complex, interests was physicians' efforts to assist women with infertility. It began early in the century, with ineffective but widely used practices such as bloodletting and advice about changing one's diet or using a vaginal tonic. By 1870, however, says Marsh, "should a childless woman happen upon a practitioner who kept up with new medical developments, especially one associated with an urban voluntary hospital, she would probably find herself diagnosed with a defective cervix, for which the recommended treatment was surgery." Women in the urban North began to gain access to medical fertility treatments that involved surgical procedures for perceived problems with the cervix, which gynecologists believed were responsible for a woman's inability to conceive, as well as experimental treatments, such as injecting spermatozoa directly into the uterus. As medicine developed new technologies that allowed access to the interior of women's bodies, surgery became a more commonplace treatment.[62]

By the turn of the twentieth century, physicians expressed great confidence in their skills and knowledge. In fact, successes in treating fertility in this time period were probably few: Marsh estimates from one physician's record that he facilitated successful pregnancies for less than 15 percent of his clients.[63] Women continued to hope, to seek medical treatment for infertility in growing numbers, and to demonstrate their faith in self-medication through advertised remedies.

CONCLUSION

By 1900, many saw the modern female body as capable, even dangerously so, of limiting reproduction. In the eyes of some, it was also a woman's responsibility to limit family size to ensure an appropriate nuclear family. On the question of women's autonomy in reproductive matters, the nineteenth century witnessed a great cultural anxiety that continues to shape debates today. In the discussions of medicine, health, and the ability of humans to control their destiny, the female body came to represent a complex set of conditions: it was driven by reproductive organs while possessing both dangerous fragility and disturbing power. Women's bodies were defined by motherhood, and these medical ideas bolstered the "motherhood mandate" and the emphasis on motherhood as women's major contribution to society. The reproductive health risks of the nation's mothers were the focus of widespread concern, especially when it came to middle-class white women, whose bodies were seen as the reproductive means of the nation. Both privately and publicly, feminist notions began to be articulated and developed in this context. Many argued that women deserved the right to choose maternity and in the process to control their sexuality. The modern mother might even be able to control what had once been God's decision by creating fertility where there had been none and limiting it where she saw fit.

It is important to realize that most women still had very minimal control over their maternal bodies, their health, or the health of their children. Though maternal and child mortality was extremely widespread, we know that the rates were higher among the most economically vulnerable populations. All evidence suggests that white, middle-class, and elite women were best situated to limit reproduction and to survive childbirth. Meanwhile, for all women, the lack of reproductive control was connected to their lack of other rights. Marriage laws based on the tradition of coverture, which also limited women's ability to terminate marriages and viably support themselves, left women vulnerable to men's sexual demands in the bedroom. Of course, for women without the legal protection of recognized marriage, such as enslaved women and unmarried women with few resources, sexual vulnerability also translated into greater maternal vulnerability.

Even with men's continued legal access to their wives' bodies, in the moral language that developed in the mid-nineteenth century we see an emphasis on the idea that men should follow women in sexual matters. Women's presumably far less pronounced and frequent sexual interests (if indeed women had any at all), could help couples conceive healthier children and preserve maternal health. Clearly these ideas left little room for the concept of women as sexual subjects in their own right. The corresponding medicalization of their bodies contributed to notions of female bodies as not only asexual but also frail and untrustworthy to perform basic functions.[64] Yet ironically the language of moral motherhood may have helped give many women a greater voice in their marriages and their sexuality and probably helped prevent the birth of additional children, perhaps forestalling many debilitating health problems and maternal deaths. Nineteenth-century "voluntary motherhood" ideas would develop broader cultural resonance. The notion would eventually be amplified and then altered by a truly modern birth-control movement in the early twentieth century, one that partially displaced ideas of female passivity.

The nineteenth century also witnessed a tension between women and physicians, who had some mutual and some opposing interests. In these relationships, both parties grappled with emerging notions of modern mothers in the age of science, changing economic incentives for family size, and the ideology of moral motherhood. Considering their stated goal of the care and maintenance of bodies, physicians' resistance to women's patterns of reducing fertility and even of stepping outside the bounds of a life defined by domesticity was oddly pronounced. By midcentury, physicians were making a mark for themselves in regulating reproductive control, in managing childbirth, and in the treatment of infertility issues, all of which had been in the province of the folk and midwifery traditions of women and all of which, a century prior, had been considered largely beyond human control. Physicians gained increasing credibility through intervention in the possibilities of the modern maternal body. They both reflected and contributed to widespread cultural fears about whether, if given the choice, women would become mothers at all. In reality, the fears were far out of bounds of the actual possibilities of nineteenth-century women, most of whom had almost no choice but to be defined by maternity and economic dependency. But even to suggest the possibility of maternity as a choice was to challenge a social fabric and a set of cultural values predicated on the idea of a moral mother, defined by her unambivalent love and willingness to sacrifice for any children she might conceive.

By the end of the nineteenth century, in law and in practice, mothers had achieved broader legal rights to their children, and women had property rights in marriage and greater rights to divorce. The nation's economically privileged women were exercising authority within and beyond the home, bolstered by the weight of religion, domestic ideology, and even a sense of national purpose. Women continued to exercise greater control over their fertility than their colonial ancestors had known, even though abortion and the distribution of contraceptive information had been criminalized. And yet economic dependency was the lot of most mothers. The loss of a male paycheck could easily mean an inability to support one's children. In addition, the centrality of mothers to national ideals and the very social fabric of American life bequeathed modern mothers with both the gift and the burden of being considered primarily responsible for a child's moral development. This moral motherhood ideology had a knack for creating distinctions, which would be elaborated in the twentieth century, between "good" mothers and "bad" mothers in ways that reinforced systems of privilege and disfranchisement based on race and class.

PART II

Modern Mothers

1890–1940

CHAPTER 4

Science, Expertise,
and Advice to Mothers

In 1918, Julia Lathrop, director of the recently formed United States Children's Bureau, received a letter from a heartbroken mother, a "Mrs. W.D.," explaining that she and her husband had lost their only child at the tender age of four months. Mrs. W.D. lamented, "My baby was sacrificed thru mere ignorance," even though she had studied child care while pregnant, had consulted experts, and had kept a sanitary home. "Money or efforts were not spared to save him. I soon found that not only mothers of large families knew nothing about the scientific care of babies, but the best Doctors of the city knew less. I could not nurse my baby, and he just faded away, never gaining, or rather losing weight all the time on the many foods which the different Doctors tried."[1] Mrs. W.D. believed that in an age when "wonderful work is being done" for infant health, such tragedies need not occur. To many other Americans, too, infant mortality seemed an appalling and outdated travesty in an era of science, mass production, and steadily advancing medicine and public health measures. At the same time, Mrs. W.D.'s reference to ignorance speaks to the thorny problem of bringing maternal care of children up to date while still maintaining the place of mothers on a pedestal of sentiment.

"Motherhood, as blind, unreasoning habit, is something we have inherited from our ancestors in the cave," wrote F. Scott Fitzgerald in 1923, in an article for the *Ladies' Home Journal*. In a letter to *Good Housekeeping*, a woman who identified herself only as "a trained mother" agreed, claiming that "a maternal instinct left alone succeeds in killing a large proportion of the babies born into this world."[2] Nineteenth-century moralists would have been shocked: mother love and its related spiritual education were thought to be all a child needed in the nineteenth century; perhaps they were all a child needed besides a male breadwinner to provide for his or her material well-being. But in the twentieth century, the idea of mothers as instinctively perfect caregivers would be taken down a peg or two by scientific efforts to modernize mothers' physical and later psychological care of children.

As the new century dawned, Americans were wrestling with the potential promises and dangers inherent in what many were now calling the "modern age." The nation was industrializing rapidly. The pace of life accelerated, and society was becoming more class stratified. Machines and standardized parts created an abundance of products and a model of efficiency that some saw as applicable to humans. Frederick Winslow Taylor's idea of clocking each worker's motion in a factory for time efficiencies found an eerie echo in physicians' advice to mothers to "make a machine of the little one. Teach it to employ its various functions at fixed and convenient times." Deliberate modernizers now focused on improving the work of individual mothers. Moral motherhood met expert-driven science, medicine, rationalism, and heady notions of progress. Many believed that through science, the nation could produce "fit" children with "modern" mothers who could save American civilization. "Study the science of motherhood," urged the Women's Christian Temperance Union. "Ignorance will not be a sufficient excuse for our mistakes in this day when so much is written on child-nature, child-culture, and child-training."[3] Childcare and infant health could be revolutionized, but that revolution required maternal education. Science, it seemed, was not so easily reconciled with the presumably untrained maternal mind.

From the Progressive era (1890–1920) up to World War II, Americans for the first time spoke of educating mothers deliberately to rear children the "modern" way. This meant control, rationality, education, and belief in science as progress, and it also meant the promise of freedom from fear of death and disease for the nation's babies and young children. In her best-selling 1909 book, *The Century of the Child*, the Swedish feminist Ellen Key praised the "light of science" for its ability to eliminate "the glamour of superstition and the glitter of false theory." Key offered to modern women an "entirely new conception of the vocation of mother." The modern mother would keep up to date on the progress of knowledge and participate in ways that would empower women and create better families. Initially, it seemed possible that scientists and physicians could work in tandem with mothers, on a similar, if not level, playing field. "Our soul is to be filled by the child, just as the man of science is possessed by his investigations," Key wrote, optimistically.[4] But in the long run, mothers' up-close observations of individual children, or even datagathering on their children, as some early child experts encouraged, were never considered scientific. As for maternal instincts, these were increasingly portrayed as inadequate and sometimes even dangerous to the task of modern mothering.

Maternal associations or child study groups had actually begun appearing early in the nineteenth century. By the turn of the twentieth century, they had become much more numerous. As the culture's fascination with science grew, their focus shifted away from religious and moral concerns and toward understanding modern, more scientific approaches to childrearing. As the newer clubs focused less on comparing the everyday experiences of mothering and finding solutions, they favored the collective study of expert knowledge, produced largely by highly educated men who based their knowledge of children on claims to scientific and medical authority.[5]

Mothers who embraced the new scientific motherhood equipped themselves with new knowledge about their children's health and their own. Many believed in the promise of science and medicine. In fact, the breathtaking progress in lowering infant mortality in the early decades of the twentieth century was justifiably celebrated. Between 1900 and 1920, infant mortality fell from 120 to 71.7 deaths per 1,000 births, a reduction accomplished before the use of antibiotics and widespread vaccinations in the 1940s. (In part because of antibiotics, infant mortality would plummet to 6.9 per 1,000 births by the year 2000.)[6] In the midst of this progress, however, mothers developed uneasy and complicated relationships with ever-changing and sometimes counterintuitive scientific advice. Class and race inequities in women's access to health care also greatly complicated these relationships, as did rural-urban disparities.

Experts in health, psychology, and the emerging profession of social work reached out to an unprecedented swathe of the population of mothers. These experts coordinated efforts on a massive scale to attack perennial problems such as poverty, infant mortality, and poor health. They created new public health schemes and scientific child-care advice as they grappled with what historian Rima Apple has aptly called "scientific motherhood."[7] Meanwhile, an emerging consumer culture generated mass advertising that reinforced these messages by appealing to mothers' insecurities as well as their aspirations for the status associated with the new scientific motherhood. Medical and psychological advice literature, directed largely at middle-class and upwardly mobile immigrant women, offers to the historian windows onto modern motherhood ideals. By the 1920s and 1930s, few mothers could escape the influence of such expertise and its cultural messages in their daily lives.

The Child Health Crisis and the Medicalization of Child-Care Advice

Throughout history, mothers had received the vast majority of advice on caring for infants and young children directly from other women. Despite the growth of print media, women remained the primary authors of child-care advice through most of the nineteenth century. Even privileged women had seen infant death largely as a problem out of their control and in the hands of God. Nineteenth-century "heroic" medical practices such as bleeding and inducing vomiting had made many parents shy away from physicians' care except as a last resort. Until the Progressive era, physicians rarely presumed to offer mothers much in the way of authoritative advice on infant and child care. Medical colleagues in more established areas of specialty initially disparaged the new "baby doctors," who developed pediatrics in the 1890s.[8]

With the entry of doctors into the nursery, female traditions of maternal advice sharing were greatly disrupted. Between the 1890s and the 1940s physicians appropriated child-care advice and solidified a near-monopoly on formal and culturally legitimate knowledge of children's health. As they transitioned from advisors to authorities, they often blamed mothers for their "ignorance," and it was not uncommon for them to suggest that this ignorance was deliberate. Mothers who did not follow physician-directed advice were now deemed responsible for child mortality and morbidity. Public health campaigns increasingly focused on mothers' role in preventing or allowing childhood maladies. For example, in 1918 a prominent physician and public health advocate claimed that the hundred thousand annual infant deaths in the United States represented babies who were "killed by feeding them with dirty, uncooked cow's milk or some other improper food, killed by weakening them with heavy clothing and then exposing them to a sudden draft, killed by letting some one who was coming down with 'a cold' fondle them and pass on to them the deadly germs of some disease." In fact, he argued, "most of these 100,000 [were] killed by their mothers or their grandmothers or their sisters, who loved them very much but did not know how babies ought to be cared for."[9]

Why would mothers increasingly seek such heavy-handed "advice"? The answer lies in part with physicians' increasing ability to augment their authority through breakthroughs in science and medicine. After scientists developed germ theory in the late nineteenth century, health experts were able to effectively target the spread of infectious diseases through water treatment, milk pasteurization, vitamin fortification of foods, and food inspection.[10] These developments meant that physicians and related experts in the health professions could increasingly offer compelling solutions to the critical problems of keeping children alive and healthy in early childhood. Because of this, mothers were often willing to accept condescension in exchange for potentially life-saving advice.

After all, mothers of all backgrounds continued to watch their infants die of diseases like tuberculosis, and pregnant women continued to face a legitimate fear of their own death or significant health problems as they approached the birth of their children. In the 1890s, one out of six children died before their fifth birthday; of these, one half succumbed before their first birthdays. Infectious diseases were the major killers of Americans generally, but infants and children were the most vulnerable: children under five accounted for 40 percent of the deaths occurring from the nation's top three killers—pneumonia, tuberculosis, and diarrhea-related illnesses. Between 1900 and 1930, maternal death rates were approximately sixty for every ten thousand births for white women and more than one hundred for every ten thousand births for women of color.[11]

Economic privilege provided some, but minimal, buffer from the loss of children in infancy. As late as 1915, the death rate for children before age one was 10 percent for all babies but 20 percent for babies of color. And in the 1910s, Children's Bureau investigators found that infant mortality was twice as high for children of parents with earnings below $521 annually as it was for families earning at least $1,200. Lack of access to running water also increased the likelihood of infant death by 40 percent. Still, infant mortality affected middle-class white women as well. Medical officer for the U.S. Children's Bureau Dr. Dorothy Reed Mendenhall was brought to her work by the tragic experience of losing two of her children before the age of three. Like so many women of her era, she also suffered from debilitating health effects after giving birth. "The tragic death of my first child . . . was the dominant factor in my interest in the chief function of women, 'the bearing and rearing of children,'" she said. "Most of my work came out of my agony and grief. . . . *A mother never forgets.*"[12]

While infant mortality and maternal health risks affected all women, the new "scientific advice" literature was initially targeted toward and mostly consumed by middle-class women, who encountered scientific motherhood advice in magazines, advertisements, and through their contact with physicians and nurses. In the burgeoning industrial cities of the North, southern and eastern European immigrants encountered this information within both ethnic newspapers and public health campaigns aimed at Americanizing infant care habits through organized programs (see discussion in chapter 5). African American women could find medical advice in black newspapers, especially directed at the small but active African American middle class, as well as through community-developed public health initiatives.[13]

Because of segregation, outright discrimination, and neglect on the part of most medical reformers, access to health care was another matter. For the vast majority of African American mothers who still resided in the South, access to physicians was extremely circumscribed. Overcrowded housing, lack of clean water, a combination of poverty and malnutrition, and lack of educational opportunities perpetuated these problems. Similarly, Mexican Americans living in substandard housing in labor camps or urban neighborhoods often lacked services, such as regular garbage removal, which made the control of infectious diseases more difficult. Segregation of Mexican Americans in urban areas like Los Angeles also meant lack of access to health care. Some hospitals refused even to admit minority women; others provided "Negro wards" that offered longer waiting periods or used the childbirth experiences of African American women as practice for inexperienced medical students. In addition, Mexican and Asian immigrants and African Americans were scapegoated as disease-carrying populations, charged with possessing "little or no knowledge of sanitation."[14] As these examples suggest, women's race, ethnicity, and class were crucial variables in how they experienced an increasingly empowered cadre of medical experts who sought to define proper modern child-rearing methods.

"MAKE A MACHINE OF THE LITTLE ONE": REGULATING CHILD CARE IN THE INDUSTRIAL AGE

Women who did receive physicians' advice encountered an increasingly authoritarian message. As Apple has observed, physician-authored advice literature in this period increasingly deemphasized women's roles as active pursuers of resources and providers of health care in their homes. Instead, physicians' writing reinforced the idea of mothers as passive recipients of medical advice. Doctors increasingly saw no reason to explain the rationale for their advice, an indication of the shift toward an authoritarian focus in physician-authored child-care manuals. Emmett Holt, leading physician and author of the widely read and influential *Care and Feeding of Children*, first published in 1894, presented his work in simple question-and-answer form. The correct answer to the question of bathwater temperature for an infant, for example, was, "For the first few weeks at 100 [degrees]F; later, during early infancy, at 98[degrees]F; after six months 95[degrees]; during the second year,

from 85[degrees]to 90[degrees]F."As is also evident in this quote, advice was specific, scientifically measurable, and did not invite variations or questions.[15]

Scientific motherhood medicalized basic infant care tasks, including bathing,
dressing, and, of course, feeding.[16] In an era obsessed with efficiency and standardization, the scientific motherhood movement went to extremes to rationalize the
physical aspects of infant care by insisting that mothers feed and nap their children
on precise schedules. The feeding schedule idea, later rejected by mothers, was born
in this era. So too could babies' and children's development be measured, with
"norms" for heights and weights. Thanks to the popular work of Dr. Arnold Gesell
in the 1920s, developmental schedules regarding physical, mental, and emotional
milestones also emerged.

Consumer capitalism in the dawning age of mass advertising also played on
mothers' fears about the proper feeding, growth, and "normalcy" of their children.
Ads for various "life-saving" infant formulas and milk products promising to promote the growth of "sturdy" youngsters proliferated in women's magazines. These
appeared alongside advertisements for doctor-approved cold remedies, reformu-
lated vitamin-packed foods, and even "sanitary" toilet paper. A Lifebuoy soap ad
from 1928 pictured a doctor and a chastened-looking mother standing over her
child's sickbed, while the bewildered mother said, "I can't imagine where he caught
it, Doctor." Readers of a two-page ad for Borden milk in *Time* magazine in 1924
would learn that even well-off parents could not rest: "Malnutrition attacks rich
and poor." School authorities, they were told, "cannot cope with it unless they have
the support of each individual mother." Scare tactics were common, as in the Borden milk ad that raised the subject of "your boy and his future. Dare you risk his
future success by neglecting his health now? And will you shoulder the responsibility then? . . . Better do it now and give him the start that is his birthright." If the
mother needed help, Borden and other companies offered to send them record-
keeping materials to track weight, height, and even hand-washing habits. The ads
promised mothers not only freedom from fear but also the prestige associated with
using up-to-date and medically approved products. Some companies combined
sobering admonishments about safety—"Mother's responsibility" appears in bold
print for a toilet-paper ad—with appeals to status: this safe, health-promoting toilet tissue was "especially sought by women of refinement."[17]

Scientific motherhood fixated on rationalization and control among those who
sought to modernize child care. The rhythms of nature seemed chaotic, and control
by science was a form of progress. Even the once revered maternal breast became
a source of cultural anxiety, and growing numbers of mothers began to doubt the
ability of their own biology to nurture their babies. Over the course of the twentieth century, a dramatic increase in the practice of bottle-feeding infants became
one manifestation of scientific motherhood. More than 80 percent of infants were
still breastfed in 1920, even though many women breastfed for a shorter period
than their foremothers. By 1972, a mere 22 percent of newborns was breastfed in
the United States.[18] Like maternal instinct, the maternal breast lost its stature in
the age of modernity.

The reasons for this shift are extremely complex, and to understand them, we must reconsider exactly who was modernizing motherhood. In the story of physician-assisted birth, women's demands for pain relief and hope for better outcomes had coincided with physicians' drive for efficiency and control in the birthing room. In the case of changing infant feeding practices, however, we initially find physicians wagging their fingers at mothers, telling them to go back to the old-fashioned breast as the best source of infant food. Physicians concerned about infant mortality blamed deaths on mothers' growing use of cow's milk for infant feeding. Their worries about the safety of cow's milk were well founded, considering the frequency of contamination in the milk supply available to a burgeoning urban population. In the period before cow's milk actually became safe through pasteurization and inspection, reformers set up clean milk stations. At the same time, physicians promoted the use of wet nurses over bottles, and public health nurses spread the gospel of breastfeeding. Urban residents saw posters with messages such as "Don't Kill Your Baby . . . Mother's Milk Is Best of All." As early as the 1920s, some doctors argued that feeding decisions were to be left to "the careful judgment of the pediatrician."[19]

Ironically, mothers were often the initial modernizers in bottle-feeding, practicing what they saw as practical patterns of infant feeding. By the 1910s, mothers were increasingly weaning their babies from the breast around the age of three months, a departure from the centuries-old practice of nursing through the infant's second summer of life. A 1912 Chicago study found that 61 percent of surveyed mothers had fed babies some cow's milk within the infants' first weeks of life. Mothers, of course, were just as concerned with infant survival as physicians. But many women claimed they resorted to bottle feeding out of fear that their milk was inadequate, either in quantity or quality, a concern bolstered by the anxiety of the industrial and scientific age. One Michigan mother who lost her first baby, despite copious reading of the latest scientific advice, believed that "the biggest mistake was probably made by our doctor, who advised against weaning, altho my milk was poor in both quantity and quality."[20]

In fact, physicians' most common explanation for the apparent failure of maternal breasts to do what they had done for millennia was that the stresses of urban life had "unnerved" mothers and disrupted their ability to produce milk. The frail maternal body of the Victorian era likely still resided in the minds of medical practitioners, but now women's vulnerable bodies faced new challenges from modernity. Concern about the inadequacy of women's milk-producing bodies appeared in not only medical journals but also the magazines read by women and the most popular infant care manual of the turn of the century, Dr. Holt's Care and Feeding of Children. Holt praised mother's milk as the best source of infant food but devoted large portions of his book to offering recipes for mixing baby formula and feeding schedules.[21]

The generally unmeasured quantities of breast milk did not fit well with scientific notions of scheduled feedings and precisely measured formulas. The U.S. Children's Bureau, which reached many thousands of mothers with its publications on child care, encouraged nursing while simultaneously promoting routinized feeding schedules and instructions for preparing formulas and sterilizing bottles.

Children's Bureau staff also urged mothers to have their babies weighed regularly, which tended to promote anxiety about underfeeding.[22]

Mothers were frequently confused on the issue. Infant feeding was the most common subject of letters written by mothers asking advice of the Children's Bureau. Mothers so agonized over the proper feeding of their children that many learned how to pasteurize milk themselves, and some had their milk analyzed by their physicians. One mother who attributed her babies' gastrointestinal problems to her own milk visited her physician every few days. She wrote, "The pictures, which I conjured up in my mind of him, suffering from malnutrition, rickets, possibly hydrocephalus were frightful. I allowed myself to be tormented by such thoughts till I was reduced to a state of melancholia." Another mother who worried her breast milk was inadequate reported, "Nothing seemed to nourish him."[23]

Increasingly aware of the role their own health might play in that of their babies, mothers worried too about milk production and overwork. "We are poor farmers and have 4 children," wrote one woman from Michigan, "so I have to over do. All so my milk leakes out. I have to give [the] baby cows milk a lot of the time, and days I wash I have *no* milk. And when I have to give him the bottle [*sic*] all together, I can hardly get his bowels [to] move at all. And my milk is get[t]ing less all the time. . . . I have follow[ed] what you Dr's and my own Dr says as near as I can. So *please* tell me what to do." Indeed, the response from a woman working for the Children's Bureau confirmed the idea that mothers could not produce an adequate supply of milk when "working too hard. Would it be possible for you to divide your washing over several days . . . so that you would not become so completely worn out?"[24]

New ideals about companionate marriage and the private family added to the cultural ambivalence about breastfeeding. Modern marital advice literature began to emphasize the good wife's availability for and interest in sex with her husband, and the success of some families in limiting births meant that couples could think about sexuality and procreation as separate. As a result, women's breasts became more sexualized. Commercial advertising for products to promote larger breasts enhanced this trend, along with other aspects of a more visual consumer culture in the age of advertising. A woman who wrote to a magazine about her pregnant daughter commented, "she wants to be more of a companion for her husband than she could be if she should nurse Baby; and . . . we wonder if it would not be best for all that the little one be fed." ("Fed" in this context meant bottle fed.)[25]

By the 1930s, clean water and pasteurized milk were more widely available, and the raging concern over infant feeding declined. With these imminent threats to infant survival diminished, a new generation of pediatricians ceased emphasizing the benefits of breastfeeding. Formula advertisements offered their own contributions as they competed with one another to alleviate women's deep anxieties about infant feeding. Eagle Brand formula, for example, offered to help in the "anxious, heartbreaking time for a mother when a bottle baby cannot digest his food. . . . In thousands of such pathetic cases, Eagle Brand has come to the rescue of a starving baby—has literally saved his life." Through Eagle Brand, a mother could "build up that tiny body into a strong, sturdy piece of human machinery."[26]

Formula companies' agendas were also advanced by a related pattern of scientific motherhood: a dramatic rise in hospital births. Though only about 5 percent of births took place in hospitals in 1900, the figure jumped to nearly half by the end of the 1930s; by 1955, the percentage soared to 95. Throughout this consolidation of modern birthing methods, hospitals alleviated the fears of mothers about the dangers of biology on three fronts: hospitals provided pain relief through powerful drugs, gave women hope for safer deliveries, and promised improved infant health through formula samples to new mothers. Women themselves advocated for heavily anesthetized births via scopolamine, the "twilight sleep" drug that became available in the 1910s. Increasing use of anesthesia ultimately helped hand over control of the birthing process to usually male physicians. Once delivered of their babies, mothers giving birth at hospitals also received a brief training in medicalized child care.[27] As a result of all these changes, by midcentury, most mothers had replaced breast milk with what had once been disparagingly called "artificial" food. More important, mothers also participated in the process of medicalizing and homogenizing the process of childbirth.

As these examples suggest, scientific motherhood increasingly cast mothers as compliant consumers of expertise in arenas once controlled by women. Just as with the rise of the "male midwives" in the nineteenth century, physicians' growing authority in areas of health care once left to women greatly complicated women's trust of their bodies and their judgment about the care and feeding of their babies. Physicians' new authority was enhanced by more demonstrable results in the form of measurably decreasing infant mortality. Establishing scientific motherhood as a kind of infant care dogma furthered the consolidation of medical authority regarding mothering.

In the decade leading up to World War II, physicians' credibility regarding child care was approaching its peak. The volume of advice increased, from government publications to popular magazines, advertising, and mothers' clubs. Infant mortality had declined; infectious diseases were being contained. Modern medicine was fulfilling some of its promise of improving children's health and chances of survival. In this context, physicians encouraged mothers to consult them on a plethora of topics and even deliberately omitted some topics from their advice books in order to encourage visits to the doctor. As one physician observed, a less informed mother might prove the best health care consumer: "In actual practice the young mother with a nutritionally untutored mind who frankly states that she knows nothing about babies and leaves the instruction to me is a treasure; the mother who has perhaps specialized in dietetics in college, or who approaches the subject with a McCollum in one hand a Gesell in the other is sometimes more of a problem than is her baby."[28]

The tone of doctors' published advice speaks to a sense of unassailable authority. Some clung tightly to their personal authority, as exemplified by assertions like these: "Unless I recommend them, do not buy books on pregnancy or infant care, as they tend to confuse"; and "please do not accept advice from friends or relatives, however well-intended. I cannot be responsible for your well-being unless you follow my instructions." An extremely popular and gently worded physician-authored book called *Let's Talk about Your Baby*, published in 1940, began with the following answer to a mother's question about setting up a baby's room: "There are some things that are really important and some that may be left to your judgment." He nevertheless gave detailed advice about everything from baby furniture to nightgowns, leaving the reader to perhaps wonder if her judgment could be trusted, even here, without a physician's advice.[29] It is not surprising, therefore, that in the postwar period the nation's best-selling child care manual of all time was written by Dr. Benjamin Spock, a man who, like the other experts discussed here, never had primary responsibility for the care of his own children.

Information as Power: Scientific Motherhood and Raised Expectations

Most Americans did not have access to physicians, even through the books they authored. But nurses and health-minded social workers did reach a wider swathe of the population than ever before. Popular magazines and newspapers also published physicians' advice. The longer-term improvements in maternal and child health must also be attributed to mothers' own demands for better health resources. Although powerfully informed by physicians and later psychologists and child development specialists, the actual changes in child-rearing practices were probably the results of conversations mostly among women. Indeed, physicians' advice was very much mediated through the women with whom they were forming new relationships. When it came to infant health alone, physicians and women knew that no amount of improvement could occur without the active participation of mothers.

The Children's Bureau, established in 1912, became an important disseminator and mediator of scientific motherhood advice. The bureau distributed medical advice to an increasingly literate and aware population of mothers using female messengers. It connected sympathetic expert women to ordinary women across the country, which lent a participatory element to the nation's modernization projects for mothers. The bureau was a federal agency, but it had a strong grassroots component and supported both Little Mother's Leagues and the National Congress of Mothers, the organization that collected, for the first time, detailed registries of births in the United States. The bureau was instrumental in developing and lobbying for the passage of the Sheppard-Towner Maternity and Infancy Act in 1921, legislation that until 1927 provided federal funding for public health nurses, well-baby clinics, and maternal education. Its demise was largely due to opposition from physicians who feared that it promoted socialized medicine and allowed nurses to encroach on physician prerogatives.

The work of the Children's Bureau continued anyway. As director of the first federal agency headed by a woman, Julia Lathrop pushed the bureau's mission on "all matters pertaining to the welfare of children" in many directions. Following on the traditions of maternalist political claims of the earlier nineteenth-century reformers, this emerging generation of Progressive era women forged a new political maternalism in part through modern ideas of science and motherhood. Progressive maternalist reformers claimed that women's special maternal qualities could be useful to the nation by providing social services to mothers in general and, for some, special services to poor women and their families. They also insisted that if government could modernize areas of economic life such as agriculture, surely it could provide resources to modernize the health and care of children. As reform leaders Lillian Wald and Florence Kelley put it, "If the Government can have a department to take such an interest in the cotton crop [the Department of Agriculture], why can't it have a bureau to look after the nation's child crop?"[30]

A federal agency headed by a woman only made sense if such an agency dovetailed with concepts of women's maternal nature. The Children's Bureau fit that bill. The bureau was staffed mostly by women. Maternalism gave Lathrop and her staff the authority and the assignment of both finding and distributing up-to-date information on child-rearing to women throughout the country. Bureau bulletins and pamphlets—especially its standard *Infant Care* bulletin—went out to women "from every geographic region, social class, and educational background," as historian Molly Ladd-Taylor points out. With nearly one and a half million copies of *Infant Care* distributed between 1914 and 1921, the bureau could claim with some confidence that half the babies in the country had benefited from the advice it distributed to mothers. And the conversation went both ways. American women sent the bureau as many as 125,000 letters a year.[31] Personal relationships seemed to develop, despite the distance; bureau staff even made personal contributions to the layettes of mothers.

The major author of the advice that reached so many thousands of mothers was Mary Mills West, mother of five and a college graduate. West was clearly a believer in rational systems of order in the enterprise of child care. "The care of a baby is readily reduced to a system unless he is sick," she wrote. This system not only keeps baby well but reduces "the work of the mother to a minimum and provides for her certain periods of rest and recreation."[32] In some ways, the bureau served as a mouthpiece for physicians, especially Emmett Holt. Perspectives from his bestselling book were very much interwoven with the bureau's widely distributed pamphlet, *Infant Care,* which even published the recipe for Holt's infant formula in the pamphlet. The Children's Bureau also knew its legal and political limits: they refused to respond to inquiries about birth control, despite the desperate pleas of women who sought such information.

But on many other matters, Children's Bureau women believed and acted on the convictions that women had something special to offer to one another as mothers and that physicians did not have all the answers. West provided the respectable caveat to readers that the advice they received was not a substitute for consultations with physicians, yet she did use her own experience as a guide in her advice giving. Her work was scrutinized by physicians, who asked that she not represent herself as the author of *Infant Care* because it was a compilation of expert advice anyway, and she herself was no expert. West responded, "I think there is a slight injustice in this attitude, for, after all, I had borne five children and as I am not a hopelessly feeble-minded woman I must have learned a few things for myself by the process. Also, everyone learns from others. Even doctors."[33] Nonetheless, she acquiesced to the deletion of her name by 1921.

Among themselves, Children's Bureau staff chafed at the paternalism of male physicians. After the bureau's medical advisory committee tried to remove discussion of "diagnosis, treatment, and etiology of disease" from the latest edition of *Infant Care*, staff physician Dorothy Mendelhall wrote to Lathrop, "Personally I believe mothers have a right to know the scientific reasons which underlie infant feeding and that the mothers our bulletins reach are capable of understanding such information. The farmers of our country are educated by bulletins from the Department of Agriculture in regard to infection diseases."[34] Why then, could mothers not understand?

There were many areas of common belief between mothers and the bureau that provided them advice. One important shared conviction was that the work of mothering was real work and that improving maternal health was good for babies, women, and the society as a whole. The bureau's studies of infant mortality were some of the era's most thorough, and they drew connections between infant health and prenatal maternal health and living conditions. As one woman physician on the Children's Bureau staff observed in response to a woman who had miscarried, "The importance of prenatal care has not until quite recently been fully realized by the medical profession as well as the general public."[35]

Bureau staff wrote frequently that "it is quite important for a mother during pregnancy to have especial care for her health." Director Lathrop wrote to a worried pregnant woman, who lived sixty miles from a physician and who was rearing the child of a deceased neighbor and another adopted child, that women's access to medical care was something "to which they are entitled." She added, "Although I am no physician, I cannot but think . . . that you must have splendid natural vigor and powers of resistance to have emerged successfully from the birth of your other children. . . . Certainly the world needs just such generous mothers as you are, and I am sure you are destined to go on helping your own and other people's children for a long time."[36] Lathrop and others made cogent arguments that women's service as mothers entitled them to better health-care opportunities.

Such compassion encouraged the continuation of honest conversations. Taking advantage of the anonymity of writing to distant, yet apparently caring strangers, women asked intimate questions about sexual intercourse during pregnancy and the appropriateness of having male physicians examine them. They shared specific medical details about their pregnancies and births. They asked for help procuring cash and medical resources. "Will you please write me a letter and tell me please what will the child Welfare and Maternity Bill that passed Congress do for us mothers and wives of farmers and working men?" asked one woman. Others asked for definitive advice from fellow women when doctors' advice conflicted. "Doctor says baby is OK," wrote one woman, "but it does not seem so to me. And as people advise me this & that, [I] don't know who to listen to and am sure your advice would be more correct."[37]

Mothers' relationships with the Children's Bureau seemed to have created, in and of themselves, a growing sense of entitlement among women to care for themselves as well as their children. In her publications for mothers, Mary Mills West encouraged mothers to rest during pregnancy and suggested that by failing to care for herself a mother could actually harm her baby. An expectant mother should "order her own life in the way that will result in the highest degree of health and happiness for herself and, therefore, for the child." Mothers clearly appreciated and even deliberately encouraged such exhortations. One mother of nine children who was "in the family way again" complained of her ill temper after working all day in the field: "What shall I do? My Husband wont sympathise with me one bit but talks rough to me. If I get tired & sick of my daily food & crave some simple article, should I have it? I have [helped] make the living for 20 years." Lathrop wrote, "I know your honest letter would help some men and women to understand why mothers ought to have better care." And another pregnant woman wrote, "My husband does not see any necessity of any extra care of my health now, and says it is only foolishness." The husband was perhaps implicated in the bureau's response about the importance of maternal health care, which once again raised the specter of men more concerned about cattle than mothers: "Farmers realize this in regard to their livestock and it is even more important to the mothers of children."[38]

Scientific Mothers Claiming Rights, Resources, and New Identities

As the letters suggest, many women saw in the modernization of maternal and child health a long overdue recognition of the work of mothering. Government funding and expert knowledge could improve farm production and the health of livestock. Why not children's and mother's health? Were they not also crucial to the nation's progress? Attention to rural health was slow in coming. But when reformers finally began to realize that maternal and child mortality in rural areas were often as high as in poverty-stricken urban neighborhoods, farm women began to demand better rural health resources. "The farmer's wife too often sees the cradle emptied for the grave," as one woman wrote. Yet "there's no farm wife who doesn't work hard enough to deserve the last notch in modern conveniences," as another observed. Farm women conveyed to researchers their wide and exhausting range of duties, such as "preparation of meals, care of the house, sewing, laundry, marketing, caring for children, poultry and dairy work, orchard and yard work, and procuring farm and household supplies," as well as care of the sick. Indiana and Illinois farm wives worked an average of thirteen hours per day, every day of the week, all year long. Perhaps influenced by the work of the widely published feminist economist Charlotte Perkins Gilman, who claimed that women's domestic work was real and economically measurable, one farm wife even calculated the value of her own labor in dollars and published the amount.[39]

The more vocal women in historian Lynn Curry's study of the rural midwestern mothers turned out to be the more privileged ones, and these women were most financially able to embrace changes in their own homes and also to make demands on public resources. They screened their windows to keep out flies (considered deadly disease spreaders), sanitized their outhouses, and demanded from their financially in-charge husbands that money be spent on indoor plumbing and electricity, in the name of child health. Like their distant advocates who established the Children's Bureau, they also argued that their husbands were not the only ones putting disproportionate resources into modernizing agriculture; the federal and state government's priorities were also wanting. As one Illinois woman put it, "the average farmer has had his county soil expert and crop advisor, cow testing association and so forth . . . while the farmer's wife, in the majority of cases is plodding on in the same old way her mother did before her."[40]

Rural women's discontentment led to the marshalling of public health funds for projects like the elimination of breeding grounds for flies. And women's frustrations undoubtedly contributed to Congress's passage of the Smith-Lever Act in 1914, which provided federal funds for "instruction in domestic and sanitary science and household art." Rural women's clubs used money earned through membership fees to provide "movable schools," supplying much needed preventive health information. And home extension programs also taught women about modern appliances such as power washing machines, no doubt contributing to additional marital discussions about resource expenditures in the home.[41]

While these women demanded improvements in country life, the invisibility of class privilege mirrored a larger problem with scientific motherhood and its promise of better health. The "progress" of science was supposed to standardize child-rearing practice and uplift everyone. But mothers' individual "failures" to embrace this advice invited the judgments of other, often privileged, mothers and of the experts, too A writer in the *Illinois Farmer and Farmers' Call*, charging mothers who did not provide proper hygiene with negligence, argued "in this day and age there is no excuse for such ignorance."[42] The rural farm women's organizations in Illinois were no exception to the general rule of maternalist activism undertaken by white women in this time period; they rarely demanded health care services for all. Instead, to go back to the example of midwestern rural women, these activists exhorted their fellow farm women to invest in sanitary upgrades of their own homes that were beyond the reach of many. The demand for more universal health care services was most vocally made by progressive African American women's groups, but, in an era of segregation and political disfranchisement, these visionary women seldom caught the ear of nearly all-white legislative chambers.

Rural women were not the only ones, of course, to play the role of modernizers and to try to define new motherhood standards on their own terms. Women often welcomed medical advice, especially when it was delivered respectfully. The appreciation of women is amply evidenced; they wrote to thank the Children's Bureau as well as individual physicians and credited the experts with sustaining or improving their children's health. One wrote of medicine that "worked like a miracle" and praised "the doctor who wasn't afraid to use it." Another woman wrote of her experiences with the Children's Bureau. "When people stop me on the street and ask the whys and wherefores of my obviously healthy baby I always say "He's a Government baby,' giving all credit to your bulletin (*Infant Care*). I was lucky enough not to know anything about babies before and not have any relatives who thought they did."[43]

A wide range of mothers could and did use the credibility of modern advice as a lever to improve their own status or gain resources. Also part and parcel of modernity were the complex negotiations between young mothers and older generations of mothers over raising a baby in a modern way. For example, a woman named Elise described a conflict with her European immigrant mother-in-law: "The baby had jaundice. So the doctor said to me, 'Fill him with water.' So I put water in a bottle and I boiled water and cooled [it] and I gave it to him. My mother-in-law, behind my back, would take [the bottle] with her dirty hands and put sugar in the thing and get it all over the nipple and stick it in his mouth. . . . When I went to school, now we had cooking lessons and they emphasized cleanliness and the washing of the hands."[44]

Differing approaches to Americanization and modernization, often perceived as the same thing, contributed to similar patterns among Hispanic mothers and daughters. Esperanza Montoya Padilla warmly recalled her mother's myriad skills in cooking, household management, and care of the sick. Still she insisted that her child-rearing methods would be more modern than those of her mother: "Poor Mother, I remember when I had my babies, I went by the book. Everything the book said, I did. And my mother would tell me to give the babies tea when they got sick, and I would say, 'No, no, no! I don't want to start your medications!' And when she would get upset with me and say, 'How do you think that all of you were raised?' 'Well I'm going to bring mine up different,' I would tell her. 'I'm going to be the modern one!'"[45]

The anonymously written song, "A Modern Lullaby," published in 1915, approaches with humor the many conflicts over child-rearing advice that must have ensued between young mothers and their female elders, both within and beyond immigrant communities:

Rock-a-bye baby, up on the bough
You get your milk from a certified cow.
Before your eugenic young parents were wed
They had decided how you should be fed.
Hush-a-bye, baby, on the tree-top,
If grandmother trots you, you tell her to stop;
Shun the trot-horses that your grandmother rides—
It will work harm to your little insides.
Mamma's scientific—she knows all the laws—
She kisses her darling through carbolized gauze.
Rock-a-bye, baby, don't wriggle and squirm:
Nothing is near you that looks like a germ.[46]

With much less irony, of course, physician authors, such as the eminent Dr. Holt, specifically urged mothers to turn a "deaf ear" to "the grandmother . . . whose influence is particularly pernicious, as she is supposed by her previous experience to know everything about babies." Indeed, some women welcomed the opportunity to claim child-rearing as their own, distancing themselves a bit from interfering mothers and grandmothers or simply proving to themselves and others that they were good mothers because they followed scientific advice. One Jewish woman recounted that during a house call from her doctor, she received an ultimatum from him. "You know you read baby magazines. How to take care of your baby and all," she explained. "And I had them on my chair in my bedroom. [The doctor] walked in, he said, I'll never forget, 'If you want me to be your doctor, you'll get rid of all those magazines.'" In deciding whether to follow his advice about discarding the magazines, which, after all, had their own modern advice distilled by the experts, she decided, "I'll see if I like him or not. Then I'll see what will happen."[47] She was pleased that the doctor had even noticed the magazines; in a way, it conveyed his attention to her efforts to seek out up-to-date advice, a hallmark of modern motherhood.

Child study clubs, justified by the new interest in scientific motherhood, also provided social and intellectual outlets for women, while confirming or enhancing their status as "modern" mothers. From the "Better Babies" clubs in small midwestern communities to Baltimore's African American branches of the Child Study Association, mothers tried to adapt their own needs to the new scientific motherhood. African American mothers' groups tended to chafe under the confines of a strictly scientific and psychological approach to the problems of child-rearing, as they well knew the structural impediments they experienced in raising their own families. Consequently, they added to their presentations on child development discussions of the need for adequate day care, safe playgrounds, and "Teaching Children Race Pride."[48]

As these examples suggest, the willingness to embrace scientific advice varied significantly with class, race, and ethnicity. Middle-class African American women and those aspiring to class mobility linked the "mothers' meetings" they organized to racial progress. Concerned about the high infant mortality and declining birth rates among African Americans, women like Atlanta University graduate Georgia Swift King referred to maternal education as a way to assure "the destiny of the Negro race." After all, as the middle-class-oriented, African American publication *Half-Century Magazine* noted, "better babies are a sign of progress. . . . A crop of puny, under-nourished infants could hardly be expected to develop into a race of robust men and women." For this reason, every mother should be educated about "the proper care of herself and her child."[49]

Those self-consciously striving to be part of the American middle class often linked modern motherhood methods to social progress. Historian Jacqueline Litt's study comparing Jewish and working-class African American women's interest in medical advice illustrated these differences. She found that as new immigrants, Jewish women often embraced medical advice as an important piece of becoming "American" and, by extension, more modern. As one woman said, "I never took my mother-in-law's remedies. She came from the other side. I mean, after all, we're American. . . . I [had] the biggest man [doctor] in the city when Phyllis was born. . . . I wanted to know what we do today. Not what we did thirty, forty years ago."[50]

African American women in Litt's study, many arriving in Philadelphia as migrants from the South, had less reason to trust physicians and apparently more reasons to trust themselves, their elders, and other experienced mothers. As one woman put it, "Why go to the doctor and ask them everything? You got a mind of your own. . . . I mean, you have to use your own judgment sometime about your own kids. You feel better to ask your mother [or] . . . somebody in neighborhood, you know, who—had more kids, instead. . . . And if somebody had about three or four kids, they know a little bit more than what my mother knew because they had more kids than she did." Having lived in a rural area, she added, "When I was raising my kids I was in the country, you couldn't run to the doctor, you know, every time they get sick."[51]

Other mothers of various ethnic backgrounds and class positions preferred traditional ways. Rebuffing the attention of a county demonstration nurse, one mother argued, "It is not necessary—all my children are well." Others encountered too much opposition from relatives in raising their babies the "modern way." Still others lacked resources, such as running water and access to doctors or to a range of nutritious food. Still others, like Peggy Gesell, a privileged woman and the daughter-in-law of the famous child development specialist Arnold Gesell, simply remained unconvinced that feeding schedules and growth charts were worth the loss of time for rest and housework. Unwilling to wake her older child with the noise of scales for daily baby weigh-ins, Mrs. Gesell quipped, "Frankly, Science is nothing to me when compared to a few minutes more sleep."[52]

Nevertheless, scientific motherhood was here to stay, even if it was embraced more quickly by middle-class women than by other groups. A major 1936 study found that 80 percent of professional-class women compared with 25 percent of women from the "laboring" class had read a child-care book in the previous year, yet more than 70 percent of all families in the survey had consulted pamphlets on child care. Although wealthier families had much greater access to physicians, more than 60 percent of laboring class women had at least consulted nurses, and female kin and other mothers did not rank as high as more medicalized sources of information. Pamphlets, books, and physicians were now popular among all classes.[53] Meanwhile, the plethora of advertisements from the emerging consumer health industry amplified the popularity of scientific advice. It is impossible to calculate the number of mothers influenced by advertisements for sanitary toilet tissue and soap or other germ-killing products and doctor-endorsed foods and formulas. These advertisements clearly appealed to a growing belief in science and medicine and created the notion that a good modern mother had to be a discerning consumer of expert advice and scientifically sound products in the modern age.

Psychological Expertise and the Modern Mother

In the 1920s and 1930s, with reduced infant mortality and improved containment of infectious diseases, medical experts increasingly turned their attention to managing the care of "normal" children. This attention included not just their physical health but also their emotional and intellectual development. "Great numbers of people are interested now in mental hygiene—more every day," wrote Dr. Karl

Menninger in *Ladies' Home Journal* in 1930. "It appears reasonable that mental health is something which can be largely controlled—like physical health—by a proper distribution of the available scientific knowledge which pertains to it." After all, Dr. Menninger said, "We all know, now, to avoid public drinking cups and be vaccinated against smallpox.... Why shouldn't we be equally fortified against temper tantrums, depressions, and such things as 'nervous indigestion' and 'nervous headaches'?"[54] Psychology would intersect with pediatrics to bring about the "child development" model of expertise. Mothers, not surprisingly, were deemed responsible for an increasingly psychologically complex management job when it came to child-rearing, but, once again, they were woefully in need of expert help.

By the 1920s, mothers were increasingly exhorted to worry about "maladjustment," cognitive and emotional, that could plague even normal childhoods. Habit formation could be conditioned, according to behavioral psychologists such as John Watson. Mothers must now be on the lookout for the dangerous habits of thumb-sucking and masturbation and must approach toilet training with nearly as much care as they had infant feeding earlier in the century. The development of toilet habits was fraught with issues of autonomy, control, and perhaps even character formation. Meanwhile, at another stage of development, the once hardly noticed stage of adolescence was now a time of "storms and stress," thanks to the work of psychologist G. Stanley Hall, the nation's first doctor of psychology.

Indeed, advice literature to mothers reflected anxiety about female adolescence and mother-daughter relationships even in the 1900s, in what could rightly be called the early infancy of popular psychology in the United States. The literature suggested that generation gaps were emerging between mothers and daughters in the modern age and that mothers would need some upgrading. Popular magazines claimed that mothers were either inadequate to the task of teaching daughters the facts of life or did not take the time to listen to their daughters' confidences. "Editorials in the *Ladies' Home Journal*," notes historian Linda Rosenzweig, "deplored the fact that American mothers tolerated rude behavior, failed to teach their offspring the skills of housewifery, and sent them out into the world with the feeling that they could have fun, go anywhere, and be the best dressed in the group." Another editorial claimed that "there should be no one upon earth to whom that daughter should feel so ready to go with every thought, every hope, every plan. If she does not it is her mother's fault." When it was time for daughters to leave the nest for college or marriage, for example, it was the mother who managed to live a full life of her own, that was "the very one they will want in their lives."[55]

The early twentieth century saw the expansion of a modern youth culture and its non-parentally-supervised entertainments as well as the advancement of a more companionable and democratic family ideal. By the 1920s, the modern middle-class family, to whom the psychological parenting advice was directed, seemed to be in a crisis. What roles should each member play in an age that celebrated more democratic relationships? Should children be sheltered and coddled for their safety and development, or should they be prepared through rigorous "habit training" and emotional conditioning for the harsh impersonal modern world? These compelling problems were reflected in the science of child development of the 1920s and 1930s.

Mothers who confronted the advice literature and advertising of the era faced at least as many contradictions as their more life-and-death preoccupied mothers and grandmothers. These mothers were alternately told to rear their children through habit training for toughness in a cold, mechanized society and to be intensely watchful about children's interior lives, all while avoiding either becoming overly involved with their children or neglecting them. After all, no parent wanted a child with a "clinging-vine" personality or an "inferiority complex."[56] Mothers should be watchful of their own problems, which were often psychological and best treated as such by none other than the experts themselves.

Even fathers were mildly implicated for their lack of competencies in the task of rearing the modern child. Some fathers were thought to be too distant and detached from their children, and this could lead to a failure to exert appropriate masculine influence on feminine-trained boys in the middle-class home. In the founding issue of *Children: A Magazine for Parents*, which set its ambitious agenda as attempting to appeal to both father and mother, the magazine pointedly advised fathers to "begin to give your child attention soon after his birth. The too intense fixation of the child on his mother is usually due to the father's neglect."[57]

This shift was part of a larger change in what the middle-class family actually did. Not only had home production all but disappeared in these families by the 1920s, but health care and children's education in grade school and beyond were, more than ever before, the responsibility of institutions and experts. Fulfilling psychological and emotional needs were now considered important responsibilities of the family. And because middle-class fathers were more often physically absent from the home, mothers were now deemed largely responsible for family discipline, a situation that created some anxiety about gender and the reproduction of masculinity in boys.[58]

With all these cultural changes, parenting became a more fraught activity. Parental inadequacies reportedly stemmed from parents' own psychological problems. Children often were not provided with "an environment in which to live that is not contaminated by the unsatisfied emotional strivings of their parents." Typical character traits associated with psychologically problematic homes included "the nagging wife . . . the neurotic mother, the phantasy-spinning nursemaid . . . the woman who hates housework . . . and wives who wear the pants." They also included "the tyrannical husband" and "the man who avoids his children" as well as "husbands who want to be God."[59]

Most parenting literature suggested that mothers had more—or at least more damaging—psychological inadequacies that could impact children than fathers. Indeed, popular child-rearing advice literature was still primarily directed at mothers, especially when it came to the care of young children, and advertisements for products other than life insurance explicitly appealed to mothers rather than the breadwinner-focused fathers. (Fathers never got a *Gentlemen's Home Journal*.) For fathers, withdrawal and tyranny were the two major issues, while women's problems spoke to diagnosable conditions like neurosis as well as the classic fears of women despising the menial labor of the home and inappropriately wanting power through wearing the pants. As is also suggested in the language above, the puzzled experts worried about a more than occasional flare-up of ambivalence about the whole enterprise of mothering. Were women sufficiently committed to mothering? Declining birth rates among white American-born women, the growth of women's labor force participation, and a vocal suffrage movement raised the disturbing specter of modern women rejecting their time-honored roles. With more women pursuing education and public roles, what would happen to the role of the mother?

At the same time, the experts also wondered about "neurotic" mothers who were too focused on their children. Were mothers up to the task of preparing adults, awash as they often were in (long culturally prescribed) sentimentalism? Was their attention to their babies really a kind of "smother love"? Did fathers need to be more involved to counter the influence of excessive femininity on their sons? Indeed, the technology that had slightly lessened women's housework responsibilities in areas such as food preparation and preservation seems to have shifted over to more time spent in child care. Echoing the advice of educators, mother-organized child study clubs of the 1920s urged mothers to undertake some activities outside the home to avoid producing the "overprotected child."[60]

Considering the skepticism about mother love, we might wonder if expert advisors ever proposed the solution of decentering the mother or perhaps providing her with a little help and even a "vocation" other than or beyond mothering. Feminists of the period offered broader visions for women, including the combining of motherhood and career. A few, like Ethel Puffer Howes, argued that pitting married life against individual female achievement was a proposition "which no normal woman of spirit and intelligence will accept for a moment." Women needed both. In claiming that social transformation would need to occur so that both sexes would "accept the twofold need of women as fundamental," Howes was clearly ahead of her time. For her, expertise could inform motherhood, but homemaking should not be a profession, rather a "potential part of life for every woman." Howes acquired funding to set up her own Institute for the Coordination of Women's Interests and shared a child-care arrangement with her husband in order to do her work. The institute provided cooperative child care for employed mothers as well as a food service to allow working mothers to bring home prepared food. Howes's ideas were best suited to privileged women who could afford hired help and could build careers on a part-time basis, relying on husbands for economic support and other women for child-care assistance.[61]

All in all though, the mostly male experts and influential social commentators rejected the idea that women—especially mothers—could expand their horizons into careers or politics. The suffrage movement, though ultimately successful, met with massive opposition in the 1910s. Antisuffrage propaganda depicted men who unhappily cared for babies and women who became aggressively masculine. One reflection of the anxiety about women's development of political roles and interests outside the home was the creation of home economics courses, funded by Congress, where mothers could learn efficient, modern, and up-to-date household management and child care. Bolstered by deep tradition, these courses reinforced the notion of the domestically focused housewife and mother.

Meanwhile, in practical terms, the responsibilities of the "woman of the house" in middle-class homes intensified in spite of new technologies, such as canned food and running water. The rapid decline in the availability and use of domestic servants meant that middle-class women were adopting a more do-it-yourself approach to both housework and child care; in fact, the ratio of domestic servants to the general population was reduced by half between 1890 and 1920.[62] Collectivist approaches to child care, though imagined by some as a boon to modern efficiency, floundered in a society that prized individualism and nuclear family-based approaches to socialization.

Despite fears of the neurotic mother, rigid gender roles were reenshrined in the ideal of the middle-class home. The 1920s saw some nods toward the role of fathers in child development and even a few admonishments against the neglectful or overbearing father. But very few social theorists of any stripe advocated a significant role for fathers in the care of young children. The notes of one child study club meeting in 1922 suggest gender conservatism even among mothers who were devotees of modern methods: "It was conceded that, as a rule, fathers play no part in the lives of children." The fact that fathers read so little of the advice literature directed at raising children provides more evidence on this point. A 1920s study found about 74 percent of mothers compared to 37 percent of fathers consulted child-rearing advice in print media. Another study found only one man out of 1,300 people attended child study groups and enrolled in a correspondence course on child rearing. Ultimately, the tradition of privatized mother care remained the norm of modern motherhood.[63]

CREATING A NEW NORMAL: THEMES IN PSYCHOLOGICAL PARENTING ADVICE

As with specifically medical advice, early psychological advice envisioned children as inputs into impersonal factory-production-like systems, with medical men serving as the crucial mediators in the production of better products. "Give me a dozen healthy infants," claimed the increasingly famous behavioral psychologist Dr. John Watson, "and my own specified world to bring them up in and I'll guarantee to take any one at random and train him to become any type of specialist I might select—doctor, lawyer, artist, merchant-chief, and yes, even beggar-man and thief, regardless of his talents, penchants, tendencies, abilities, vocations, and race of his ancestors." Watson cautioned strongly against playing with babies and even reproached mothers for hugging children when a handshake would do. Watson's harsh and brazen advice reflected an emerging branch of the modern notion of the extreme fallibility of maternal instinct and even maternal love. He wrote pointedly of "The Dangers of Too Much Mother Love" with claims that it "is a dangerous instrument" and that most parents "should be indicted for psychological murder"; Watson castigated mothers who cuddled and kissed their children. Through examples such as his observation of how many indulgent kisses mother, grandmother, and nurse showered a baby with in the course of one car ride (thirty-four kisses in all), he lambasted maternal sentimentality and even argued that kissing baby was "at bottom a sex-seeking response."[64]

A businessman at heart and an academic set adrift in part for his personal habits (he was asked to resign from Johns Hopkins University after an extramarital affair), the audacious Dr. Watson experimented boldly with the technique of insulting his maternal audience in his books and lectures. Watson provoked deliberately, and, though he received significant attention in the 1920s, there is much evidence that his theories were greeted with significant skepticism by his colleagues, popular purveyors of expertise, and not surprisingly mothers themselves. Some mothers rebelled explicitly, as did the woman who said to Watson, after one of his lectures for a group of mothers, "Thank God, my children are grown—and that I had a chance to enjoy them before I met you."[65]

In the trenches, in actual homes across the country, Watsonianism was greatly watered down, often ignored, and, even more often, unknown to mothers. Watson was also challenged even in his day by experts, from Maria Montessori to John Dewey, who touted individual personality development rather than standardized parental conditioning for children.[66] Still, the fact that Watson found an audience at all suggests the ambivalence about the once so-admired emotional sensibilities and impeccable motives of mothers. Fueling these concerns was the dawning Freudian preoccupation with sexuality, the unconscious, and the dangerous motives of the psyche.

The behavioral psychology of habit training did get under women's skin. Mothers wrote to the Children's Bureau with worries about their children's potentially harmful habits, such as thumb sucking and masturbation. These preoccupations were quite different from those of nineteenth-century moralists, who had focused on children's spiritual and religious development. Mothers who covered their children's thumbs with tape and aluminum mittens or consulted "baby specialists" about baby girls who rocked and crossed their legs expressed intense worry, claiming that such problems were "making a nervous wreck of me." Rather than advise "emotional conditioning" and extreme behaviorism, the still prolific Ms. West and other bureau women counseled distraction of children, tolerance for "phases," and the provision of physical restraint, such as pinning "small splints of wood on the child's arms" to prevent thumb-sucking, a restraint that also freed the mother from constant supervision.[67]

The influence of behaviorist psychology faded somewhat with the onset of the Great Depression. Mother love looked less dangerous in the more subdued 1930s. Strongly rejecting the notion of child-rearing as parallel to factory production, the era's child development guru Dr. Gesell advised mothers, "Don't watch the clock; watch the child." Mothers again had a role in child care, but more in the capacity of observers of children's wonderful unfolding, rather than as authoritative adults. Dr. Gesell, more kindly but less remembered to history than Dr. Watson, profoundly influenced notions of child development. The precise physical care instructions of the early twentieth century had corresponded to the measurement of "normal" physical milestones, such as height and weight. Dr. Gesell, working with a loyal cadre of female research assistants, developed the ages and stages concepts of psychological development and the mastery of developmental tasks. Child development required mothers to closely observe their children, "attune and adjust their own growth to that of the child," and work with the experts to maximize what Gesell saw as the "almost inexhaustible opportunities for guidance of growth."[68]

As with children's physical health, advertisers capitalized on the situation, reminding mothers of those inexhaustible opportunities. Parents could pay for behavioral consulting: "Habit Training: the Home Psychological Service," invited one ad in 1928, including "Psychiatric Case Work . . . for All Children, Normal or Handicapped." Just a bit more subtly, advertisers reinforced messages about children's emotional and intellectual development through consumer products and educational services. A discerning mother was told she should be sure to choose "the *right* camp" so that her child would return "healthy and happy and keen in his observations, sure of himself or herself among schoolmates." Encyclopedia ads asserted that "children at the age of five have EIGHT MILLION MILLION BRAIN CELLS . . . But those brain cells are worth absolutely zero UNLESS THEY HAVE ALL THE MATERIAL THEY NEED TO WORK WITH." And the magazines' advice literature complemented the advertising. If a mother read the magazine in which such ads were embedded, she would be asked by the authors to be introspective about psychological issues in her parenting. For example, in "The Co-operative Parent's Catechism," written by a female schoolteacher, parents were encouraged to consider questions, such as, "Am I watching for the development of special proficiency in any kind of skill?" and "Am I careful to suppress my own preferences regarding my children's careers?"[69]

Mothers' judgment in the emotional guidance of their children was forever disrupted by the impact of psychology's contribution to scientific and modern childrearing. Despite the detached observation method proposed by Gesell or the introspective tone of popular advice literature, watching for norms and questioning their own motivations while observing the minutiae of their children's aptitudes created anxiety in mothers. The work of Gesell and others of his era became deeply embedded in every aspect of modern motherhood: worrying over the development of "normal" children, psychologically and physically. In our fixation with normal numbers, from Apgar scores to height and weight charts to measures of developmental milestones, we are living out Gesell's work. We are also living out the consequences of the turns taken by consumer culture in popularizing the notion of purchasing solutions to psychological problems or creating developmental opportunities through specific products.

The early psychology era also bequeathed mothers with insecurities about their own motives. The popular child guidance movement of the 1920s and 1930s provides a compelling example of this process. The movement's clinics brought psychological expertise to bear on the problems of children's disruptive behavior at school and at home. Working in a hierarchy of expertise with psychiatrists and psychologists at the top and female social workers recording personal family histories of clients, the clinics often recommended individualized therapy for mothers to treat children's problems. As they sought advice, mothers became introduced to terms like "maternal overprotection" and "maternal rejection." Unlike Watson, who dismissed and insulted mothers, experts on the ground worked with them and diagnosed them. But their clinical work was undergirded with ambivalence toward mothers. Many believed that a "nagging or anxious mother" might produce a "rebellious son or daughter . . . [who] may even become unfit for taking their place in any scheme of harmonious social life." In the child guidance clinics, even the occasional worries about fathers as ineffectual or authoritarian, says historian Kathleen Jones, "were quite often traced back to the errant mother. Domineering wives, for example, created spineless husbands who stayed away from their children to avoid confrontations and thus deprived children of necessary guidance."[70]

The mostly middle-class women who came to the clinic hoping for help with rebellious or troubled children were sometimes taken aback. "I'm not on trial here," one woman said to her social worker. And many mothers appear to have had short-lived encounters with such clinics when they refused the clinic's diagnoses. At the same time, some mothers used these clinics to talk through family relationship issues for therapeutic reasons, whether or not they accepted the diagnoses of themselves or their children. Like mothers who consulted physicians for medicalized child care, at the clinic these women took the opportunity to access expertise in the form of conversations about their family lives. Talking with female social workers, they explored solutions to children's behavioral problems. Using the relative anonymity of the expert-client relationship, they also frequently redirected these therapeutic conversations toward issues related to their marriages.[71]

The need for a therapeutic outlet made sense. After all, this was the era of rapidly changing childhood norms, evidenced in not only the form of conflicting advice literature but also a new youth culture, which allowed for unchaperoned dating, movie going, and general individual youthful initiative. Also, women were supposed to suddenly be interested in sexuality within their marriages and to serve as good companions for their husbands. The child guidance clinic records, though filled with evidence of broken appointments and cases closed from mothers' lack of cooperation, provide evidence that many mothers wanted some expert help and tried to use it for their own purposes, whether for negotiating new forms of parental authority with their children or for easing the stresses of new familial expectations and women's ambivalence about motherhood.[72]

Here, as in our evaluation of the ability of mothers to appropriate medical advice to their own purpose, it is important not to overstate the case for mothers' ability to extract dignity from condescension or even condemnation. Psychology helped create and then diagnose and give a particular credence to one of the key cultural dilemmas of modern motherhood: negotiating the twin poles of maternal overinvolvement and underinvolvement. In between, there was little room for maneuvering. The rejecting mother and smothering mother archetypes became much more widely discussed and feared in the 1940s and 1950s, but, even in this earlier era, psychology suggested mothers' inability to find a happy medium.

Psychological theories conflicted and changed markedly over the first several decades of the century, but they shared some common characteristics. First, mothers were still expected to be the primary caregivers. Even though the language of "parents" supplanted exclusive references to mothers in the child-rearing literature, then, as now, the audience of such magazines was intended to be women. And women were the primary consumers of it. As with physical care of children, experts increasingly claimed that mothers needed psychological guidance. Yet the experts often and sometimes deliberately insulted the very mothers they sought to influence. With the emergence of the study of child development, the experts shared a conviction that early childhood, though mysterious to the untrained eye, was profoundly important, whether for habit training or for meeting the milestones of normal development. The complexity of it all meant that mothers' potential mistakes were manifold, from failures to regulate potentially harmful behaviors to missed opportunities to encourage growth and individuation. Anxiety was the lot of the well-informed modern mother.

Conclusion

In both medicalizing and psychologizing child care, science presented a prospect of certain results, even if it could not always deliver. It did so in ways that differed from the religious perspectives and cultural practices that had informed the rearing of children in previous centuries. Science could offer promise, and science could create the anxiety that still plagues modern motherhood today. At least initially, mothers could appropriate medical advice and use it for their own purposes. Not only did they experiment with such advice in hopes of preventing infant death and illness, but many also used their consumption of medical advice to symbolize their own status as modern, up-to-date mothers. As mothers' groups continued to proliferate in the twentieth century, new information and the act of seeking it helped mothers find community among other mothers their age by moving beyond or enhancing traditional female networks.[73] Additionally, consuming and acting upon ever more widely available health advice literature was part of dignifying the work of mothers. In the process, women raised expectations about the health and material needs of mothers by drawing attention to the vitally important role they played in properly caring for babies.

Scientific child-rearing advice contributed to the creation of an ideal modern mother: a woman who sought up-to-date advice, educated herself, studied her child, but deferred to the experts. By the 1930s she was still the ever vigilant primary caregiver, who, as Ann Hulbert aptly put it, should "walk—and speak—ever so softly, and carry a big chart."[74] She managed her household and tried to direct family resources toward children's health, education, and social development and increasingly toward the realization of a child-centered home. She was advised to attend to individual differences and psychological problems in children, even while keeping an ever-watchful eye on their physical health. On top of all this, she had to become a discerning consumer of both expert advice and marketing. The modern mother chose her female networks in the spirit of maternal communities seeking, the newest and best child care methods, and she either left behind or tried to bring along a more "old-fashioned" set of female elders.

Paradoxically, at the same time that scientific child-rearing advice insulted mothers, it also subtly helped create a sense of entitlement on the part of mothers to pay attention to their own health and perhaps even to their own emotional well-being. What some historians have called the "therapeutic culture" of advice-seeking about children and family elevated women's voices in certain respects. Like the nineteenth-century religiously inspired ideal of modern motherhood, scientific motherhood both burdened and privileged mothers with the notion that what they did mattered more than what fathers did for children's emotional development.[75] Taken from a different angle, notions of modernization fostered criticism of mothers' heavy workloads in the home. Drudgery and modernity did not go together, and mothers' drudgery was perhaps even inimical to the lofty job of bearing and rearing the next generation. Modern mothers who could afford to do so were able leave the most menial household labor to hired help or to modern appliances and concentrate instead on their children's multifaceted and complex needs. Observers sometimes praised modern mothers for their contributions to civilization, but critics also warned about the dangers of problems as yet unseen in their children. Eternal vigilance was clearly the price of mothers' hard-won places on the pedestal of scientifically nurturing a teetering civilization.

CHAPTER 5

Grand Designs

UPLIFTING AND CONTROLLING THE MOTHERS

Between the 1890s and the 1930s, the foundations of the American welfare state began to take shape. The United States created a small governmental safety net, for not only mothers and children but also workers. In that era workers were culturally defined as male, although the female ranks were growing. By international standards, the United States had a sparse welfare structure. Nowhere is this more evident than in the inadequate social policy accessible to mothers and, of course, the people who lived with mothers. The origins of the American welfare state contained grand designs indeed, and reformers' notions of mother-informed politics, or "maternalism," strongly infused both the rhetoric and the reality of social policies. This was a much more expansive vision of what social policy could do than nineteenth-century maternalist reformers had foreseen. Undergirding the maternalist social imagination of this generation of new reformers was the idea of dignifying mothers' work and expanding the opportunities of scientific motherhood.

"We cannot afford to let a mother, one who has divided her body by creating other lives for the good of the state, one who has contributed to citizenship, be classed as a pauper, a dependent," declared Mrs. G. Harris Robertson, president of the Tennessee Congress of Mothers. "She must . . . stand as one honored." Mrs. Robertson proclaimed her support for state funds, "mothers' pensions," for families "shattered by the loss of father, the bread-winner." Indeed, it was in this era that Woodrow Wilson made official the annual celebration of Mother's Day, in 1914. He did so in response to a concerted national campaign for the holiday undertaken by Anna Jarvis, who wanted to honor the life of her own mother and all mothers with a day of sentiment and memory. Jarvis's mother, a pacifist during the Civil War and an activist with fellow mother on issues of health care access and sanitation, had lost eight of her twelve children before the age of seven.[1]

Mother's Day's origins and its conflicted meaning in the early twentieth century reflected the tensions between an individual, sentimental view of motherhood and notions of maternal dignity and sacrifice as a catalyst for a broader ideal of a just society. Charlotte Perkins Gilman argued that motherhood was the nation's highest calling: "A new standard is rising—the woman's standard. It is based not on personal selfishness but on the high claims of motherhood, motherhood as social service instead of man-service." The "woman's standard" could define a society that cared for all, like a mother. Gilman contributed to a rising chorus of demands for progressive public policy for mothers.[2]

Maternal economic security and dignity were not always so well imagined, especially when it came to mothers working outside the home. For example, Florence Kelley, leader of Progressive organizations to help women workers, and Frances Perkins, Franklin Delano Roosevelt's secretary of labor during the 1930s, knew well that most mothers were one paycheck—usually one male paycheck—away from poverty. But what these highly educated and compassionate women were not able to imagine was a situation in which the majority of mothers could earn wages by working jobs that took them outside the private sphere of the home. In fact, despite their great sympathy for mothers, some of Progressive-era reformers' most vocal energy went into supporting a social policy structure that discouraged combining paid labor with motherhood. In public policy—regarding welfare, labor, and in the spotty and relatively unpopular attempts at creating institutional day care—such maternalist assumptions about domestic mothers and breadwinning fathers were pervasive, even among feminist reformers. Architects of the emerging American welfare state offered struggling mothers some critical new resources, but they also installed some long-standing hindrances to women's ability to claim full economic citizenship.

A related limit on these reformers' imaginations was the "new standard" of motherhood. In an increasingly multicultural society, establishing scientifically influenced mothering norms became the work of energetic reformers, including some within the emerging profession of social work. Social workers' interventions, however, were sometimes experienced not as uplift, but as cultural imperialism. Middle- and upper-class Anglo American women did not control very much in the public world (after all, they could not even vote until 1920). But an important segment of these women did exercise significant control over the dispensation of charity and even the shaping of public policy on questions pertaining to family life. They did not all think alike. But the most influential among them wanted to extend what they saw as the benefits of middle-class moral and scientific motherhood ideals to a much larger portion of the population, including the nation's ever-growing immigrant communities.

During the Progressive era, the energy of political maternalism spurred on community and policy initiatives, including anti-child-labor campaigns, the creation of the U.S. Children's Bureau, and state-funded "mothers' pensions" for widows deprived of the support of a male breadwinner. These bold projects, many believed, would improve family life by putting social supports in place, thereby securing and unifying the nation through the healthy and sustainable reproduction of family life. To secure the social supports reformers envisioned, many believed it was essential that mothers have the right to vote. "If woman would fulfill her traditional responsibility to children, then she must bring herself to the use of the ballot," insisted the well-known reformer Jane Addams. After all, argued Gilman, men had had their opportunity: "you have worked your will—you have filled the world with warfare, with drunkenness, with vice and disease. . . . Now we will have a new world . . . a mother-world as well as a father-world, a world in which we shall not be ashamed or afraid to plant our children." Growing numbers of reform-minded women, no longer content to engage in locally bound projects and petition campaigns, also demanded that the government "give the ballot to the mothers."

Women's reform projects were both self-serving and directed toward the female "charity" tradition. Clinging to high ideals of motherhood and social progress provided cover for the brash demands that women's voices be heard on public policy issues. Many reformers of the era, especially feminists, saw dignified motherhood as a lever for women's social and civic influence as well as claims to citizenship. Among feminists and labor activists alike, a radical few used this historical moment to demand other new rights for mothers, such as the right to decide when and whether they would become mothers through contraception and to the dignity of well-paid work for women. Crystal Eastman, for example, declared that "love and home and children," as well as "work of her own for which she is paid," were "equally natural desires."[3]

Most maternally inspired reformers had more modest claims. Rather than seeking to create gender equality in either the home or the workplace, most reformers focused instead on providing mothers with the scientifically based education and modest resources to care for their children in ways that continued the nineteenth-century focus on the centrality of mothers to children's development, appropriate to the modern age. As Progressive-era state welfare policies developed into national programs, the mixed legacy of those reformers concerned with poverty and family life is something we need to understand today, for both the bold—if culturally bound—social imagination about motherhood and the limited but important policy victories in creating a small safety net for the nation's mothers and children.

New Conditions for the Work of Mothering in the Industrial Age

Italian immigrant Fabbia Orzo's description of family life in the early twentieth century revealed some of the social and economic problems that animated the work of maternalist reformers of the time: "It was pretty hard to make a living at that time. My father worked in the building line—his work was seasonal—he didn't work much in the winter. Women who couldn't go out to work took in home sewing. Women who could go out did factory work. Women with young children couldn't go out to work, there was no one to take care of the children."[4] In the nation's growing cities millions of Americans like Orzo were experiencing the ravages of rapid industrialization: social instability, grinding poverty, and minimal infrastructure. With nominal sanitation in burgeoning cities, the swift spread of infectious diseases claimed the lives and health of family members and burdened women with providing makeshift health-care arrangements for their families.

Over the course of the nineteenth century and well into the twentieth, families accustomed to rural survival strategies on farms or in artisanal home production were transforming into urban clusters of wage earners, who often could not make ends meet even when men and children worked long and grueling hours in factories. The late nineteenth century saw an enormous influx of children into the labor force; in the last three decades of the century, approximately one-sixth of children between ages ten and fifteen worked for wages. In addition to stretching paychecks and raising large families, usually without access to information about how to stop bringing more hungry mouths into the family, many urban working-class mothers also needed to bring in cash of their own. Between 1890 and 1940, the rate of women's labor force participation grew from about 18 percent to approximately 25 percent. Americans' participation in World War I spurred this development, as women stepped in to fill a labor shortage occasioned by the war.[5]

Meanwhile, owing to the extreme instability of available jobs and a generally volatile capitalist economy, families became increasingly vulnerable to paternal abandonment, especially during the Great Depression of the 1930s. Industrial accidents also contributed to the population of mothers without male breadwinners and intensified women's need to be breadwinners themselves. In 1930, while only about 12 percent of married women worked for wages, 34 percent of widowed and divorced women and 46 percent of single women did so. Though urban life contributed to single motherhood, according to statistics, single mothers headed only 8.4 percent of families. Many single mothers were not counted in this figure because the absence of a male breadwinner often forced mothers to move in with relatives, lest they face enormous financial vulnerability. The social stigma of single motherhood also contributed to undercounting. Regardless, maternal financial ruin, as a result of either widowhood or "desertion" (or separation in today's terms), was a serious concern among both reformers and the struggling urban poor.[6]

At the same time, ordinary mothers' workload in this period, whether or not they worked outside the home, was staggering, and poverty greatly exacerbated the situation of millions of women. In the 1910s, washing machines and refrigerators were not the only conveniences mothers lacked. The vast majority of poor rural families managed without access to running water. Daily chores included carrying buckets of water for laundry, bathing, and other needs. Typical urban families also did without reliable heat, ventilation, closets, cabinets, and screens. Even among middle-class women, household chores were onerous and time consuming. More affluent urban families were beginning to enjoy the benefits of electricity and running water, and a larger segment of the population saved time because of the availability of canned food.[7]

In the industrial economy, growing one's own food and bartering services were seldom viable economic strategies. Cash meant survival now, and mothers had limited opportunities to earn money outside the home while still keeping their children safe. Many opened their cramped tenement apartments to boarders, usually immigrant men. Women traded more cooking and cleaning, their privacy, and possibly the safety of their children in the home, for small but essential additions to the household budget from boarders' rent. Mothers also took in laundry and sewing for other families or did light assembly at home, such as making artificial flowers for factory-made garments. One investigator documented the situation of a family of seven: "grandmother, father, mother, and four children aged four years, three years, two years, and one month respectively. All excepting the father and the two babies make violets. The three-year-old girl picks apart the petals; her sister, aged four years, separates the stems, dipping an end of each into paste spread on a piece of board on the kitchen table, and the mother and grandmother snip the petals up the stems." The need for cash made for a very different kind of home space and mother-child relationship than the one imagined by nineteenth-century moralists and many of their Progressive-era descendants.[8]

Mothers who had to earn wages outside the home struggled as well. Women's wages averaged between 56 and 60 percent of men's between the mid-1910s and the mid-1930s, and nearly 90 percent of all wage-earning women were clustered in just ten low-paying occupations. Lack of reliable child care contributed to the limited range of cash-generating activities for working mothers. Keeping up with work at home made for relentless and exhausting labor. Although mothers used the labor of children old enough to help, as both babysitters and wage-earners, studies of the period found that women typically shouldered the vast majority of housework. During the beet-growing season, for example, only 14 out of 454 Colorado mothers who engaged in fieldwork had help with meal preparation from another adult in the household; only 42 had even a child to help them. Similarly, more than one-third of wage-earning mothers in a Chicago study did all the housework themselves; an additional one-third had help from their children, and only one-fifth had help from their husbands, a figure that may reflect the large proportion of single mothers engaged in wage work.[9] Women's wage-earning raised concerns about maternal health. Many were deeply troubled by stories like this one of a Polish immigrant woman in a Pennsylvania steel town:

> At 5 o'clock Monday evening went to sister's to return washboard, having just finished day's washing. Baby born while there, sister too young to assist in any way; woman not accustomed to midwife anyway, so she cut cord herself; washed baby at sister's house; walked home, cooked supper for boarders, and was in bed by 8 o'clock. Got up and ironed next day and day following; it tired her, so she stayed in bed two days. She milked cows and sold milk day after baby's birth but being tired hired someone to do it later in week.[10]

In the early twentieth century, families in which mothers worked for wages also faced increased health risks to their children. Studies of the time showed that infant mortality was considerably higher for these families. A dearth of reliable child care compromised children's safety as well. Child-care centers, or day nurseries, as they were then known, were few and far between. A mere 205 existed in the whole country in 1906, mostly in urban areas, and poor mothers were reluctant to use them. Instead, mothers relied upon older siblings, neighbors, and relatives as child care providers and also took their children to work with them at times. These children were at risk for industrial accidents, while those left at home in the care of siblings faced their own hazards. Investigators found situations in which babies were left at home alone for entire work days or in the care of children as young as four.[11]

Necessity continued to drive millions more women into the labor force. Nearly two million more married or previously married women were earning wages in 1910 than in 1890. Among these, mothers of small children were probably well represented, though exact data on maternal status is hard to find in available records. As one immigrant woman put it, "How can we help it? The man he no works two days, three days maybe in one week, two weeks. Sunday no work, no money. Well what can we do? My girl we maka da feathers. The children must have to eat." Indeed, fathers usually could not support families with their own wages in industrial America, despite a lot of political energy put into the goal of men earning a "family wage." Nonwhite men faced special obstacles because of rampant and legally sanctioned discrimination. For at least a generation, discrimination also limited the wage-earning opportunities of eastern and southern European immigrants who flooded the nation's northern cities and were considered by many native-born people to be separate "races" of people. Because discrimination against African Americans in housing, credit access, education, and the legal system was much more entrenched and pervasive, African American women worked outside the home at nearly twice the rate of white women in 1920. Families of color often needed to rely on children's labor as well. One 1933 study of Mexican American families found that children typically contributed 35 percent of a family's total household income.[12]

African American, Hispanic, Asian American, and Native American wage-earning mothers were very often confined to low-paying domestic service positions in the homes of white families. In 1930, 33 percent of Hispanic women worked in the low-paying, virtually impossible to unionize, and exploitative area of private household service, while only 12 percent of European American women did so. Often these women had no choice but to board with their employers, who expected round-the-clock availability. If they were mothers, then private household workers maintained two households. Live-in domestic servants were often barely able to be present with their own families. An African American woman recounted her situation in 1912, "For more than thirty years—or since I was ten years old—I have been a servant . . . in white families. More than two-thirds of the negroes of the town where I live are menial servants of one kind or another. . . . I frequently work from fourteen to sixteen hours a day. I am compelled . . . to sleep in the house. I am allowed to go home to my children, the oldest of whom is a girl of 18 years, only once in two weeks, every other Sunday afternoon—even then I'm not permitted to stay all night."[13]

When possible, working-class families attempted to piece together a patchwork of wages between a male breadwinner, who could command the most wages, and children old enough to work, leaving mothers to do the heavy housework and find other ways to bring cash into the home. Maternal labor, child labor, and the other economic strategies most used by working-class families did not always mesh with the social welfare approaches being orchestrated by a more privileged class.

SETTLEMENT HOUSES AND THE POSSIBILITIES OF
CROSS-CULTURAL MATERNALISM

A new approach to addressing industrial urban poverty began in the United States in 1889. Bringing the British idea of the "settlement house" to the northern urban immigrants was the brainchild of college graduate Jane Addams. Addams was looking for a meaningful role for herself and other college-educated women in a world that denied them traditional professional avenues. The idea of the settlement house was to live among and provide services to poor urban neighborhoods in places like Chicago and New York City. Mary Simkovitch, who worked in the settlement house movement of New York's Lower East Side, expressed the hopeful possibilities of women cooperating with one another in settlement communities to improve family life: "The settlement ought to be the matrix of a more adequate understanding of what goes on . . . its permanent value is not so much in the rendering of specific services . . . as in the fruitful knowledge obtained through firsthand contacts with the people in the neighborhoods. To voice their wrongs, to understand their problems, to stand by their side in their life struggles, to welcome their leadership, to reveal to others who had not had the opportunity of direct contact . . . is the primary task."[14]

Significantly focused on helping mothers and children, the settlement house workers tried to improve the conditions in which women mothered. Addams, Simkovitch, and others in this profoundly influential network of educated women sought to understand the structural conditions that contributed to poverty—from grossly inadequate wages to the crowded, unhealthy living conditions in the immigrants' tenement neighborhoods. While spreading their vision across the country, these women helped create nearly four hundred settlement houses in the urban North by 1910.[15] Well before they had the right of the elective franchise, such maternalist reformers inserted themselves into city politics through the settlement house movement by demanding that poor neighborhoods have clean milk, libraries, playgrounds, safe drinking water, legal services, better housing, and protections for workers. Settlement house women, effectively sociologists on the ground, conducted the nation's first urban survey research that detailed wages, living conditions, and family situations in the country's burgeoning immigrant neighborhoods. In addition, they expanded their influence to Washington by providing political energy for the creation of the Children's Bureau and eventually translating state-level welfare and labor protection legislation into federal programs and law.

The settlement houses themselves, however, fell far short of being able to put a significant dent in urban poverty. The problems were too large for four hundred small settlements to address, even as the settlement house leaders grew more effective in moving city government to action over time. In terms of health activism alone, industrial living and working conditions contributed so much to the problems faced by new immigrant populations that often the best reformers could only provide stop-gap solutions.[16] Still, the movement created important cross class conversations between women about what was needed to do the work of mothering. How much in the way of social and economic resources, such as health care and job training, was necessary? And how much in terms of the reeducation of mothers, especially immigrant mothers, toward a modern American standard?

Settlement house workers in the Progressive era gradually supplanted their foremothers' more missionary, religious-conversion-focused work with an effort to understand and illuminate the social and economic conditions of the poor. In those early years before social work became professionalized, relationships were often based on genuine friendships, sympathy, and learning. Founder Mary Simkovitch remembered her time on New York's Lower East Side: "How much there was to learn about family life in our early days." In contrast to later views of the poor, in which family pathologies were again identified as the reasons for poverty, many Progressive-era settlement house women tended to see resilience, community building, and adaptation rather than dysfunction. Simkovitch, for example, reflected on immigrant families:

> The family pattern had a conservative cut, but on the whole it worked. The position of the mother was a strong one, much stronger than often obtains in families of a higher economic level. She paid not only the rent, insurance and food, but also bought the family's clothing and gave the husband and children enough for carfare and lunches. This built up a solid family life where each was dependent on the other . . . there was something loving about such a home life in which no individual could live for itself. It made of sacrifice not a beautiful thought, but a common custom.[17]

Settlement house workers on the Lower East Side attended family events with immigrants, shared meals with local families, and deliberately honored the heritage of Italians, Poles, and other European immigrant groups. They celebrated a form of multiculturalism at a time when *The Dictionary of Races of Peoples*, published by the U.S. Immigration Commission, listed "races" from most to least advanced, where Anglo-Saxons led and southern Italians were very low on the list.[18] The workers also tried to develop settlement houses into community centers for health and educational needs and hubs of political activity to lobby city governments for improved public infrastructure. Working with the burgeoning General Federation of Women's Clubs and its African American counterpart, the National Association of Colored Women, settlement houses built programs such as legal aid societies, protective agencies for women and children, and child care centers. Out of the settlements came the National Consumer's League, which promoted fair labor practices for women and children.

At the same time, there were important tensions between middle-class Anglo American values and the family values of immigrants and other working-class Americans. Settlement house workers sometimes admired the work ethic of immigrant families, but many worked hard to convince immigrants of the values of individualism for all family members, and the superiority of American food and health practices. They inserted themselves into core aspects of family life that had been the province of immigrant parents. Often the settlement workers were oblivious to their own privileges of class and ethnicity and to their cultural biases. After all, immigrants were not invited into middle-class neighborhoods to give child-rearing advice.

Immigrant parents often experienced a double threat from the settlement house workers and the public schools, where children learned English, ate strange foods, and learned that their parents' ways were old-fashioned and un-American. "A godless country, America," said one immigrant father. "All wrong side up. The children are fathers to their fathers. The fathers, children to their children." Accustomed to relying on children for labor and earnings, immigrant families often expected deference from their children. Meanwhile, the forces of American consumerism, education, and the settlement house charity organizations advocated a more child-centered, individualist approach to parenting. Stories like this one, told from the perspective of a social worker, make the point: "By having the children with us constantly, we are able to further our plan of teaching them American manners and customs. The reaction, at times has been irritating to the child, for it is really difficult to bridge from peasantry to City life. Parents are being criticized as to their mode of cooking and eating, until one desperate mother sent word to me to please tell her where to buy an American cookbook."[19]

Even if immigrant women disagreed with some of the cultural prescriptions of Anglo American reformers and felt coerced by them, they often accessed and benefited from the settlements' services in their communities. For example, in the city of El Paso, with its large Mexican population, Mexican women received health care for their families, including prenatal visits, free immunizations, well-baby checks, and by 1930 a maternity facility. In New York, immigrant communities benefited from projects like one in which nurses provided medicine to midwives to confront a now preventable disease that could lead to blindness in newborns.[20]

As immigrant mothers sought to preserve their culture and their authority in families, they had to figure out how to tolerate, or adapt to their own purposes, the imposition of new values into their family lives. The El Paso, Texas, Houchen Settlement, for example, offered citizenship classes, which might have obvious appeal to new immigrants, and Protestant Bible classes, which could lure children away from their own religion. One woman recalled of her relationship with the settlement house, "My Mom had an open mind, so I participated in a lot of clubs. But I didn't become a Protestant."[21] Some Anglo American antipoverty crusaders continued to offer the Bible, but just as often they offered the latest infant feeding advice or suggestions on disciplining children that promoted the "American" way of parenting.

White Anglo women, even the most progressive, resisted as "foreign" some basic tenets of child-rearing among immigrant families. These differences became starker with the professionalization of social work and the intrusive practices of public policy administrators intervening in the name of good mothering and scientific charity. The development of mothers' pensions programs illustrates this pattern.

Welfare Policy and Scientific Motherhood: Uplift and Regulation

In 1909, at the urging of women reformers, President Theodore Roosevelt held the first White House Conference on the Care of Dependent Children. Those in attendance found some principles upon which they could agree: "Home life is the highest and finest product of civilization," their collective statement asserted. "It is the great molding force of mind and character." Because of this, "children should not be deprived of it except for urgent and compelling reasons. Children of parents of worthy character, suffering from temporary misfortune and children of reasonably efficient and deserving mothers who are without the support of the normal breadwinner, should, as a rule, be kept with their parents, such aid being given as may be necessary to maintain suitable homes for the rearing of children."[22] The earnest Progressive advocates for children who gathered at the conference expressed their preference for private charity, stopping short (for the time being) of a broad push for public aid. Nevertheless, they were singing a new tune compared to nineteenth-century would-be poverty problem solvers: Impoverished mothers should be kept with their children, they claimed. At least, "worthy," "deserving," and "reasonably efficient" mothers deprived of the "normal" (male) breadwinner should be kept with their children.

These reformers wanted to end the nineteenth-century practice of "placing out" children into institutions like almshouses and orphanages. Building on nineteenth-century concepts of childhood innocence, a previous generation of reformers had separated poor children into orphanages, a practice viewed as an improvement over simply lumping parents and children into all-purpose "poorhouses." With the hardships caused by the expanding Industrial Revolution, however, the population of half-orphans and children of destitute single mothers had grown rapidly in the last quarter of the nineteenth century. Desperate parents themselves, especially single mothers, also sometimes placed their children in orphanages while hoping to retrieve the children when mothers could provide for them. Typically, late nineteenth-century orphanages contained more children with at least one living parent than children who were actually orphaned. At the same time, state and local governments took a greater role in seizing custody of the children on the basis of parental behaviors, such as "neglect, crime, drunkenness or other vice." Although such removal was sometimes in the best interest of children, in many cases it happened with scant provocation, especially for female-headed and immigrant households.[23]

Maternalist reformers of the Progressive era hoped that such desperate situations, in which good mothers simply ran out of money, could be averted by endowing and educating the nation's mothers. This Progressive view challenged the old (and recurring) notion that parents were generally to blame for their own poverty. Some Progressive-era Americans still argued that the bad personal habits of the poor caused their own poverty; perhaps the children of the poor were salvageable, but only if they were removed from their parents' homes. Others blamed poverty on hereditary "defects." But most maternalist reformers, active in developing welfare policy, tended toward a more environmental view; most believed in some combination of maternal education and reform of structural situations, such as housing, wages, health care access, and charitable support.

For the most social justice-oriented crusaders of this era, state support of mothers meant that women would have their work as mothers dignified and their rights to their children protected. Mothers would receive "pensions" from the state, just as veterans did, in the event that they were left without male support. Embracing the modernizing possibilities of good government, an increasingly influential group of reformers saw public aid as superior to private help because it could be rationalized and regulated.[24]

Through legal reforms and experiments in collective housework and sometimes child-rearing arrangements, the more feminist-minded maternalists sought ways to free mothers from economic dependence on men. Male breadwinners might abandon a family, suffer frequent unemployment, be abusive, or just die prematurely, but these situations all produced the same result: an impoverished widowed mother. These risks made the male breadwinner model increasingly problematic for those who were trying to keep children under maternal care. Feminist Crystal Eastman advocated rewriting laws on marriage, divorce, and illegitimacy to provide women more freedom and less dependence. Through a better endowed motherhood, childrearing could be "recognized by the world as work," she said, "requiring a definite economic reward and not merely entitling the performer to be dependent on some man." Similarly, Katharine Anthony saw political equality for women and economic support of mothers as working "together like the right eye and the left eye in a single act of vision."[25]

Such soaring visions did not come to pass in Eastman's lifetime (nor in ours). But, in the form of mothers' pensions, reformers did create an opening wedge to relieve mothers of the utter vulnerability they faced in a world in which men's wages usually determined their survival. Written into state laws, mothers' pensions empowered local governments to make payments to impoverished mothers to support their children in their homes. Beginning in Illinois, these laws proliferated throughout the country and affected thirty-nine states, mostly in the North and West, within just eight years of the first model law. Such laws initially enjoyed great public support.[26] A broad coalition of maternalist reformers advocated for and helped design the mothers' pensions, which established the model for the long-standing federal public aid program for women, Aid to Dependent Children (ADC). ADC, part of the Social Security Act of 1935 (later renamed Aid to Families with Dependent Children, or AFDC), lasted from 1935 to 1996.

In reality, mothers' pensions were stingy, discriminatory, and reached only a fraction of the population of single mothers. States were generally unwilling to match the idealistic rhetoric with actual public assistance funds, and, to the extent that they did, many, many strings were attached. Historian Gwendolyn Mink found that in the 1920s the average mothers' assistance grant in thirty-nine of forty-two states was at least 20 percent below the cost of living; in twenty of the states, the annual pension was just over half the estimated cost of living. Children's Bureau research from the 1920s estimated that only about 37 percent of needy children actually received aid. Given the failure of mothers' pensions to make a significant dent in familial poverty, Progressive reformers failed spectacularly in their goals, at least in the short term. The number of children residing in institutions rather than single-mother households actually tripled during the Progressive era.[27]

For most mothers of color, mothers' pensions were simply unavailable. States and localities discriminated freely on the basis of race and ethnicity. Los Angeles officials, for example, citing a "feudal background" that would likely lead Mexican immigrants to "abuse the principle of regular grant money from the state," categorically refused to provide pensions to Mexican widows. Many southern states did not even create mothers' pension programs, but those that did generally refused them outright to African American families, at a time when about 90 percent of African American women lived in the South. Northern states also rationalized racial discrimination. In Illinois, for example, lawmakers argued that African American women were potentially self-supporting and therefore did not need public aid.[28]

Mothers' pensions were also limited because they were "morals tested" as well as "means tested," to use the language of welfare historians. A soldier's pension was based on the fact of his service. And the mostly male and white beneficiaries of unemployment and workmen's compensation programs had only to prove they worked for wages in recognized occupations throughout most of the year. But to receive state funds, mothers' work was subjected to an energetic and multifaceted army of judging gatekeepers of the public coffers. Although laws varied, states typically denied pensions to all but "worthy widows." Divorced or "deserted" women were usually ineligible, as were the many who did not keep "suitable homes." A mother's character was always under scrutiny. States empowered social workers to investigate questions of church attendance, use of the English language, mothers' wage-earning outside the home (which was considered harmful to children), and information that might suggest a mother's sexual impropriety. Full-time work that took mothers out of the home made mothers ineligible in many states, while seasonal labor or piecework in women's homes—often the most exploitative, poorly paid work—was acceptable because of the notion that such mothers stayed at home with their children.[29]

To survive, mothers who partook of these small bits of public assistance still had to bring in cash and have their children work. One 1923 study of nine different locales found 52 percent of mothers receiving aid were actually working for wages as well. While the maternalist reformers who advocated for these programs did not have this in mind, local administrators actually expected such patterns. For example, an Illinois court found that a "Mrs. C." needed thirty-four dollars a month to live, but the state, determining to pay her only twenty dollars a month, noted that she could earn the difference through cleaning work. Despite the antipathy of many maternalist reformers to the use of child labor, when mothers' aid stipends were administered by states, women were also often rejected if their children could earn money.[30]

Still, mothers' pensions were rationalized and widely supported because they advanced this era's notions of moral motherhood combined with science-based maternal uplift. Administrators poured significant energy into the education and supervision of needy mothers and, for many, the Americanization of immigrants. "Go after the women," claimed those who sought to reshape Mexican American families. Anglo American reformers urged the mothers to avoid tortillas and beans in favor of "American" foods such as bread and lettuce and to change the way they served their children food. "A folded tortilla with no filling" could lead children to crime by encouraging them to "take the food from the lunch boxes of more fortunate children."[31] In many states, Americanization programs were bolstered by mothers' pensions. To meet eligibility guidelines for state aid, mothers often needed to take classes in English as well as modern child care.[32]

The modernization efforts directed at Native American families were significantly harsher. They involved removal, often coerced, of children into off-reservation boarding schools with the deliberate goal of breaking intergenerational bonds between parents and children. In 1879, reformers created the first off-reservation Native American boarding school, run by a man with the destructive educational philosophies: "Kill the Indian and save the man"; "immerse him in civilization and keep him there until well soaked." Approximately 12,000 children from 77 tribes attended the most famous boarding school, Carlisle, in Pennsylvania, usually at a huge distance from their parents and tribes. Thousands of other Native Americans attended similar schools across the country, especially between the 1890s and the 1930s. Even with reform during the New Deal, which moved federal policy away from the project of assimilation, the Great Depression contributed to the use of the schools by parents desperate to give their children an education and room and board. By the early 1930s, 15 percent of all Indian children in school were in off-reservation boarding schools.[33] The law allowed Bureau of Indian Affairs agents (non-Indians almost exclusively) to remove children as young as age five from families. BIA agents could and did withhold government assistance from families if they refused to surrender their children.

Because of the explicit goal of breaking up Native American families and assimilating Indian children, boarding school students were not allowed to speak their native languages and were often pressured to convert to Christianity. Most of these children were deliberately prevented from having contact with their families; one school forbade visits to parents for a full five years. Letters to parents were read aloud to the class, and letters from home passed through teachers. In 1900, Native American activist Zitkala-Sa, who opposed the schools, wrote in the *Atlantic Monthly*, "On account of my mother's simple view of life, and my lack of any, I gave her up, also. . . . Like a slender tree, I had been uprooted from my mother, nature, and God. I was shorn of my branches, which had waved in sympathy and love for home and friends."[34] The deliberate denigration of all that was Indian caused enormous trauma for many generations.

Though male government officials instituted assimilation policies, white women were likewise instrumental to assimilation efforts. Their role was to persuade Native families, which they saw as backward, to relinquish their children to become educated and "civilized." In the minds of most Progressive reformers, the goal of family unity simply did not apply to Native American families. Estelle Reed, super-intendent of Indian education from 1898 to 1910, argued publicly that her role with Indian women was to "gain their confidence and liking and make them see how much better it is to trust their children to the training of civilization."[35] As historian Margaret Jacobs has shown, white women developed relationships with families, which furthered the aims of a government determined to undertake a new phase of colonizing Native Americans by destroying their culture now that most of their land had been conquered.

Operating mostly in the American West, these reformers appealed to Native American mothers in ways similar to reformers of immigrants in other parts of the country; the reformers were persuaded that "among the wildest, most degraded peoples, it is still the mother who has the say concerning the children." White maternalist views of Native homes were similar to their views of immigrant tene-ments. One missionary said she found two very young babies without "any article of clothing. One baby was wrapped in a piece of cheese-cloth and crying with colic; and the baby two days old was wrapped in a piece of old calico and lying on the ground on a piece of an old quilt. . . . The women do not seem to make any provi-sion for their little ones."[36] Many such reformers were moved by a desire to alleviate chronic American Indian poverty through assimilation, although the U.S. military had dispossessed Native American people of most of their land and created the very conditions of this poverty. Unlike immigrant mothers or impoverished moth-ers generally, Native American mothers were not seen as up to the task of accom-plishing modernization themselves.

For their part, American Indian communities often resisted the removal of their children, especially when they could see other options, such as day school educa-tion or preservation of Native forms of education and socialization of children. Some parents hid their children when government agents came to take them away. Though the project of assimilation itself did persuade some Native Americans that these programs had value, by the 1920s some Native American activists used their connections to the schools' operations to reassert the value of Native childrear-ing traditions. Chippewa tribe member Marie Baldwin, for example, argued pub-licly that in many tribes the Indian woman "was industrious, frugal, loving and affectionate and performed her duties willingly and cheerfully" and that within her culture "she was treated with the respect, the esteem, gentleness and loving consid-eration she so richly merited and appreciated."[37]

Throughout the era of the boarding schools, Native American parents wrote to officials about the conditions of the schools, which a 1920s government study even-tually found "grossly inadequate." This study exposed "dietary deficiencies leading to malnutrition, overcrowded and unsafe dormitories, substandard health care, poor sanitation, high incidences of tuberculosis and trachoma, poorly qualified teachers, an overly uniform curriculum . . . routinization, and cruel discipline and punish-ment." Acknowledgment of these conditions came too late for the Springer family, Omaha Indians who in the 1880s lost their daughter to illness in a distant board-ing school in the East. Mrs. Springer, in a letter to Carlisle school founder Captain

Richard H. Pratt, expressed anger about not being notified of their daughter's illness. She and her husband wanted their other two daughters returned to them:

> We are anxious to have our children educated, but do not see the necessity of sending them so far away to be educated, when we have good schools at home, where we can see them when we wish, and attend to them when sick. . . . I had no idea of sending my children there, but Miss Fletcher got round Elsie and persuaded her to go and then Alice wanted to go with her . . . and now my husband is grieving all the time. . . . Please do not deny our request, if you have any regard to a Father's and Mother's feelings.[38]

Pratt denied the request. As for Miss Fletcher, a white government recruiter for Carlisle and Hampton boarding schools, she could barely contain her indignation toward the parents about "the words you wrote about me and my efforts on behalf of the Omahas. I am sure you did not realize in your grief what you were saying or you would not have written so unjustly."[39] Although a few white women, often citing the importance of the maternal-child tie, did protest the removal of American Indian children, their opposition went largely unheeded, even in a culture that had long sanctified maternal-child bonds.

Of all American populations, only Native Americans endured these particular forms of state-sponsored, highly orchestrated break-ups of parent-child bonds. Still, for non-Native populations, intervention in family life was a prominent theme. This was especially true as social work became more professionalized in the 1920s and used the new technique of casework to reform families in the process of administering charity. Environmental causes of poverty, so important to the Progressive-era generation, now tended to be overlooked or deemphasized. In these ways, private charities and public administration of mothers' pensions tended to share similar methods. The complicated case of an African American working mother named Rosa makes the point.

In 1905, approaching the Minneapolis Family Welfare Society (MFWS), Rosa looked not for charity, but for assistance finding work. Her subsequent relationship with MFWS would extend over twenty-three years. Like other women living on the edge of poverty, Rosa used the institutional resources in her community when times got hard. Over the years, MFWS supplied her and her family with fuel, food, clothing, a liaison with the Society of the Blind to secure a small monthly disability stipend for Rosa's husband, assistance with an eye operation, and, later, funeral expenses when Rosa's husband died. Throughout this relationship, Rosa was subjected to harsh judgments of her family and relentless badgering by her caseworker about the "problem" of Rosa's working outside the home. Rosa's family was described by an MFWS "fact sheet" in this way: "Problems— William—husband—cataracts, old age, shiftlessness, laziness, uneven employment, and blindness; Rosa—wife—dirty, poor housekeeping, works too much, and neglect of family: Louise—eldest daughter—heart trouble; Edward—eldest son— delinquency; Marion—youngest daughter—not bright." Continuously, the caseworker complained, "It seemed impossible to make any headway with the family as they seem quite contented to live in their dirt and filth. The man did not seem responsible mentally to talk intelligently and the woman seemed quite willing to work and support the family."[40]

The juxtaposition of the husband's presumed incapacity and the wife's wage work speak volumes to the discomfort of this caseworker with nontraditional gender roles, despite the economic logic of these roles for this family. Rosa's blind husband had been born into slavery and suffered other physical disabilities related to his advanced age. Rosa worked six days a week and, according to the caseworker, "right after work would rush home, get the evening meals, make a fresh fire, put the children to bed, and rush to a dressmaking establishment where she worked every night." The caseworker urged Rosa to admit that her son's "delinquency" was caused by her wage-earning and admonished Rosa both to rest more and to improve her housekeeping. In one report, the caseworker indignantly noted that Rosa "did not intend to do more" with her housework: "She would do it once a week and that was all. Visitor then went on to explain to her that her daughter Marion should not have been sent to school with two sweaters on. She should have had a coat. Rosa said she would send her in whatever she wanted. She would not tell Visitor any of her affairs and became quite indignant and left the office."[41]

The antipathy continued when the caseworker urged Rosa to put her husband in institutional care. Although the caseworker threatened to discontinue Rosa's MFWS funds for noncompliance, she did not follow through on the threat. The record does not show that Rosa was ever threatened with removal of her children from her care. Had there been any hint of sexual impropriety or drinking, Rosa might have been vulnerable to this threat from local organizations like the Society for the Prevention of Cruelty to Children.[42] But Rosa shared with many working-class women an experience of charity agencies or government programs that combined access to resources with onerous intrusions into family life.

When looking back at this time period, it is difficult to fathom how much energy Americans were willing to put into the project of reforming mothers in order to rationalize providing them such small amounts of economic assistance. Yet many believed they were preserving children's health and the health of the community, preventing poverty, bringing the nation together by creating a melting pot, and educating mothers. Sometimes these efforts came together to confront problems like the spread of infectious diseases. The case of the Germani family shows the convergence of public health fears and immigrant mothers' extreme vulnerability to the judgments of public and private helping agencies at this time.

The Germanis' daughter, Maria, had tuberculosis. Though the Germanis agreed to medical testing, they refused the Charity Organization Society's recommendation to hospitalize their daughter. Maria's parents planned to remove her from the city by sending her to New Jersey to be cared for by relatives. But the charity appealed to the Society for the Prevention of Cruelty to Children (SPCC) for assistance in forcibly removing Maria to a hospital. The SPCC refused, and Maria apparently received good care with her relatives. During one of her visits home, a truant officer visited the home and found Maria there. Maria was then hospitalized via court order. Mrs. Germani appealed to the judge, but "no one seemed to pay any heed" to her. "When they got into the automobile, she thought they were going to take Maria to the hospital for an examination, but when they arrived there she was told that the child would have to remain." Maria died within a few months of her admission into the overcrowded Metropolitan Hospital. As historian Emily Abel astutely observed, charity workers, reflecting broad cultural beliefs, regularly expressed their belief that mothers were primarily responsible for children's health. The Germani case "reveals the chasm between the responsibility attributed to the mother and her ultimate powerlessness."[43]

These struggles illustrate a complicated truth: mothers' need of any form of public assistance often made them willing to endure such intrusions and judgments, and many were unaware of the risks they took in accepting assistance. The subjection of impoverished mothers to moral judgments and intense family regulation as a condition of assistance became further enshrined into social policy in the 1930s. The Aid to Dependent Children (ADC) provisions of the Social Security Act of 1935 were modeled on state mothers' pensions programs. Like those programs, ADC provided some overdue recognition of maternal economic vulnerability while imposing strict moral and mother-care regulations on mothers.

Unlike the more generously funded unemployment and "old-age" insurance programs that were also part of the Social Security Act, the mother-focused ADC was both poorly funded and left to discriminatory state guidelines. Through compromise with powerful racist southern Democrats, the vast majority of African American women were ineligible for the benefits of the Social Security Act. The act's authors included exemptions for workers in domestic and agricultural work, where most African American women worked. A decade after the passage of the Social Security Act and after several amendments expanding entitlements, two-thirds of African American women were still excluded from benefits. In the 1930s many western states "repatriated" Mexican Americans to remove them from the labor market and the relief rolls, and several western states tried to prevent American Indians from any benefits of the Social Security Act.[44] Equally important, ADC was associated not with the dignity of work through which recipients purportedly earned their benefits, like unemployment and old-age pensions. Instead, ADC was linked with the indignities of continual supervision of women's private lives on which their paltry allowances depended.

The work of Progressive-era welfare activists stands as an important reminder of the homogenizing tendencies of those who wanted to modernize family life. Modernizers sought a uniform motherhood, newly scientific but anachronistically and prejudicially conceived in middle-class standards of domesticity. Historian Gwendolyn Mink referred to the whole project as "uplift through conformity."[45] This was an unsustainable agenda. Cultural diversity, the necessary survival strategies of financially strapped mothers, and the evolution of a capitalist labor market that pushed mothers into labor force participation changed the conditions of women's lives. Cultural attitudes and social policy were much slower to change.

The social policies directed at mothers reveal some important limits of modernization programs and policies. They represented a kind of insurance against female vulnerability, designed to keep the mother-care tradition intact, preserve moral motherhood ideals, and promote scientific motherhood. As a result, maternalist assumptions in welfare policy complemented the limited provision of child-care options for women through an emphasis on limiting women's labor force participation. The ensuing policy structure did not alleviate the needs of many women to work but did make it difficult for mothers to patch together a life of subsistence for their families. Historian Linda Gordon imagined what might have been: "A more generous ADC program would have kept more mothers at home but more likely it would have improved the overall labor-market position of women: fewer would have been forced to take the worst kinds of work, casual labor and home work. . . . A nonmaternalist welfare policy might have encouraged some of the supports that make it easier for mothers to earn, notably child care."[46]

Still, even the very modest provisioning of single mothers within the nation's signature federal welfare legislation was a consequential achievement. For more than sixty years, ADC and later AFDC provided a small life raft for impoverished women. Gradually, these programs allowed women to keep their families together at rates much higher than those among early participants. Through amendments to the Social Security Act, growing numbers of women became eligible for benefits, including mothers who found themselves rearing children without men for reasons other than widowhood. Also, widows gained even more generous rights through survivors' benefits. For some women, these programs offered an escape route from abusive relationships, and the aid generated a limited but important sense of entitlement to assistance from the government for doing the work of rearing children.

EXPERIMENTS IN CHILD CARE

The idea of continuous mother care for children also slowed the development of child-care programs to assist mothers who had to work outside the home. Founded by maternalist reformers, the nation's first "day nurseries," as they were called, sought to provide an alternative for poor wage-earning mothers, many of whom had to place their children in almshouses, board them with relatives, or house them in orphanages. The nurseries had the important advantage of allowing low-wage-earning mothers, usually without male breadwinner support, to live with their children. But even the designers of these institutions believed strongly in continuous maternal care of children whenever possible, and so they undermined their own cause. Josephine Dodge, who for thirty years served as president of the National Federation of Day Nurseries, repeatedly insisted that such institutions existed only for family crisis situations and that the best care of children occurred in the home, by mothers. Her views on gender roles were so conservative that she actually founded the National Association Opposed to Woman Suffrage in 1911.[47]

Much like mothers' pensions, the day nursery programs were inadequate to the needs of the growing numbers of working mothers. In order to rationalize the always questionable project of enabling mothers to go out to work, day nursery advocates justified their work as improving the bad habits of poor mothers, rather than facilitating their wage earning. One day nursery superintendent for the Women's Christian Temperance Union explained: "It is indeed a grand work to rescue from sin those whose lives have been spent in wickedness; but to take the *sinless* little ones of these parents and train them for God, is labor which will yield a much more abundant harvest." Day nursery leaders argued that they were eradicating the need for charity by improving the poor, one family at a time, and leaders like Dodge promoted only a private charity approach to day nurseries. These strategies ultimately helped forestall a widespread demand for child care as a public right.[48]

Even progressive and nationally known advocates of government programs to improve living and working conditions did not believe mothers should be encouraged to do paid labor. Jane Addams described the day nursery as a "double-edged implement" because it encouraged poor mothers to try the impossible task of being "both wife and mother and supporter of the family." The Children's Bureau, also discouraging such endeavors, cited the higher risk of infant mortality for working mothers.[49] And advocates for child care lost further ground as public support grew for mothers' pensions because the pension programs encouraged mothers to stay home with their children. Day nursery leaders, on the defensive, further downplayed their role in enabling mothers to go to work.

The conditions at the day care centers reflected their ancillary status in the arena of social supports for families and their agenda in promoting middle-class prescriptions of motherhood. Across the spectrum, subtly or not so subtly, day nurseries demeaned the women and children who needed to use them. Well into the twentieth century, day nurseries had high child-adult ratios and usually inadequate play areas; meals were often served in silence at long tables, similar to practices in orphanages. Some children were excluded on the basis of religion, race, or ethnicity, and children born out of wedlock were often excluded as well. Those who were admitted were subjected to daily medical inspections and baths, with the none-too-subtle suggestion that their mothers did not keep them clean.[50]

Mothers paid a price for charity-funded child care: applicants had their homes inspected and their lives regulated. For example, Russian-Jewish immigrant Leah Nadel, who suffered through her husband's alcoholism and then his death, was a factory worker. She tolerated home visits as a condition of her child-care arrangements. When a social worker told Mrs. Nadel that her children should not sleep with her in the same room, the social worker reported that Mrs. Nadel "did not understand our point of view and said that she believed that having the children in the same room would strengthen their moral standards. She promised, however, to make other adjustments."[51] Poor women's child-rearing, their type of employment, their efforts at enrolling older children in school, and generally their fitness as mothers were all judged and considered as conditions of use of these poorly equipped institutions.

Of course, beyond the institutional rhetoric, working mothers developed real human relationships with the child-care providers of that day, relationships that probably mediated the harsh social control ideas suggested here. Women sometimes expressed enormous gratitude to day nursery personnel, as when young mother Goldie Rokofsky wrote to a day nursery staff member Marion Kohn, "I will never forget what you try so good for me." Rokofsky later wrote to Kohn with a request for advice on child care. "You are the only person in the world that could give me good advise [sic]."Others wrote that their encounters with the Neighborhood Centre day nursery had given them sympathy and courage.[52]

At the same time, the rhetoric reminds us that day nurseries were institutions designed for the poor, not generally sought by more affluent or even economically secure parents. From its origins, then, child care was associated in the public mind "with dire poverty and family crisis," as historian Elizabeth Rose has observed. Indeed, the president of one day nursery made clear that mothers could only use these facilities in dire circumstances: "If the support of the family no longer falls to the mother, those children must withdraw ... ; the Nursery must never deteriorate into a mere receiving station for children, to free mothers from their duties."[53]

Along with orphanages, almshouses, and arrangements with neighbors and kin, day nurseries provided one more tool for working mothers, but one that most did not rely upon long term. A 1927 newspaper found that "65 percent of Philadelphia's wage-earning mothers left their children with relatives, 13.5 percent with neighbors, and 15 percent without any supervision." Immigrant women especially turned to family members and neighbors if they needed to leave their children for wage work: a 1930 study found that 90 percent of immigrant women relied on relatives, older siblings, and neighbors for child care.[54]

The need for child care increased over the course of the twentieth century. By the 1920s, compulsory schooling laws lessened the availability of older siblings to do child care. Declining immigration meant that working-class women had fewer opportunities to bring cash into their homes by caring for boarders, and thus more women had to leave their homes to go to work. Employers were becoming less tolerant of situations like those in the southwest canneries, where mothers encouraged their children to play near them while they worked. Later in the twentieth century, the population of at-home grandmothers and other relatives would decline, while maternal employment steadily increased.[55]

When the institutions themselves eventually began to become more educational and less regulatory and punitive, mothers and reformers would leverage the benefits of day care to argue for expansion and even public support, but they never achieved a great deal of success. The ambivalent origins of the whole project continued to hinder the development of publicly endowed child care right up to the present. Even as the twentieth century closed, other industrialized societies were far ahead of the United States in moving toward universally available child care.[56] The modern industrial economy drew women into the "land of dollars," but the reformers who influenced policy clung to older ideals. Modern motherhood could not mean a rational and efficient use of a woman's labor in support of her family because such a pattern violated nineteenth-century ideals of ever-available mother care.

Protective Labor Legislation and the "Burdens of Motherhood"

Laws limiting women's wage-earning work hours in the name of motherhood, what historians have broadly labeled "protective labor legislation," provided reformers another avenue to protect moral motherhood ideals, even as women's labor force participation continued to increase. So-called protective labor legislation gained national legitimacy from a significant Supreme Court case, *Muller v. Oregon*, in 1908. Speaking for the majority on this decision, which concerned limitations on women's hours in the workplace, Justice David Brewer observed: "That woman's physical structure and her performance of maternal functions place her at a disadvantage in the struggle for subsistence is obvious. This is especially true when the burdens of motherhood are upon her."[57] In *Muller*, Brewer and his colleagues upheld an Oregon law that limited women's wage work to ten-hour days. The case was path breaking. Just a few years earlier the court had rejected a similar case concerning a maximum-hour law for male bakers in New York. Women workers, it now claimed, were categorically different from men because of their motherhood, either actual or potential. Therefore, for women, protective labor legislation was constitutionally acceptable.

This ruling opened an important wedge for government regulation of any kind of labor, challenging the "freedom of contract" notions that had prevented the Court from intervening in the right of employers to set any terms they chose. It also cast women as a special class of workers and promoted state action well beyond Oregon. The case carried forward state laws, accumulated over decades, which kept women out of certain occupations on the basis of dangers to women's health and morals. Previous laws had restricted women's work serving alcoholic beverages or delivering messages, all for fear of their potential association with unsavory men. Maximum-hour laws were based on similar protective and gender-conforming notions, with special emphasis on protecting mothers. With the Supreme Court's green light, the laws gained ground in the majority of states. Within fifteen years, all but five states had maximum-hour legislation for women, often accompanied by restrictions on heavy lifting and night work for women and other practices justified in the name of motherhood.[58]

Male unionists generally supported such legislation, in part because it restricted women's competition for men's jobs. They frequently cast the working-class struggle as a fight for the "family wage" for the male breadwinner, which would allow him to keep his wife out of the workforce and support his family. As one American Federation of Labor columnist put it, "Women may be adults and why should we class them as children. Because it is to the interest of all of us that female labor should be limited so as not to injure the motherhood and family life of a nation."[59] Based on the records of trade unionist men on this issue, the commitment to the domestic roles of women was widespread. In light of the realities of the long and onerous days of wage-earning women, many men and women believed family life could be better maintained without dragging women, already burdened with enormous labor in the home, into the paid labor force.

The *Muller* ruling was also supported directly by female reformers such as Florence Kelley, who threw the weight of the National Consumers' League (NCL) behind the sociological research that informed the case. Like a growing number of advocates for women laborers, Kelley believed the state should protect women from rapacious employers who would ignore women's "double duty" at home, but the NCL researchers fell right into arguments about women's biological inferiority to make their case, claiming that "women are fundamentally weaker than men in all that makes for endurance: in muscular strength, in nervous energy, in the powers of persistent attention and application." The brief even cited physicians who lamented "the periodic semi-pathological state of health of women" and their generally more fragile constitutions.[60] Investigators of women's working conditions emphasized the night shift's moral danger to women and their consequential exhaustion during the day, both of which had an impact on the family.

What *Muller* and the legislation it upheld did for women was certainly more complex than protection. This legislation prevented women from participating in not only labor that required long hours, heavy lifting, or night work but also significant categories of skilled labor. Often jobs with these requirements paid better or, in the example of night work, allowed women to stagger wage-earning and child-care duties. Some women, realizing that the consequences could mean losing their jobs or finding themselves ineligible for particular work, protested the laws. A forty-seven-year-old widow, Mrs. Ella Sherwin, lamented, "We are forced to compete with the worker who is not restricted as we are."[61]

There is no doubt that some women were also relieved by the passage of such laws. Married women who did not need to serve as the sole or primary breadwinners in their families could now keep jobs that might otherwise have been impossible to hold alongside their other responsibilities. As one woman said, "I think ten hours is too much for a woman. I have four children and have to work hard at home. Makes me awful tired. I would like nine hours. I get up at 5:30 when I wash. I have to stay up till one or two o'clock." Women's testimony at the time showed that those who worked ten hours or less, day or night, were better able to manage their double duties.[62] Single women, including widows like Mrs. Sherwin, were more likely to suffer for these legal work restrictions.

In the long run, protective labor legislation helped broaden government labor regulations, preventing some of the most egregious exploitation of any workers. But there was another long-term outcome. By making women a special class of employee, regardless of whether they were actually mothers, protective labor legislation contributed to women's secondary and segregated roles in the workforce, just as Mrs. Sherwin suggested. The laws reinforced the cultural idea that women were essentially and always mothers and were the weaker sex as a result. Justice Brewer's words about women's disadvantage when suffering under the burdens of motherhood make this point, but so do the words that follow in his opinion. Even for women who were not, at any given moment, weighed down by such "burdens," Brewer pointed out, "by abundant testimony of the medical fraternity, continuance for a long time on her feet at work, repeating this from day to day, tends to injurious effects upon the body." The same might well be said of men, such as the New York bakers who might have enjoyed a ten-hour work day instead of a twelve-hour one. But gender distinctions were critical in allowing the court to interfere with employers' traditional rights. Justice Brewer claimed that because "healthy mothers are essential to vigorous offspring . . . the physical well-being of woman becomes an object of public interest and care in order to preserve the strength and vigor of the race." For this reason, "differentiated by these matters from the other sex, she is properly placed in a class by herself, and legislation designed for her protection may be sustained, even when like legislation is not necessary for men and could not be sustained."[63]

For more than half a century after the *Muller* decision, such restrictive laws remained in place, dislodged only by the provisions of the Civil Rights Act in 1964. Employers who could justify paying less money to a special, dependent class of worker benefited from this legislation. As unionized men increasingly empowered themselves to negotiate reduced hours through organizing, they simultaneously enjoyed preferential access to highly skilled and better-paid jobs, many of which were barred to women. Meanwhile, protective labor legislation also slowed feminist gains in both the workplace and the larger political arena, in part because the issue divided feminist activists for many decades. National Woman's Party activists pointed to the inequality of women in the workforce, and more labor-oriented feminists claimed that they were safeguarding women's lives within the real-world constraints of overwork and motherhood responsibilities by supporting protective laws. Mary Anderson, head of the Women's Bureau, remarked, "I consider myself a good feminist, but I believe I am a practical one."[64]

Maternalism, then, limited the possibilities for improving women's conditions in the workplace. In fairness, so too did the hostility of many powerful business interests to workers having any legal protections—whether hours limitations, minimum wages, or safety conditions. Women reformers advocating for these laws were relatively empowered spokespersons for working women, who were so often denied access to both unions and, until 1920, the vote. Through the Women's Trade Union League, some women even organized together across class lines to develop an agenda to empower women workers. The League supported working-class women in their rights to unionize and to gain the vote. Their work resulted in genuine improvements in women's workplaces, including health and safety advancements. They were bounded by the ideology of moral motherhood, which, as in other areas of welfare policy, framed the conditions in which women could be both breadwinners and nurturers for their children. Nevertheless, their commendable championship of working-class women represented an important public voice for the concerns of working-class mothers. Taken together, these maternalist reforms, from mothers' pensions to protective labor legislation, created a foundation upon which antipoverty, labor, and women's rights activists could build. The movement for women's suffrage was energized by such activism on working mothers' issues, and the achievement of suffrage in 1920 provided the powerful tool of the franchise, through which women might address these issues on a broader scale.

THE ROAD NOT TAKEN: MATERNALIST VISIONS
OF AFRICAN AMERICAN REFORMERS

All areas of social policy for mothers that became law or well-funded charity stemmed from the privileged position of white policy makers. Class-privileged white women, like Florence Kelley, Julia Lathrop, and Jane Addams, could get their voices heard at the city, state, and national levels. Officials read their policy briefs, while the reformers sometimes ran agencies and earned national recognition for their approaches to maternal and child health and related concerns. In a racist society, however, such power was largely denied to African American women and other women of color. Even the achievement of the vote for women in 1920 had limited impact for them, especially in the South, where Jim Crow disfranchised African Americans, and the Southwest, where Mexican Americans' vote was limited. Even northern women of color, who were solidly in the middle class financially, had far less direct access to the white men who wielded significant political and economic power than did their white counterparts.

This complicated landscape did not stop African American women from trying to put a floor under struggling mothers of what they called "the race." African American women organized on a national scale as early as 1896 in the National Association of Colored Women (NACW), nearly a decade before the formation of the National Association for the Advancement of Colored People (NAACP). Informed by the motto "lifting as we climb," this largely middle- or aspiring-to-middle-class group of African American women took up a very broad agenda of "welfare" work. Like the work of white reformers, their efforts were often directed at the welfare of mothers and children. They included creation of settlement programs, day nurseries, and community projects such as clean milk campaigns as well as "talks on social purity and the proper method of rearing children."[65]

Like white women, African American reformers were inspired by the lofty ideals of maternalism: "A stream cannot rise higher than its source," noted Anna Julia Cooper. "The atmosphere of homes is no rarer and purer and sweeter than are the mothers in those homes. A race is but a total of families, the nation is the aggregate of its homes." And the keepers of the homes were women. African American women were part of "a mothering influence" that was "leavening the nation." As one of Cooper's contemporaries observed, the "civilized world has been like a child brought up by its father. It has needed the great mother-heart to teach it to be pitiful, to love mercy, to succor the weak, and care for the lowly." Because they were confronting a society that they often found hostile to themselves and their families, African American women believed the stakes of their mothering were high. Cooper declared, "Woman, Mother,—your responsibility is one that might make angels tremble and fear to take hold!"[66] Such powerful motherhood, indeed a privilege, required preparation and support.

The mostly middle class and disproportionately well-educated reformers of the NACW understood the need for programs that did not stigmatize, programs that were modeled on universal access rather than moral code. Though not without their own middle-class biases, NACW activists were aware that, as Mary Church Terrell put it, even black women with privilege "cannot escape altogether the consequences of the acts of their most depraved sisters." Therefore, "both policy and self-preservation demand that they go down among the lowly . . . to whom they are bound by ties of race and sex, and put forth every possible effort to reclaim them."[67] As a result, the programs they designed, though often privately funded through their hard-won fund-raising efforts in the community, tended to be far less "morals tested" than those designed by white women. African American clubwomen concentrated a great deal on broadly accessible education and health initiatives. They also extended the notion of parental care into the community by founding schools in the South as an alternative to segregated education.

In this era of high rates of infant mortality and morbidity, health care as a piece of social welfare was a significant focus of African American clubwomen. By one count, African Americans created, often with female fund-raising leadership, about two hundred hospitals and nurse training schools between 1890 and 1930. Women's clubs also initiated health surveys, established clinics with free treatments, and launched immunization programs in poor rural and urban areas. Their fundraising success for these initiatives can likely be attributed to the urgency of the situation and to arguments like that made by *Half-Century Magazine*: "better babies are a sign of progress. The future of the race . . . in numerical strength and its physical fitness depends wholly on its babies. A crop of puny, under-nourished infants could hardly be expected to develop into a race of robust men and women."[68]

Additionally, middle-class African American women were well aware of the necessity of most women of "the race" to work outside the home. Many believed that higher wages for men could help relieve the strain on working mothers and their families. Because labor force participation was much more typical for African American mothers than for white mothers, the NACW threw its organizational support behind projects like the National Association of Wage Earners to try to improve wages and working conditions for women doing domestic work. African American reformers spoke of "the hope of an economic independence that will some day enable them [African American women] to take their places in the ranks with other women." Also advocating for child care with more urgency and less ambivalence than did white women, African American women expressed a version of maternalism that was, overall, less contradictory.[69]

The social welfare efforts of Hispanic, Asian American, and Native American women in this time period are poorly documented, but even the racial comparisons that historians have made between white women and African American women are instructive. Linda Gordon assessed the climate: "Had black women activists had their way, the working mothers of the past few decades would have been much better supplied with child care and other measures to lighten the double day. ADC would have been more balanced and the demand for it possibly reduced."[70] African American women, based on their own experiences combining wage work and child care, pioneered a vision of social supports that a much broader swathe of working women came to imagine later in the twentieth century, when the demands of work-family balance and the inadequate labor market opportunities for women were more evident to the enormous numbers of women who struggled to combine caring and breadwinning.

CONCLUSION

Despite their limitations, the initiatives of Progressive era reformers inspired broader attention to the conditions in which women mothered, especially urban women experiencing the social and economic transformations of the Industrial Revolution. These generations of reformers brought genuine material benefits to some of the nation's struggling mothers and raised expectations for millions more. Maternalist activism created a place of advice, resources, information, and arguably even empowerment for the nation's mothers in the form of the U.S. Children's Bureau. Although short-lived, the Sheppard-Towner program for maternal and child health was a public-health precedent set by mostly female maternalist reformers. However flawed and incomplete, the direct-relief welfare programs of the Great Depression-era New Deal also had their roots in the maternalist visions and the crossclass negotiations of mothers in the Progressive era. So, too, did labor legislation that at least acknowledged the double day of working mothers. In the first four decades of the twentieth century, mothers came to expect some role for government in helping hold families together when they lost a male breadwinner, when men could not or would not provide, and eventually in situations of domestic abuse.

How much motherhood was actually dignified through American social policy is a question we could continue to debate today. Many mothers—disadvantaged by poverty, language, immigrant or indigenous status, or racism—experienced charity and education as forms of cultural imperialism. Some of these programs directly challenged the mother-child bond or the survival strategies upon which mothers relied. Because of conservative opposition to public aid for the poor and ambivalence about single and working mothers, the positive impact of the nation's welfare state was very limited. Maternalism weighed down the needs of modern mothers with nineteenth-century notions of mother care, even as maternal activists were unable (and sometimes unwilling) to wrest broad and generous provisions and higher wages for struggling mothers from the male legislatures that controlled public funds. Mothers living in modern times, in family situations defined by the need to bring in cash, often needed to earn a wage. The social policies described here did not do a great deal to facilitate this need. As Gwendolyn Mink aptly wrote, social policies of welfare and labor legislation "modernized gender inequality."[71] This is partly because poor and working-class women had so little voice in the public sphere and were largely absent in the debates over the policies that impacted their ability to provide for their families. Still, mothers negotiated such powerful obstacles and used the resources they had through their own patterns of maternal resilience.

CHAPTER 6

Modern Reproduction

THE FIT AND UNFIT MOTHER

As late as 1940, the most popular form of "contraceptive" in the United States was the antiseptic douche, a profoundly unreliable method. With the Comstock laws still in place, douches were covertly advertised, not labeled as contraceptives, and packaged by multiple companies in an unregulated marketplace. Some versions contained very little besides water and salt; others were unsafe, sometimes even deadly.[1] Despite a century of declining birth rates and all the progress made in infant and child health and in the prevention of maternal mortality between the 1910s and the 1930s, most women still could not reliably control their fertility. Nevertheless, the historical record of the first decades of the twentieth century shows in rich detail women's pleas for useful information and reliable reproductive choices. Over these decades, Americans debated about, experimented with, and legislated on the issue of reproductive control and its connection to modern motherhood. Nineteenth-century fears about women's unwillingness to be mothers now combined with newer anxieties about their potential for sexual autonomy and about the reproduction of the American population by "fit" mothers.

"Now what I Want to know," insisted a married mother of three in Kansas in 1928, "is Why can't We poor people be given Birth Control as well as Dr's. & the Rich people. . . . We need help to prevent any more babies," Mrs. E.S. insisted. "Don't you think it better to be Parents of 3 which we are willing to work & do all we can for them, to raise & provide food for us all, then to hafto [sic] have 6 or more that would take us down into the grave & leave 6 or more for poverty to take & be Motherless?" She was even willing to consider sterilization to prevent more pregnancies. Nineteenth-century voluntary motherhood advocates, mostly middle class, had argued that putting women in charge of fertility would create better babies. This twentieth-century argument from a working-class woman emphasized the economic struggles of large families, as well as the risk to maternal health from repeated pregnancies and poverty. But, like others writing to the U.S. Children's Bureau about contraception, Mrs. E.S. would not receive the information she sought because of legal restrictions on this information. Her demands represented an ongoing conflict between women desperate to control their childbearing and the laws and economic barriers that prevented them from doing so.

In the twentieth century, more women were willing to take on the struggle publicly, especially by demanding access to effective contraceptive devices. At their most radical, these demands were nothing less than a call for reproductive freedom and even sexual freedom that had a much wider impact than the nineteenth-century radicals had managed. As Margaret Sanger, founder of first birth control clinic in the United States, said: "No woman can call herself free who does not own and control her body."[2]

Limited birth control technology certainly presented its own barrier to reproductive possibilities for women and their male partners in the early twentieth century. But this problem was greatly compounded by the law. The Comstock laws proved so prohibitive that Sanger and her activist sister went to jail protesting them in the 1910s, and Children's Bureau officials tacitly agreed to a contraceptive and abortion "gag rule" in their response to health and poverty concerns of women that it was their mission to address.[3]

In simple legal terms, circulation of birth control information and devices remained at least partially criminalized for a very long time. In 1936, the Supreme Court ruled that doctors, but only doctors, could acquire contraceptive information. Meanwhile, marketers of contraceptive products had to pretend their products had other medical uses, and consumers had little knowledge of product effectiveness. Not until 1972 did the Court effectively invalidate all the "Little Comstock" laws of the states and finally allow even unmarried women access to openly advertised birth control. Abortion remained illegal via state laws until 1973. Between the 1900s and the 1970s, however, eugenic sterilization laws to promote "selective breeding" of the American population meant that state agencies took a remarkably active role in coercively sterilizing women whom authorities believed should not be mothers. Women's actual access to reproductive choice is more complicated than this simple chronology suggests. By the 1960s, though perhaps not quite in the way Sanger imagined, the majority of married couples had access to safer, more reliable birth contraceptives than ever before, in part because of improved medical research and in part because the market provided what the law would not.

The groundswell of women's rising expectations from the 1910s to the 1930s also shaped the direction of change. Advertisers encouraged modern mothers to protect their marriages through reproductive control. Thanks to modern medicine, more women than ever before also felt entitled to protect their own health for the future of the children they already had, and birth control was one way to do this. Nevertheless, modernizing women's access to reproductive choice met with stiff resistance. For a variety of reasons, women's reproductive choices were deliberately limited in ways that distinguished between the fit "mother of the race," who should reproduce for the stability of American civilization, and the "unfit," who should not. Reproductive freedom, more broadly conceived, was still on the distant horizon when Mrs. E.S. wrote her letter in 1928.

MODERN REPRODUCTIVE RIGHTS AND AMERICAN CULTURE

As the twentieth century dawned, generations of women had already been privately attempting to exert broader control over their fertility by experimenting with new methods. In the new century, women were vocally demanding, or just quietly assuming, more public roles as well, campaigning for voting rights, entering the factory labor force, and pursuing higher education in unprecedented numbers. The popular press announced the arrival of the "New Woman," who was ready and eager to be her own person. Meanwhile, Sanger's nascent birth control movement, begun in the 1910s, attracted national attention and galvanized a parallel strand of feminist thinking that claimed women's reproductive freedom as part of their overall citizenship and potential for human development.

On the surface, advancing birth control might have been seen as an obvious step for a culture enamored of scientific progress, and embracing new reproductive choices for women would seem to fit beautifully with Progressive-era emphasis on uplift of the nation's struggling mothers. For some Progressives, this was true. After all, women's capacity to prevent pregnancy had a direct bearing on some of the most pressing concerns of maternalist reformers: maternal health and poverty. Practically everyone in this period made the connection between large families and poverty. In terms of maternal health, the risk of infant mortality declined by nearly 25 percent if women spaced their children just twelve months apart, compared to spacing of less than one year.[4]

Yet, unlike the medicalization of child care, arguments linking infant survival and birth control would do little to sway the law. When Margaret Sanger testified before the Senate Judiciary Committee in favor of a birth control bill in 1931, she cast birth control as part of a "Mothers' Bill of Rights." But she failed to persuade legislators skittish about the topics of sex and women's rights. Arguments in favor of women's sexual freedom were even less effective: they provoked powerful backlash. Most nineteenth-century "voluntary motherhood" advocates had eschewed "artificial" contraceptive devices and asked only that a woman have the right to say no to sexual intercourse within marriage. But twentieth-century birth control feminists such as Sanger, Emma Goldman, and Mary Ware Dennett demanded more: recognition of women as individual, and even sexual, beings. However much Sanger tried to tame her message for conservative audiences, she was also known for arguing that women should refuse to be "passive instruments of sensual self-gratification on the part of men. . . . In increasing and elevating her love demands, woman must elevate sex into another sphere, whereby it may subserve and enhance the possibility of human expression." In her radical youth, Sanger's *Woman Rebel* publication, produced to support birth control, boldly declared on its masthead, "No Gods, No Masters."[5]

The fear that white, American-born women were embracing too many modern freedoms and public roles led many Americans to oppose any effort to lessen the motherhood mandate or potentially promote sexual freedom for women. Even in the 1930s, in the midst of the Great Depression—when millions of American families could not afford to have more children and when religious liberals and growing numbers of physicians offered vocal support for birth control—the resistance was fierce. Some opponents referred to contraceptive advocacy as a Soviet plot, designed to subvert the morality of the young. One physician author considered birth control "An Insult to True Womanhood," "A Degradation of the Female Sex," and "A Menace to the Nation." Echoing the nineteenth-century physicians who warned that women's education would provoke dire consequences to the maternal body, this doctor also argued that use of birth control could cause fibroid tumors, neurosis, and permanent infertility. Catholic opposition was especially well organized and included associations between birth control and pornography. Birth control activist Mary Ware Dennett found that congressmen's most frequent objection to allowing access to contraceptives was that women would not guard their chastity without the fear of pregnancy.[6]

In an era of large-scale immigration, xenophobia and racism added to the hysteria about which women were opting out of motherhood. In 1905, Teddy Roosevelt referred to white, American-born, middle-class women when he said that those who avoided having children were being "criminal against the race." His remarks prompted widespread discussion of the "race suicide" of such women. Roosevelt also publicly declared that he wished "very much that the wrong people could be prevented entirely from breeding."[7] Much like the welfare projects that began in the Progressive era, the reproductive-control struggles of this period reflected deep anxiety over who was to participate in motherhood and on what terms.

The notion of stopping the reproduction of the unfit emerged and developed simultaneously with the question of whether the "right" women were getting too modern (and free) and seeking to avoid motherhood. Many feared that putting reproductive decisions into the hands of privileged women would only exacerbate the problems of the modern age, while leaving too much freedom to reproduce in the hands of poorer women and women of color meant weakening the nation's genetic stock. One pattern is clear: few people with the power to distribute resources believed that women should be in charge of these maternal decisions. Even those who did, like Margaret Sanger, eventually rationalized the cause of reproductive freedom through the rhetoric of a eugenic notion of population control, partially eclipsing women's freedom in the name of controlling the reproduction of the poor and otherwise "unfit."

The irony is that most women knew what they wanted and needed in terms of family limitation, and for the most part their wishes were far from radical: the overwhelming majority wanted simply to stop having more babies than they could afford or than their health could sustain. "I have never rebelled at motherhood and no one on earth is more devoted to their home and children than I am," wrote one woman who sought contraception. "I feel like I've had enough children."[8] In the throes of growing industrial capitalism, and especially during the Great Depression, many were sufficiently desperate to acquire control over their reproduction that it mattered not whether the means were contraception, abortion, or even, for a few, permanent elective sterilization.

Accessing Birth Control: The Activists, the Law, the Doctors, and the Entrepreneurs

When Margaret Sanger opened her pioneering birth control clinic in a largely immigrant neighborhood in New York City in 1916, her intention was to directly confront the Comstock laws that prohibited information on birth control and to put information in the hands of women. As a practicing nurse, she had seen women die from both botched, often self-induced, abortions and repeated pregnancies that their bodies could not support. She was determined to provide women with real control over their reproductive lives. She and her cause became known to untold numbers of women around the country because, over time, newspapers published reports of her project. Writing from all over the country to the Children's Bureau and to Sanger directly, women begged for advice on how to prevent pregnancy. During the Great Depression women's letters repeated the same themes that they had contained in the 1910s. Again and again, women feared for their lives, pointing out in their pleas to Sanger, "my last baby almost cost my life." One woman wrote in the 1930s, "My husband works on relief, because his job is shut down. Please tell me the secret about birth control. When you write about it, please write to me in plain words because I don't know what it means in big words."[9]

Hounded by the law through her first decade of activism, Sanger bravely broke the silence on birth control. She traveled to Europe to research new contraceptive methods. She appeared in court to face obscenity charges even after having lost her young daughter to illness. Sanger championed reproductive self-determination for women and safe, effective methods of birth control with single-minded determination. She founded the American Birth Control League in 1921, which later became the Planned Parenthood Federation of America. She spurred the development of birth control clinics across the country and contributed significantly to emerging world-population research and planning. Yet the goal of women's reproductive self-determination was partially undermined by the birth control movement's compromises: a gradual acceptance of a medicalized model of contraception availability, the drawing of a sharper moral line between contraception and abortion, and a willingness to embrace some rhetoric of population control or "eugenics" as a rationale for contraceptives.

Sanger expended great resources to maintain her leadership and national prominence in the birth-control movement. Ultimately one of her strategies to gain credibility for her cause was to ally with physicians. From early on it was clear that the only way to make her birth control clinic project work was to engage medical supervision of the project. When she appealed her conviction in New York for violating the Comstock law by distributing birth control, the court reinterpreted state law to allow for physician-supervised distribution; Fortunately, Sanger and her allies were able to find forward-thinking physicians and nurses to staff birth control clinics. With such legitimacy, birth control clinics spread across the nation's cities, numbering 145 by 1932. Women who came to the New York facility and some other progressive clinics also received sex education, access to fertility and marriage counseling, and even some discreet referrals to relatively safe abortion providers.[10]

Sanger and the American Birth Control League gradually gave up the idea of launching an outright attack on the Comstock laws and focused instead on winning physicians to the cause. The League eventually did succeed, in part by bankrolling research on the diaphragm and proving to physicians that it worked. In 1937, a year after the Supreme Court made it legal for doctors to prescribe contraception, the American Medical Association endorsed the use of birth control as prescribed by physicians. By the 1940s, the majority of physicians were receiving training in contraception, and physicians recommended the diaphragm more than any other contraceptive method.[11]

Convincing willing physicians that there was a safe and effective method certainly helped the cause in the long run, and, even in the short term, medicalizing birth control probably kept alive Sanger's movement. For most women in the period before World War II, however, this strategic alliance did little to expand their options because most women in the United States did not have access to medical care. In the early 1930s, a study found that in some poor rural counties the ratio of physicians to residents could sometimes be as high as 1 to 20,000, and access was very much determined by ability to pay. In 1941, an estimated one-half of the southern population was unable to pay for medical care. Another study in the early 1940s showed that only about 6 percent of working-class families had learned about contraception from physicians, compared to about 31 percent of middle-class families. Pharmacists often recommended diaphragms, but research showed that customers frequently bypassed a fitting with a physician. Cost was an issue even for purchasing the one contraceptive device that women could control in the bedroom with demonstrated effectiveness: a tube of contraceptive jelly for use with a diaphragm cost between four and six dollars, a relative fortune compared to the one-dozen box of condoms or douching solution yielding four liquid gallons, either of which could be purchased for a dollar.[12]

Some women found birth control options through the efforts of medical entrepreneurs, such as Clarence J. Gamble of the Procter and Gamble Company. In the late 1930s, the economic stresses of the Great Depression helped lessen public opposition to contraception in some areas of the country. With varying levels of support and cooperation from Sanger and the birth control movement, Gamble used North Carolina's public health clinics to dispense and test birth control technologies by targeting poor women whose reproductive activities the state wanted to restrict anyway. As nurse Doris Davidson put it, "We all know the ever-present need for a simpler method for unintelligent, illiterate, lazy, and poverty-stricken patients."[13]

At public expense, visiting nurses came to the homes of poor North Carolina women and even to migrant labor camps. Some distributors, including some physicians and nurses, provided contraceptive devices to poor women with genuine sympathy about their lack of access to physicians, privacy, and money to pay for devices like the diaphragm. But programs like the one in North Carolina were driven by interests in both controlling the perceived overpopulation of the poor and testing products for the market, rather than proving genuine reproductive health care. For women in these generations, new birth control technologies came, if they came at all, with numerous strings attached. Those in contraceptive trial studies were not informed of the risks of the devices, and their options were limited. Gamble supplied public health officials with free contraceptive foam powder and asked them to collect data on the effectiveness of the product. Providers could discuss other methods with women, but the vast majority of clinics only offered foam powder. As a result, women who either disliked foam powder or jellies or found them ineffective had few other options, even though many did complain to the public health nurses. When research programs ended in their areas, women were often left stranded again when it came to contraceptive devices. Meanwhile, because health officials were so afraid of opposition, they often neither advertised their services nor distributed birth control through the logical channels of maternal and child health services. The Children's Bureau, anxious about negative publicity, even threatened to discontinue funding for maternal and child health programs for states that distributed birth control.[14]

Eugenic notions of population control were well established by the 1930s. Gamble himself was a lifelong proponent of eugenic sterilization as well as simple contraceptive technologies to help reduce the population of the poor. In an effort to promote "positive eugenics" to encourage breeding of the fit, Gamble offered cash prizes to Harvard alumni who produced large families. While Sanger worked with African American health advocates toward community-run clinics in some areas, racism combined with class prejudice in the philosophy that undergirded the testing and distribution of devices. "The mass of Negroes, particularly in the South, still breed carelessly and disastrously, with the result that the increase among Negroes, even more than among whites, is from that portion of the population least intelligent and fit, least able to rear children properly," noted Gamble. Nonetheless, he and other distributors held racist assumptions that African American women were not intelligent enough to use birth control, an attitude that meant African American women were more underserved than coerced in the period before World War II. This pattern helps explain why they were also more likely than white women to seek abortion services.[15] Because they were frequently deemed unfit, the white poor were certainly targets of the eugenics movement as well.

Beyond the range of coordinated contraceptive experiments, the marketplace of contraceptive possibilities expanded rapidly with the development of modern advertising. Women were targeted as both the major consumers of the family and the more responsible party for preventing pregnancy. Some product standardization occurred in the 1920s, especially for condoms, and condom sales soared during the Great Depression. Still, most women relied simply, and often to their regret, on "feminine hygiene" products. In the late 1930s, douches, vaginal suppositories, and one-size-fits-all nonmedical diaphragms constituted 85 percent of contraceptive sales, while medically fitted diaphragms accounted for only 1 percent of such sales. "Hygiene" products were covertly advertised with hints about their contraceptive value and overtly claimed medicinal benefits. The advertisers of these products were under no obligation to either test for or explain contraceptive effectiveness. While this was true of many products in the relatively unregulated consumer marketplace of the early twentieth century, these products were not even being advertised as contraceptives, given the Comstock law. Advertising was often patently fraudulent, as when companies created fake European female gynecologists to serve as product spokespersons.[16]

Contraceptive ads raised expectations for modern motherhood while also playing on fears, just as did ads for products to protect babies from germs. "It amazes me in these modern days, to hear women confess their carelessness, their lack of positive information, in the so vital matter of feminine hygiene," remarked a product spokeswoman (billed as a European gynecologist). "They take almost anybody's word . . . a neighbor's, an afternoon bridge partner's . . . for the correct technique." Instead, women should have used "scientific research and medical experience" as befitted their modern status. Other ads warned of "Calendar Fear" and asked "Can a Married Woman Ever Feel Safe?" and "the Fear [of pregnancy] that 'Blights' Romance and Ages Women Prematurely."[17] Modern mothers, said the advertisers, should protect their marriages and their health by preventing pregnancy. Though many women lacked valuable information and medical access to make this possible, the medical and consumer messages of the era raised expectations.

In the long run, contraceptive testing and medicalization would improve women's access to reliable contraceptives. The daughters of the women whose reproductive lives spanned the early twentieth century would have better options. By 1940, birth control research was gaining legitimacy. In the throes of the Great Depression, the first public opinion poll on contraception already showed that 70 percent of respondents nationwide were in favor of medical birth control.[18] Sanger's movement had gained legitimacy in part through embracing modern medicine and advocating for contraception during a time of dire economic crisis.

Drawing the Line: Birth Control and Abortion

In their attempt to legitimate contraception, birth control activists drew a sharp distinction between birth control and abortion. Birth control was safe, claimed the contraceptive advocates, while abortion was dangerous. Women were not to blame for seeking abortion. If the laws against birth control were eliminated and physicians would cooperate, Sanger and her colleagues reasonably argued that the need for abortion would greatly diminish.[19] Even as the New York City birth control clinic did discreetly refer women for abortions, the public face of the movement sought to dissociate the birth control cause from that of abortion. Highlighting this distinction meant that reproductive self-determination for women could only go so far.

In the age of what Sanger called "Comstockery," the birth control movement was not alone in parceling out the kind of reproductive services or even advice it gave. Women who wrote to the Children's Bureau learned even less than those who wrote to birth control advocates. When they did respond to women who brought up abortion, bureau women showed sympathy. One woman wrote that she had terminated a pregnancy, and her own attitudes demonstrate how the culture was in flux on the question of abortion: "I have regretted the day I ever went to that doctor . . . now I am afraid I can never have any more children. . . . My only goal in life is to be a mother." Ethel Watters, of the bureau, wrote, "I am very sorry that you should have so unfortunate an experience but nature is usually very kind and she does not always punish by depriving women of children when they have destroyed only one child." Here and in other responses, the bureau reinforced the notion that terminating pregnancy was morally wrong. One Oregon woman asked first how a woman could tell she was pregnant, and then, "Do you think it right if one knows how to stop a childs birth to do so?" Anna Rude of the bureau responded, "It is not right to stop a pregnancy. It is not only dangerous to the mother herself, but also the taking of another life."[20]

Women's information on the topic was extremely limited, and they had few other reproductive control options. It is no wonder, then, that many women apparently continued not to differentiate between birth control and abortion or to accept the traditional view of when a pregnancy and a life begin, despite the concerted efforts of physicians to make these distinctions for more than a century and a half. In the early twentieth century, leading physicians sought to discredit midwives, in part by associating them with the practice of abortion. Yet physicians frequently lamented that they could do little to change broader public attitudes. "The laity," as one physician complained in 1922, still believed "that there can be no life until fetal movements are felt."[21]

Many women likely refused to differentiate between contraception and abortion because their reasons for seeking them were the same: protecting the living, providing for the children they needed to feed right now, and sustaining their own health. Though there were always women who conceived out of wedlock, the vast majority of women did marry, approximately 92 percent of those born between 1910 and 1934, for example. And married women seldom sought to avoid having children altogether. The poorest women were most likely to seek birth control, abortion, or even sterilization, whichever tactic worked, when they felt they had enough children. Middle-class women tended to attempt to delay childbearing early in their marriages to establish themselves.[22] When birth control failed, women, especially those with little money, frequently attempted self-induced abortions. If they had the resources, they might also seek out doctors or midwives through informal underground information networks on abortion providers.

There was significant public sympathy for poor, unmarried women who sought abortions. Married women, however, received greater vitriol for exercising the abortion option, much as they did for pursuing contraceptives. One judge declared, "A woman who would destroy life in that manner is not fit for decent society. It is the duty of any healthy married woman to bear children." Overall, though abortion remained criminalized, between 1890 and 1940 midwives and physicians performed the operation more commonly than we might expect. Physicians considered a fairly wide range of health conditions, including then common diseases like tuberculosis, grounds for a therapeutic abortion. Then, too, until the late 1930s, enforcement of state laws restricting abortion was somewhat limited. Juries, including male jurors, often proved sympathetic to women seeking abortions; usually prosecution occurred only in the cases where a woman had died from an illegal abortion.[23]

By many accounts, the Great Depression led to a large spike in the incidence of abortion. Though numbers will always be hard to capture in an age of illegality and self-induced abortions, various reports confirmed an upward trend. One New York physician reported that abortions among poor, white women at his hospital increased 166 percent just between 1930 and 1931. The desperation of the population in the 1930s led some outspoken physicians to talk about reforming or repealing the abortion laws while the profession as a whole moved toward a broader range of acceptable medical conditions warranting therapeutic abortions. One example of physicians' interest in reform comes from a woman doctor, Regine K. Stix, who interviewed nearly one thousand women in the early 1930s. Dr. Stix discovered that only 24 percent of women who reported self-induced abortions did not have complications, in contrast to 91 percent of those who had had the procedure performed by physicians and 86 percent of those who had used the services of midwives. Even as early as 1939, a poll of medical students nationwide showed that 68 percent of the students "were willing to perform abortions if they were legal."[24]

In 1940, legal abortion was, of course, decades away, and women were, in fact, on the cusp of an age of great repression and more aggressive prosecution. In retrospect, however, it seems that procedures and technologies placed under physician control in the name of science had the potential for cultural legitimacy. In the long run, this was true for both birth control and abortion. A later generation of physicians actually contributed vocally to the liberalization of abortion restrictions by the 1960s. Medicalizing the options for women's reproductive bodies left much control in the hands of doctors, but it likewise increased the acceptability of birth control, abortion, or sterilization.

Not surprisingly, the exercise of choice in preventing or terminating pregnancies was most available to women with money. If ordinary women were often unable to make good on their hopes for reliable reproductive control, then they were still increasingly aware of what they needed and felt entitled to pursue. The possibilities of reproductive freedom existed even in an age of repression.

Eugenic Sterilization and the "Unfit" Mother

Meanwhile, reproductive control in an entirely different direction emerged as a celebrated cause of prominent members of the American elite, leaving a powerful imprint on cultural notions of who should and should not be mothers. Between the early 1900s and the mid-1970s, an estimated 63,000 people were surgically sterilized and thus prevented from future motherhood or fatherhood in the United States. The majority of those sterilized—approximately 61 percent—were women.[25] For most, these sterilizations were performed under the orders of institutional or other state authorities, rather than at the request of the women or men whose reproduction was at stake. The primary victims were poor women and men and, in later decades of these state-sponsored programs, a very disproportionate number of women of color. Many sterilization surgeries were performed with minimal or nonexistent consent, sometimes without the patient's knowledge.

The number 63,000 does not represent a large percentage of the population, and only a few states account for the majority of the coerced sterilizations. But eugenic sterilization of so-called genetic "defectives" greatly impacted the culture and contributed to the notion of population control directed at presumably unfit mothers. With the nation's growing emphasis on the importance of motherhood to national purpose and to child development, it became an important national project to ensure that only "fit" mothers would reproduce.

Modern eugenics—the promotion of reproduction by those of "good birth" and the discouragement of reproduction by those labeled unfit—was the brainchild of elite intellectuals. Following the late nineteenth-century work of Francis Galton, the United States Eugenics Research Organization, formed in 1910, included luminaries such as the president of the American Medical Association, a Yale economist, a Nobel Prize–winning geneticist, and a Harvard Medical School psychiatrist. The related Eugenics Record Office had the mission of researching the "best method of restricting the strains that produce the defective and delinquent class of the community."[26] Much initial interest focused on preventing reproduction by men deemed unfit due to criminal behavior, but, over time, the focus shifted toward potentially unfit mothers. Rhetorical support came in many forms, including public statements by Theodore Roosevelt, Thomas Edison, and Woodrow Wilson.

There was always diversity of opinion on the matter, including dissent from nervous state legislators, skeptical physicians, the Catholic Church, and prominent figures such as the president of the American Bar Association. Nevertheless, support for a program of eugenic sterilization to improve American "heredity" and "genetic stock" was astoundingly wide-ranging and rose greatly in the 1920s and 1930s. Support could be found among state legislators, physicians, clergy, and attorneys, as well as psychiatrists, directors of mental and penal institutions, social workers, nurses, public-health officials, academics, judges, journalists, newspaper editors, and civic organizations. Even Margaret Sanger declared that reproductive control was geared toward "more children from the fit, less from the unfit." In the same years that the American public demonstrated growing support for birth control, citizens also warmed to the idea of coerced sterilization. *Fortune* magazine asked readers in 1937, "Some people advocate compulsory sterilization of habitual criminals and mental defectives so that they will not have children to inherit their weaknesses. Would you approve of this?" In response, 66 percent favored sterilizing "mental defectives," and 63 percent favored sterilizing criminals; less than 17 percent opposed sterilization altogether.[27]

Like other reforms originating in the Progressive era, eugenic sterilization was a quintessentially modern program for social change. It purported to be rational, scientific, and based on controlling what nature could not: the reproduction of the "socially inadequate," the "high grade moron," the "feeble-minded," and the "worthless stock," to use a few choice phrases of the era. Such words, as historian Martin S. Pernick has noted, were understood to have scientific meaning and to connote measurable variations of abilities. The movement was driven by decades of purportedly scientific research that was increasingly challenged academically even as it was embraced socially and legally.[28] Begun in 1907, state eugenic sterilization laws initially floundered in the courts because of public squeamishness about "castration" operations, especially on noncriminals, and concerns about due process and equal protection. But sustained advocacy on the part of a number of well-positioned men eventually resulted in the creation of model state laws.

Over the course of the 1910s and 1920s, sterilization advocates developed concerted arguments to reduce opposition to sterilization. They claimed that sterilized people could be "liberated" from institutions and allowed to live normal lives once they were surgically prevented from endangering society with their potential reproduction, a move that would also save states money in institutionalization costs. Supporters claimed that newly developed IQ tests could scientifically determine the feeble-minded, even though actual assessments were often made on much more subjective criteria, and, over time, "moral deficiency" came to just as easily qualify a person for sterilization as IQ tests. Advocates asserted that sterilization protected society, reduced welfare dependency, proved therapeutic to patients, and could be humanely done through surgeries that neither castrated nor removed ovaries. They insisted that such surgeries could be used with both institutional and noninstitutional populations, and included procedures of due process.[29] These carefully developed and well-funded arguments were driven by educated and ideologically motivated men like Charles Davenport, who held a Ph.D. from Harvard University, his protégée Harry Laughlin, and American Breeders Association President Bleecker van Wagenen, who declared that some 10 percent of the American population should be prevented from reproducing due to "inferior blood."[30] (Inferiority included not only blindness, deafness, and epilepsy but also "feeblemindedness" and pauperism.)

In 1927, the transformative Supreme Court decision *Buck v. Bell* upheld coerced sterilization in Virginia and spurred additional similar legislation. Seventeen states created or revised sterilization laws within just four years of the verdict. By the early 1940s, two-thirds of the states had enacted sterilization laws, which complemented marriage restriction laws, including those on the books in thirty states to bar interracial marriage.[31] "Heredity" was the buzzword, but the point was to control the reproduction of vulnerable populations and those who digressed from conservative social norms.

Increasingly, as eugenicists sought to legitimate the sterilization laws and practices that were gaining ground in the early twentieth century, the weight of expertise was so strong that authorities did not even need to provide direct evidence to secure an order to sterilize. The Supreme Court decision, like the Virginia trial that preceded it, was based on extremely subjective evidence. Carrie Buck's "illegitimate" seven-month-old baby was declared "feebleminded" based on a cursory statement from a nurse that baby Vivian was "not quite normal."[32]Accepting abundant though strikingly indirect expert testimony on Carrie Buck, her baby, and Buck's own mother, Judge Oliver Wendell Holmes Jr. declared that "three generations of imbeciles is enough" and empowered Virginia to expand its program of sterilization.

The state laws that followed *Buck v. Bell* were expansive. California, which boasted of its enormous sterilization program, allowed sterilization for those "suffering from perversion or marked departures from normal mentality or from disease of a syphilitic nature"; in fact, California accounted for nearly one-third of the total sterilizations recorded in American history. The likeliest targets of sterilization were people who came into contact with institutions, including prisoners and those confined to epilepsy "colonies," homes for the feebleminded, and other asylums, of which there were many in the Progressive era and subsequent decades. Some laws even expanded the police power of the state to advance the project of controlling reproduction. In Idaho, for example, legislators gave the state board of eugenics the authority to "order the sterilization of anyone it believed had an inherited tendency to feeblemindedness or would probably become either a social menace or a ward of the state."[33]

Class, Race, and Gender in the Eugenics Movement for "Fit" Motherhood

Racial anxieties shaped eugenics initiatives from the beginning. Some eugenic promoters linked the sterilization of the feeble-minded to "the Indian question." It was best, argued a Boston physician, to "stamp out the whole breed," as was being attempted with Native Americans through assimilation programs. At a time when darker-skinned Europeans were also considered separate races from "sturdy Anglo Saxon and Germanic stocks," a physician who worked at Ellis Island promoted study of the practical application of eugenics to Jews in an article in *Popular Science* monthly. His reasoning went that "the Jews are a highly inbred and psychopathologically inclined race." By midcentury, sterilization campaigns disproportionately targeted African American and Native American women. In North Carolina in the 1950s and 1960s, African American patients represented between 59 and 64 percent of sterilizations.[34] Native American women disproportionately faced coerced sterilization well into the 1970s.

At first, eugenic sterilization was as much about class and gender as about race. Major test cases for the laws, including *Buck v. Bell*, involved poor southern white women, although because the South had few institutions, outside North Carolina, these southern states did not contribute significantly to the overall number of people sterilized. One of the most ardent and well-connected advocates for such laws was Dr. Albert Priddy, surgeon, moralist, and director of the Virginia Colony for the feebleminded. Priddy, one of the masterminds behind the use of Carrie Buck as a legal test case, insisted, "These people belong to the shiftless, ignorant, and worthless class of antisocial whites of the South." Historian Wendy Kline has observed that the sterilization programs before World War II probably focused on white women in part because "the ultimate concern was the preservation of female sexual morality in the white race."[35]

Eugenic sterilization was also very much about gender; the procedures initially targeted problematic male behavior (hence the castration of criminals beginning in the nineteenth century) and later enforced proper motherhood. Women who were promiscuous or who had children out of wedlock were potentially unfit mothers. In addition to the deaf, persons afflicted with epilepsy or syphilis, and men accused of sexual crimes, social scientists targeted girls and women more for their sexual behavior, their poverty, and their family members' behaviors than for what would today be considered genuine mental disabilities. In North Carolina, 85 percent of those sterilized were women; of those women, 73 percent were unmarried or separated from spouses, and 50 percent were single and had given birth to at least one child out of wedlock.[36] Perceived sexual deviance got vulnerable women, especially poor women, in trouble and jeopardized their right to future motherhood. Female sterilization patient records in institutions frequently noted words like "passionate," "immoral," "promiscuous," or "oversexed." Unlike men, women were very seldom sterilized for actual crimes. "Sexual licentiousness" was a hereditary trait, argued eugenic scholars, and one that cost states significant amounts for care of such "wantons" and "ne'er-do-wells."[37]

The range of terms to describe women who should be sterilized reflected intense ambivalence about both women's sexuality and the impossible juxtaposition in the popular imagination between maternity and sexuality. Such women had a "fondness for men," suffered from "sexual degeneracy" or "nymphomania," or had tested positively for sexually transmitted diseases. Terms associated with poverty compounded prejudices about out-of-control female sexuality: "wayward," suffering from "general backwardness." The zealous Dr. Priddy often found reasons to sterilize women he did not actually consider feeble-minded, as in the case of a woman whom he believed had had an "immoral" mother. The woman's relative, requesting that she be released from Priddy's colony, was told that "for the protection of defective girls who leave the institution and to prevent harmful heredity we have sterilized a great many of them."[38]

The potentially unfit mother resided in communities, many eugenicists warned, not just in institutions. When Stanford University psychologist Lewis Terman, developer of the IQ test, investigated a state home for unwed mothers, he found that these women had "a marked inferiority to average adults," although they could "pass for normal in almost any community." Psychologist Henry Goddard (like Terman, a prominent eugenics advocate) developed the term "moron," to describe people with a mental age ranging from eight to twelve. This term was adapted for scare campaigns. One publication warned, "Attractive morons abound within the community." It pictured a well-dressed young woman who lived at a "state training school" and noted, "Girls like these, who come from defective stock yet who are trained sufficiently to pass for normal by those with superficial judgment, are the greatest menace to the race when returned to the community without the protection of sterilization." A 1926 report from one "training school" made the presumably alarming assertion that 99 percent of the "high grade" feebleminded "lived outside of institutions, and were 'mixing and mingling with the general population.'"[39]

In this anxious age changing definitions of female sexuality combined with fear of the lower classes and people of color. All this led to the notion that girls and women who engaged in sex outside marriage were no longer the victims that nineteenth-century maternalist reformers had claimed; instead, these women were genetically flawed, not redeemable through rehabilitation or education, and morally contagious.[40] In 1915 Goddard himself noted: "It is no undue sentimentalism that assures us that we need to take care of this group of people. We need to study them very seriously and very thoroughly; we need to hunt them out in every possible place and take care of them, and see to it that they do not propagate and make the problem worse, and that those who are alive today do not entail loss of life and property and moral contagion in the community by the things that they do because they are weak-minded."[41]

Such sentiment helps explain the case of Willie Mallory, a woman who, by all available evidence, was entrapped by police in her home. Police alleged she was running a brothel because she had shown an undercover informant a room in her home when he claimed to be looking for a place to board. In 1916, Mallory was involuntarily committed to the Virginia Colony, along with two of her daughters. She and one daughter were sterilized. Mallory's younger children, whom the juvenile court said had been "exposed to vicious and immoral influences," were placed in the Children's Home Society. Mallory recalled that a social worker helped a doctor come up with criteria to commit her: "Put on there, 'unable to control her nerves,' and we can get her for that." Colony records accused Mallory of having a career in begging, using public charity, and "streetwalking" and noted that her father had multiple marriages and her mother was feebleminded. Mallory's "mental deficiency" was attributed to heredity.[42]

Willie Mallory's confinement and the sterilization of the two Mallory women occurred against the heartbreaking objection, ultimately fruitless, of George Mallory, husband and father. George Mallory sued Dr. Priddy, who had performed the sterilizations. Begging for the release of his child from state custody, the father lamented, "Dr what business did you have opreatiding [sic] on my wife and daughter with out my consent . . . she is not feeble minded."[43] The Mallory suit lost in court.

In the 1930s, with growing demands on the public coffers, sterilization skyrocketed; nearly three times the numbers of sterilizations were performed in the 1930s as had been done in the 1920s. In 1935 Nebraska even instituted a law requiring that all feebleminded persons register with the state and allowing the state to deny these persons a marriage license without proof of sterilization. The American Eugenics Society recommended sterilization even in situations where "there is no certainty that the traits of the parents will be passed on to their children through heredity." So-called heredity was no longer the only justification for eugenic sterilization. Home environments, culturally assigned as mothers' domains, could also lead to institutional commitment and sterilization. In 1930, Fred Butler, who ran the Sonoma State Home in California, said that the institution was no longer really concerned about whether sterilization candidates were the "hereditary or non-hereditary type"; either way, problem mothers would not care for their children properly. "The saddest of them all, in my opinion," he observed, "is a feebleminded mother trying to care for normal children."[44]

Restricting motherhood to the fit became an even more compelling argument than restricting genetic defects, especially as prominent academics were challenging the hereditary-conditions arguments made by eugenicists. And the issue even went beyond controlling the poor. The wealthy Ann Cooper Hewitt sued her mother and the two surgeons who, at the mother's request, had sterilized her without her consent. In the widely publicized 1936 trial, Ms. Hewitt was portrayed as "dangerously oversexed." The defendants drew on eugenic ideas about protecting society from such a "high grade moron"; Ms. Hewitt lost the case. Wendy Kline astutely observed, "The determining question was no longer, Will she spread her genetic defect to her children? It was, Will she make a desirable mother? This change paved the way for widespread use of sterilization as a way to regulate motherhood."[45] Indeed, like the opposition to women's self-determination in contraceptive use, eugenic thought about regulating motherhood was part of a larger response to women's perceived new freedoms and potentially declining attachment to the motherhood role.

Resistance and Compliance

"She was not feeble-minded when she left home," declared one mother, after her seventeen-year-old daughter had been committed to the state "training school" and deemed a candidate for sterilization. Another mother described her daughter: "She is not more feebleminded than anyone in this building." These mothers' voices stand out as two of the very few that historians have uncovered to document the resistance to sterilization by women and their families. And organized opposition to the laws seems to have been truly minimal. One exception was Lora Little, the mother of a child who died at age seven. Little blamed doctors and compulsory vaccination for her child's death and felt compelled to challenge the prerogatives of governmental health orders. Through the Oregon Anti-Sterilization League, Little led a referendum drive that successfully killed Oregon's sterilization law in 1913. This delayed coercive sterilization in the state by several years, but ultimately the variety of state laws made a national movement difficult. The weight of expert opinion helped prevent popular protest.[46]

The tens of thousands of sterilization cases received scant public attention, even when they were opposed legally. Newspapers rarely covered the cases themselves until the Hewitt trial. Even after the trial, there was no great public outcry against the procedure. As evidenced in the 1937 *Fortune* survey, public approval for sterilizing an ill-defined group of "mental defectives" was strong. Despite documentation that the charge of feeble-mindedness rested on meager evidence, in practice, appearing before a eugenics board to contest a charge of feeblemindedness was probably sufficiently intimidating for both women and men and their family members that most decided to forego protesting. It is hard to imagine a working-class, possibly impoverished, already committed woman in this era facing down a board of mostly male physicians who have made it clear they believe she is mentally challenged and, very likely, morally reprehensible as well. In fact, most patients and guardians did not attend the hearings to determine a woman's reproductive future. Then, too, it was not uncommon for patients or their guardians to give consent without understanding the operation, and some did not even find out until later that they had been sterilized. One woman who had been discharged from Virginia's Colony wrote to Dr. Priddy asking for his permission to marry, a gesture that spoke volumes about her limited sense of personal autonomy; her letter made clear that she did not know she had been sterilized while under Dr. Priddy's care.[47]

When sterilization candidates or their family members did appear before these boards, they took pains to assure board members of the patient's willingness to conform to behavior befitting a proper mother. An eighteen-year-old woman named Pattie was defended by her mother, who did not want her daughter sterilized. Pattie herself promised to find a way to marry, to refrain from sex outside marriage, and to defer to her future husband's wishes about the advisability of additional children. Pattie's mother also promised to discipline her daughter and make sure that she would not become a charity case for the state. The board gave Pattie "another chance." Indeed, when patients actively resisted, it was not entirely unusual for eugenics boards to stay the execution of a woman's reproductive capacity. But the board warned Pattie, "You might come before us again if things don't work out."[48]

At the same time, some women appear to have chosen sterilization; they approached eugenics boards themselves or pursued information about sterilization they received from case workers. Historian Johanna Schoen found that about 20 percent of the petitions filed in North Carolina between 1929 and 1975 appeared to have been voluntary sterilizations. Of these, approximately 80 percent were petitions received from women. Some of these apparently believed that they had reached an appropriate family size. As one woman put it, "I've had my pile. I've done my share." But the context in which most women asked for the procedure in the first half of the century is paramount to understanding their choice. Those who approached the board tended to be extremely poor, and most lacked the support of a male breadwinner. One woman's petition notes contained the detail "even with assistance given the children are . . . hungry to the extent that they eat out of garbage cans." Most had several children already, and African American women requested the procedure significantly more often than white women.[49] These patterns reflected not only the lack of available birth control and abortions but also the lesser resources of African American women to otherwise protect their reproductive health.

Public Opinion on Eugenic Sterilization

The story of sterilization is difficult to tell in any way other than top-down: powerful people imposed their will on women and men who had very little voice in society. To understand the impact of approximately 63,000 sterilizations on a much larger American population, however, we must know a little about the way that eugenic ideology weaseled its way into American social thought. Well-funded organizations like the Human Betterment Foundation distributed publications such as *Human Sterilization Today* across the country to promote the cause. In the 1930s, the pamphlet went out, by request, to some seven thousand college professors in just one year. Teachers, too, requested information on sterilization for use in the classroom, and textbooks carried the message to younger people about the menace of the wrong breeding, reinforcing class prejudices and taboos on interracial mixing.

Generations of social workers, as well as physicians and academics, were trained in eugenic thinking. The Human Betterment Foundation also funded books written for nonspecialists, such as *Sterilization for Human Betterment: A Summary of Results of 6,000 Operations in California, 1909–1929* and *Twenty Eight Years of Sterilization in California*. Kline found support for eugenic sterilization in "thousands of letters from students, professors, ministers, rabbis, social workers, public health and welfare workers, Rotary Club members, physicians, librarians, birth-control advocates, and Parent Teacher Association members."[50]

Eugenics also received some support from women in the "helping professions" and in reform work. In North Carolina, social workers sometimes threatened removal of welfare benefits to women who refused sterilization. These kinds of practices unfortunately were related to the idea of the new special training presumably required in the age of "scientific motherhood." Some women even nominated their neighbors as candidates for sterilization. *Los Angeles Times* columnist Fred Hogue noted in 1936, "In casting over my correspondence on Social Eugenics . . . I find there is a growing interest in a more extended enforcement of State sterilization laws. This increasing interest comes chiefly from women, most of whom are mothers. Many letters come from women who confide to me . . . conditions of families in their immediate neighborhood. They see families of subnormals, both mentally and physically, increasing without let or hindrance."[51]

Margaret Sanger's own writings on eugenics support the connection between well-trained "modern" motherhood and the desire for healthy bodies as well as healthy minds. In a piece called "No Healthy Race without Birth Control" she claimed, "Our girls must be brought up to realize that Motherhood is the most sacred profession in the world, and that it is a profession that requires more preparation than any other open to women." Quoting her friend Marie Carmichael Stopes, British author of the scandalous sex advice book *Married Love*, Sanger claimed one of the basic rights of babies was "to be given a body untainted by a heritable disease."[52]

The support for eugenics from Margaret Sanger and the American birth control movement probably had limited impact on enhancing public opinion. The men of eugenics largely wanted nothing to do with her cause. They found birth control too controversial as it was associated with women's potential freedom from motherhood. Still, Sanger was willing to associate herself and her agenda with eugenics. The record shows that she not only failed to object to coerced sterilization, but she also actively sought support from eugenicists, including the scientists and academics, because she believed their scientific credibility would help protect her from religious opposition to birth control. Eugenics also had the advantage of providing a language of "racial betterment" of the population and of "fitter families," as opposed to the more controversial discussions of women's sexual freedoms. Sanger modified her own language accordingly. Birth control was where "a true eugenic approach to social change must begin," she claimed. She argued that eugenic research showed that "uncontrolled fertility is universally correlated with disease, poverty, overcrowding, and transmission of hereditable traits." She even proposed in an address to female college students that the government should provide a bonus payment to "obviously unfit parents" who chose to be sterilized and take "the burdens of the insane and feebleminded from your backs."[53]

Nevertheless, echoing her socialist and feminist roots, Sanger leaned more toward blaming the harsh environments of the poor than their genes, even as eugenic mania ascended in the 1920s and 1930s. She also objected to the racial and ethnic stereotyping used by eugenic supporters of immigration restriction. The American Birth Control League, when given the opportunity to align with the American Eugenics Society, rejected the idea. Sanger tempered her language about the "unfit" with frequent assertions that, in general, women would use the opportunity of real reproductive choice wisely, if it were given, by adjusting their fertility to their income and circumstances. Her primary emphasis remained on freeing women from "enforced maternity," and she made the case that doing so would not only address the weaknesses in the American population but also save families by saving women:

> Equipped with the instrument of birth control, the mother regains not only mastery of her procreative function, but an immeasurably increased sense of power over life itself. Thus quite aside from its economic and eugenic aspects—the importance of which I am in no sense seeking to minimize—the practice of birth control brings with it inestimable physical benefits. A whole sphere of life—the sexual—is elevated from the level of the purely instinctive and fortuitous and submitted to intelligent direction. . . . And so between husband and wife mental and spiritual bonds are strengthened and vitalized.[54]

Though ordinary women rarely asked for birth control with reference to spiritual bonding, some did draw on eugenic thinking as a rationale for their pursuit of contraceptive information. Mrs. T.M. of North Dakota, for example, wrote, "The other day I read a letter in a daily paper from a woman who said parents have no right to bring more children into the world than they can properly take care of and educate." She suggested that with seven children already at the tender age of twenty-two, she might be one of these people. Meanwhile, in an era of heightened attention to heredity, we also see eugenic thinking in the way women began to worry about whether they would have "normal babies." Some women seemed to have made sense of their own situations in the language of eugenics. One woman who had been sterilized said she was no longer afraid "of giving birth to kiddies who would or might not be normal" even though she already had three "bright wholesome youngsters." Another woman, who had never run afoul of institutional sterilization programs, wrote to the Human Betterment Foundation expressing her concerns about being engaged to "a young man who is very brilliant mentally and in very good health physically" but did have "one physical defect. His ears are smaller than normal." She herself had "somewhat the appearance of being upside down . . . I have been advised by a physician that if we have children it may result in something degenerate."[55]

Eugenic attitudes also affected parents of children with abnormalities at birth and with a range of disabilities. In the 1910s, Chicago physician Harry J. Haiselden created a stir when he admitted to having secretly withheld surgical treatment from a number of infants with severe problems (some of whom might well have not lived through the surgeries). The case to which he publicly confessed was that of Baby Bollinger. The baby boy's problems included the absence of a neck, as well as bowel abnormalities that would require surgery, which Dr. Haiselden persuaded the parents not to pursue. The baby died six days later. The debates that followed Haiselden's admission revealed that Americans were deeply ambivalent about whether children who were then labeled "defectives" could have meaningful lives. Many newspapers ran editorials on the subject. Of those taking public positions, a sizable minority—35 percent—believed that all babies should be medically treated at birth via any available means; the other 65 percent had reservations.[56]

These anxieties were not, of course, entirely attributable to eugenics. Inoperable conditions influenced decisions about trying to save very fragile babies, as did the enormous dearth of resources available to parents whose children's challenges ranged from spina bifida to the inability to walk. For children with severe physical or mental disabilities, institutionalization was widely promoted. Haiselden in fact justified his practices with the claim that children like the ones he admitted to allowing to die had a better fate than those subjected to the often horrific conditions of institutions that housed a variety of children with disabilities.[57]

We also know that eugenic thought heightened the onus on children who did not measure up to genetic norms and that such norms were clearly not objectively measured. Most prominent eugenic spokespersons, preferring sterilization of prospective parents, stopped short of advocating euthanasia for "defective" infants. Eugenicists John Harvey Kellogg and Paul Popenoe found it old-fashioned to "kill off the weakling's born," which was "nature's way, the old method of natural selection." Modern sterilization practices could now do this work instead. Parents who knew they had defects should permit themselves to be sterilized. Heiselden wrote, "Sterilize defectives for three generations, and we shall have no Bollinger baby cases to worry us. When parents come to realize fully that a child is deficient—I do not mean insane to the point of idiocy alone, but whenever the child is subnormal—they should permit sterilization."[58]

Though physicians and psychologists claimed they could chart normal developmental milestones for babies and children in this new modern era, in reality, distinguishing normal from "degenerate" or "defective" was anything but simple. Perhaps most important for the history of motherhood, what Wendy Kline has called a new "reproductive morality" took hold in this period: only fit mothers should reproduce. Historians of eugenics duly acknowledge that there may have been women and men who benefited from sterilization, but it is clear that as a whole the movement was about reproducing class and racial hierarchies as well as policing women's sexuality. Eugenics' stain on American history even includes the fact that Nazi Germany modeled its sterilization laws to deal with its "unfit" populations on California's law. The German legislation led to the sterilization of more than 350,000 Germans. One prominent American eugenicist, Paul Popenoe, even praised Adolf Hitler's German government for developing a eugenics program that was in "accord with the best thoughts of eugenicists in all civilized countries."[59]

Conclusion

For a brief moment in the 1910s, social visionaries and radicals envisioned not just reproductive control but also reproductive freedom as an essential component of women's full personhood and citizenship. But the ink was hardly dry on the radical phase of Sanger's incendiary publication *The Woman Rebel* when conservative opposition, eugenic arguments, and physician-controlled birth control and abortion access began to undermine the cause of genuine reproductive choice for women. Similar to the way that the high hopes for the settlement house devolved into surveillance over poor families, a movement promising uplift of women through reproductive control happened simultaneously with and contributed to one of the bleakest chapters in American social and cultural history. Eugenics, the science of "racial betterment" through selective breeding, trumped arguments for either female self-determination or improved maternal health. Gender, race, and class anxieties forestalled an expansion of the range, effectiveness, and practice of available reproductive technologies that women could control. The underlying anxiety about who was to participate in motherhood and on what terms continues to inform public debate up to the present day.

Yet this era's story of reproductive control and hopes for reproductive freedom can be understood triumphantly as well as tragically. Some of Margaret Sanger's more optimistic vision came to be realized over the course of the century. Modern women did indeed take reproductive control into their own hands. Between 1900 and 1929, the birth rate declined by one third, continuing the long-term trend documented over the course of the nineteenth century.[60] By the middle of the twentieth century, some battle lines drawn over women's reproductive rights would give way, at least for a time. As the nation emerged from the Great Depression in the early 1940s, it was becoming the sensible and modern thing for mothers to use "family planning" to space their children. More concerted feminist and antiracist efforts were necessary to budge the restrictions on abortion and finally end the practice of coerced sterilization that greatly limited the choices of women made vulnerable by poverty and racism. Yet the advocates for birth control, however contorted their message, opened doors that would eventually liberate many women from "compulsory maternity." Through reproductive rights, more women than ever before would ultimately enjoy at least the partial fulfillment of the modern promise of freedom for humans, even mothers and potential mothers, to exert more control over their destiny.

CHAPTER 7

Mothers' Resilience and Adaptation in Modern America

Remembering her years with her children in the early twentieth century, Mrs. Nishimura, a first-generation Japanese American (*issei*), told an interviewer, "My happiest time was then, when my children were small. I was poor and busy then, but that might have been the best time. It was good to think about my children—how they'd go through high school and college afterwards." Similarly, an African American mother reminisced, "I tell you I feel really proud and I really feel that with all the struggling that I went through, I feel happy and proud that I was able to keep helping my children, that they listened and that they all went to high school. . . . I really feel proud, even though at times the work was very bad and I came home very tired."[1]

By now it is clear to readers of this book that the realities of mothers' lives were shaped by powerful forces over which they sometimes had no control. The historians who reveal to us the laws, cultural attitudes, and economic conditions that either hindered women's ability to care for their children to the best of their ability or forced women into—or out of—the role of motherhood do a great service. These researchers illuminate patterns that are still very much with us in today's world: mothers, and women generally, still have little say in social policy, command less economic power than men, and confront various cultural norms that shape a continued motherhood mandate and a constrained, arguably impossible, definition of good mothering.

But as these examples suggest, there is always more to the story. Even with limited documentation of mothers' identities and relationships in their own words, social historians, collectors of folklore and letters, and writers of memoirs and poetry have also left other kinds of stories about motherhood in this modernizing era before World War II. Some strands of what we have collectively saved in our cultural memory speak to powerful and life-affirming patterns of maternal resilience, resistance, and joy. Motherhood was central to the identities of the vast majority of women who lived in this and other historical eras. Then, as now, mothering children was a labor of love, a source of pride, a sense of accomplishment, and an expression of connection to humanity.

Deep attachments to children continued well beyond the years of babyhood and childhood and spanned divergent experiences of race, class, and ethnicity. Mothers of grown children often expressed how deeply their lives were grounded in motherhood. One middle-class mother who learned that her daughter was expecting a baby wrote, "I just cried tears of joy, for I know now my little Darling will never be lonesome again, and with such a dear Husband & baby why Lydia you will come into your joys at last." Another wrote candidly to her daughter, "Daughters are wonderful luxuries; they are well worth a bad husband in my opinion: at least mine are." Grandmothers often continued the work of mothering, helping to rear another generation of children. Jewell Prieleau, an African American woman who worked in white women's kitchens throughout her life, helped take care of her grandchildren and invested energy and hope in her involvement with them. She recalled, "I went to three nice department stores and I opened up credit for them so I could send them to school looking nice. I got up early in the morning and sent them off to school. After school I would pick them up in a taxi and bring them here [to her job]."[2]

To see history through mothers' eyes, we must explore these stories. They are all the more meaningful in light of the challenges mothers faced while doing the cultural work assigned to them. By focusing attention on maternal resilience and adaptation in the late nineteenth and early twentieth centuries, we can also learn much about the limits of social welfare programs, anxiety-producing medical advice and advertisements, and even the exclusively mother-focused caregiving ideal that was imagined and promoted by the dominant culture. When looking at the evidence through this lens, we find that most mothers were not passive victims of modernization and its challenges. Indeed, many proved quite adept at developing familial strategies to help them gain new resources, both within and beyond their communities. Mothers preserved cultures, reconfigured family life, maintained family and community ties, and sometimes found new tools to protest as they navigated the shifting roles of women and conflicting cultural messages about motherhood.

LABORS OF LOVE: SUSTAINING FAMILY AND COMMUNITY

Mothers' extensive labors in industrial America were often unpaid, undercounted by economists, and undervalued in a culture enthralled with the image of brawny "working men" (the *real* workers) and railroad and banking magnates (the *real* wealth producers). Family memories, however, suggest another story. At a time when millions of families still worked together on farms, in small shops, and in labor-intensive housework, children appreciated their mothers' work and frequently participated in it. Agnes Smedley, for example, writing in 1929, recalled her time doing laundry with her single mother in her autobiographical novel, *Daughter of the Earth*: "I wrung and hung out clothes or carried water from the hydrant outside.

She and I were now friends and comrades, planning to buy a washing machine as we worked. We charged thirty cents a dozen pieces for washing and ironing, but the women always gave us their biggest pieces—sheets, tablecloths, overalls, shirts."[3]

Children whose mothers played indispensable roles in maintaining family and community ties often had keen memories of the traits they admired in their mothers. Their memories suggest something of the pride the mothers themselves must have taken in their work. "My mother was always very hardworking, even as a child," Soccorro Felix Delgado recalled of his childhood in 1930s Arizona. "She would get up real early in the morning and wash the dishes in a *tina*. They had to draw water from a well because they had no sink." A Hispanic daughter remembered her mother's extensive labor running a boarding house, selling chickens and turkeys, making *carne adobada* from pigs slaughtered by her father, and serving as a midwife for women in the community. During butchering and preservation time, she recalled, "Everyone pitched in. The fat would be strained and collected in cans and saved. This is the lard that my mother used for cooking. I tell my kids that I love all those foods because I was raised with them." Across the country, in rural Wisconsin, Ho-Chunk (Winnebago) women recalled that their mothers "did everything," from preparing food over open fires and gathering sap for maple syrup to beadwork and basket-making, and they taught those skills to their daughters. From her mother, Ruth Cloud remembered, "I learned how to do a lot of things. I'd watch her and she'd be down there by the river . . . [gathering maple sap, with help from the kids]. . . . We'd sit down there and cook our bread down there."[4] The admiration of daughters in particular came in part from being socialized into roles as future mothers, wives, culture keepers, and workers for the family's survival. Especially in the early twentieth century and among more rural families, daughters did not doubt that they would use these same skills in their lives.

The connections between mothers and their children, and often other intergenerational female connections, were maintained through the cultural preservation work of mothers. Mothers may have disagreed widely on the issue of whether and how much to embrace the new modern American cultural norms, but they still took significant responsibility for acculturating their children. Fathers and other kin were of course involved as well, and often men's cultural authority was greater than women's within their communities, even for groups that were not part of the dominant culture. Jewish men, for example, were the official keepers of religious knowledge as the readers of the Torah. But across the segments American society culture flowed from and was sustained by mothers in countless ways. Women created fiestas, organized family weddings and other community events, and served as models and guideposts for their children in changing times. The son of immigrants, Mike Gold remembered the role his mother played in sustaining community life in rich detail. She "was always finding people in trouble who needed her help. She helped them for days, weeks and months with money, food, advice, and the work of her hands. She was a midwife in many hasty births, a nurse in sickness, a peacemaker in family battles." An immigrant daughter, Letitia Serpe, recalled her mother's role in her wedding, always a highly charged moment for intergenerational bonds: "I got married in Mama's store," she remembered. "Mama went all out for my wedding. Even though we didn't have a lot of money, she gave me a beautiful wedding. Everyone was there, the whole family, all the friends, practically the whole neighborhood. Mama gave me a beautiful trousseau . . . all kinds of beautiful linen that she embroidered herself."[5]

Mothers and grandmothers transmitted culture through songs, stories, and the teaching of skills, especially during time spent with children doing shared work. Ho-Chunk women in Wisconsin could recall many years later the songs their mothers sang to them as children. One Ho-Chunk woman, Irene Thundercloud, described the sense of belonging created for her by spending time with both grandparents, though she focused on the beadwork skills her grandmother taught her:

> In the summertime my sister and I used to go visit, stay with my grandparents all summer. . . . My grandpa woke me up real early. He was singing the morning song. I knew he'd done that every morning. . . . I got up and my grandma and I went to bathe in the crik. That was a ritual we had to do every day. So her and I went swimming and we come back and we got breakfast ready and the fastest dishwashing I ever did was that morning, 'cause I was so anxious to get started with the beads. I was so impatient, trying to hurry, that right away I cut the thread . . . she said take your time, she said, so she showed me again with her second needle.

A daughter of Mexican immigrants remembered, "My mother . . . never tired of telling us stories of our native village in Guanajuato; she never let us children forget the things that her village was noted for, its handicrafts and arts, its songs and its stories. She made it all sound so beautiful. . . . From the time I was a small child I always wanted to go back to Mexico and see the village where my mother was born."[6]

It was also incumbent upon less privileged women to socialize children, perhaps especially daughters, to be resilient in the face of hard work and uncertain results. The novelist Zora Neale Hurston expressed the patterns she saw in African American culture in her story of a young woman whose mother told her: "You got de spunk, but mah po' li'l' sandy-haired chile goin' suffer ah lot 'fo' she git tuh de place she kin 'fend fuh herself. . . . And Isie, honey, stop cryin' and lissen tuh me. Don't you love nobody better'n you do yo'self." Daughters, however, sometimes expressed ambivalence in their descriptions of their mothers' seemingly endless labor. Jewish writer Anzia Yezierska remembered that her mother "dried out her days fighting at the push-carts for another potato, another onion into the bag, wearing out her heart and soul and brain with the one unceasing worry—how to get food for the children a penny cheaper."[7]

Daughters from impoverished families could especially see that sacrifice was the lot of mothers of little means. Even the social science research on immigrant families of the early twentieth century documented this reality. For example, researchers found that Italian immigrant mothers, who handled the family cash flow, habitually shortchanged themselves on small discretionary purchases, such as clothing, even when their family's income increased. The Japanese American mothers interviewed by Evelyn Nakano Glenn showed great pride in their abilities as mothers, including their capacity to sacrifice and to "bear it all."[8]

The dominant American culture, social welfare policies, and the incorporation of immigrant and Native American groups into American legal definitions of the male-headed nuclear family made it difficult for many women to claim their bread-winning roles. For example, both Native American women and Hispanic women lost traditional property rights through the imposition of American legal norms. But it was harder to squelch the sense of entitlement to the fruits of women's bread-winning labors. One Hispanic woman boldly claimed a right to half the property in her husband's estate in 1900 even though it was all in his name because "all know that I worked as much as my husband and spent less than he and our son. My husband always told me that for my work half was for me, that it was not owed me except that I had earned it."[9]

WORKING-CLASS MOTHERS, MOTHERS OF COLOR, AND FAMILIAL SURVIVAL

These stories remind us of the continuing need for collective survival strategies of the majority of mothers in the United States—those mothers who were working-class, poor, and/or not part of the dominant Anglo American culture. An under-developed social welfare state and the absence of a strong union movement before the 1930s to lift the floor of industrial wages meant that families had to try to pro-vide their own insurance against disaster.[10] This was true for struggling rural families as well. For families of color, racism compounded the necessity to create flexible familial roles for familial survival. Indeed, in all areas of production, exploiting labor was a higher national policy priority than familial preservation. To cite two prominent examples, most Chinese Americans were not even allowed to form families for decades: only men were permitted to enter the United States, and anti-miscegenation laws prevented their intermarriage with white Americans. Similarly, in the Great Depression, thousands of Mexican American families were disrupted by coerced deportation. They or their ancestors had been invited in as inexpensive labor, but in the 1930s they were seen as competition for struggling white workers. In these situations, family ties were strained sometimes to the breaking point.

Essentially the working-class nuclear family unit was too vulnerable—to illness, industrial layoffs, death, eviction, deportation, and other manifestations of eco-nomic insecurity—to go it alone. Unlike the middle class, Stephanie Coontz has observed, "the working class family . . . put forward neither privacy nor escape from community obligations as an ideal." Kin, neighbors, ethnic organizations that pro-vided noncommercial life insurance, and community organizations were necessary to provide a security net. For working-class and poor families of color (that is, the vast majority of families of color), the family and ethnic community could be a haven from Anglo American hostility and ignorance and a resource base.[11] To the best of our knowledge, all cultures assigned the care of young children to women, especially mothers, when possible. But flexible roles—breadwinning, caregiving, and all the rest—were necessary for most people outside the white middle class.

Figure 1: Surviving portraits of motherhood in the American colonies are often stiff, formal, and much less sentimental and suggestive of physical closeness than more modern images. Babies and children often have adult proportions. The baby's posture also suggests Puritan notions of a quick babyhood, in which children are encouraged to stand on their own and become independent.

IMAGE © WORCESTER ART MUSEUM

Figure 2: By the 1830s, motherhood had become highly sentimentalized in the popular culture. Many commentators emphasized mothers' unique influence on babies and children and insisted that women's "sphere" was domestic and maternal, while men's domain was public and concerned with breadwinning and politics. The isolated middle-class home depicted in popular imagery was far from the norm in American society. Such ideals coexisted uneasily with the realities of early industrialization in the North, in which women needed to earn wages, and of slavery in the South, where families were frequently separated.

Figure 3: Officers of the Women's League of Newport, Rhode Island, these women represent the millions of African American women organized into clubs, many of which operated under the umbrella organization, the National Association of Colored Women, founded in 1896. Through such civic organizations, African American women developed a strong tradition of public motherhood by organizing to meet the needs of their families and communities in areas such as health care and education.

AFRICAN AMERICAN PHOTOGRAPHS ASSEMBLED FOR 1900 PARIS EXHIBITION.
PRINTS AND PHOTOGRAPHS DIVISION, LIBRARY OF CONGRESS

Ask Your Doctor First, Mother

Before You Give Your Child An Unknown Remedy to Take

According to any doctor you may ask, there is one duty every mother owes her child. The duty of asking *him* before giving her child an *unknown* remedy to take.

Yet, unthinkingly, every day mothers violate this simple rule. Take the advice of unqualified persons—instead of their doctors'—on remedies for their child.

If they knew what the scientists know, they would *never* take the chance.

Doctors Say PHILLIPS' For Your Child

When it comes to the very frequently used "milk of magnesia," authorities stand solidly together.

Ask your own doctor about

Safety for You and Yours

You can assist others by refusing to accept a substitute for the genuine Phillips' Milk of Magnesia. Do this in the interest of yourself and your children—and in the interest of the public in general.

this. For over 50 years, doctors, whose life work it is to study the safety and quality of drugs that go into the home, have said "PHILLIPS' Milk of Magnesia for your child."

For "*Phillips'* " is the result of over a half century of continuous laboratory experiment. And is rated among the finest products that science knows in its field, the kind of product your child deserves.

So *Always* Say "Phillips' " when you buy. And see that your child *gets* what you ask for—Genuine *Phillips'* Milk of Magnesia. Do this for your own peace of mind.

PHILLIPS' *Milk of Magnesia*

Figure 4: Around the turn of the twentieth century, physicians claimed increasing legitimacy in the arena of infant and child nurture. Public health campaigns and advertising reinforced physicians' authority and gave women the message that the modern mother deferred to expert advice.

"STEP ON IT, MOTHER ► THIS ISN'T THE POLKA"

MODERNIZING MOTHER ... *Episode Number Four*

THE HAPPY RHYTHM of her youth, the buoyancy, sparkle and zest of all her ways, her self-reliance and sanity — it is these charms of the modern daughter which are tempting the world away from old-fashioned ideas — preaching the new thought of not growing old.

In a gloomier age, women were resigned to drudgery. Today, young womanhood does not permit drudgery to cloud her joy of living. She is the champion of every new device which adds to the pleasure and ease of existence.

It is this eagerness of youth for something better which has won for Modess, in so short a time, a nation-wide popularity. For Modess is infinitely finer — more comfortable, safer.

The softness, pliancy and gracious ease of Modess are due to the remark-able new substance of which the filler is made. This filler is as fluffy and downy as cotton, amazingly absorbent and instantly disposable. There are no square edges to irritate — the sides are smoothly rounded. For still greater comfort, the gauze is cushioned with a film of cotton.

Modess is made in one size only because its greater efficiency meets all normal requirements without readjusting size of pad. A box lasts longer.

Modess is deodorizing. Laboratory tests prove it to be more efficient in this respect.

You are sure to prefer Modess — every woman does. Since it costs no more — why not try it?

Johnson & Johnson
NEW BRUNSWICK, N.J., U.S.A.
World's largest makers of surgical dressings

Modess

(Pronounced Mō-dess')

Figure 5: Consumer advertising repeatedly sent a message to mothers: they needed to accommodate their adolescent children's more modern sensibilities in fashion, hygiene, entertainment, and even dating, rather than dragging children down with old-fashioned ways. Modess created a large advertising campaign around this theme in the 1920s.

AD* ACCESS ON-LINE PROJECT—AD #BH0110, JOHN W. HARTMAN CENTER FOR SALES, ADVERTISING & MARKETING HISTORY, DUKE UNIVERSITY DAVID M. RUBENSTEIN RARE BOOK & MANUSCRIPT LIBRARY HTTP://LIBRARY.DUKE.EDU/ DIGITALCOLLECTIONS/ADACCESS/

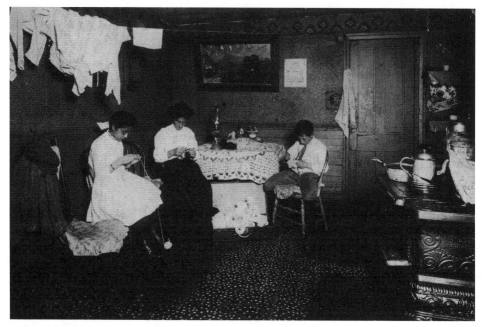

Figure 6: Between about 1890 and 1940, the pace of modern industrial life increased rapidly. Urban working-class mothers needed to find ways to bring cash into their homes while also fulfilling their caregiving duties. Children often helped with cash-producing activities like light assembly work at home (known as "homework"). These children were working on crochet slippers. Older girls were also expected to help care for younger children.

Figure 7: This photograph was captioned "A menace to society." The family was illiterate, the mother and children were employed, and there was no mention of a male breadwinner. An "investigator," probably a social worker, had found this family's "Home in utter neglect; filthy and bare." The mother had left the children inadequately supervised, the investigator claimed. The situations of impoverished mothers and children provoked for many Progressive-era Americans the ideas of either uplifting them through education or financial assistance or eliminating their "defective" genetic stock through eugenic sterilization programs (see chapters 5 and 6).

Figure 8: Margaret Sanger, pictured here holding her son, was the twentieth century's most famous crusader for contraception for women. She coined the term "birth control" and defied the laws that prohibited distribution of contraceptive information. Sanger opened the nation's first birth control clinic, founded the organization that would become Planned Parenthood, and contributed to research into new contraceptive methods, including the Pill. She linked birth control not only to a modern, free motherhood but also to disturbing notions of population control.

Figure 9: Despite efforts to homogenize motherhood in the name of modernization, many mothers continued traditional mothering practices, which were connected to their multifaceted familial, community, and cultural roles, as described in chapter 7.

PRINTS AND PHOTOGRAPHS DIVISION, LIBRARY OF CONGRESS

Figure 10: Well into the twentieth century, rural children continued to help mothers with various kinds of labor-intensive domestic and agricultural work in the era before modern conveniences, such as washing machines and indoor plumbing.

Figure 11: First issued in 1946, Dr. Benjamin Spock's best-selling *Baby and Child Care* was the most widely read child-care advice book ever. It influenced generations of mothers and epitomized the twentieth-century trend of male experts instructing mothers in all matters of child care.

Figure 12: Carolyn Teach Denlinger, pictured here with her family in the 1950s, epitomized the baby boom era's trend of youthful marriage and the creation of large nuclear families. Women of this era bore more children, on average, than their grandmothers had, despite widespread access to birth control for married couples. Yet many women chafed at the confines of rigidly defined gender scripts for mothers. Their sense of confinement fueled Second Wave feminist activism on a variety of issues related to motherhood.

Figure 13: The National Welfare Rights Organization represented one many of social movement challenges to the public policy structures that left mothers' work underresourced and undervalued. A wide array of related mothers' protests challenged established expertise and entrenched power structures in the 1960s and 1970s, as women demanded abortion rights, an end to sterilization abuse, more autonomy in childbirth, and improved community resources for child care, child safety, education, and more.

PHOTO BY W. H. SPRADLEY, NATIONAL PARK SERVICE U.S. DEPARTMENT OF INTERIOR, MAY 13, 1968. JACK ROTTIER PHOTOGRAPH COLLECTION, COLLECTION #C0003, SPECIAL COLLECTIONS AND ARCHIVES, GEORGE MASON UNIVERSITY

Figure 14: By the 1980s, it was becoming increasingly common for mothers with young children to participate in the labor force. Many women embraced the possibilities of expanded juggling acts and professional opportunities, but Americans also displayed deep ambivalence about the rapid changes in female life patterns around work and caregiving, which occurred simultaneously with new rights for women gained through feminist activism.

© CLASSICSTOCK/MASTERFILE

Figure 15: By the 1990s, American families were rapidly diversifying. Lesbian mothers, mothers whose families crossed the age-old boundary of race, and mothers who did not marry all pioneered new family forms and pushed for more rights for their families and for broader definitions of motherhood.

© GIGI KAESER, FROM THE BOOK/EXHIBIT *LOVE MAKES A FAMILY: PORTRAITS OF LESBIAN, GAY, BISEXUAL, AND TRANSGENDER PEOPLE AND THEIR FAMILIES* (AMHERST: UNIVERSITY OF MASSACHUSETTS PRESS, 1999). COURTESY OF FAMILY DIVERSITY PROJECTS. WWW.FAMILYDIV.ORG

Even the small and perpetually vulnerable African American middle class had high rates of labor force participation for mothers. Self-employed Asian American agricultural producing families in the West relied heavily on the labor of every family member. Most Native American tribes, in the midst of massive social and economic transformation in the reservation era, continued to rely on both the reproductive and frequently shifting income-producing labor of women. White working-class families also used mothers' wage labor or "piecework" at home when necessary, especially for families in which the male breadwinner worked in low-paying, volatile, or seasonal industries. On average, such women's work contributed one-quarter of their families' income.[12]

For working-class women, devotion to their children was often expressed in different ways than the model lauded by the dominant culture. Providing for children often involved the creation and maintenance of extensive ties beyond the nuclear family. Approaches to family and community networks differed significantly by culture, but the variety does not overshadow the common theme of going beyond the nuclear family for support with childrearing. For example, Hispanic families in the Southwest continued traditions of appointing comothers for their children by formalizing bonds of emotional and practical interdependence among families. Japanese American families sometimes sent children back to Japan to be cared for by relatives so that both parents could earn money in the United States. In African American communities, grandmothers, aunts, and community members participated in othermothering, as they had done since the era of slavery. Ella Baker, a civil rights activist who grew up in poverty as a sharecropper, recalled, "My aunt who had thirteen children of her own raised three more. She had become a midwife, and a child was born who was covered with sores. Nobody was particularly wanting the child, so she took the child and raised him . . . and another mother decided she didn't want to be bothered with two children. So my aunt took one and raised him . . . they were part of the family."[13]

As we have already glimpsed in the power struggles over the distribution of charity, when mothers knew they had to earn wages to support their families, little could stop them—not charity caseworkers, not the dominant culture's glorification of the at-home mother, and not even the limited availability of work that paid them a living wage. Indeed, the notion of women providing materially for their families was traditional in many cultures that made up the industrial United States. Evelyn Nanako Glenn says, "The ability to provide for their children fulfilled *issei* [first-generation Japanese American] women's deeply ingrained belief in *oyakoku*, the reciprocal obligation that existed between parent and child." She described an example of a woman who "felt less victimized than her mother because in America she was able to work to support herself and her children," despite the fact that her husband frequently drank away the family paycheck.[14]

Mothers' flexibility in pursuing wage-earning when necessary was reflected in the ways in which they arranged for and shared child care within their families and neighborhoods. Working-class mothers used shifting strategies to accommodate their need for help with child care while they worked within and beyond the home.

Illness, widowhood, accidents, and financial destitution forced some mothers to seek temporary or permanent relief from the financial and physical burdens of caring for young children. Mothers boarded children with neighbors or nearby kin, a situation that allowed them flexibility and frequent contact with their children. Some mothers, historian Ruth Porter Benson found, also foisted their offspring "on unwilling kin." More common was the hope of mothers to be reunited with their children; for example, an Oklahoma widow's children were in different places, and she told a Women's Bureau agent that "when she can get caught up, the mother would like to find a house where she could have all the children at home together."[15]

While today's older siblings are generally expected to be attending to their own education and personal development, so mothers and fathers can count on only limited help from them, expectations were quite different just several generations ago. Families often relied on older siblings to do child care, especially in times and places where compulsory school attendance was not in place or in which a mother's labor force participation made more sense than sending an older child into the workforce. Mothers relied on older girls as "little mothers," even when the mothers did not need to leave the home to earn wages. This was especially common in large families or in situations when the mother was busy tending to piecework or laundry for cash, the needs of boarders, or simply the heavy demands of household production and cleaning described in chapter 6. Sydney Stahl Weinberg points out in her study of early twentieth-century urban Jewish immigrant families, "Generally, older daughters were expected to act as their mothers' chief assistants in caring for the home and younger children. Many older daughters felt overworked by their duties, cooking and cleaning and watching over their siblings. Some even took charge completely while their mother was out earning a living." One such daughter lamented that she had "no freedom," and others in similar situations said they had "no childhood at all." The famous trade union organizer Rose Schneiderman, whose father died when she was nine, had to do housework, prepare meals, and care for her younger siblings while her mother worked a shift that left Schneiderman without her from 7:30 A.M. to 6:30 P.M. each day. Not until an aunt started taking care of her younger siblings could Schneiderman pursue some schooling.[16]

Though working-class boys frequently foreshortened their schooling to work for wages, they were not usually expected to participate in the care of young children.[17] For example, first-generation Italian Americans often resisted sending their daughters to school more than their sons. Sons' schooling could pay off, through the availability of vocational opportunities for skilled jobs, whereas daughters' adolescence seemed better spent bringing in income or helping with the care of younger children. Only the more financially secure Italian American families were likely to send their children to school. Similarly, Mexican American families blended cultural traditions of keeping daughters closely tied to the family, even when their labor was not immediately needed. A Hispanic San Antonio schoolteacher remarked, "Among the poorer class, the girls always do all the housework, and nursing . . . when the mother is ill. Among the middle and upper classes, the mother strives to teach the girl how to make all kinds of fancy work. . . . The daughters were usually kept in the home more than the sons, and the sons were given more responsibility and independence."[18]

In midwestern farm families, preindustrial patterns of family cooperation meant that children's labor was needed for work on the farm as well as for care of younger siblings. Mari Sandoz, a Nebraska writer who was a child at the turn of the century, recalled that "the eldest daughter of a sizable family was often a serious little mother by the time she was six, perhaps baking up a 49-pound sack of flour every week by the time she was ten." Mirroring the experiences of urban immigrants, older farm children sometimes deferred schooling in order to care for younger children or to earn wages that would allow their younger siblings to attend school. In contrast to the urban situation, the adolescent labor of boys on the farm was often valued more than that of girls so families were more likely to make schooling available to girls than to boys. One woman recalled of her adolescence in the 1920s, "Going to high school was quite a thing in those days. Very few farm girls got to go on to high school. Very, very, very few boys [did], because when they became high school age they didn't have the chance to go to school. They had to stay home to help farm."[19]

In the absence of older siblings or other adult caregivers, child care arrangements sometimes reflected mothers' desperation, stuck between family financial survival and the safety of their children. Social workers found situations in which mothers resorted to extreme measures, like Anna Lippman, who tied her baby to a chair all day and left his preschool age siblings to care for him and themselves while Lippman helped her husband with the family produce stand. One mother said that before leaving each day for her hosiery factory job, "I give them their breakfast, put the meal on the table for them, hide the matches, knives and everything that could hurt them, lock the front door and the gate in the back yard and go away." A survey of Philadelphia's immigrant neighborhoods found one-quarter of the children, most between the ages of seven and twelve, of working mothers were unsupervised during the day. During the Great Depression, Salvation Army workers found an abandoned three-month-old baby with a mother's note attached. Unemployed and single, she had gone to find work: "I will send money every week if I have it," she had written.[20]

By the 1920s and 1930s, the expansion of social work and state involvement with families discouraged the practice of leaving older siblings in charge. A family, no matter how economically desperate, risked having children removed from the home if a mother left them without adult supervision while she went to work. Combined with child labor laws and compulsory school attendance laws, attitudes toward what parents expected of older children were changing. The little mother pattern declined.[21] Safety for young children increased with these changes, but sharing the work of home care and child care between mothers and children became less common. By midcentury, mothers of young children became more isolated in their homes, without the company and assistance of older children.

In the meantime, quietly defying the breadwinner-father/caregiver-mother dichotomy, working-class fathers participated more than we may ever know in child care in the industrial era. These men were continually at the mercy of seasonal lay-offs and economic downturns that threw them out of work and washed them up on the shores of the familial home during the day while their wives worked for wages. A study of immigrant women in Philadelphia in this time period showed that "over half of these men participated in child care" and "a quarter were simply described as being helpful around the house." Unemployed fathers as well as brothers sometimes cared for younger children in New York's tenements while their wives or sisters continued the light industrial piecework that brought in a little bit of cash. Working-class men were likely to spend more time with their children than middle-class men. Class-privileged men were more likely to have steady work that kept them away from home for long hours throughout the year, leaving them less in touch with their children's daily lives.[22] In addition, white middle-class mothers were seldom pulled outside the home for labor force participation. But when mothers were absent, servants were more likely to fill in the gaps than fathers for most of this period.

WOMEN FINDING RESOURCES AND MAKING NEW DEMANDS: CREATING THEIR OWN MODERN MOTHERHOOD

The maternal strategies discussed above speak to the continuity of the roles of women, especially working-class women, as family providers and community sustainers. Industrial wage-earning was part of a tradition of using the labor of every member of the family for survival and sometimes upward mobility. But part of the story of resilience in this era can also be seen in mothers' novel adaptations to modern life. Mothers of all backgrounds saw new means of appealing to people outside their communities for assistance and guidance in performing their labors as mothers, and even in creating the kinds of family lives they wanted. Some mothers refashioned cultural ideas about family life to make new demands on state and national governments and on their husbands; some became activists in gaining resources for women's assigned role of feeding and educating their children, from organizing rent strikes to consumer boycotts to founding alternative schools.

In addition to requesting information, as mothers across the country did from the Children's Bureau, many mothers insisted on material assistance from their government. They often cited their responsibilities to support their children and keep them in school rather than in the labor force. "I am writing you to state my case to you," Mrs. J.W. Spence wrote in 1929. "I am a woman with a husband and 4 children but my husband has been down sick for two years and my oldest boy is 16 years old and I had to take him out of school . . . to help me make a living and have not been able to get any help and I have taken in washing to help make a living until my health is a wreck now." Like many other women seeking assistance in the 1920s, Mrs. Spence drew on her claims as a citizen. "Governor Carlton I certainly did all I could for you in the June primary and the very county commission I voted for in Volusia county pays no attention to the condition I am in now."[23] In their letters, women often tried to stake claims to the mothers' pensions about which they had heard but could neither find nor qualify for. They frequently justified their request for resources on the basis of the inadequacy of the male breadwinner arrangement. As "Mrs. W.S." put it in a letter to the Children's Bureau, "I have a very good husband but he has such poor health . . . [prices are] so high that we can not save a penny. . . . I can and would gladly do sewing to earn some money but can find no work like that in these times. Can you show me a way out or a way I can help myself?"[24]

During the Great Depression, mothers wrote to Eleanor Roosevelt, who reached out to American women constantly with her "My Day" column in *Ladies' Home Journal* as well as her prolific correspondence, speeches, and activist projects. Women ashamed to ask for charity felt that Mrs. Roosevelt would understand their needs as mothers, as in the case of Mrs. H.E.C. of Troy, New York, who wrote, "Please, Mrs. Roosevelt, I do not want charity, only a chance from someone who will trust me until we can get enough money to repay the amount spent for the things I need." As security on the loan she requested from the First Lady, Mrs. H.E.C. offered two family rings, one from her courtship days with her husband and another from her own mother. "Perhaps the actual value of them is not high, but they are worth a lot to me. If you will consider buying the baby clothes, please keep them (rings) until I send you the money you spent. It is very hard to face bearing a baby we cannot afford to have, and the fact that it is due to arrive soon, and still there is no money for the hospital or clothing, does not make it easier." Mrs. H.E.C. provided an entire list of clothing, blankets and diapers, asked Mrs. Roosevelt to buy them for her, and implored the first lady, "I would *rather no one knew* about it."[25]

For most mothers, resilience and adaptation meant taking advantage of opportunities that presented themselves to help rear their children. For some, however, making new demands on government and business as mothers was part of a broader activist politics that sought to put human needs above profit and to empower women in their responsibilities as stretchers of the family paychecks. As one Farmer-Labor party woman saw it, "A woman's place may be in the home but the home is no longer the isolated complete unit it once was. To serve her home best, the woman of today must understand the political and economic foundation on which that home rests—and then do something about it." On the Lower East Side of New York City, in the 1910s, socialist ideas and a volatile capitalist economy that affected rents and food prices helped fuel sporadic female-initiated rent strikes and picketing of high-priced food vendors. "My mother suggested a rent strike," remembered one immigrant daughter. "The neighbors agreed with enthusiasm."[26]

During the Great Depression, a "housewives' movement" organized on a broader scale. In cities across the country, women sought to protect themselves, their families, and their neighbors from economic ruin by organizing food boycotts and antieviction protests. They developed networks through which to barter goods for families who were strapped for cash. They voted, sometimes even ran for office on their interests as purchasers of the family goods in a cash economy, and they also insisted that government could regulate housing and food prices as well as wages.

Clara Lemlich Shavelson, a leader in this movement, provides a striking example of a mother who combined intense activism with the work of motherhood. Putting consumer and educational issues on a par with labor union empowerment, Shavelson carted her toddlers to socialist meetings. She became a "soapboxer," a speaker on neighborhood corners, and brought other housewives to her causes. She organized one rent increase strike that got her family evicted. Shavelson was one of the founders of the United Council of Working-Class Women in Brownsville, New York, an organization that developed branches in industrial cities across the country during the Great Depression. Shavelson and the United Council appealed to mothers to organize against economic injustice in the consumer realm on the basis of their interest in doing right by their children. One leaflet read, "The working class mother finds it impossible to provide her children with proper food and clothing, to which our children have a full right. The unsanitary conditions in the tenements, the poor clothing in wintertime, the lack of playgrounds and healthy recreation, lack of proper food is the reason for many diseases among the children of the working class."[27]

The movement, launching a major meat boycott that spread nationwide during the Depression, forced the closure of 4,500 butcher shops in one summer in New York City alone. In related activity, Chicago housewives gathered on the city's meat-packing plants and claimed that they knew it was not meat shortages that caused high prices. To dramatically make their point, historian Annelise Orleck recounts, "they doused thousands of pounds of meat with kerosene and set it on fire, filling the streets of Chicago with the smell of burning meat." Over that summer of 1935, housewives, activating the boycott in nearly a dozen major cities, gained national attention.[28] They organized a National Consumer's Congress in Washington, D.C., and in Washington State and Michigan elected "housewife" activists who called for government regulation of prices of essentials such as food, housing, and utilities.

The voices of similarly minded people emerged in the national Farmer-Labor party in 1936. Its platform included not just governmental price regulation but also "construction of more low-cost public housing and public schools; reform of prostitution laws; unemployment insurance; job security for working mothers; and an end to discrimination against married and older women workers; and free access to birth control devices." The movement's *Working Women* magazine published the opinion of one Bronx housewife that husbands and wives should share child care "as they share bread. Perhaps two evenings a week father should go, and two evenings, mother." Although they fell short of their often revolutionary goals, these activists did contribute to the reduction of food and rent costs and to the creation of additional public housing, schools, and parks. New York City's rent control laws and federally funded public housing were in part results of the housewife movement.[29]

Activism for many women meant time away from family life. Shavelson's children and husband supported and took pride in her work, but they also complained of her frequent absences. Shavelson's daughter remembered, "My mother didn't have to fight to be a liberated woman because my father expected that everyone would pull their own weight," but "the thing that finally upset my father was . . . he was tired of not ever seeing us. We'd never be home." Shavelson did not stop her activism. She saw her duties as a mother, family member, and activist as all of a piece. A family friend remembered that when presented with a choice between "things in the house" and "speaking in a way that [would] benefit her own children and other people around her, Clara felt she had to make the choice of going out to speak." However complex her legacy with her own family, as her friend Rae Appel said, Shavelson helped women "to become conscious of . . . their role not only as mothers and wives, because that they knew, but as part of the overall picture . . . helping to create a better world for their children."[30] In doing so, she and her fellow housewife activists helped women claim the importance of their work in the household.

Shavelson serves as a bold example of a broader sense of entitlement felt by mothers to demand the resources from government to enable them to provide for their families. Historians have told us little about the personal lives of most activists who demanded a more humane society for the next generation, besides illuminating the fact that motherhood or maternalism informed the housewives' efforts. Many of the white women who designed the social welfare programs described in chapter 5 were not mothers, though they used the maternalist rhetoric freely. African American women were more likely to combine mothering in their personal lives with activism in the public.[31] Many shared the difficulties and triumphs of Shavelson: advancing a broad social and political agenda while struggling to balance the demands of family life.

For some mothers, organized activism or individual efforts to improve their children's lives centered on educational opportunities. As high school became more available in the 1920s and 1930s, working-class parents knew that schooling offered skills for more lucrative jobs and better futures for their children. In women's letters to Eleanor Roosevelt and New Deal agency leaders, children's education was one of the most often mentioned worries. In letter after letter, mothers appealed to state and federal governments to help them find a way to keep their children out of the labor force and to pay for clothes or books required for school. Mrs. Bessie Mallett wrote to the governor of her state, "I am a widow, unable to get any employment—no income and a boy of 16 to educate and support. I am denying myself in every possible way, to put him through the last 2 years on [sic] High School, so that he will be equipped to earn his own living, and also if necessary to help me." Second-generation European immigrants increasingly placed value on their children's education, and education could be a resource for farm women hoping for different lives for their children. Especially with the stresses of the Great Depression, family farm life was in jeopardy, and mothers, more than fathers, envisioned alternative futures for their children.[32]

Despite the obstacles in their way, schooling figured into the American dreams of many families that faced discrimination on the basis of race and ethnicity. Hispanic mothers in Colorado in the 1920s confronted opposition from rural white mothers to the social mixing of children in the high schools and Parent Teacher Association meetings: "The Americans made it so plain that they were unwelcome that they didn't come again." Between 1925 and 1930, however, Hispanic youth increased their presence in Denver's public junior and senior high schools from 15 to 174, a trend that would continue.[33]

African American female activists took up the cause of founding schools in the segregated South, and individual African American women sacrificed to provide better lives for their children through schooling. One woman who worked in domestic service explained, "Strangely enough, I never intended for my children to have to work for anybody in the capacity that I worked. Never. And I never allowed my children to do any babysitting or anything of the sort. I figured it's enough for the mother to do it. . . . So they never knew anything about going out to work or anything. They went to school." Historian Bonnie Thornton Dill found that this approach to children's upward mobility was typical of the African American mothers in domestic service. But she also noted an emphasis on the dignity of all work; women encouraged the notion of children "moving up" but not looking down on their elders. The community pattern, she says, was "reinforcing the idea that while domestic service was low-status work, the people who did it were not necessarily low-status people."[34]

Mothers were not only interested in reforming a government that too often left them without resources. But many also wanted to reform the fathers of their children. Put another way, they wanted to reform the private patriarchy that, in concert with the public male-dominated world of government and the economy, shaped the conditions in which they mothered. We have already seen how some mothers vented their frustrations to the women of the Children's Bureau about husbands who did not see the need for prenatal care and caution. Other mothers wrote to the bureau about husbands who would not provide for them and asked that someone in government do something.

A woman who had given up food for her two children while pregnant with a third wrote that she had begun looking for work the fourth day after giving birth. With her newborn unable to keep down his mother's milk, Mrs. H.B. had grown frantic: "My *baby starved* and my husband *refused to provide* for us. At the end of one month my milk had dried up. . . . After Christmas, the loss of my position [made me] now unable to buy food for the baby, I must starve and also see the rest of my children do the same. At the end of 3 months my chubby little fellow that weighed 11 lbs at birth now was just merely a skeleton." A local nurse linked her to United Charities, which helped her survive. Pregnant again, with her youngest child now aged five, Mrs. H.B. was telling her story after having read an editorial titled "Save the Babies" in her local paper. She said she had experienced "only *abuse* and *torture* at the hands of the man who *promised to provide and protect woman. And no law to enforce this promise.*" Like the more privileged women who wanted to endow motherhood with financial support, Mrs. H.B. understood that public policy priorities were part of the problem: "The Soldier receive [*sic*] his pension, What do mothers receive? Abuse, torture, slurs. . . . Mothers deserving receiv[e] nothing." She suggested to the Children's Bureau that they start "an association to protect mothers who are to give birth and after that help them to help themselves, and enable them to do for their babies." Another mother asked "if there is any law in this Bureau that will help me to locate and make my husband support myself and two children, a girl aged 10 and Boy 11 yrs: he deserted his family."[35]

Some mothers in similar positions did more than write. They contested husbands' financial abandonment in court. For example, in the wake of the passage of a Texas law that facilitated lawsuits to compel support of deserted wives and mothers, many wives used these new legal means to try to obtain resources from their spouses. One woman, who had already been to court to seek custody of her children and lost, wrote to her governor, "I have no employment and am living with my Brother. And I just want to know if there is a law that can give me my children and make my Husband provide for them. I am a good mother. And as all mother's Love my children very dearly. Willing and wanting to do everything I can to make their little lives happy."[36]

Obviously, not all married women were so unhappily tied to their husbands. But these examples speak to the reasons that women seldom sought divorce, even in bad circumstances. Economic necessity kept most women married; so too did cultural and religious traditions that sanctified the maintenance of marriage. Women took great social and economic risks when they left marriages, and they often experienced guilt and shame. Minnie Ortiz divorced her husband after many years of tolerating his infidelities and lack of adequate financial support. When he hit her, Ortiz was ready to leave; once she filed for divorce, she remembered, "crying my eyes out, thinking of my shattered home life and my fatherless children."[37]

Still, women in relationships with violent men exhibited a growing willingness to seek outside help for their situations. In Linda Gordon's study of family violence between 1880 and 1960, she found that not until the 1930s did women in these situations demonstrate a broad sense of entitlement to be free of that violence and trust outside agencies to help them. For example, "In 1910 a mother who was permanently crippled by her husband's beatings, who had appeared to the police and her priest so badly bruised that they advised her to have him arrested, complained to the [social welfare agency] only about his failure to provide." This pattern began to change by the 1930s, when popular understanding of the marriage contract was also changing The mystique of the provider role became less salient because more men had greater difficulty providing and more women were earning wages. Throughout this period, women tried to protect their children from abuse even more so than themselves. Women who sought help from social service agencies, says Gordon, "believed that they were obligated to protect their children and that they could expect help from outsiders in doing so, even when they did not seek or expect help for themselves."[38]

On a more subtle level, mothers in modernizing America also sought changed relationships with the men who continued to partner with them in rearing children. Research on immigrant families provides fascinating examples. Italian American Carmella Caruso disliked her husband's control and was triumphant about the change she saw in her daughters' marriages. "I didn't like my husband ordering me around. . . . My daughters used to see how I hated the way I was treated, and now they are the boss, not the men—especially my little one. Her husband's a piece of bread. Sometimes she tosses so many words at him—this and that—and I tell her, 'Mary if your father was alive and I say words like that—bing! My teeth would be on the floor.' But Mary says, 'Hey, Ma, it's how you train 'em.'"[39]

Immigrant women often saw fathers' involvement with child care and mothers' demands for autonomy as part of the American way. Japanese immigrant Mrs. Sugihara had a husband who worked around the house, including doing dishes. She said, "He was considerably Americanized. He was young when he came over. . . . Even when we quarreled, he wouldn't hit me, saying it's bad in this country for a man to hit a woman, unlike in Japan. . . . 'Japan is a man's country; America is a woman's country,' he often used to say." Similarly, a Mexican-born man complained that his American-born wife "does not want to stay home and take care of the baby. She learned how to work in a beauty parlor and now she wants to start a parlor and make money." In another case an American-born wife said of her Mexican-born husband, "My husband is a good man—but too many kids. I am twenty-three years old and I have five. American women do not look old and tired when they are twenty-three. They are still girls. Look at me. My father picked out this husband for me, but he should have sent to Mexico for a girl."[40]

In spite of growing middle-class preoccupation with companionate marriage, many working-class women continued to define a "good husband" as a man who did his best to provide for his family, prioritized his family over other relationships, and was not abusive. Even into the 1970s, when sociologist Lillian Rubin did her research on white working-class families, these ideas persisted. As one of Rubin's informants, said, "I guess I can't complain. . . . He's a steady worker; he doesn't drink; he doesn't hit me. That's a lot more than my mother had, and she didn't sit around complaining and feeling sorry for herself, so I'm sure haven't got the right."[41] This is not to suggest that there were not deep emotional connections and effective partnerships between husbands and wives. The point is that the economic realities of women's financial dependence greatly impacted the way they viewed the social contract of husband and wife and, consequently, the complementary but precariously situated roles involved in parenting and ensuring the family's survival.

As working-class families and those on the margins of the middle class continually accommodated changing family needs, women's new marital demands were tied in part to their increasing labor force participation. All of this created conflict between traditional family ideals and reality, especially during the Great Depression. For instance, long discontent with the isolation and other limitations of farm life crystallized for many Nebraska farmwomen in the 1930s. Historian Deborah Fink observed, "Women said 'no' to the agrarian pattern in a number of ways: they left the farms in large numbers; more women who stayed remained single; more married women divorced their husbands; and women who stayed married were less tied to the farm economy than they had been previously." In an increasingly cash-dependent economy, women's need to exert some control over the discretionary spending of the male breadwinner also contributed to these patterns. Similarly, with a more interventionist state and growing urbanization, fathers continued to lose the legally sanctioned authority over their children and their wives to which they had long been entitled. For example, many fathers vocally opposed child labor laws that would deprive them of their children's labor on the farm, but over time, they lost that battle.[42]

Despite women's rebellions, there was considerable continuity in the patriarchal roles of family members. For example, though Italian and Jewish immigrants adopted the American pattern of letting children choose marriage partners in the second generation, until World War II Japanese American families continued to rely on a tradition of arranged marriages. Similarly, it was not uncommon for white midwestern farm women of the early twentieth century to remember that men had the final say in their families. "Back in those times," said one woman, "I believe the man just managed things mostly on his own. I think he was the boss. The women, I guess, more or less went along with it." Especially for poorer farmwomen, isolated by rural lives and enmeshed in family economies from which it was difficult to extricate themselves, there was often little opportunity to reshape familial relationships.[43]

More broadly, the development of a grassroots collective voice for mothers, like that seen in the housewives' movements of the Great Depression, was all too rare.[44] Few women had a say in the policies and the economic practices that shaped their family lives, and, without public power, private rebellions could only go so far. Nevertheless, the growing autonomy of family members, the increasing opportunities for and necessity of mothers' labor force participation, and a broader sense of the entitlements of mothers to recognition and resources established important precedents and contributed to the way in which ordinary women modernized the ideas of mothers' rights.

Mothers and Daughters: Friction, Flexibility, and Connection

At a time of confusing and conflicting messages about the role of women in modern life generally, mothers' ambivalence about their own lives complicated the ways in which they socialized their children, especially their daughters. In all classes, we find examples of daughters whose mothers seemed to either support patriarchal roles or resign themselves to them. In Tillie Olsen's famous short story, "I Stand Here Ironing," a mother reflects poignantly on the future of her daughter, a lively young student who sees her mother as always ironing: "'Let her be,' the mother says to herself, 'So all that is in her will not bloom—but in how many does it? There is still enough left to live by. Only help her to know—help make it so there is cause for her to know—that she is more than this dress on the ironing board, helpless before the iron.'"[45]

Historian Linda Rosenzweig found excellent evidence of the closeness between middle-class mothers and daughters in her study of letters and diaries in the Progressive era. But she also found struggles over tradition. Mothers tended to be more supportive of daughters' education and career aspirations than they were of daughters' straying from conventional sexuality or even appearance and manners. One woman remembered her mother's opinion that a woman needed to "submerge her personality" once she married. Daughters chafed under the influence of mothers who appeared to defend the sexual double standard or prescribe ladylike behavior. Bryn Mawr College founder M. Carey Thomas, never a traditionalist, wrote in her journal when she was twenty-two, "I have just had a talk with Mother and I do believe I shall shoot myself."[46] Thomas preferred studying to traditional feminine activities and questioned her family's religious beliefs; her independence in both areas apparently led to family friction. Nevertheless, Thomas's mother borrowed money to help her go to Europe for graduate education and clearly took pride in her daughter's educational accomplishments.

Resignation to traditional patriarchal family patterns was not the only issue. Mothers of older children often felt threatened by the consumer culture. Many believed their children and their family lives could be better protected from threatening modern or "American" values through the maintenance of tradition. Here the deference of children to parents was sometimes wrapped up in the deference of wives to husbands and the limitation of daughters' privileges compared to sons. "In the new and more anonymous urban world, maternal concern was tied to a fear of strangers and of unpredictable experiences," notes historian Elizabeth Ewen. Italian American Fabbia Orzo remembered that her mother was less strict with her sons than her daughters on curfew times. Jewish mothers often tried to prevent their daughters from going to dance halls. Mexican American mothers tried to exert influence over daughters' leisure activity by chaperoning them at dances.[47] Safety was a concern here, but not the only one. Parents often felt the need to guard the sexual virtue of their daughters, which was a way of protecting their marriage prospects. Across varying situations of class, race, and culture, mothers rarely wanted to gamble with what was still the best hope for economic and social stability, or even upward mobility, for their daughters: marriage to an economically stable man.

By the 1920s, with the rise of flapper culture and admiration for American movie stars growing, Mexican American young women frequently conflicted with their mothers over issues of dress and appearance as well as courtship. Bobbing hair was a statement of modernity, as was make-up. Daughters argued with both mothers and fathers about fashions such as bathing suits and bloomers and debated skirt length. The larger community also guarded tradition. "They were always spying on you," said Ruby Estreda, speaking of relatives and neighbors in her small town. Tight-knit communities and families often contained these conflicts though. Estreda said, "We took it in stride. We never thought of it as cruel or mean."[48]

Moreover, immigrant youth responded to parental concerns in part by arguing that they were embracing American traditions in order to fulfill their parents' dreams. In 1939, Dora Ibanez expressed the concerns of many second-generation Mexican Americans: "What is happening with our children? Why do they reject our behavior? . . . Don't they feel the warmth of our traditions and customs like we do?" But Ibanez encouraged parents to begin a "parallel march" with their children, who were, after all, taking advantage of opportunities in the United States. Many Mexican American parents were already on that march, but there was a constant tension between maintaining Mexican traditions and promoting Americanization.

Class made a difference. For example, in San Antonio, Texas, middle-class Mexican American organizations promoted children's education for the advancement of the community. At the same time, residential and occupational segregation promoted the maintenance of cultural traditions, as did the cross class rallying within the Mexican American community around Mexican holidays and traditions. Many mothers, especially in working-class families, kept a Spanish-speaking home, even when children went to an English-speaking school.[49]

For white middle-class women, the new consumer-oriented culture was also sometimes threatening. A generation gap emerged by the 1920s; the famous Middletown study of middle-class Indiana families found sources of contention between parents and children. These included "cigarettes," "boys," "petting parties," "bobbed hair," "playing cards," "reading too many books," "Dancing," "machine riding to other towns at nights with dates," and "evolution." One mother lamented, "You see other people being more lenient and you think perhaps that is the best way, but you are afraid to do anything very different from what your mother did for fear you may leave out something essential or do something wrong." Mothers could not remain mired in such indecision; most accommodated and compromised. One mother, for example, encouraged her daughter's membership in a limited number of high school clubs in an effort to "minimize the boy interest" by filling her daughter's time. Mothers also did their best to accommodate daughters' demands for new clothing, and some took it upon themselves to talk to their daughters about sex education, then called "sex hygiene."[50] In general, mothers tried to adapt in their childrearing to help their daughters navigate a world of new opportunities and dangers.

If mothers were ambivalent about the consumer culture, they frequently promoted new educational and occupational opportunities for their daughters. One Mexican American woman remembered that she always wanted to "be a beauty operator," and this goal was supported by her mother: "My mom pushed the fact that she wanted me to have a profession—seeing that I wasn't thinking of getting married." Mothers who were uncertain about the economic prospects of the men their daughters might marry felt it important to help daughters secure livelihoods that would offer them security. As the new century dawned, African American activist Fannie Barrier Williams observed the efforts of African American mothers to help their daughters escape domestic service occupations in which they were extremely vulnerable to sexual exploitation. "I am constantly in receipt of letters from the still unprotected women in the South," she wrote, "begging to find employment for their daughters . . . to save them from going into the homes of the South as servants as there is nothing to save them from dishonor and degradation." Historian Paula Giddings has observed that the many thousands of African American mothers who moved from the South to the North during the Great Migration, or sent their daughters north, linked daughters' safety to their hopes for their daughters' new employment possibilities.[51]

In general, the daughters of white middle- and upper-class women had the most opportunities to pursue nontraditional paths, including higher education.

Research shows a notably strong pattern of maternal support for what was, at the time, an unconventional path for daughters. When only a minuscule percentage of college-aged young women attended higher education (3 percent in 1900, for example), these women's mothers expressed extraordinary pride in their daughters as "new women." "I believe you have a future before you," wrote Eleanora Wheeler Bosworth to her college daughter. "I am proud, proud, proud of my girlie. . . . I am so glad you could go to college." Most of these mothers had not gone to college themselves, but they often provided precollege encouragement and stayed in regular contact with their daughters while they pursued higher education. "I enjoyed reading the clipping you sent," wrote one mother to her daughter, who was training for social work. "I feel proud that I have a child who can do much good."[52]

In families that could afford college, mothers also frequently encouraged daughters to pursue public life after completing higher education. "If any plan comes up that really tempts you, you and your life work, that which you have to offer the world, must be considered as of most importance," Ethel Sturges Dummer wrote to her daughter, while congratulating her on her college accomplishments. Career-oriented daughters very often continued to enjoy maternal emotional support, consulting their mothers on matters ranging from dress to romance. Crystal Eastman's unconventional life as a feminist activist was supported by her mother, and the younger Eastman never forgot it. "Oh, the unhappy people who have not you for a mother! My heart goes out to them," she once wrote.[53]

In light of the mother-teen friction resulting from new youth culture opportunities for dating, hair bobbing, and cigarette smoking in the 1920s, Rosenzweig finds more ambivalence and sometimes hostility expressed by daughters toward their mothers in this decade and beyond. Helene Harmon, for example, penned in her diary something nineteenth- and early twentieth-century daughters would have been very unlikely to express, even privately: "I have a fear of turning into the kind of person Mother is, who suddenly in middle age remembers all the things she wanted when she was young." Her words suggest how the youth culture generally would create challenges between mothers and children for decades to come. At the same time, daughters who were young in the 1920s were actually more likely to settle down and become wives and mothers themselves than women who came of age in the 1890s, 1900s, and 1910s. This pattern served to again create commonality of experiences between mothers and daughters.[54] For the time being, ties of mutuality, support, and shared experiences kept many mothers and daughters in relationships in which both parties often took great pleasure.

Conclusion

In the first half of the twentieth century, mothers' adaptability had its limits. These limits were often structural, for reasons we have been exploring for several chapters. But sometimes they were personal and idiosyncratic. In every era there surely existed mothers who were cruel, selfish, or neglectful, just as there were exceptionally loving, courageous, and inspiring ones.[55] Mothers' psychology was also shaped by their own tenuous role in a patriarchal society, and mothers' ambivalence and the compromises they made in their own lives affected how they socialized their children. Still, the strength and flexibility of maternal-child relationships is truly a striking thread in the sources we have for this transitional era in industrial America. Equally striking is mothers' general adaptability and resourcefulness when it came to mothering. They often enjoyed self-confidence in their maternal roles, in spite of all the cultural messages pushing in the opposite direction. Mothering practices and motherhood as institution often diverged.

Class, race, and cultural differences deeply influenced how women used the resources at their disposal. Racial-ethnic minority women, as well as poor and working-class women, had to be the most inventive because they faced greater obstacles and higher stakes and often suffered more devastating losses in all aspects of their family lives. Yet they persisted in using and adapting strategies for survival, including the socialization and education of their children through reliance on networks beyond the nuclear family. Although they were often at odds with the makers of social and economic policy, mothers made adaptations that kept families and communities going. They emphasized sacrifice and resourcefulness as essential to good mothering and attempted to define the meaning of those concepts for themselves. Some mothers, most notably African American and socialist-influenced women, developed broader notions of a public mothering role, one that would give women a voice in securing resources for their families.

Commonalities of experience among mothers are also significant. Mothers organized their lives around providing for their children, emotionally, materially, and culturally; in some cases, they also devoted energy to an intergenerational agenda of social change. There is no distinct body of historical literature on mothers' resilience and adaptation, but such resourcefulness is evident in every part of these stories, a thread running through the still inadequately documented history of mothering in all eras.

PART III

Mothers of Invention

WORLD WAR II TO PRESENT

CHAPTER 8

The Middle-Class
Wife-and-Mother Box

Between 1941 and 1945, the United States participated as a combatant in World War II. Mothers were expected to sacrifice on the home front, and Americans sentimentally honored the sacrifice of mothers' sons to the larger cause. Meanwhile, the nation encouraged less traditional roles for women and mothers, asking them to adapt their domestic roles with greater labor force participation to keep industrial production moving while men were at war. At the close of the war, however, many Americans grew fearful and reactionary, as they tried to come to terms with the developments of a turbulent decade and a half—the years spanning the Depression and wartime. In the immediate aftermath of the war, a McCarthyist hunt for communists and suspected subversives expressed a culture of fear and conformity. The postwar backlash was a reaction to not only the perceived excesses of leftist activists from the 1930s but also the social and cultural changes of modern life, especially in the form of nonmarital sexuality and married women's labor-force participation.[1]

Nevertheless, during and especially after the war, Americans hurtled into neo-traditional family life, exploding onto the suburban landscape and creating the twentieth century's great demographic bump: the baby boom. They did so in perhaps the century's most rigidly enforced definitions of masculinity and femininity. Despite the increasing similarity of the education of middle-class women and men, cultural commentators insisted on portraying masculinity and femininity as utter opposites. Maintaining gender distinction was a primary assignment for both parents, but mothers most especially felt the pressure to shape appropriate gender norms and to conform to those norms themselves. Experts in books and popular magazines and on television carried a relentless message to women: "accept your role" as wife and mother.

Consider the story of Jennifer Colton, who told her fellow wives and mothers "Why I Quit Working" in a *Good Housekeeping* article in 1951: "At first I found it hard to believe that being a woman is something in itself," she wrote. "I had always felt that a woman had to do something more than manage a household to prove her worth. Later, when I understood the role better, it took on unexpected glamour. Though I still wince a little at the phrase, 'wife and mother,' I feel quite sure that these words soon will sound as satisfying to me as 'actress' or 'buyer' or 'secretary' or 'president.'"[2] Ambivalence rings throughout this exposé on the life of a reformed (or almost reformed) woman who had engaged in interests that society deemed too absorbing for a true wife-and-mother.

This message of acceptance was reinforced throughout the culture, with the help of the nation's new pastime: television. Even in its early years, television was an American dreamscape, enticing viewers with the family life and products they really wanted—or were supposed to want. Programming reflected Americans' hopes and fears and, in a continuous loop, fed them new ones. Tightly scripted narratives and visual confines, in a box, seem to be an appropriate metaphor for this era in motherhood, the period roughly from 1940 to the early 1960s. The visible families who developed into archetypes by this new technology were almost uniformly white and middle class, and usually suburban. They were also deeply ensconced in rigid gender roles assigned to Mother and Father, the latter parent being the one who "knew best." TV mothers were always married, financially supported by a man, prolific in their reproduction (this was, after all, the baby boom era), and content with a life that revolved around serving the needs of children and husband. These women exercised very little initiative even within that realm. Jane Wyatt, who played the mother in *Father Knows Best*, later recalled, "My only complaint was you never saw her reading a book, or going to the office, or playing tennis. Mom always had to be around with nothing to do . . . just to say, 'wash your hands.'" She was available, but not too involved, and she exercised little real authority. Mothers who did not fit this domestic ideal, or women who were not mothers, were either invisible, suspect, or problematic characters in television and in films.[3]

In real life, of course, things were more complicated. The cultural prescriptions for motherhood were riddled with contradictions, and yet most women threw themselves into trying to be good mothers and wives. The embrace of domestic nuclear family ideals by many Americans had to do in part with their celebration of greater opportunities and safety. Many who had been children during the Great Depression of the 1930s now experienced a postwar age of affluence, better health, and economic opportunity. With the availability of antibiotics, immunizations, and other medical developments, both infant and maternal mortality had declined to all-time lows, which meant that women were able to contemplate childbirth without the fear of previous generations. They also enjoyed longer life spans and a host of modern conveniences, from the washing machine to the automobile. Yet, with the cultural emphasis on perfect homes maintained by happy housewives, even middle-class women still did as much housework, even with their new washing machines, as their mothers had done.[4]

A strong postwar economy and significant support from government policy meant that the nuclear family ideals were available to a larger swathe of the American population than ever before. The national GNP increased 250 percent between

1945 and 1960s. Between 1940 and 1960, the percentage of Americans who owned homes increased from 43 to 62. White working-class families moved to the new affordable suburbs, where 85 percent of new homes were built. Suburban living became the new ideal, though it was not available to African Americans and, in many areas, Jews. Tax exemptions for dependent children and incentives for home ownership encouraged large families. Federal financing made possible nearly half of the nation's suburban housing.[5]

This was a period of great upward mobility for Americans as real wages improved sharply, rising for men by a striking 50 percent between 1947 and 1966. Federal GI benefits, available to 40 percent of young adult men, helped millions go to college and improve their earning power. More Americans than ever before enjoyed middle-class income level, and unprecedented numbers were able to make ends meet on just one male income. Second incomes, brought in by wives, were often the key to the more comfortable middle-class lifestyle now defined as the norm. By 1960, 75 percent of Americans possessed a car, and 87 percent owned a television; women's "extra" wages helped pay for these things, along with piano lessons and family vacations.[6]

The rising tide did not lift all boats. Poverty still affected 25 percent of Americans, who at that time had neither food stamps nor federally supported housing programs and were disproportionately nonwhite. The poverty rate for two-parent African American families was 50 percent, but there were still strikingly similar family patterns across divisions of race and class. Across the board, "people married at a younger age, bore their children earlier and closer together, completed their families by the time they were in their late twenties, and experienced a longer period living together as a couple after their children left home," says historian Stephanie Coontz.[7]

This was also an age of mass psychology, and the role of motherhood became deeply imbued with psychological meaning. Midcentury mothers were charged with maintaining a precarious balancing act of availability and distance from their children. Psychological management roles had expanded to fill the energy vacuum created by freedom from the physical drudgery and the survival imperatives of their mothers and grandmothers. Mothers were also responsible for orchestrating "togetherness" for their families. They were encouraged to involve fathers in child care, especially for boys, without challenging fathers' authority and masculinity.[8] And they were expected to cultivate and carefully manage their all-important "femininity" and their roles as wives.

As childhood became more structured by organizations and experts beyond the family, mothers were also supposed to coordinate relationships with the many bureaucracies of modern life, such as schools, scout troops, and summer camp. With the advent of television and the expanded consumer culture it promoted, mothers had their work cut out for them in managing both television viewing and their children's new demands for the consumer goods they saw on TV. Although television was originally touted as a medium to bring families together, problems with children's overexposure worried mothers, and the experts reinforced their fears. A *Ladies' Home Journal* cartoon in 1950 showed a little girl who had grown "bugeyed" from watching too much television.[9]

The professional experts now gained their largest audience ever with the pervasiveness of print media as well as television and radio. Dr. Benjamin Spock's baby and child care literature became a cultural phenomenon like nothing before it. Because the suburbs were primarily made up of unrelated, young nuclear families, many young mothers were cut off from extended kin networks. This made them more open to relying on medical experts, from their prenatal care to the end of their child-rearing years. In keeping with the times, most of these experts promoted the values of pronatalism and subservient femininity; and they urged women to squelch any ambivalence about marriage and motherhood. These were the prescribed paths to female happiness and social stability. From buying the right products to looking good when a husband came home from work, mothers were repeatedly told that their job was to conform and to serve.

THE NEW MOTHERHOOD MANDATE AND THE SHAPE OF THE POSTWAR MIDDLE-CLASS FAMILY

Bearing children represented the ultimate fulfillment in postwar culture, and women in the United States far out-rivaled their nineteenth-century great-grandmothers when it came to fertility. Birthrates hit twentieth-century highs. The baby boom began to take off even during the war. Women who started their families in the 1930s bore, on average, 2.3 children, while parents in the 1950s averaged 3.2. The rate of childlessness among women fell dramatically. Couples who could not conceive sought adoption in record numbers. Another boon to fertility was the fact that marriage ages hit twentieth-century lows; it was 20.3 for women in 1950.[10]

To not be a parent meant enduring a sense of not quite being a "mature" adult or even a full member of society. Indeed, studies from the time found that only 9 percent of Americans believed a person could be happy and single. Even for men, fatherhood became, as historian Elaine Tyler May put it, "a badge of masculinity." Partly because of the era's homophobia, unmarried men (assumed not to be fathers) were characterized as "immature" or "deviant."[11] But the experts expended far more energy packaging women into motherhood than chastising men; writers and reporters linked marriage and motherhood to female normalcy as well as to psychological, physical, and sexual health.

While the ideal nineteenth-century woman was fundamentally maternal and without sexual instincts, the ideal woman of the mid-twentieth century was sexual. But she channeled her sexuality into both marriage and motherhood. In their best-selling book, *Modern Woman: The Lost Sex*, Dr. Marynia Farnham and journalist Ferdinand Lundberg explained that femininity meant "receptiveness and passiveness, a willingness to accept dependence without fear or resentment, with a deep inwardness and readiness for the final goal of sexual life—impregnation." Meanwhile, self-styled marriage saver Paul Popenoe, an advocate of "positive eugenics," published the "Can this marriage be saved?" column in *Ladies' Home Journal* for more than a decade. Popenoe argued that fertility was critical to both marital health and women's health: "children are especially needed by the wife for her own health and mental hygiene." Indeed, "a woman's body is made for childbearing and is not functioning normally unless it bears children." Echoing nineteenth-century fears about the rising rates of higher education for women, magazine articles declared that "books and babies don't mix." Educated women who chose not to have children, said one woman writer in the magazine *American Home*, were "ignorant, lazy, or selfish" and had "no place" in American society.[12]

Women's behavior in marriage was linked to the pronatalism of the era. Women were encouraged to pour their emotional energy as much into the nurture of men and the maintenance of heterosexual couples as they put into mothering. Some people even wondered if women's two occupations, wife and mother, were in conflict with each other. "Are Good Mothers 'Unfaithful' Wives?" a male author asked the readers of *Better Homes and Gardens* as early as 1941. One reformed mother whose babies "were becoming an obsession" confessed, "And as for Jim, I didn't have any time or energy left for him. He'd become part of the furniture." Ambivalence about either role was expressed in subtle ways. In one early 1960s poll, 60 percent of wives told the Gallup organization that their marriages were happier than the marriages of their parents. Yet a staggering 90 percent of women in that same poll said they wanted their daughters to live different lives than they had lived: they wanted them to marry later and achieve more education. Despite all the positive attitude toward marriage and all the conveniences, health advantages, and increased affluence of American society, about two-thirds of mothers in that poll did not believe they were doing a better job rearing their children than their mothers had.[13]

Mom's Evil Empire: Momism and Midcentury Mother Blame

Meanwhile, the confused messages about how to mother meant that getting "the role" right required at least as much care, thought, and emotional self-policing as ever before. A deeply psychologized and malicious form of mother blame emerged with the publication of *Generation of Vipers* in 1942. Author Philip Wylie's stinging diatribe castigated American mothers, demoting them to the demeaning status of "Moms" and vesting them—or at least those who deserved the label of "Mom"—with a sinister mission: depriving sons of their rightful masculinity through controlling and even monstrous mother-love. As American culture became deeply influenced by Freudian psychology, Wylie claimed to be uncovering the darker side of mother love and its negative impact on the entire society. "Disguised as good old mom, dear old mom, sweet old mom, your loving mom, and so on, she is the bride at every funeral and the corpse at every wedding," he wrote. Now "deprived of her social usefulness," thanks to modern conveniences, Mom spent her free time interfering in the lives of her sons and bringing her one-dimensional perspective to the ballot box, all in service to what Wylie called the "gynecocracy," controlled by sentimental mothers who demanded obedience or even worship.[14]

Wylie's best-selling book received enormous attention. The press covered it extensively and magazines ran excerpts; both women and men wrote him many letters. The book was revised and reprinted in the 1950s, and indeed the *Oxford English Dictionary* editors chose to offer a definition of Momism: "an excessive attachment to, or domination by, the mother."[15] Equally important, Wylie's work was complemented by similarly unsubtle, alarmist invectives against Mom. Other best-selling authors, often with more expert credentials than Wylie, blamed Mom for a range of social problems in ways that previous generations would have been shocked to imagine.

It was one thing to say, as earlier generations of experts had, that mothers did not know how to fight germs without expert help or even that their own psychological issues could affect children's psychology. It was quite another to lay at the feet of mothers (or more rightly, Moms), the problems of juvenile delinquency, neurosis, "immaturity," lack of combat readiness in soldiers, alcoholism ("mom in a bottle"), homosexuality (then defined as a social problem), and rape (the rapist's mother raised him wrong). In books like psychiatrist Edward Strecker's *Their Mothers' Sons*, Farnam and Lundberg's *Modern Woman: The Lost Sex*, and David Levy's *Maternal Overprotection* the experts did just that; they blamed mothers for a host of social ills. Connecting motherhood to national security, FBI Director J. Edgar Hoover claimed that communists and other "subversives" were frequently the products of "neurotic" mothers.[16]

Meanwhile, psychiatric and medical experts claimed that the "refrigerator mother" and the "schizophrenogenic mother" created, through either inadequate or inadequately expressed mother-love, autism and mental health problems in their progeny. The idea that mothers' and sometimes fathers' deviant sexual pasts could create birth defects had been around for some time, but by midcentury, many experts suggested that children with physical disabilities probably became that way through no fault of parents. Nature had created these problems, and many of them could be solved through science. Experts, however, frequently advised parents of neuro-atypical and developmentally delayed children to institutionalize their progeny, much as they had long advised for deaf and blind children.[17] Most ominously for mothers, between the 1950s and the 1970s, experts considered autism and schizophrenia, conditions not readily visible at birth, to be caused by a deficiency of maternal love and bonding.

The term "refrigerator mother" as a label for mothers of autistic children was coined in the 1950s by Dr. Leo Kanner. Psychologist Bruno Bettelheim further popularized Kanner's notions in his chilling but widely lauded book, *The Empty Fortress: Infantile Autism and the Birth of the Self* (1969). Bettelheim advised institutionalization and removal from the offending mother. Indeed Bettelheim ran his own institution for autistic children, the results of which he publicized, though apparently with significant exaggeration as to his success. Most mothers seem to have suffered silently through this blame. But in an era when children with disabilities lacked educational rights and related family stress frequently resulted in divorced parents, some mothers resisted expert advice and continued to work with their children. In the 2003 documentary, *Refrigerator Mothers*, Marie Boldt, mother of one child without autism and one child with the diagnosis, recalled: "I was getting treatment as a parent with this social worker and got hit with Bettelheim. So I knew what they were looking for. But I remember getting the results of all those tests and seeing for the first time what these professionals were saying about me. And it was very, very disturbing. . . . The word psychotic was mentioned at one point, a couple of times. And that was appalling to me. . . . I was nervous and overburdened and things were tough. But I was not psychotic." Even when Bettelheim's theories began to be discredited, some physicians and educational authorities still considered such children to be the broken examples of faulty mothering well into the 1990s.[18]

In the heyday of antimother ideas, some liberal authors even blamed both white and African American mothers for racism by reducing vast institutional structures and cultural attitudes to the mistakes of mothers who improperly raised sons, either as racism's victims or its perpetrators. "Matriarchal" black mothers, academic and popular writers charged, reared sons who were either too submissive or too aggressive. While earlier castigations of African American mothers had largely targeted the working class and the poor, now middle-class African American mothers were just as likely at fault. As with white women, class privilege could not protect African American mothers from charges that their adult sons might still be engaged in "a struggle for the maternal breast." At the same time, African American mothers could be blamed for qualities of self-assertion valued in white children. Mamie Bradley Till, whose fourteen-year-old son was brutally lynched in 1955, bravely exposed his mutilated body to the public in order to publicize the racism that made him a victim. But she also felt compelled to insist to the public that she had taught her son to "humble himself" to white people when necessary.[19]

Psychological critiques of mothers who were too affectionate or "smothering" began in the 1920s. Readers should recall John Watson's accusation (see chapter 4) that mother love was "at bottom, a sex-seeking response." But, as historian Rebecca Jo Plant has aptly illustrated, "antimaternalism had gone mainstream" by the 1940s, as had psychology itself, for that matter. Now even maternal self-sacrifice, the stuff of legend, was being derided in psychological terms. In Philip Wylie's youth, open affection between mothers and children was a culturally valued expression of the famed "silver cord" of love that bound them, often much more explicit—and warmly received—expressions than can be imagined today.[20] The Freudian-influenced midcentury experts, however, were appalled by such affection, which presumably damaged their sons' masculinity.

Meanwhile, in a blow to a century of assumptions about women's moral superiority due to their motherhood, midcentury critics argued that mothers wrongly and manipulatively pointed to their sacrifice, even the pains of birth, to demand emotional obedience from their children. As Strecker explained it, mothers were often "spoken of as 'giving their lives for their children.'" But "in return . . . they exact in payment the emotional lives of their children. Usually moms are paid in full." Indeed, many experts and social critics used the fact of increasingly anesthetized birth experiences to undermine old notions of maternal sacrifice. Early twentieth-century Americans had compared the national service of soldiers to that of mothers who risked their lives giving birth; many commentators now had a different view.[21]

Mothers were also no longer accorded much moral authority in the larger public world. Wylie the extremist put it this way: Mom at the ballot box and through her civic organizations "snaps independent men out of office and replaces them with clammy castrates." The most severe authors—and these were widely read—linked "Mom" and her domination to the dictatorship of Hitler. "Nazism *was . . .* a mom surrogate with a swastika for a heart," claimed Edward Strecker. He need not have worried about "Mom's" public power: women could be found in a mere 5 percent of public offices during the 1950s. In the Cold War era of macho posturing in world politics and McCarthyist finger-pointing at home, "the great mother heart," or the mother who would clean up government, could no longer move the masses. Indeed, progressive organizations often purged themselves of women to survive the McCarthyist witch hunt for communists. A fine example is former maternal agitator for working-class rights, Clara Lemlich Shavelson, discussed in chapter 7, who actually came under investigation from the House Un-American Activities Committee for her relentless pursuit of economic justice.[22]

The diatribes against mothers are striking, especially as they came within a few decades of the cultural glorification of the mother as the pinnacle of civilization, the good force in government and society, and one whose love, if not her preservation instinct, was rarely impeachable. The Momism critique provided another fulcrum on which the midcentury version of modern motherhood turned. Motherhood needed youth and vitality in this era. Sentimentality and the lionizing of maternal sacrifice were out, as were the parasitic and middle-aged women with grown children, tainted with Freudian fixations, who received the harshest judgments in the writings of Wylie and Strecker. Youthful, "detached," but ever-available mothers, feminine and even a little sexy (though only to their husbands), were in.

Wylie's book and its subsequent publicity seem to have inspired many women to try to avoid becoming Moms. As Plant points out, in the long run, Momism may have played a twisted role in suggesting that motherhood was not a lifelong occupation and that women should be individuals as well as mothers. When the children of the baby boom came of age, actual feminists took up this point with vigor. But in the short run, this was not the case. Those with cultural authority, the ones who wrote the books, nevertheless continued to chain women to domesticity by offering no viable alternative to domestic lives. They just blamed the Moms.

The criticism of Mom has to be understood in light of the fact that there were equally powerful messages to women that motherhood and marriage should be the focus of their lives. Dire consequences followed if women abandoned their "feminine role," and many experts seemed to suspect they wanted to do just that. In *Modern Woman: The Lost Sex*, the authors delineated four kinds of mothers who were responsible for the creation of "neurotics." Three of them overmothered their children: the "oversolicitous or overprotective mother," the "dominating mother," and the "over-affectionate mother, who makes up for essentially libidinal disappointments through her children." The fourth type did not mother her children enough. The "rejecting mother" was "usually too busy with something else—she may leave her [her baby] alone for long periods as it squalls in hostile protest or lies in terrified silence; or she may relegate it to the care of others." Farnam and Lundberg made no bones about their contention that women who rejected femininity or embraced feminism in any way were likely to ruin their children:

> If the girl has the good fortune to have a mother who finds complete satisfaction, without conflict or anxiety, in living out her role as wife and mother, it is unlikely that she will experience serious difficulties. If, however, the mother is beset by distaste for her role, strives for accomplishment outside her home and can only grudgingly give attention to her children, has regrets for whatever reason at being a woman, then, no matter how much or little of it she betrays, the child cannot escape the confused impression that the mother is without love, is not a satisfactory model.

Such a mother would give her daughter "no sure grasp on the solid satisfactions inherent in feminine development," and this daughter might well be poisoned in her gender attitudes by a mother that "will inject into her attitudes her own covert strivings toward masculinity." Fear of embattled masculinity was everywhere connected to fear of women's rejection of "femininity." With the significant increase in women's employment outside the home during World War II, the alarm bells had begun to sound early in the 1940s. Writing in the *Woman's Home Companion*, J. Edgar Hoover claimed that mothers who worked outside the home risked creating children who were "driven first to perversion and then to crime."[23]

After the war, British psychologist John Bowlby gained fame in the United States through his study in war-torn Europe of displaced homeless children deprived of "mother love." Bowlby liberally applied his observations to American children whose mothers were not constantly available to them. He claimed that this "partial" deprivation, resulting, for example, from mothers leaving their children to go to work, could also harm children. A mother's daily absence might suggest to her children a lack of love. The consequences were "acute anxiety, excessive need for love, powerful feelings of revenge, and, arising from these last, guilt and depression." By the 1950s, with the war crisis passed, working mothers were more psychologized than berated. "Why," wondered one anonymous "successful career wife," did some women have "this suicidal hunger for success outside the home?" After all, "The young woman who is giving her best to her work cannot give her husband and home all they deserve."[24]

Attitudes toward working mothers were more mixed than some of these writings suggest. Widespread circulation of such ideas, however, regularly drove home a key point: domestic women were "normal" women; ambition was unfeminine, and unfeminine women were a menace to society because being both wife and mother required deference, subordination, and "acceptance" of a role. According to Farnam and Lundberg, the only good mother was "the feminine mother," whose motherhood was intricately linked to her dependent status as a wife. This kind of mother, in contrast to the other four neurotic types, "accepts herself fully as a woman" and "knows . . . that she is dependent on a man. There is no fantasy in her mind about being an 'independent woman,' a contradiction in terms. She knows she is dependent on the phallus for sexual enjoyment, which as she is genitalized, she is in need of. Having children is to her the most natural thing possible, and it would never occur to her to have any doubts about it."As could be seen over and over again on *Ozzie and Harriet, Father Knows Best, Leave It to Beaver,* and *The Donna Reed Show,* the family home was really the place where women should find their happiness. More positively, modern motherhood was happiness and fulfill-ment. As one enthusiastic female writer explained, "The new philosophy of child guidance makes of parenthood not a dull, monotonous routine job, but an absorb-ing, creative profession—a career second to none."[25]

How, then, did mothers walk the line between becoming heartless, rejecting mothers and smothering monstrosities that might be called Moms? As Plant points out, the experts provided a kind of resolution: children needed mothers' unremit-ting attention only in the first few years. As one woman psychologist wrote, a new-born baby "is helpless and needs and demands your constant attention . . . but nature does not permit this state of helplessness to last for long."[26] After those first few years, children needed not endless attention, but constant—or near constant—availability. Over subsequent decades, Americans became somewhat more willing to settle for near-constant availability as a prerequisite for mothering. In the post-war decades, most commentators erred on the side of constant.

Farnam and Lundberg's "Feminine Mother" did not "dominate" her children. "Instead, she watches with somewhat detached interest to see what each one takes to. She can tell, without reading books on child care, what to do for the children by waiting for them to indicate their need." The passively feminine mother, wait-ing for someone else's needs, was articulated mostly in the negative, via caricatures of the kind of "Mom" a woman did not want to be, such as the kind who lives on "the emotional satisfaction, almost repletion, she derives from keeping her chil-dren paddling about in a kind of psychological amniotic fluid rather than letting them swim away with the bold and decisive strokes of maturity from the emotional maternal womb," to quote psychiatrist Strecker.[27]

"Trust Yourself"—Maybe

The experts were not all united in deriding mothers. Accompanying all the distress, the calm child care advice "Bible" of the era suggested a broader range of accept-able behaviors and even feelings. The first edition of Dr. Spock's book, *The Com-mon Sense Book of Baby and Child Care,* hit the presses in 1946 and quickly became the most widely read child care book ever written, an influence for generations of mothers. Spock became a national icon. His book sold as many copies in its first ten months as the illustrious Dr. Holt's book had sold in thirty-nine years. Within the first three years, a million copies were in print, and, over the decades since publication, many millions more circulated in revised and translated editions. Dr. Spock opened his first and subsequent editions of the book with these oft-remembered words: "TRUST YOURSELF. You know more than you think you do."[28]

As a softer and more flexible expert than most of his predecessors and many of his contemporaries, Spock peddled modern child care in a friend-next-door kind of way. "This book only tries to give you sensible present-day ideas of the care of the child. . . . It's not infallible." His mission included upgrading earlier "modern" ideas of childcare, such as Watsonian behaviorism, as well as reassuring mothers and dignifying their work. He openly disapproved of an "overemphasis at present on making parents, and especially mothers, the scapegoats for anything that goes wrong with children." Spock freely acknowledged that expert advice was contradictory, as were the suggestions of other well-meaning people in the mother's life. "Don't be overawed by what the experts say. Don't be afraid to trust your own common sense," he assured mothers. "Bringing up your child won't be a complicated job if you take it easy, trust your own instincts, and follow the directions that your doctor gives you."[29] Here and elsewhere, Spock skillfully straddled the line between maternal "instincts," which he encouraged women to reclaim, and doctors' authority.

Dr. Spock was also an interactive expert. He based his work on years of clinical practice, and he encouraged women to write to him. In his "Talks with Mothers" series, which ran in *Ladies' Home Journal* through the 1950s and 1960s, Spock printed mothers' letters and then incorporated their viewpoints into his revised advice literature. In an important departure from the more authoritative prewar child-rearing texts, Spock saw himself as a partner with mothers in some important respects: "Every time a mother told me something even slightly different from my previous concepts," he demurred, "I revised my ideas accordingly."[30]

Spock was neither the only expert in the field nor the only interactive one, but he was the best known. Unlike the women child-care advisors who continued to reach out to fellow mothers and sometimes referred to their own mothering, Spock remained the disembodied expert. He neither referred to his experiences as a father nor credited his wife Jane (until many years later) for her critical contributions to *Baby and Child Care*.[31] The implied objectivity and his male privilege likely contributed to his mystique.

Similar to Spock in their relaxed approach to child-rearing, the two single mothers of grown children, Louise Bates Ames and Dr. Frances Ilg, solicited letters from mothers and responded in print. In, doing so, they too contributed to more forgiving attitudes that acknowledged a diverse array of mothers and children. Their syndicated column, "Parents Ask," ran from 1951 to 1973 and reached nearly nine and a half million people. Ames and Ilg defended working mothers: "These women are not lazy. They are not slackers. They are not unnatural mothers." They were also far ahead of their time in refusing to blame mothers for problems like autism and developmental delay by arguing these were biological issues, not a result of a deficit in maternal nurture. Like Spock, Ames and Ilg inspired hope and angst in mothers. "I burn with the passion of self-improvement," one woman wrote to the two columnists. "I would do anything to help our children learn all they must know to become happy, useful adults. My great desire—part of this improvement plan—is to become a more ideal mother—more relaxed, patient, calm-voiced, less demanding."[32] In the child-centered—and husband-serving—culture of the post-war period, self-effacement was part of what many women believed they were supposed to aspire to, reassuring experts notwithstanding.

Historians have debated the meaning of Spock's partnership with mothers and of their response to him. It is clear that some mothers found Spock singularly empowering. "We had an expert on our side!" exclaimed one woman, who credited Spock with helping her and other young mothers break away from their elders' child-rearing ways. Another wrote, "That book to a mother was knowledge—confidence—you could lean on it and know what you were doing."[33] In an age of widespread credibility of experts, many women felt that to trust themselves they needed the validation of experts. One woman wrote to Spock about the charged issue of pacifier use, "Now I know that an authority has the same opinion as mine."[34] Reinforcement by the experts was valued in part because kin networks were more attenuated, and many mothers had not experienced caring for younger siblings.

Many women also appreciated these experts' positive view of expressiveness and their gentler, child-development-oriented approach to discipline. Although modern behaviorism may have promoted harsher forms of discipline, midcentury mothers tended to ascribe strictness to "old-fashioned" values. Spock-era mothers were the self-styled new modern mothers: "My mother was too strict," wrote one mother to the kindly expert, "so I've never tried to imitate her methods." Indeed, one woman journalist exclaimed that Spock, especially in his 1957 revised edition of *Baby and Child Care*, was just what was needed for "the modern mother . . . paddling frantically about in a dark pool of Freudian implications, torn between the embattled forces of Discipline and Permissiveness, dazed by the potential perils of rejection, affection, early weaning, late toilet training and chronic thumb-sucking, traumatized by the fear of causing a trauma and helplessly stuck with the suspicion that a little psychiatric orientation is a burdensome thing."[35]

To the extent that Spock inspired mothers' confidence, he did so in part by providing a small space for honesty about the challenges of child-rearing and the contradictory advice of the experts. He wrote about "that blue feeling," what today would be called postpartum depression. He told women that breast-feeding was "natural" at a time when formula feeding was becoming the norm, but he also assured mothers who did not want to breastfeed that their babies would be okay. He discussed discipline with similar balance and again took the opportunity to absolve mothers of blame for their foibles and mistakes; he suggested that mothers were simply human beings doing a complicated job. "No parent (or non-parent, either) is always happy and reasonable. We all have our troubles, great or small, and we all take them out on our children to some degree. Come to think of it, it wouldn't be good training for a child to be brought up by perfect parents, because it would unsuit him for this world." Spock even included in his earliest edition a section on "the handicapped child," in which he offered models of a "sensible" maternal attitude toward such children, one that maximized their opportunities for happy childhoods.[36]

Children themselves were reasonable in Spock's world view, Freudian fears notwithstanding. Spock's advice literature made less worrisome habits that had deeply disturbed the interwar-era experts and mothers, such as thumb-sucking in babies and toddlers, Spock felt that these children did not require restraints, although they did warrant eight pages of his advice. A worried parent could even look up "Masturbation" in *Baby and Child Care*'s handy index and find that such behavior springs from "wholesome curiosity" and should not be met with threats. "Though masturbation itself doesn't need to cause nervousness, excessive worry about it can certainly cause nervousness," he opined, letting the potentially worried mother know that worrying in itself was the problem.[37]

Spock's critics, including some vocal mother letter-writers of the time, said he made it all look too easy. "Don't you realize," asked one irritated Texas mother, "that when you always emphasize that a child basically wants to behave well, and will behave well if he is handled wisely, you make the parent feel responsible for everything that goes wrong?" Her feelings about child-rearing after reading his book were "more burdensome and discouraging and oppressive than I can ever express. Can't you see that a parent is a human being, too?" Another insisted that parents were not meant "to be burnt offerings" to their children and that too much security could backfire. It would not do to keep children "in cotton-wool—safe from the cruel world, which, when he gets out in it won't give a hooray about his complexes and frustrations."[38] Some also complained of what Spock's much later critics would call the "permissiveness" of his approach. In fact, Spock revised his 1946 edition in part to take into account complaints that he portrayed children as *too* reasonable and not in need of firm discipline.

Other mothers could be called critics of Spock in the sense that they ignored him. Spock confessed to a colleague that a group of African American women who attended his family clinic frustrated him with their unwillingness to heed his advice. "They don't seem to expect or want medical advice on infant feeding, weaning, toilet training, sleep arrangements, sleep problems. In fact they silently but firmly refuse to take advice which is pressed on them."[39] Like many mothers before and after Spock, especially outside of the white middle class, some mothers still preferred to rely on cultural traditions in raising children and took medical advice with a grain of salt.

Taking the long view, historical writers like Ann Hulbert point out that Spock's work betrayed his own anxiety and that of other experts, in what Hulbert astutely calls the "awkward age of the expert": "Don't be anxious, the experts anxiously insisted." The modern mother at midcentury was the confused mother, in part because the experts raised concerns even as they soothed them. Hulbert also shows that ambivalence about the predictive value of psychology—and all science—was part of the coming of age of the experts. Science was beginning to run amok in the form of the atomic bomb, and Freudian fears about the unconscious made the simplistic, behaviorist formulas of the interwar years seem naïve at best. Mothers still wanted answers, but they also wanted acknowledgment of the inherent complexity. At the same time, the experts, from psychologists to medical doctors to social workers, could afford to be more sensitive, even therapeutic toward their clientele. They were now established cultural authorities, even though, as one psychoanalyst admitted, they were perhaps not yet capable of "fulfilling the wonderful promise of better mental health through better psychological care." Hulbert observed about parenting expertise in the era: "Modesty was an ingratiating gambit in a crowded market, designed to disarm skepticism."[40]

In spite of some skepticism, the experts maintained a strong hold on women's experiences of mothering, and that hold began early. Prenatal visits were now medically recommended. These consultations developed relationships between expecting middle-class women and their doctors, who led them toward hospital births. In 1940, only a slight majority of women gave birth in hospitals, but, by 1955, 95 percent did so.[41] Building on decades of experimentation with anesthesia and drugs for prompting or altering the course of labor, physicians solidified their authority in childbirth in an unprecedented way. The effective use of antibiotics and blood banking to facilitate transfusions meant that maternal mortality dropped precipitously as hospital births rose.

Women could increasingly approach their birthing experiences with very little fear of death. But a culturally conditioned fear of the pain of childbirth, combined with a trust in medical experts, led most women to rely willingly on a passive experience without questioning doctors on their recommended procedures. Women were generally so sedated that they had no memory of the experience of giving birth. A fear of spreading disease, left from the era before antibiotics, led to the wearing of face masks by pediatric nurses and even mothers.[42] This was one of many hospital protocols that heightened the sense of urgency about following the rules of a medicalized environment. In the charged, potentially life-and-death situation of childbirth, medical control was easier to maintain and harder to question than was the case for day-to-day child-rearing questions. The experiences with maternal and child mortality from their mothers' and grandmothers' generations could not have been far from the minds of midcentury women, who gave birth in the presumably sterile hospitals with take-charge doctors.

Few women in this generation had witnessed childbirth so they did not know what to expect. One woman remembered her experience: "The doctor was in command . . . the doctor was God. And when the doctor told you this is how it's going to be, you don't worry. You let the doctor worry." By this time, many obstetricians held the core belief that birth was a pathological process. When Ina May Middleton explained to her doctor in 1966 that she did not want anesthesia while giving birth, he responded that he could not condone an "uncontrolled delivery." Without medical management, a baby's head could become a "battering ram" that could leave the mother—and the baby's brain—damaged.[43]

There were some dissenters. The British obstetrician Grantly Dick-Read gained fame in the United States after the publication of his book, *Childbirth Without*

Fear, which became a best-seller. Influenced by Dick-Read's work, the *Ladies' Home Journal* reported in 1958 on "Cruelty in Maternity Wards." The article challenged practices like strapping women down to delivery tables with steel cuffs and other "tortures that go on in modern delivery rooms." The magazine received a barrage of letters from women who, amplifying these complaints, told of "assembly line techniques," "lonely labor rooms," and nurses' orders to refrain from pushing until physicians arrived. As a result, new conversations about birth emerged among women.

But before the feminist health movement, the medical profession as a whole did not concede much to complaining women. One physician even wrote to *Ladies' Home Journal* readers that most women in labor were "spoiled, hysterical and full of fears" and therefore clearly in need of the command and control model of physicians' care. Demands for natural childbirth could get a woman labeled a "hostile patient" quite quickly. One physician openly described a woman who had already defied postwar norms by postponing marriage and earning a Ph.D.; the doctor, who committed the woman to a psychiatric institution, blamed alternative birth ideas and essentially implicated this woman for defying gender codes.[44]

At the same time, though he was less immediately influential than Dr. Spock, Dick-Read did for birth what Spock did for child care: he held out the idea of "natural" birth. He claimed that nature had not intended birth to be painful, just as Spock claimed that nature had not intended child-rearing to be excessively complicated. The famous anthropologist Margaret Mead set out to prove the point about childbirth. As early as 1939 she argued that pain in childbirth was a "male myth." With the help of young Dr. Spock, Mead arranged a widely publicized birth experience for herself without anesthesia, though she was still separated from her baby right after delivery and subjected to other hospital protocols.[45]

As a physician proponent of childbirth without fear or pain, Dick-Read enjoyed the gratitude of mothers who wanted an alternative but also wanted an expert to validate their choices. One woman wrote to him, "I can't tell you what it meant to me to read your book and know that there really is a path open to me heading to the end I *know* is right—happy, content pregnancies and lovely births for my children." Dick-Read argued that fear caused pain and that, if women learned about their bodies, then the vast majority would never need anesthesia, and he argued against routine use of forceps and episiotomy. For Dick-Read, childbirth was natural because women were naturally meant to be mothers. A neotraditionalist and pioneer at the same time, he sought to return to women an experience that was "the crowning moment" of their lives.[46]

Dick-Read also encouraged compassionate physician care for birthing mothers at a time when they were routinely shaved, strapped to tables, anaesthetized, and often not even in contact with their doctors until the moment of delivery. "Your patient may wish to hold your hand," he told his fellow physicians, ". . . she may call for you to be beside her, but most certainly she desires the unwavering strength of the confidence that you share with her in the successful issue of her trial."[47] But even for Dick-Read, the physician-woman partnership was one in which the physician was in control and mothers remained isolated from the comforts of loved ones and routines, the patterns in which women had labored naturally for a millennia before medicalized childbirth.

When it came to advice literature from the medical experts, friendliness (or perhaps an ingratiating style) probably made it harder to take the areas of judgmentalism that even the gentlest experts refused to contain. Spock, for example, joined most of his expert peers, past and in some cases all the way up to the present, in wagging a finger at mothers who worked outside the home. "Some mothers *have* to work," he observed. "Usually their children turn out all right, because some reasonably good arrangement is made for their care. But others grow up neglected and maladjusted." Anticipating (wrongly) that European social welfare policies would make their way to the United States, Spock claimed, "It would save money in the end if the government paid a comfortable allowance to all mothers (of young children) who would otherwise be compelled to work. You can think of it this way: useful, well-adjusted citizens are the most valuable possessions a country has, and good mother care during early childhood is the surest way to produce them. It doesn't make sense to let mothers go to work making dresses in factories or tapping typewriters in offices, and have them pay other people to do a poorer job of bringing up their children." Those who "had to" or "chose to" work were reminded that "the average day nursery or 'baby farm' is no good for him." Spock also peppered his advice on finding caregivers with fear-inducing caricatures: "An adult who is too bossy will make him balky and frantic. One who lacks self-confidence may be helpless to control him. One who smothers him with too much attention will hamper his development." If a mother had to work, Spock encouraged her to at least find work that left her free for her children in the afternoons, and he encouraged working mothers not to indulge their children, not to "bow to all his wishes" because of guilt.[48]

Perhaps Spock's vacillation sprang from his awareness of the cost of women's isolation in the home with young children. The women who wrote to Spock—perhaps disproportionately worriers—often did experience intense anxiety and frustration with child-rearing and with child-rearing literature. One mother who pretended to leave the house after her four-year-old son said he did not want her "as a boss" was guilt ridden for "needlessly causing my child one minute of terror." Another felt she had not read enough about child care when her daughter was young, and she worried that, "We didn't hand rock her much and she usually had her bottle propped and as she got older I made her listen . . . if I would slap her hand once she would usually stop and I always made her take a nap in the afternoon . . . all the articles I read lately have me worrying that maybe she doesn't know we love her . . . is there anything to do that can make up for not being as close to her although she seemed contented most of the time."[49] Mothers wrote of their intense desires to make their children happy: "It is because I want her to be so happy that I am so distraught and incompetent," wrote one. And they despaired of their power struggles with children. One mother said that she and her young son were "both fighting for control. . . . Surely there must be something for troubled mothers as AA is for drinkers to call SOS when they need help."[50]

Antimaternalism, the frustrations of isolated stay-at-home mothers, and the assurance that mothers were fallible individuals doing a job for a short time probably contributed considerably to feminists' later assertion that women were "trapped" in domestic roles. Betty Friedan made this assertion with significant fanfare in her 1963 book *The Feminine Mystique*. These patterns also contributed to an already growing trend of validating mothers' labor-force participation, at least for mothers of older children.

Working Mothers: The Wave of the Future

Contrary to popular assumptions, many 1950s housewives worked, though usually during the hours children were at school. Between 1948 and 1958 there was an increase of about 80 percent in the number of employed married women with children under age eighteen. In fact, even within the postwar "box," there was some acceptance of combining paid work and motherhood. Married wives and mothers who worked for that something "extra" for the nuclear, child-centered family were sometimes publicly praised in the 1950s, as in a 1953 *Life* magazine photo essay focusing on the working wife. Unlike the "strident suffragettes" who had worked to "prove their equality" with men, the editors claimed working wives today were different. "The typical working wife of 1953 works for the double paycheck that makes it possible to buy a tv set, a car—or in many cases simply to make ends meet."[51]

Working women had advocates, even among some child care experts, like Ames and Ilg. Husbands sometimes showed public support of their working wives as well, in spite of the potential diminishment of their masculinity that came with not being the only breadwinner. In 1956 David Yellin wrote an article in *Harpers* magazine titled, "I'm Married to a Working Mother." He noted that "our two salaries have provided economic sanction for having children sooner and oftener." Yellin, like many others, emphasized that working wives could contribute to family fertility and comfortable middle-class lifestyles. Some also spoke out for combining work and family for other reasons, and these advocates benefited from the experts' worries about obsessive and smothering mothers. Dorothy Barclay, a family columnist, found experts who agreed that, "if for her own morale, a mother feels she must have a job, it is better to do so than to fret and strain at the tasks of full-time homemaker to the detriment of her disposition and ultimately her family's happiness." Similarly, another popular magazine celebrated the story of Mary, a working mother, who "feels that being a working mother can be a good thing, provided you have a husband sporting enough and youngsters smart enough to permit it all."[52]

As the young parents of the baby boom aged, many mothers of grown children in this generation would return to work. A growing demand for women workers, especially in the lower-paid and usually nonunion clerical, retail, and service sectors, combined with other economic and demographic factors to pull women into the labor force. This expansion happened well before feminists successfully demanded more meaningful work roles and opportunities for women. In the mid-century decades it was already becoming more acceptable for married women to work before the children came. With childbearing confined mostly to a woman's twenties and with the population enjoying longer life spans, married women often worked when their children were older as well. Women over thirty-five were the largest growing group of married women workers; usually their children were in school or no longer living at home.[53] Without knowing it, these women were creating a pattern that would expand throughout the rest of the twentieth century. The age of the children when a mother returned to work continued to get lower, and employers continued to demonstrate their willingness to hire the more poorly paid half of the potential adult labor force.

Women who worked in this period struggled with more than just the mixed messages of the national culture. They often had few familial or social supports for combining their work and family roles. Federal support for child care was an important wartime innovation, but it scarcely touched the needs of working mothers and was discontinued after the war. Women in some industrial unions, especially the auto industry, were beginning to make demands for contract language that included child care and maternity leave, but it was decades before such options affected most working mothers. Even those voices that praised working mothers acknowledged that they needed to be more or less superhuman to make family life run smoothly and continue the all-important gender conformity on which proper family life depended. The authors of the popular book *Marriage for Two* warned women that husbands would not support their working wives if they shirked their at-home duties; they had to become "those wives who are able to dismiss their business interests and become all wife during home hours." There is scant evidence of any significant uptick in the amount of housework done by fathers during this time period. So mothers who worked generally shouldered a "double day" with which future generations would become increasingly familiar. Historian Sonya Michel has observed that Americans clung to the notion that solving these problems was a private concern. Individual women were supposed to manage work and family with neither policy supports nor outside assistance. These convictions slowed demands for true social supports for families with working mothers, such as universal high-quality child care and paid family leave.[54]

Adaptations within the Wife-and-Mother Box

The trend toward combining labor force participation with mothering continued to grow in the decades after the Second World War. In the 1950s, however, more than 90 percent of mothers in the suburbs—the women for whom the ideals were most rigidly enforced—did not work for pay. This was another reason that many people did not notice and often do not remember mothers' increasing labor force participation.[55] These non-wage-earning mothers were indeed restricted to a confining domesticity. Middle-class wives and mothers were told that they had it all—beautiful homes, modern conveniences, husbands who supported them, healthy children, and easy lives. Complaining was a symptom of a psychiatric disorder. Because much historical literature on the postwar era focuses on these women, we have some fascinating clues about how they adapted to the rigid domesticity to which they were assigned.

For all the repression and fear, there creeps out from postwar sources an uncanny optimism that links family life to both citizenship and personal fulfillment. Oral histories show that even many women who remember the 1950s and early 1960s as a time of great repression also recall the era with fondness for its straightforwardness: The suburban family world was "warm, boring, completely child-centered," remembers Carol Freeman. "We sat around in each other's kitchens and backyards and drank a lot of coffee and smoked a million cigarettes and talked about our children. There was some competition, yes, but mostly we were young mothers and we were learning from each other and getting support from each other. We took care of each other's children, too, so that we were able to get away some." Even women who later became frustrated recalled their joy in their pregnancies, especially with first babies. Another mother remembered the thrill of moving to the suburbs. "I thought I'd died and gone to heaven. Green grass, places for the children to play, good schools, a nice house, with an automatic washer and dryer. . . . We even had a car." But, she noted, "the houses were all alike. The people were pretty much alike, too, and everybody was trying to achieve middle-class status. Everybody had to have the same things everybody else had. . . . We went on the same kind of vacations, read the same books, we even had the same bubble hairdos."[56]

However narrow the prescribed purpose of women's lives, in their own memories and in our more distant view, that purpose was reinforced for them by the structure of their lives and the dictates of the culture. As Julia Harmon remembered, "I felt extremely happy if everybody was happy: if I'd had a good dinner, and the children were scrubbed and happy and doing well in school and their clothes were clean and I was looking good when it all came together—that was pleasing, that was good. It was best when all these good things were happening for everyone else and I was managing it." Julia gave up her passion for painting and often managed her household alone while her husband traveled for work. But, as she recalled, "honest to Pete, I really think this was what I wanted." June Tavern remembers, "I was determined to make homemaking represent a good job. I was constantly trying to live up to some expectation about being a good mother and homemaker," though "after awhile that wasn't enough." Indeed, middle-class women tended to minimize the closing off of other opportunities in favor of marriage and motherhood, often referring to "the role" as a "career" in itself.[57]

Women's memories express a common belief that the pursuit of the familial good life was part of American progress and connected to the civic good. One woman reminisced about the time:

> As dissatisfied as I was, and I was restless, I remember so well this feeling we had at the time that the world was going to be your oyster. You were going to make money, your kids were going to go to good schools, everything was possible if you

just did what you were supposed to do. The future was rosy. There was a tremendous feeling of optimism. You were working for good causes, you believed that
politicians were, on the whole, honest. You believed in this idea of good government and you believed you could have a part of it through political activities. . . .
Much as I say it was hateful, it was also hopeful. It was an innocent time.[58]

Educated middle-class women, even with family responsibilities, often participated in civic life. In large numbers women volunteered, creating "good government" through participation in organizations like the League of Women Voters
and energizing their communities with the gift of their free hours. Young mothers
with large families had little time for community involvement, but many of these
mothers completed their childrearing by age thirty; once the youngest child was in
school, they had much to give to their communities.

In a less celebrated, but no less important development, birth control gained
widespread acceptance and use within marriage. Although they bore more babies
than their mothers, midcentury married women took some control of their family
lives by confining their childbearing to a smaller portion of their lives. In one large
sample survey of middle-class couples, 98 percent said they used birth control.
They delayed their first babies according to their own needs and spaced children
thereafter. Gender roles were straightforwardly defined, children were relatively
affordable, and childrearing was considered the defining achievement of adulthood
for both women and men. Because of all this, middle-class married couples appear
to have had little friction over childbearing decisions. Between 1940 and 1960, in the
sample mentioned above, couples agreed a remarkable 90 percent of the time on
the number of children they wanted.[59]

But many women adapted at great cost to both themselves and perhaps the ideal
families they were trying to create. The story of Carolyn Teach Denlinger, who had
seven children between 1950 and 1960, illustrates some of the frustrations. Denlinger, who died in 2010, left behind detailed diaries about her isolated life with
children. A very bright student with a love of learning, Denlinger attended college
for one year but dropped out after contracting rheumatic fever. She did not return
to school and instead married Dean Denlinger in 1949 at the age of nineteen. She
and her husband, an attorney-in-training and then a lawyer, settled in a rural home
near Dayton, Ohio, where she stayed home with children and was out of the labor
force until 1978.

Despite the availability of birth control, it is not clear that Denlinger and her
husband were able or willing to use it successfully. "I don't see how I can be pregnant," she wrote in 1955, "we didn't take any chances until the 24th day!" Once she
knew for sure that she was pregnant with her fourth child, she wrote, "I don't see
how I will manage with two babies so close, but I won't be the first one to do it."
Denlinger clearly had trouble managing and was deeply frustrated by the confines
of her life. She expended considerable energy in her diary lambasting herself for
her lack of drive, her weight problems, and her inability to be the kind of mother
she thought she should be. True to the ideals of the 1950s, she also believed she

needed to portray a certain image as the wife of a successful attorney. Referring to her struggle with her weight, she wrote in 1955, "I don't want Dean to be ashamed of me . . . I really have let myself go."[60]

Denlinger often wrote that she was "so lonesome" with her husband gone on business. In 1955, with three young children and another on the way, she worried, "I am surely not a very good mother. I seem to put almost everything before my children. I growl and snap at them, especially when I'm reading a book. I must try to cultivate a more pleasing personality and more patience." Denlinger blamed herself for her unhappiness in the domestic role, even deciding at one point to see a psychiatrist. This was typical for women in her situation, and they often used the language of psychology. Clara Jones, another 1950s housewife, for example, explained her problems with her husband's long absences and her busy family life like this: "My overanxiety has made some problems seem bigger than they were." She was plagued by "anxiety and guilt from overly severe and strict treatment in childhood, according to the psychiatrist who is helping me now."[61]

Beyond a lifelong habit of reading fiction, Denlinger had given up a deep love for the world of ideas and people with whom to discuss them. She recorded her feelings of loss on many occasions in her diary. One evening, after listening to her husband and a male friend discuss philosophy and theology late into the evening, she lamented, "I wish I could follow conversations like that better, but they use terms I don't know. I served popcorn and Kool-Aid." Her children and housework were the next most commented-upon topics. Her frustration with her expatriation from the outside world was clear on many occasions, such as when she returned to her college, ten years after dropping out, for someone else's graduation: "I was very unhappy . . . remembering what a glorious year I had and how bitterly disappointed I was that I didn't get back. I could have cried."[62]

Although Denlinger does not seem to have commiserated with other housewives about these problems, she might have been comforted to know about the many women who shared her plight. A woman named Dorothy Glenn, for example, remembered, "I was doing a lot of reading about metaphysics and one day while I was rinsing out dirty diapers in the toilet, I thought, these things are incompatible. So I stopped the reading—I couldn't stop the diapers."[63] These women's struggles help us understand why the "happy housewives" of the 1950s admitted, en masse in surveys, that they wanted their daughters to have different lives than their own.

Denlinger's isolation, compounded by her rural location, also makes her a fine example of the ways in which women in her situation relied on experts to mediate their discontent. Denlinger was fortunate to have warm and caring physicians. "Went back to Dr. Heery today," she wrote in 1955. "He just talked to me—didn't examine me or anything. He says he wants to see me every Sat. just to make sure I get out of the house." Another doctor became Denlinger's connection to a coping aid for housewives of the 1950s, a mother's-little-helper of a drug called Dexamil. The drug was both an amphetamine and a barbiturate. Another housewife of the time recalled that her physician brother-in-law supplied the drug for her housewife friends. Approved as a diet drug, it was marketed to housewives in ways that suggested they would be happy doing their household chores. One ad showed a woman in a glowing sunshine image, smiling while pushing a vacuum. For Den-linger, the drug worked, at least for a while. "Took a pill and made the work fly," she wrote in 1959. "Folded clothes, washed dishes and scrubbed the floor, cleaned the rest of the house."[64]

By the 1970s, when her children were older, Denlinger completed both her bachelor's and master's degrees and became very involved in her church. As these activities expanded, her marriage fell apart. Her husband left her and married his secretary; Denlinger was regretful for many years, especially because her time out of the labor force probably disallowed her the opportunity to work in her field of historical preservation as well. As her daughter Elise, who compiled and analyzed her mother's diary evidence, observed, Betty Friedan's book *The Feminine Mystique* could have been written for Carolyn Denlinger. "She, along with millions of other women, spent many miserable years trying to find fulfillment in her role as wife and mother alone. As a person who actually did not like children, and a woman, like many others, who had much to offer intellectually and creatively, she was sti-fled by expectations that she actually did not even question. Instead she believed, again, like millions of other women, that she was at fault somehow because she couldn't be happy in that circumscribed role." Indeed, when women began writ-ing to Friedan in response to her critique of domestic life, they echoed Denlinger's complaints but finally felt they had a framework to understand their frustrations.[65]

In the 1950s, however, such complaints were suppressed; they just leaked out privately. From survey research, historians have found that housewives' most con-sistent grievance was that their husbands did not participate enough in child care and housework. As a whole the contemporary culture celebrated fathers' involve-ment in playful, nonspecific ways. Historian Jessica Weiss found striking evidence that baby-boomer fathers held themselves up to these new "Dad" ideals and often found themselves wanting. Their wives often found them wanting as well; in fact, middle-class women in one national sample reported dissatisfaction with their marriages at twice the rate of men. Both husbands and wives admitted that women had to make more adaptations to wife and mother roles than men did to being hus-band and father. Elaine Tyler May aptly noted, "After making so many adjustments, women may have felt some measure of accomplishment or, at the least, a sense of personal investment in the relationship."[66]

At a time when suburban communities were extremely age- and gender-segregated, one of Denlinger's contemporaries remembered, "We moved to the suburbs and I went into the house and started having babies and hardly ever came out—or so it seemed." Another remembered that she had "no adults to speak to during the day, totally iso-lated, nervous. It was awful." When men either traveled for business or took the tradi-tional prerogative of hiding behind a newspaper in the evening, it meant that women had long hours alone with children. When Denlinger's physician suggested that she hire household help to alleviate her domestic workload, she complained, "I don't want more help—I want my husband home more!"[67] Out of frustrating experiences like these, says historian Jessica Weiss, came new expectations and accommodations between baby boom-era husbands and wives. Some of these changes would not be realized until the late 1960s and early 1970s, when these couples were in middle age. At that time, many women reentered the labor force; others divorced, as Denlinger did. These women's marital rebellions, though often invisible to their daughters, were critical to raising expectations about egalitarian marriages that would be lauded by the next generation, who created the feminist movement.

REPRODUCTIVE NONCONFORMISTS

In the tightly contained cultural script of the postwar era, emotionally healthy women conceived babies within wedlock, wanted lots of babies, and accepted economic dependence and confinement to the domestic sphere. One of the best ways to understand this particular manipulation of the motherhood mandate and the tight constriction of motherhood and marriage is to look at what May has called the "reproductive misfits" of this era: those women who conceived children out of wedlock, who could not have children, and who made the radical choice of childlessness in an era of pronatal fervor. For a surprising number of girls and women the marriage and motherhood mandate did not work. Their stories speak volumes about the lengths to which people went to preserve the fiction that all babies were, or should be, the product of married mothers and fathers. In so many ways, reproductive choice was in the hands, once again, of practically everyone but the woman involved: boyfriends, parents, doctors, psychiatrists, social workers, religious authorities, courts, schools, employers, and politicians; they all had far more say in women's reproductive choices than women who might or might not carry a baby to term and perform the social role of motherhood. Both the unhappy acquiescence and the quiet rebellions of this era reveal women's efforts to exercise their own choices about their reproductive life.

Sexuality and the Potentially Maternal Young White Woman

Out-of-wedlock pregnancies were a problem for more women and girls than Americans wanted to admit. A hasty marriage, still the most common solution for premarital pregnancy, occurred in an estimated 50 percent of cases of out-of-wedlock conception. Some women also continued to seek out abortion. Most women had no idea how to procure an abortion, and those who did faced a significantly more dangerous situation than had women in the 1930s. Even at a time when the average age of marriage remained very low (below twenty-one from the war years until the early 1970s), nonmarital pregnancies were extremely common. In the mid-1950s, 40 percent of first babies born to girls ages fifteen through nineteen were conceived out of wedlock; by the early 1970s, the figure was 60 percent. The percentage of women who had babies outside of marriage tripled between 1940 and the late 1950s. The proportion of unmarried teenagers engaging in sex rose, from around 39 percent in the 1950s to 68 percent by the early 1970s.[68]

Whatever happened as a result of this nonmarital sex, most people believed that the woman or girl bore the brunt of responsibility and shame. Why did young women risk the consequences of nonmarital sexuality? Certainly the postwar era was one of great preoccupation with sexuality. Enjoyable, nonprocreative sex was widely approved—within marriage. Popular films suggested that sexual repression was harmful, even to young people. New dating norms in the era of the automobile offered privacy to hormonal teenagers, and girls were encouraged to increase their social status by dating. Yet girls walked a fine line, practicing what Elaine Tyler May has called "sexual brinkmanship." Many tried to keep their boyfriends attached to them without "going all the way," risking pregnancy and a ruined reputation. While "petting" and noncoital sexuality tended to escalate in committed relationships, it was the girl's job to put a stop to any situation that could result in intercourse. As a 1945 book titled *How to Win and Hold a Husband* put it, "Remember the average man will go as far as you let him go. A man is only as bad as the woman he is with." Indeed, young women themselves disapproved of nonmarital sex well into the late 1960s. One 1964 survey of college students showed 68 percent of college seniors believed that it was "morally or ethically wrong" to have premarital sex with one's fiancé.[69]

Birth control was largely unavailable to single women, even well into the 1960s. One woman who later relinquished a child for adoption explained: "If you wanted to get birth-control pills, you had to be flashing a diamond solitaire. Doctors really didn't give them to you. Why would you need those? You shouldn't be having sex anyway." As for condoms available at the drugstore, "The boys would maybe buy them, sneak them, or something. But as a female? To go and buy rubbers? Oh, my God that did not happen." In the memories of women who "got caught" (became pregnant out of wedlock), boys often perpetuated this myth. One remembered, "He kept saying, 'It's okay . . . It's really hard to get pregnant.'"[70] Of course, boys also knew little about preventing pregnancy, but the double standard made them more willing to take chances to satisfy teenage sexual desire. They were much more often spared having to face the consequences, such as ruined sexual reputations or the forfeiture of education.

The risks of nonmarital pregnancy were enormously high for women, and a new emphasis on relinquishing babies for adoption especially shaped the experiences of white girls and women in these situations during the postwar period. For the first time in American history, the majority of white mothers who gave birth out of wedlock surrendered their babies for formal adoption, and the upward trend that started after World War II continued apace until 1970: 70 percent of children born out of wedlock were relinquished in 1963, and 80 percent in the peak year of 1970. There was an enormous demand on the part of white couples who could not have children. And in this pronatalist era, married women almost never relinquished babies for adoption; a sharp contrast to the prewar period when approximately 65 percent of adopted children had been born to married women.[71] Meanwhile, African American babies born out of wedlock were more likely to remain with their mothers and within the community, in part because of community norms among African Americans and in part because of the greater difficulty placing African American babies with adoptive parents in a racist society.

An important way to avoid social shame and expulsion from school for white girls and women was to discreetly disappear to a maternity home, where they endured quiet isolation and a hurried birthing experience, often followed by separation from their babies. Some never actually saw their babies, and many were coerced into signing adoption papers. These girls returned to school with a story about a sick aunt who had needed them for a few months and without a baby. The result for the relinquishing mothers was often a lifetime of heartache, as Ann Fessler discovered when she invited mothers of that era to share their stories for her 2006 book, *The Girls Who Went Away: The Hidden History of Women Who Surrendered Children for Adoption in the Decades before Roe v. Wade.* The stories Fessler gathered speak to the personal pain inflicted on women for the sake of the cultural ideal of maritally confined motherhood. Women felt immense and lasting guilt: "I let somebody take my child. That's the guilt," said one. Most felt that they had neither voice nor choice in the decision. They felt pushed along by parents and social workers through a script in which they were told that the pregnancy was their fault, that their babies would be better off with two parents, and that they would forget and move on. As one woman said, "I never felt like I gave my baby away. I always felt my daughter was taken from me." And yet Fessler found that the women generally described these moments of nondecision as "the most significant and defining event of their lives." One woman spoke for many when she said, "I never made it through a night without wondering how [my daughter] was." Later in life, the shame of these experiences, both sexual and maternal, often led to entrenched habits of secrecy, from husbands, children, friends, and even families of origin, who typically never discussed the relinquished child again after the event. One woman remembered "that little wet ink across a piece of paper made me *not* a mother in the eyes of society. . . . My personality changed."[72]

Dorothy's experience illustrates the difficulties of girls and women trying to make actual choices about sex and reproduction outside of marriage. Promised by her boyfriend that she would not get pregnant because he would "pull out," she remembers that he "stopped trying to convince me and just took over and sort of pushed me back, and again I felt unable to act." When she found out she was pregnant, she "was very ashamed. This was not something that good girls did. Because I came from a very kind of poor family, I was more acutely aware than most people, maybe, about reputations and how easily they are lost. . . . Your best hope in those days was to marry the boy and have done with it. . . . The thing was, I was fifteen. I didn't love this boy. This was 1966—abortion wasn't an option. I mean, we didn't even think about it."[73]

Dorothy's mother said that together they would "get through this." Dorothy's priest told her that marriage was the best way, but the church would not support the marriage because the baby's father was not Catholic. Her baby could thus not be baptized without a marriage, a situation that would consign her baby to purgatory. The priest suggested the maternity-home plan, and Dorothy's mother eventually agreed. The isolation there was excruciating, and the birth itself was "the loneliest thing I've ever gone through in my life." Dorothy was told she had

had a baby, although she remembered nothing because of the anesthesia. She wanted to see her baby but was told she could not until the next day at feeding time. When she finally saw her child, Dorothy remembers, "I knew what real love really was."[74]

After a postpartum illness and a necessary surgery, Dorothy was asked to sign the papers for adoption, but she resisted. A social worker said she had not bonded with the baby anyway, and, "as far as we're concerned, she's only known the foster mother at this point. The adoptive family is waiting for her. And why would you want to just do this to *them*? They've been waiting all this time while you were sick to get this done." When Dorothy continued to argue and asked to see her baby, she was told that the baby's location could not be disclosed and reminded that "the state paid for you to go to St. Agnes [maternity home]. That's quite a bit of money that we put out in good faith. Do you have the money to pay for that?" Her mother, supportive though she was, admitted they did not have the money. "For every question I asked this woman," remembered Dorothy, "I got the answer I didn't want to hear: that I had no rights. That I had already given her away. That it was the best thing. And that it was all my fault."[75] Dorothy hung onto this experience, escaped into drug use and cut herself off from relationships for many years. These responses were not predicted in a postwar climate that clung to the idea that the experience of premarital pregnancy for white women could be washed away, forgotten. These women could be "redeemed" and made marriageable, made real mothers once they had a ring on their fingers. In following their parts in the adoption story, they could make married parents—deserving parents—happy and provide their babies with a better life.

The relinquishment script was relatively new. Prewar maternity homes had encouraged unwed mothers to keep their babies with them. To reinforce this notion some states even legislated that unwed mothers would breastfeed for six months.[76] A letter passed around maternity homes in the 1930s blatantly chastised mothers-to-be who would consider leaving their babies. "Written" by "The Baby you didn't want," the letter intoned,

> Just as I had become used to your arms and begun to know your voice and to recognize . . . your movements and your smile you are walking off and leaving me. Whose arms will pick me up from my coop tomorrow? Into what home shall I be consigned and who will give me that bottle you taught me to pull on when you decided that I must stop getting my milk from your rather thin breast? Anyhow, what have I done to you that you should walk off and leave me like this? I never asked you to bring me into this world . . . I thought I belonged to you . . . I think you should have thought about me in the first place.

References to the "rather thin breast" and the things the young woman "should have thought of in the first place" cast the "illegitimate" mother as more sexual than maternal. The appropriate punishment for her sexual sin was to keep her baby and face social stigma both for herself and her baby. Indeed, one woman who did keep her baby in the postwar years recalled, "I am an unwed mother who kept her child.

And I fear no hell after death, for I've had mine on earth. Let no man or girl deceive herself—hell hath no punishment like the treatment people give a 'fallen woman.'"[77]

Between the mid-1940s and the mid-1960s, social work practice shifted toward encouraging adoption, supposed to be a liberating and progressive option for unwed mothers. But freedom was not really the issue, as it turned out. As historian Rickie Solinger and others have shown, the white unwed mother was, much like other reproductive nonconformists, cast as neurotic. "Every unmarried mother is to some degree a psychiatric problem," wrote two Harvard psychiatrists in 1965. A social worker who saw unwed mothers as psychologically challenged but capable of rehabilitation said, "Her pregnancy is often a purposive acting out of her inner drives." Academic perspectives confirmed and reinforced the new ethos of social work by providing psychiatric rationales for assuming that such mothers were "overly dominant, aggressive, narcissistic and bitterly hostile, but are covertly passive, inadequate, and masochistic."[78]

Often the problem was cast as one that seemed to plague practically every woman who ran into an expert in this era: ambivalence about feminine roles, in either the offending unwed mother or her mother before her. The mothers of pregnant unmarried girls and young women were often described as controlling, unhappy in their marriages, not sufficiently feminine and subordinate in their relationships with their own husbands. One psychiatrist noted "the pregnant girl and her mother must both be given a decisive, 'no!' The girl's mother must be dealt with as if she is a child herself."[79] The unwed mother was by definition an inappropriate mother.

However objectionable and reductive it seems today to cast every white girl or woman who found herself pregnant out of wedlock as neurotic, social work and psychiatric thinking of the day emphasized the possibility for redemption in the scripted story of pregnancy and relinquishment. The girl could forget the pregnancy and marry later. She just needed to follow instructions and learn, like every other woman, to form a proper mature relationship with a future husband and to accept her femininity. Most homes even offered classes on charm, hair-dressing, and make-up as well as cooking and sewing as a way to direct women toward future married life, when they could become legitimate mothers. One woman wrote from a maternity home in New York, "I want a home. I want to be married. I want children I can keep and love. Maybe that's why I'm here. Maybe I just need someone to love."[80]

The pressures on white girls and women to relinquish their babies reveal how their lack of power as mothers reflected their social status as young, unmarried women. Even for couples who wanted to marry, parental consent was required before age twenty-one, and parents were not often willing to give it. Boys and men who tried to take responsibility were sometimes prevented from doing so by parents or religious authorities skeptical about "that kind of girl." When they did not want to take responsibility, there was little compulsion to do so. Their denial of paternity was rarely questioned, and there were no reliable DNA tests to determine paternity before the 1980s. Boys and men could face negative emotional consequences, knowing they fathered a child for which they would not or could not take responsibility, but research is lacking on their stories.[81]

Parents' attitudes varied. Some were supportive of their daughters emotionally, but many overrode their daughters' choices. Some made their daughters crouch in the back seats of cars on their infrequent visits home from the maternity homes so that none of the neighbors would see them. Middle-class parents and those anxious about their class status were most likely to make these decisions, and this was the case for many in the conformity-conscious 1950s and early 1960s.One woman remembers her mother's fear that she would lose her job if people knew her daughter was pregnant.[82] They feared for their daughters' sexual reputations, which were linked to family status, and some apparently took it as a personal affront or failure that their daughters had engaged in out-of-wedlock sex.

Some pregnant girls and women exercised what few options they had by refusing to marry the boy or man who had gotten them pregnant. One woman said of her boyfriend, "My mother and father knew his whole family and everybody thought he was Mr. Wonderful. He's the one who got me pregnant. But he had slapped me and I didn't want to be with him if he could be that mean. I told him the baby wasn't his." Another said she feared that if she revealed her pregnancy to her boyfriend, she would be "forced to marry him and I didn't want to marry him. I didn't know if I ever wanted to marry anyone. I had not seen that marriage had done much for my mother."[83] Their determination to avoid marriage to men who did not represent the future they wanted suggests a sort of underground trend of this era: women's belief that they could make choices in their lives about motherhood and marriage. Their choices were unfortunately more limited than these young women, living in a culture of secrecy about unwed motherhood, actually knew.

African American Single Mothers

Race was often a determining factor in how a young woman experienced an unexpected out-of-wedlock pregnancy. We know the most about this from research, especially historian Rickie Solinger's work, contrasting the experiences of white and African American single mothers. Unkept promises from boyfriends, limited access to contraception and abortion, and the enormous economic and social challenges of single motherhood influenced women of all races. Unwed African American mothers, however, faced special constraints and often encountered a coercive and punitive state apparatus. As late as 1959, unwed white mothers were using Aid to Dependent Children (ADC) benefits at a higher rate than African American mothers because of racial discrimination in the administration of welfare benefits, but increasing rates of ADC enrollment by African American women in the 1950s and 1960s made their "illegitimate" pregnancies a political issue. Studies failed to find a link between increased rates of unmarried motherhood and ADC costs, but state and city governments nevertheless targeted African American women who became pregnant out of wedlock. Some states required women to "produce" the father as a condition of being awarded ADC. Solinger's exhaustive research into state laws revealed that "in one state, if the unmarried mother wanted to put her child up for adoption, she had to get the father to sign his agreement, or she had to publicly state on the record that she had no idea who the father was or what his name was, thus 'confessing' in open court that she was promiscuous." Some cities evicted women with out-of-wedlock children from public housing. In some states, such as Illinois, unwed mothers who received ADC and had an illegitimate child were threatened with jail time.[84]

State-sponsored sterilization, increasingly directed at women of color rather than white working-class women, constituted yet another threat. In 1958, a Mississippi state representative proposed "An Act to Discourage Immorality of Unmarried Females by Providing for Sterilization of the Unwed Mother." Though this bill was not enacted, in states that continued to promote sterilization, politicians referred in coded terms to the fertility of African American women as a rationale for such initiatives. A North Carolina state senator explained, "We are breeding a race of bastards."[85]

As these examples illustrate, single African American mothers felt the long arm of the law in their lives and very frequently faced limitations everywhere they turned, limitations that had as much to do with race (and sometimes class) as with gender. As one woman said, "When I needed financial assistance, all Welfare did was to give me a hard time. . . . They made matters worse for me by trying to drag the baby's father to court. I probably would have been able to work if there had been a daycare center where I could have left the baby." Meanwhile, the ostensibly more rehabilitative institutions were generally closed to African Americans. There seems to have been a stronger sense of the moral imperative to keep one's child among African Americans than among whites: placing a baby for adoption "would be throwing away your own flesh and blood," as one mother of a single teenager put it. Still, many pregnant African American girls and women asked the Children's Bureau about maternity homes, and African American mothers sometimes saw these homes as safe places for their pregnant daughters.[86] They were very often turned away on the basis of race. Not until the late 1950s did the homes begin to desegregate and offer more spaces to nonwhite girls and women.

Adoptive parents for African American women's babies remained in short supply. White Americans in the 1950s, the most connected to the adoption infrastructure, retained a strong racial bias for white babies. Indeed, the only interracial adoptions that even made a tiny dent in this pattern occurred in the aftermath of the American bombing of Japan and the Korean War. Small numbers of orphans from these conflicts were adopted by white Americans. Within domestic adoption, agencies, believing they could not place African American babies, often refused to accept them. The National Urban League expanded outreach to African American communities to increase adoption, but adoption agencies often set unrealistic income and age requirements and bans on maternal employment. These policies contributed to a situation in which the need for African American adoptive parents always exceeded the supply.[87]

Single motherhood was more often forced on African American women than on white women during this era, and it was no easy road. The marriage box that was so glorified by the dominant culture had different meanings for African American women facing out-of-wedlock pregnancies, especially among the poor and working-class. Given the limited job prospects available to African American men, most young women could not look to husbands for economic security in the way that white women could. In one study, 93 percent of unwed African American mothers agreed with the idea that "a girl must pick her husband carefully because most men turn out to be no good as husbands." During the second half of the twentieth century, acceptance of single motherhood became more prevalent among low-income women. Even at midcentury, having a baby was a marker of adulthood in African American communities; marriage, while respected and promoted, was not the same rite of passage into economic partnership and prescribed gender roles that it was for more privileged whites. Class mattered in these patterns: middle-class African Americans, for whom economic stability within marriage was a more realistic hope, more often resembled white families in negative attitudes toward out-of-wedlock motherhood.[88]

Abortion in the Era of Secrecy

A woman named Barbara, who in the 1950s had an abortion performed on a kitchen table by a man with unknown credentials, remembered that "when something is illegal and you have to go through all this subterfuge to get it, you really *feel* like a criminal." Afterward, "when I got back to college, I told a few of my close friends the real reason and they turned against me. . . . You see, this just wasn't done. In college, if you were actually sleeping with someone you kept it totally secret because we all lived this pretense that 'nice girls don't do it.'" She said that "if you did get pregnant, you simply got married—or you left school. You disappeared. What you *didn't* do was to go have an abortion and then come back and expect everyone to treat you the same."[89]

Abortion, as we have seen, had expanded during the Great Depression, along with greater acceptance among physicians. But with abortion options, as with carrying out-of-wedlock babies to term, women with problem pregnancies faced a sea change in attitudes in the postwar period. Historian Leslie Reagan has shown that this era saw more heavy-handed state policies, including raids on clinics, requirements that women come to court to face juries (a very rare occurrence in interwar America), and the creation by nervous hospital administrations of stricter rules to police physicians' practice of abortion. In a pronatalist culture, seeking abortion was cast as a crime against femininity. Some experts even recommended shock treatments for these women.[90]

Once again, the threat of gender nonconformity by would be-mothers (which is to say, women generally) fueled a postwar tightening of options. Rising abortion rates in the 1930s and rising rates of maternal labor force participation in the 1940s combined to elicit old fears of women's rebellion against motherhood. After the war, McCarthy-era anticommunist hysteria fueled a willingness to use police force to squelch subversive activities. At a time when police raided suspected gay and lesbian bars to root out potential subversives, they also broke into surgical rooms during abortion procedures, seized patient records, and sometimes forced women to undergo gynecological exams. Newspapers provided lurid coverage.

Some published the names of patients or witnesses, thereby casting abortion as part of a criminal underworld and exposing women to suspicions about their sexual behavior.[91]

Physicians who performed abortions were no longer protected unless operating under strict hospital guidelines; otherwise, they risked revocation of medical licenses and imprisonment. Hospitals increased their use and surveillance of in-house therapeutic abortion committees to police themselves and women. Outside of hospitals, physician abortion providers, who may have been more likely to be holistic and consider family and personal situations in agreeing to an abortion, were largely compelled to stop this part of their practice. They were the victims of McCarthy-esque professional conservatism. Within the profession itself, those in favor of tightening abortion access referred to Russia's "amoral and unethical" society as a counterpoint to a moral, abortion-restrictive America, and some tried to rename the procedure as "abortion-murder."[92]

The face of the problem was defined by that demographic group that became such a thorn in the side to postwar sexual morality: single pregnant women. Indeed, among therapeutic abortion patients, the proportion of unmarried women skyrocketed from 7 percent in the 1940s to 41 percent by the early 1960s.[93] Abortion, however, remained inaccessible to many married women who sought it for family, personal, or health reasons. At the moment when demand increased, and, as we now know, not terribly long before abortion reform would force a change in the law, abortion seems to have become more dangerous and more humiliating.

For the minority of women who had access to a physician's care and were willing to make their situation public enough to seek that care, abortion was a new labyrinth. Securing the procedure was no longer a matter of finding a reference for a physician provider, something relatively easy to do for an illegal procedure, at least for urban women, in the 1930s. Now a woman had to have her case reviewed by a hospital committee. Sometimes she even had to appear before the committee for an interview, and often the committee reviewed her sexual history. In the era of psychologizing about nonconforming behavior, such as out-of-wedlock pregnancy, a pregnant girl or woman was unlikely to escape without a psychiatric label being placed on her as an official rationale for performing the abortion. Threats of suicide were often helpful to the case. One sympathetic psychiatrist who believed women should make their own decisions, facilitated the situation by writing letters saying women were suicidal, whether they were or not.[94]

Women's lack of autonomy in the situation was taken for granted by most of the medical establishment. At a time when poor women and women of color were disproportionately sterilized without their consent, abortion admissions became a venue for this practice. Public ward patients were sterilized far more frequently than private patients. Hospital abortions, like medical care generally, were rationed by income and race. One study of abortions in New York City found that 91 percent of the hospital abortions were performed on white women. Very few were performed, however, because most women who pursued this option underwent illegal, rather than hospital-sanctioned, abortions.[95]

Outside hospital structures, obtaining the procedure was a different and more dangerous obstacle course. Nonhospital abortion providers now needed to protect their secrecy. Unlicensed and unethical abortion providers proliferated, which drove up the financial cost of the procedure and greatly increased women's medical risks. Women who recalled their postwar abortion experiences described secret meetings, being blindfolded and driven to an unknown place, and having the abortion performed by an unknown person. Women's memories included an abortion provider smoking during the procedure, another smelling badly of alcohol, and an abortion performed without any anesthesia. One woman whose pregnancy was the result of a rape said she was offered a $20 refund on her $1,000 abortion in exchange for a sexual favor, and her experience was not unique. Follow-up care was usually the woman's responsibility. One woman remembered going to an abortionist who "said not to call if I had problems."[96]

Women's own desires for secrecy increased their risks as well. Rose S., pregnant despite using a diaphragm, found a gynecologist in the phone book, used a false name, and pretended to be married: "What seemed of paramount importance to me . . . was the secrecy: I not only didn't want anyone in authority to know, I was also anxious that no word leak out to any of my friends and, certainly, family." Such secrecy cost some women their lives, as it did one woman's college acquaintance who died from postoperative complications. "She was too frightened to tell anyone what she had done . . . [she] tried to take care of herself. She locked herself in the bathroom between 2 dorm rooms and quietly bled to death."[97]

The enormous social, cultural, and professional energy combined with the secrecy and the control that went into denying women the opportunity to make their own choices about motherhood is somewhat staggering. Reagan has astutely observed that the cultural climate around abortion reflected the era's obsessions: "Silencing, forced speaking, naming names, and public exposure of subversive behavior and beliefs were all characteristics of the McCarthy era."[98] The same could be said of the situations of white women who were shunted into maternity homes and all pregnant women coerced into suing for paternity as a condition of future financial assistance from either the state or their families. The stories of women lying about their neuroses before abortion committees, suffering from infection from illegal attempts to terminate pregnancies, languishing in maternity homes, or fearing jail time for conceiving out-of-wedlock babies all speak volumes about their relative powerlessness and lack of autonomy. Yet the very presence of nonconforming women, pregnant out of wedlock, could not be denied.

At a time when childbirth became dramatically safer owing to the use of sulfa drugs, abortion caused a significant proportion of maternal deaths. For example, abortion-related deaths composed more than 42 percent of the maternal mortality in New York City by the early 1960s, up from about 14 percent of the maternal mortality rate in the 1920s. At the same time, wards devoted to caring for women with complications from abortion burgeoned: Cook County Hospital in Chicago, for example, saw the number of women treated for such complications triple between the late 1930s and the late 1950s. As Reagan has noted, "Abortion was institutionalized in hospitals in two interrelated structures: the therapeutic abortion committee and the septic abortion ward. While a very small number of women came in through the hospital's front door for scheduled therapeutic abortions, many more abortion patients entered the hospital through the emergency room door."[99]

By the mid-1950s, the contradictions of this situation were becoming increasingly glaring to medical professionals, and a cadre of physicians began envisioning reform for reasons of humane care. As I discuss in chapter 9, the cause of abortion reform would be taken up by feminists as well. In the postwar era, the seeds of this reform lie in not only the medical situation but also ironically the rise in psychiatric "exceptions" for abortion, no matter how rare those exceptions were in practice. Not just physical risk, but attitudes toward pregnancy and motherhood mattered in a psychologically saturated culture, even if women's own choices, their own version of the relationship between motherhood and mental health, were not yet taken seriously. "Most psychiatrists recognize that the woman who states she does not wish to have a baby is unlikely to be a good mother," said one psychiatrist in 1955.[100] It was a leap from here to the idea of women making their own reproductive decisions; nonetheless, women's voices and problematic reproductive situations were becoming visible despite every attempt to silence and erase them.

Infertility, Adoption, and Motherhood: The Other Side of Reproductive Nonconformity

White married women's inability to have children was cast as a tragic situation in which marriages could not thrive and women in particular could not assume true womanhood. This attitude contributed to a doubling of adoption rates between the mid-1940s and mid-1950s. By 1957, there were an estimated 91,000 adoptions annually, and that number rose to a peak of 175,000 in 1970. Meanwhile, the idea of infertility as a medical problem with a potential solution became visible to more and more Americans. Between 1952 and 1955 alone, the number of fertility clinics nationwide nearly doubled.[101]

Not surprisingly, women of this era agonized over the problem of infertility. Despite the long-term gains in women's public roles, women who could not conceive in the 1950s echoed almost precisely the language of similarly situated women a century earlier, such as Civil War era Mary Chestnut Boykin who lamented that because she did not have children, "no good have I done—to myself or anyone else." A mid-twentieth-century woman named Pamela wrote in the same vein, "Being childless has been an ongoing cause of great sadness in my life—nothing else ever made up for that loss. To me children are the greatest source of happiness in life." Infertility affected approximately 10 percent of married couples in this era. While men were also very pained by infertility, especially at a time when fatherhood was more highly linked to identity and masculinity, women were more often devastated.[102]

Relatively few women had made themselves the pioneers of nineteenth- and early twentieth-century medical experiments in addressing infertility. But by the mid-twentieth century, more women pursued promises like this one, which appeared in the magazine *The American Weekly*: "Maybe you CAN have a Baby. . . . Doctors are able to help up to half of all sterile couples to have children." Interviews with physicians and testimonials from women who had conceived added to the appeal. Modern medicine significantly raised people's hopes. Physicians tested, sometimes with success: hormone therapy, donor insemination, and the surgical reconstruction of damaged fallopian tubes. The promise, however, was much greater than the success rate. Diagnosis occurred in only about half the cases, and only one-third received treatment that resulted in carrying a pregnancy to term. At the same time, the treatment often contributed to pathologizing both a woman's mind and body. Pronatalism underlay medical approaches to women's potentially infertile bodies: "For conception to take place a woman must be a woman," noted Abraham Stone, medical director of the Margaret Sanger Research Foundation; "being a woman means acceptance of her primary role, that of conceiving and bearing a child." Some even argued that a lack of readiness for motherhood accounted for infertility and miscarriages. Indeed, a prominent obstetrician argued in 1953 that "an unconscious rejection on the mother's part of repeated pregnancies and of motherhood" could be the cause of miscarriage and that "psychiatric treatment will do more to help these women achieve happy motherhood than such prescriptions as vitamin E, sex hormones, or complete bed rest."[103]

Though certainly not all infertility specialists subscribed to them, psychological explanations could be especially damning in this Freudian-influenced era. An article in the *Journal of the American Medical Association* written by a sociologist, a psychologist, and a gynecologist, claimed, "Most people who do not truly want [children] have personality defects—for example, infantilism. . . . Women totally lacking the desire for children are so rare that they may be considered as deviants from the normal." And infertile women might be in the situation they were in precisely because of that problematic female ambivalence about the assigned role of femininity.

> The masculine-aggressive woman insists on having a child of her own body cost what it may. She is a ready, though rarely ideal, candidate for donor insemination, sometimes obtaining her husband's reluctant consent by species of emotional blackmail. Second, there is the wife who accepts childlessness and lives on good terms with her sterile husband but demands from him constant proofs of his masculinity. . . . And, third, the truly motherly woman compensates for her lack of children by directing her motherliness toward other persons or objects, real or symbolic.[104]

Peppering their explanation with psychologized labels for gender rebellion, the experts also betrayed a pervasive bias about all reproductive health: it was the responsibility of medical experts to determine the appropriate course of action for a woman's reproductive life. In their professional literature, physicians called for consideration of the "emotional maturity of the patient" in making decisions about whether to offer treatment. Questions to ask included: "Is the patient a cold, selfish, demanding person, or is she a warm, giving woman?" "What are her deeper meanings underlying her surface attitude toward pregnancy, motherhood, and sterility?" For some critics, career women who might "wear the pants" in a family were suspect candidates for fertility treatment. "We have all seen a long-desired pregnancy follow the renunciation of a career. This may be the result of the development of 'motherliness' and the consequent hormonal changes." Elaine Tyler May has pointed out, however, that men escaped such pathologizing: "Experts in the field never suggested that men thwarted their own potential for parenthood by 'unconscious wishes' or 'a rejection of their masculinity.' On the contrary, specialists frequently reassured men that infertility did not mean they were lacking in masculinity."[105]

Women's bodies and sexuality were linked to their minds in this medical discourse. Some neo-Frueudian explanations included the notion that sexually "frigid" women who were not sexually adjusted often could not conceive. "Medical terminology was filled with metaphors of the 'incompetent' female body, while presenting the male reproductive system as robust," says May. Medically accepted phrases included "defective cervix" and "incompetent cervix." One woman wrote to Eleanor Roosevelt that her heart ached to have a child and lamented that she could not "have any children because my uterus is deformed."[106]

Researchers, knowing that men's role in conception was important, even issued guidelines about examining the man before running the often invasive suggested tests on the woman. But the association between men's virility and their ability to father children was a sensitive topic, and physicians often rationalized attempts to treat a woman before even testing a man. One medical scientist explained that he and his colleagues were aware of "the responsibility of the male in infertility, but the incidence of primary male infertility is variable but relatively low and, in our culture, it is usually the women who initiate the request for assistance." Women often protected their husbands, too. One woman whose spouse was "depressed and angered" at the suggestion that the conception problem might be his, said, "He couldn't take it . . . it might break up our marriage. Rather than risk that I'll reconcile myself to going without a family."[107] Shielding their husband's egos sometimes meant undergoing painful and prolonged attempts at treatment rather than bringing their partners into the medical system. Postwar infertility treatments clearly reflected pronatalism, medicalized notions of a faulty female reproductive system, and antiquated ideas of the "barren" woman as the problem.

Meanwhile, as growing numbers of Americans pursued adoption as a means to parenthood, adoptive motherhood in the postwar period became another expression of modern motherhood: expert driven, socially engineered, and reflective of tightly defined "normal" families. Informal and broadly open practices of the prewar era gave way to a more formal closed adoption system. An infant's past was erased, along with that of his or her biological mother. A new family that looked "normal" was created; the happy two-parent married couple was the mirror image of the presumably neurotic biological mother who had conceived the baby.

Through adoption screenings, women were required to prove their psychological worthiness to participate in the institution of motherhood. In an era when mother love was such a charged and suspicious concept, the experts reminded one another to ask: did an adoptive mother really want the "normal, genuine satisfactions of motherhood"? Or was she pursuing adoption to "perpetuate [her own] early neurotic relationships . . . or to realize . . . immoderate specifications for love"? Of course, women who were not good wives might well be suspected of not being good potential mothers. Women like "Mrs. C." were approved by the social workers who served as gatekeepers to parenthood in this situation: "Mrs. C . . . seems to accept completely and with great satisfaction her role as a feminine person, as a wife, homemaker and potential mother. She shows great admiration and pride for her husband and certainly seems ready to put his career ahead of other considerations." Feminine dress was noted, positively, in case records of prospective adoptive mothers, while adoptive fathers—unlike biological fathers—were also evaluated, though their necessary proof of masculinity and normalcy basically involved their capacity for breadwinning.[108]

Mothers who wanted to adopt were often required to quit their jobs as a precondition of the next step: the home study. As one social worker reported, "I let Mrs. W. know that we felt it important that there be a period when she was dependent on her husband's income and at home for awhile before she had a child." As previously suggested, this practice was especially challenging for African American women. One prospective adoptive mother explained, "We were moving along nicely and then they told me I would have to give up my job."[109] The irony of suggesting that every unmarried pregnant white mother was "neurotic" while also scrutinizing the gender conformity of conventional married women (whom those young, unmarried women were told would be ideal mothers) seems to have been lost on postwar experts. This scrutiny occurred despite the fact that experts promoted adoption as a positive good.

The postwar fixation on the appropriately gendered couple also limited opportunities for single women, women in relationships with other women, older couples, and divorced and widowed women. Single women had long faced the unflattering designation of spinster, but in the Progressive era it had been assumed that, as women, their motherly instincts could positively benefit children. Professional women who could support themselves, even some who lived with female partners, did adopt children earlier in the century. The labor activist Pauline Newman and prison reformer Miriam van Waters were among the most famous of what we would now see as lesbian mothers. Over the course of the 1920s and 1930s, increasing homophobia, Freudian suspicions about unmarried women's potentially misplaced affections toward their children, and the cultural critique of moral motherhood all made women who were not in committed married relationships suspect in their claims to mothering. By 1945, one expert article opined that "'unmarried people' were 'obviously disqualified,' along with the 'mentally ill' and 'alcoholics.'"[110] Among adoption placement professionals, the overwhelming emphasis came to be on helping young married couples, the anchors of ideal nuclear families, who could not biologically bear children.

This is not to suggest that married adoptive mothers had an easy time. By the time they adopted children, most had endured fertility treatments and the sometimes harsh judgments from people who had children. Some withstood suggestions that their children were not really their own after the adoption was complete. Janice Stiles (who ultimately chose not to adopt) recalled that, while trying to conceive a child, she would "cross the street, sometimes, to avoid walking past a pregnant woman; I'd go to baby showers (and this was during the baby boom— there were LOTS of showers) and come home and cry . . . I even used to daydream while we went on long drives that I'd see a baby in a blanket by the side of the road and take it home." Florence Barkley, a married woman who adopted children during the postwar years, remembered, "It was hard to adopt. It took 7 years to get my first son and three years for my second one—and I did go through a lot of painful infertility treatment—I'd do it again, I'm not sorry—and I get very angry when people say, 'Oh you got yours the easy way.'"[111]

Perhaps because adoption was a privilege, a role for which women had to prove themselves worthy, adoptive mothers often spoke in idealized terms about motherhood. Yet they asserted a challenge to strict biological definitions of motherhood and family and contributed to enlarging the idea of motherhood beyond biology.[112] They helped push Americans toward a broader acceptance of adoption as a legitimate way to construct a family. In this way, adoptive mothers, of whom there were more than ever before in the population, represented the more expansive possibilities of midcentury United States. There were other connections besides the actual babies between adoptive mothers and the women who relinquished their babies for adoption. Both were offered a second chance in a culturally acceptable family life after circumstances, relational or biological, threatened to bump them off the path to the traditional American family.

Conclusion

Many of those who lived through the midcentury decades sought to contain what ultimately could not be contained. The wife-and-mother box, like Pandora's, would burst open in the 1960s. The suppression of nonmarital sexuality and of mothers' labor force participation, the rigid prescriptions for the nuclear family, the squelching of cultural and political dissent, and women's acquiescence to the experts—all this would be roundly challenged by the time the young parents of the baby boom reached middle age. Those who lived on the margins of the white middle-class suburban ideal, including the racial and ethnic minorities systematically barred from the suburbs, would help shatter the illusion of unity, conformity, and boundless opportunity that shaped the mainstream postwar American culture. The pervasive mother blame that characterized this era would be difficult to dislodge, but a revived interest in the social and economic conditions of family life would create some additional space to reduce the finger-pointing at Mom. As the tight nuclear family script began to unravel and feminists challenged rigid gender roles and the motherhood mandate, women gained a broader voice in defining the terms of motherhood. To understand these dynamics of historical change, it helps to appreciate the social contradictions of the period from the 1940s through the early 1960s: for mothers the era was expansive as well as repressive. It was, in retrospect, a tinderbox, in which the contradictions of modern gender roles were forcibly contained and stoked until they ultimately exploded.

CHAPTER 9

Mother Power and Mother Angst

As a spirit of rebellion swept the nation in the 1960s and 1970s, many who considered themselves experts on women and motherhood were not sure what was hitting them. Women who were supposed to have "adjusted" to their wife-and-mother roles were launching a widespread feminist movement. They were simultaneously demanding access to the public world and criticizing the American family for infantilizing and restricting them. Betty Friedan's best-selling book *The Feminine Mystique*, the formation of the National Organization for Women in 1966, and young women's 1968 protests against the Miss America pageant's objectification of women were only widely visible pieces of a much larger whole. This was a veritable earthquake under the pedestal of privatized, underresourced, and rigidly prescribed American motherhood. The momentum of social movements demanding real provisions to mothers and challenging the cultural construction of motherhood and womanhood continued into the 1980s, although it then faced a powerful conservative backlash.

When Daniel Patrick Moynihan, who considered himself a liberal and a well-informed policy analyst, published the famous Moynihan report in 1965, he referred to African American families as a "matriarchate" and a "tangle of pathology." He seemed somehow completely unprepared for the pushback from African American activists who found fault not with families, but with racist and classist social policies that targeted women. In Harlem, mothers like Rita Martinez told assemblymen: "You're going to tell me I need a playground, and I'm telling you I need better schools. The playground will come later. . . . You can't tell me what I need if you don't live in this community. . . . Come and ask me what I need. And I'll tell you what I need is a job."[1]

Within the same span of time, most obstetricians were equally flabbergasted by a rising alternative birth movement in which some radical women took on their own "inspections" of maternity wards. They protested the use of excessive drugs, episiotomies, forceps, and forcible restraint and isolation of laboring women. The natural birth advocacy group, Mothers of the wHole [*sic*] Earth Revolt (MOTHER) declared, "Birth is normal and hospitals are terrible. . . . We are reclaiming motherhood. We will reclaim birth."[2] Similarly, a majority of physicians supported legalization of abortion by the early 1960s, but what most had in mind was that physicians would have more professional autonomy in deciding when abortion was warranted. Many were surprised by an advancing feminist argument that the decision should ultimately belong to women, not to physicians or to legislators.

Even the venerable Dr. Spock, who shocked many people with his late life conversion to antiwar activism, was bowled over by accusations like the one leveled at him by feminist Gloria Steinem. "I hope you realize," the normally gentle Steinem asserted, "you have been a major oppressor of women in the same category as Freud!" And Steinem was not alone. Another feminist, Jo Ann Hoit, insisted that Spock's presumably generic use of the term "parents" was deceptive because, in Spock's examples, children's problems ended up being the mother's fault. After all, in 1970, Spock was still praising women in his child-care advice literature as specially qualified for "working at unexciting, repetitive tasks," part of the skill set that made them "indispensable as wives, mothers, nurses, secretaries."[3]

Around the same time, John Mack Carter, publisher and editor of the *Ladies' Home Journal*, found himself the victim of a feminist occupation of his office, where he headed up the gold standard of domestic advice to women, including motherhood articles often written by men. The women who challenged the magazine's practices were tired of "slanted romantic stories glorifying women's traditional role." The *Journal* agreed to a feminist insert in a special issue, a space in which women could finally say to a large female audience who read domestic magazines: "We are not only not paid for our work, but are considered less than human when we perform it." The issue also featured a "Housewives' Bill of Rights," which included a call for maternity leave, free child care, Social Security benefits for housewives, health insurance, and paid vacations.[4]

Challenges to the silencing, privatizing, pathologizing, and economic disempowering of women came from a variety of directions. Experts who had based their influence on science and male authority now stood more uncertainly on their pedestals. In addition to the creation of the atomic bomb, the hyperrationalism of the first half of the century seemed partly responsible for atrocities like Hitler's "final solution." Meanwhile, science itself had traveled from Newtonian certainty to Einstein's relativity theories and Rachel Carson's argument that scientific progress could partly be blamed for environmental destruction. In that context, beginning in the 1960s, new forms of maternalist activism challenged entrenched, usually male power structures and cultures of expertise: welfare policies that left women and children hungry, schools that marginalized children of color and poor children, industries whose pollution poisoned children and entire communities, and military policies that threatened the future of the world. At the same time, Second Wave feminism developed stinging and multifaceted critiques of women's confinement—psychologically, economically, sexually, reproductively, and culturally. Feminists also questioned the motherhood mandate more extensively than ever before and drew attention to the ways in which motherhood in a patriarchal society was part of the oppression of women. They also pushed, often successfully, for policy changes to empower women.

These protests did much to transform cultural attitudes toward women and motherhood. Feminist critiques also shaped and were shaped by a changing economy in which extensive labor force participation for mothers began to become the norm. The old division of mothers as private, emotional, and noneconomic caretakers and fathers as breadwinners, disciplinarians, and public representatives of the family was disrupted. The continued pattern of privatizing women's struggles as mothers, as well as the divisions within feminism and backlash against it, forestalled many liberating possibilities of these profound transformations. Still, some changes would be lasting.

MATERNALISM REVIVED
Economic and Racial Justice for Mothers

Envisioning a Great Society and reacting to both pressure from and inspiration by the civil rights movement, President Lyndon Johnson persuaded Congress to enact a sweeping agenda of economic opportunity in the mid-1960s. In a burst of legislative activity scarcely imaginable today, Congress authorized the creation of Medicare, Medicaid, Head Start, a new GI Bill, and a Department of Housing and Urban Development (HUD), Upward Bound, and a Manpower Development and Training Act, as well as expansion of Social Security benefits, legal services, student loan programs to increase college opportunities, and the enactment of a Voting Rights Act to ensure the citizenship rights of people of color. Declaring a War on Poverty, Johnson also launched the Office of Economic Opportunity (OEO), out of which grew Community Action Programs (CAPs). Those programs departed from Progressive or New Deal era social provisions because they emphasized participatory democracy in keeping with the new antiauthoritarian ethos of the 1960s. Community residents were invited to have "maximum feasible participation" in the design of antipoverty initiatives.

Impoverished and social-justice-oriented mothers and like-minded activists took this idea and ran with it; indeed, they ran with it quite a bit further than the president or Congress had in mind and certainly much further than entrenched urban politicians appreciated. Along with civil rights protesters in the South, women working on the intertwined issues of poverty and racism in New York City engaged in what sociologist Nancy Naples calls "activist mothering." Like the activists of Clara Lemlich Shavelson's generation, who took up consumer price issues in the desperate 1930s, New York resident Wilma North, an African American mother of three, did not need President Johnson's declaration to know that a war on poverty was necessary. She also knew that it would take mothers' energy to fight the battles. "There was too much to be done . . . if you need crossing guards, or if there are dilapidated houses, or if you're not getting the kind of response from the police department that you feel the community needs to get."[5] It was time to get involved. As her words suggest, mothers of color in working-class and poor communities saw problems such as housing, education, and community policing as intertwined.

Compared to the Great Depression era, 1960s maternalist activists had a broader platform, a more expansive media system, a government and general public suddenly alert to the issue of poverty in the midst of plenty, and the benefit of civil rights, antipoverty, and budding feminist social movements. One important facet of the OEO program was New Careers, a program that promoted the hiring of community members whose educational credentials were less important than their knowledge of the community. This was a striking challenge to a long-held reverence for experts in American society. Naples's research showed that these programs "created a point of entry into the social welfare establishment for workers from poor communities," allowing them, at least for a time, to expand and elevate the moral authority of the unpaid community caregiving work many women were already doing, while challenging power structures at a neighborhood level. Nationally, an estimated 250,000 to 400,000 people were hired as paraprofessionals in human service fields during the War on Poverty. By one estimate, 125,000 poor residents gained employment in CAPs in community organizing, teachers' aide roles, day care workers, and similar positions.[6] The CAPs hired professionals, too. Educated community-based professionals shared schools, housing opportunities, and concerns about community policing with their neighbors and relatives. They also continued their unpaid work alongside paid employment.

Mothers or not, community workers explained their motivations in terms of children's needs. Educational issues in the public schools catapulted even apolitical women into activism. Japanese American activist Paula Sands believed that "educational institutions were not really prepared to teach youngsters in low economic neighborhoods. There was not a will to learn about minority youngsters, nor a will to protect minority youngsters and their potential and to assume they had the potential if it was encouraged." For many, dreams for their own children fueled the fire. Maria Calero described her aspirations for her children: "I wanted them to go to college . . . and I think I had many more dreams for them than I had for myself. . . . I began to ask questions about the Board of Education, about the public schools, about how were Hispanic children being educated. . . . I wanted them to be educated, but I also wanted my children to be thinkers."[7]

Jewish community worker Teresa Fraser, who came from a union and Communist Party–affiliated family, felt the need to advocate for her son in the Bronx public schools because of his special needs. But because he was white, "somewhere I realized that while he was getting . . . [some] attention or there was an expectation that he was going to learn, that was not true with black or Hispanic kids." Consequently, she joined with other public school parents, mostly mothers, to address a range of issues connected to educational inequity. "You found that you couldn't work on schools and leave out housing," she said. "You couldn't work on housing and leave out welfare." Similarly, learning was difficult for children who went to school hungry and did not enjoy nutritious meals while at school: "We once took a couple of vans and picked up the garbage outside about three schools, and we took it and dumped it at 26 General Plaza having called all the radio stations, TV stations, and newspapers. We got tremendous coverage . . . we tried to point out that the food was so bad that the kids weren't eating it, and it was a waste of money and the government was throwing its money down the drain."[8]

When Fraser's group invited Bronx elected officials to lunch and one became very sick, publicity increased. Going further, these parents proved that they themselves could provide kids more nutritious food in the schools at the same cost. "We did all these things they said they couldn't do such as get rid of frozen meals, put totally fresh meals in all of the schools that had kitchens, brought them to the other schools that didn't have kitchens. . . . We did ethnic meals. . . . We increased the breakfast program from next to nothing to six thousand kids eating breakfast a day. . . . We had school food committees, which included the kids and school staff."[9]

For women involved in these neighborhood and city-level struggles, maternal activism was a way of claiming citizenship for themselves and their families. Nina Reyes, for example, a mother of three who had moved to the Lower East Side from Puerto Rico at age ten, became active in a push for child care within her community as well as in initiatives to register Puerto Rican voters. The traditions that informed these women's work often included othermothering practices and the habit of community service among African American women, as well as involvement in the African American church, where, said community activist Ann Robinson, "you had responsibilities" that developed leadership.[10] In addition, the challenges to authority in the civil rights, feminist, student and other anti-racist movements spurred these women to action. Also new were the visible models throughout the country of confrontational tactics that gained media attention, made politicians listen, and sometimes exposed the experts as not so knowledgeable or invulnerable as many once believed.

Community mothers gave a lot of credit to their own mothers' traditions of community caregiving. This suggests that they saw themselves as not so much recently awakened as finally slightly more empowered. For most of these women, racial discrimination and poverty experienced by their parents helped drive them forward. Many of their mothers had served as what Naples calls "informal caretakers in their communities," engaged in "taking neighbors to the hospital, helping care for the elderly, advocating for increased childcare programs, fighting school officials to expand educational opportunities for young people, struggling with landlords and police officials to improve the housing and safety conditions in their community, and interpreting for non-English-speaking residents." Josephine Card remembered her mother as a person whom "everybody in the community came to. . . . If they had problems with bills, if they had problems with burying somebody that lived somewhere else, they'd come to my mother. My mother knew all the funeral directors, and she knew all the ministers. . . . she knew everybody." These networked mothers also modeled how to ask the hard questions. At a time "when it wasn't right for parents to get involved, to be in the classrooms, and to question teachers," Carmen Hernandez's mother did so anyway. "She'd ask, 'Why?' 'How come?' 'Give me a reason.' 'I won't take it just because you said it.' 'Show it to me.' . . . And she would fight for different children's rights, and she didn't care whose child it was." As Naples notes, community care work was devalued by the larger culture in ways similar to mothering work generally, but that was not the case within the families from which these women drew their strength.[11]

Perhaps even more remarkable were the long-standing successes of a similarly situated group of women whose activism came to focus on welfare rights. The African American hotel workers and mothers of Las Vegas, whose stories have been beautifully told by historian Annelise Orleck, shook the foundations of city and state government policy. The women embarrassed the casino owners who paid them poverty wages and founded highly effective and pioneering community programs for poor families. The fruits of their labor survived sustained and often vicious opposition and, for a while, Reagan-era political backlash. The six women at the center of Orleck's research were very poor southern migrants, with very little education, who came to Las Vegas. All had relatives who were attacked or killed by whites in the South, and they shared experience with domestic violence and their inability to convince physicians to prescribe birth control.

These women had numerous kids, were paid pitiful wages in a city that glorified wealth, and lived in segregated substandard housing. When they sought public assistance, they encountered even more ways in which poor mothers of color could be demeaned. One woman who was laid off from her hotel job in the mid-1960s and rejected from AFDC because she had not lived in Nevada long enough was told she could put her children in a shelter. She was also turned down for emergency food assistance.[12]

The health status of these children in the American age of affluence was shameful. Later, when welfare mothers launched a community health clinic, health-care providers documented that 80 percent of the children needed dental work and half had never once been to a dentist. (Dental care was considered cosmetic and not part of Medicaid coverage.) Although Congress had authorized funds for hot lunches for kids in school back in 1946, many states and localities failed to develop programs for poor children. In Clark County, Nevada, the home of these Las Vegas women, fewer than three hundred hot school lunches were being served in a district with eight thousand students on public assistance. Children were so hungry and malnourished that scurvy was not uncommon, and some mothers withdrew their children from school because of lack of funds for food or clothing.[13]

On all these issues, mothers on the ADC program were organizing nationally as well as locally, advocating for livable wages, jobs training, child care programs, and voter registration to politically empower their communities. Until arthritis made her work impossible, Johnnie Tillmon, for example, had ironed hundreds of shirts a day in California while doing community improvement projects with other mothers in public housing. Once subjected to the indignities of ADC, Tillmon quickly organized other mothers to begin challenging the system. By the mid-1960s, Tillmon had a vocal and well-connected ally in George Wiley, a chemistry professor turned civil rights activist. Together they founded the National Welfare Rights Organization (NWRO).

Tillmon, Wiley, and other activists gained national attention and some prominent liberal allies, pushing for a federal guaranteed annual income. Meanwhile, Las Vegas poor mothers continued to organize at both city and state levels. They came armed with new NRWO handbooks on welfare rights and ready to directly confront state legislators: "You're the one that's keeping us from getting shoes for our children," Ruby Duncan said to her state senator, Floyd Lamb. Because of this mobilization, one mother said, "No one had to go to the welfare office alone."[14] Moreover, much to the frustration of the more conservative guardians of the public coffers, more women did participate in AFDC and related programs. Despite relentless opposition from the state Welfare Department, including threats of losing welfare benefits because of protesting the system, the results of these poor mothers' efforts were breathtaking.

In 1972, in the heart of their impoverished neighborhood, the Las Vegas women developed "Operation Life," much like the settlement houses of the Progressive era, but it was run by residents themselves, not by well-meaning outsiders. Like the college-educated settlement house workers of the turn of the century, Operation Life workers surveyed residents about their food needs, crime issues, homelessness, and general concerns. Operation Life also ran workshops to help women understand their rights to public assistance and developed grant programs to serve the community in innovative ways, including services for the elderly, job training and tutoring programs, and the creation of day care centers. They also brought the community its first library, which included a large dose of African American history, and at one point the largest collection of African and African American studies books in Nevada. As one of the Las Vegas women leaders, Ruby Duncan, explained, "It was just like giving food to our children. They were hungry and we wanted to feed them."[15]

These community mothers fed the children literally as well. Knowing that children went hungry during the summer, they successfully applied to the USDA for a summer lunch program. With those funds they provided fifteen thousand lunches to kids in 1974. Using their evolving organizational genius, they forced Nevada to implement the Women and Infant Children (WIC) nutrition programs authorized by Congress in 1972, against major opposition and continual state harassment on the question of welfare fraud. Congress had approved funds for protein-laden foods, medical screening, and nutrition education for low-income pregnant women and those with young children. But President Richard Nixon and the USDA resisted releasing these funds until poor mothers and the Food Research and Action Center filed a class-action lawsuit. Then, the Las Vegas mothers of Operation Life won a federal grant to open a WIC program on the Westside, making theirs the first WIC clinic in the country run by poor mothers. After Congress appropriated funds for medical screening of poor children and, once again, Las Vegas welfare rights activists forced the actual release of this money into the state through a lawsuit, Operation Life women also opened a clinic in 1973. Its success catapulted Nevada, long near the bottom of the list for its medical care for children, to the very top. Operation Life was nationally recognized by Congress twice for its success in preventive health.[16]

Working in concert with the National Welfare Rights Organization and an inspired generation of antipoverty lawyers, welfare activists were able to secure important victories. They persuaded the Supreme Court to declare unconstitutional many states' "man in the house" rules that allowed for unannounced searches of the homes of public assistance recipients (*King v. Smith*, 1967). For mothers these were significant reforms to the regulatory welfare state that had been established in the Progressive era and developed during the New Deal. The Court also struck down AFDC state residency requirements. And back in Nevada, women who objected to questioning about their sexual history as part of an application for public assistance reached their limit; Nevada women said they would sue in federal court if the state did not stop forcing them to take lie detector tests and blood tests to determine the paternity of their children, and the state backed down.[17]

At the national level, welfare activists fell far short of their goal of a guaranteed annual income, which would have been a major acknowledgment of the need for genuine social provisioning of the work of mothering. President Nixon had considered a Family Assistance Plan, even though it would have represented far less than a living wage. But the plan faced too much opposition, and Nixon began to see a brighter political future in promoting workfare rather than in expanding welfare. American society had long resisted both the idea that mothering was work and the notion that the paid labor of mothers was necessary to many families. The idea of women supporting children outside of marriage was also anathema. In Senate hearings on the proposals of the National Welfare Rights Organization in 1967, Louisiana Senator Russell Long revealed another dimension of resistance, by complaining that welfare benefits had made it difficult to find someone to iron his shirts.[18] Indeed, opposition to welfare benefits went hand in hand with opposition to labor rights and the expansion of Social Security benefits to the African American labor force that had supplied labor deliberately kept cheap by federal and state laws.

One piece of the backlash to welfare rights was a growing racialization of the media image of welfare recipients. In contrast to the 1960s, when President Johnson had stressed the widespread nature of poverty among white Americans, the 1970s image of poverty was largely African American, and a demonization of welfare mothers escalated in the 1980s under President Ronald Reagan. Even in the 1970s, with federal help and a strong national social movement, state legislators relentlessly cut welfare expenditures, especially as the expenses of the Vietnam War overshadowed the War on Poverty. With the counterattack against government programs in the 1980s, the value of welfare dollars declined. Ronald Reagan's 1981 Omnibus Budget Reconciliation Act drastically reduced public assistance programs, barred striking workers from the programs, and provided the flexibility many states wanted to implement wage work requirements (even though many women had already had to combine paid work and AFDC). Program cuts removed three million children from school lunch programs and another million from food stamps. African American families were especially hard hit, falling below the poverty line at twice the rate of whites.[19] These reductions contributed to what many now called the "feminization of poverty" and to high rates of child poverty as well.

By 1996, under President Bill Clinton, Democrats and Republicans reached a compromise that ended the sixty-one-year-old Aid to Families with Dependent Children program. A program called Temporary Assistance to Needy Families (TANF) was created instead, under the Personal Responsibility and Work Opportunity Reconciliation Act (PRWO/HR 3734). The legislation rewarded states for reducing their recipient numbers and for reducing out-of-wedlock birth. It limited benefits to two consecutive years and five years total, tightened Food Stamp eligibility, and left greater latitude to states to deny public assistance to immigrants. The PRWO froze cash assistance benefits at 1996 levels and left millions of women and children without public assistance. Within the first three years of this unprecedented "welfare reform," there was a 40 percent reduction in the number of recipients of cash assistance, and the consequences of this enormous withdrawal of commitment to poor mothers is ongoing. Immigrant and refugee mothers were especially hard hit, along with those trying to flee violent relationships with male partners. This situation continued to leave many mothers trapped in poverty with very few resources.[20]

In light of these developments, the long-standing success of welfare rights activists in Nevada is even more striking. The Operation Life women ran their programs for more than twenty years. Ruby Duncan gained a national voice on issues of welfare rights and job training for poor mothers and served as a delegate to the 1975 Mexico City International Women's Conference. Operation Life survived what can only be described as continuous harassment by Nevada's Welfare Office Director George Miller, who gained national prominence himself as an antiwelfare warrior. Unlike so many other programs, the Operation Life organization sustained itself during the Reagan administration's attack on the antipoverty initiatives of the 1960s. As Orleck's research demonstrates, even after Operation Life was forced to close its doors in the early 1990s, poor families in Nevada continued to benefit from what was left of the welfare rights movement, including the WIC programs brought to the state by Ruby Duncan and her friends and allies and job training programs that Duncan had convinced the Carter administration to develop for women of color and poor women. Poor mothers' efforts to resist the pathologizing of African American welfare mothers planted seeds of pride in future generations. Johnnie Tillmon remembered, "As we talked to each other, we forgot about that shame [of receiving public assistance]. . . . And as we listened to the horrible treatment and conditions all over the country, we could begin thinking . . . that maybe it wasn't us who should be ashamed."[21]

Maternalism in Peace and Environmental Activism

Maternalism in the 1960s and the decades that followed was an expansive and malleable political approach that continued to take on new forms. In 1961, an estimated fifty thousand housewives and mothers, left their homes and their jobs, participating in a one-day "strike for peace." Women Strike for Peace (WSP) quickly became a social movement. Frustrated with men's leadership and feeling a need to be a voice for children, women developed local WSP chapters across the country. WSP was a group composed largely of middle-class white women, very few of whom had personal livelihoods in jeopardy because of their protest. But they challenged a pervasive anticommunist stranglehold on social protest by subverting traditional male politics. They wanted worldwide disarmament and national budgeting that planned for peace, not just for war.[22] The spark for their nonhierarchical, extraordinarily flexible women's organization, free of member lists (and therefore, they hoped, of government surveillance) was their intense frustration at the old-time peace organization National Committee for a Sane Nuclear Policy (SANE). SANE had purged itself of communists in order to survive the postwar anticommunist hysteria and had failed to protest the jailing of peace activist and philosopher Bertrand Russell. In fact, all but one of the venerable and sometimes radical maternalist peace organizations that had formed in the Progressive era had disappeared with the Second World War and the ensuing Red Scare.

Those progressive groups had been inspired by sentiments like that of Julia Ward Howe, who had insisted, back in 1870, that "our husbands shall not come to us, reeking with carnage, for caresses and applause. Our sons shall not be taken from us to unlearn all that we have been able to teach them of charity, mercy and patience. We women of one country will be too tender to those of another country to allow our sons to be trained to injure theirs. From the bosom of the devastated earth a voice goes up with our own. It says 'Disarm, Disarm! The sword of murder is not the balance of justice.'"[23] Generations of women had acted on this notion, infusing peace platforms into women's civic organizations that encompassed hundreds of thousands of members and organizing groups like the Women's Peace Party.

But by the early 1960s, after the Second World War, a Red Scare, the Korean War and the beginning of the Cold War, only the Women's International League for Peace and Freedom remained active among women's peace organizations. For the WSP activists, this represented a failure of traditional political ideas and male political leadership. WSP drew on the now century-long tradition of rhetorically placing mothers above the political fray. "We're not politicians," they declared, "we're housewives and working women. . . . We don't make foreign policy—but we know to what end we want it made: toward preservation of life on earth." The national media, perplexed by traditional women's outrage, perpetuated the image, quoting a Los Angeles woman in the 1961 strike, "I don't belong to any organization. I've got a child of ten."[24]

Just a little over a year after the national strike for peace, WSP had mobilized women across the country in protests, vigils, and community forums. They actually developed significant knowledge of the health effects of nuclear testing, of the status of international agreements, and later of laws regarding the draft for the Vietnam War. But they reveled in their novice status and used a ladylike image to their advantage. In 1962, a number of WSP activists were summoned to appear before the House Un-American Activities Committee (HUAC) for suspected communist activity. Through their unthreatening appearance, humor, and bold refusal to answer questions about others, they flummoxed a feared authoritarian committee. They came wearing white gloves; some brought babies and children.

All the women stood when the first WSP witness was called. When the committee tried to argue that WSP was a highly structured organization controlled by the Communist Party, WSP women laughed out loud. Press coverage embarrassed the committee. Although some critics claimed that the "pro-Reds have moved in on our mothers and are using them for their own purposes," others in the press used the women's rebellion to poke fun at HUAC. A *Washington Post* cartoon pictured three committee members at a table, with one asking another, "I Came in Late, Which Was It That Was Un-American—Women or Peace?"[25] Though three WSP women were convicted of communist activities by HUAC, the courts refused to uphold the conviction, and many in the national press credited WSP with an irreversible tarnishing of the esteemed committee's image and power in American life.

WSP continued its highly visible protests throughout the 1960s and 1970s, holding Mother's Day marches, building coalitions with feminist and civil rights activists, and broadening their maternalist mandate. Their opposition to the Vietnam War and the draft continued to emphasize maternalism: Expressing their opposition to the draft, they insisted, "Not Our Sons, Not Your Sons, Not Their Sons." WSP women also helped publicize the impact of Napalm on Vietnamese children, with photographs and with the slogan, "Children are not for burning." Increasingly influenced by Second Wave feminism, they also drew attention to war as a "feminist issue," noting the brutal impact of the war on Vietnamese women.[26] WSP would remain active and be joined by other groups, such as Women Against Military Madness, which emerged in 1984.

The idea of saving a world on the brink of destruction also animated maternal activism on environmental issues. In the mid-1960s, groups like the Pittsburgh-based Group Against Smog and Pollution (GASP) emerged, propelled by the leadership of women. Like WSP, GASP drew on the volunteer labor of middle-class women who defined themselves as wives and mothers; they asked their neighbors, "What will you tell your children when they ask why they can't catch their breath while playing in the yard?" Also like WSP, GASP women used and expanded middle-class female networks. They raised funds through the production and sale of cookbooks, did environmental education through the schools and civic groups, and linked with other organizations working on women's issues, racial justice, and the environment. More radically, they gained publicity for their cause by presenting the chairman of the board of U.S. Steel with a "Dirtie Gertie" award for the worst polluter. GASP produced alarming educational films highlighting the problems of pollution, such as *Don't Hold Your Breath (Fight for It)*. One of their films showed a nurse walking children to school buses; the children wore air masks on their faces.[27]

Some press coverage of GASP's activism minimized the women's threat by casting them as apolitical mothers. Other coverage praised women's competency, as when the *Christian Science Monitor* noted, "Everyone knows that if you want something accomplished, you turn it over to a busy woman." Still others in the media disdained maternal activism. While WSP women faced charges of communism and welfare activists endured racist charges of laziness and promiscuity, maternal environmentalists were called "hysterical" and "emotional."[28]

Working-class environmental activists became motivated by direct threats to their families' health, and the "hysterical" label tended not to faze them. Lois Gibbs and Patsy Ruth Oliver, for example, both discovered that they and their families were becoming very ill while living in extremely toxic communities. The situation seemed dire enough to warrant a little hysteria. Gibbs, a working-class white woman, lived in Niagara Falls, New York, a city in which Hooker Chemical company had dumped significant amounts of contaminated waste back in the 1950s into what would later become the infamous Love Canal. Hooker Chemical later sold the abandoned waste site to the local school board for one dollar. In the 1970s, Lois Gibbs's two children spent years enduring seizures, enzyme deficiencies, asthma, and immune disorders; her young daughter displayed a blood disease that made her body bruise with the slightest bump. When Gibbs began to discover what city and county officials already knew, that her son Michael was attending school on a toxic waste site, she took action as a private mother. She attempted to work with her pediatrician, who she says was also unaware of the toxic history of the community, and a reluctant school principal to try to get her son moved out of the school.

Soon Gibbs decided to start a petition to close the school and essentially act as a public mother. Gibbs recalled, "For many years I had honestly taken pride in being the best mom on the block. My kids had the right sweaters for the right temperature. Their faces weren't dirty. I prided myself on being a responsible mother. And yet when it came to doing something to protect my children that was not within my norm, I was afraid." Gibbs shouldered the burden of blame in this regard. "As a result of being afraid, I helped to put Michael into that [hospital] bed, I contributed to his sickness." Gibbs set out to investigate and organize. She was beginning to understand that the problem was much larger than her son's school and the local playground. She knocked on her neighbors' doors and talked to women and men. "They talked about how their wives had babies that were malformed, how a thirteen-year-old had a hysterectomy due to cancer, how a twenty-one-year-old died of 'crib death,' according to her death certificate. And then we had three women in a row with children who had to have surgery so that their skulls could grow normally. And I realized, this is not about the school. This is about the whole neighborhood."[29]

Gibbs and the women of Love Canal eventually drew national attention. Their tactics also became radical. At one point, says Gibbs, "women—blue collar, law-abiding women—were pouring gasoline on lawns across the street and saying that the EPA was burning them." Aware of the power of media attention for their cause, the Love Canal women also enlisted their children, donning them with signs that said, "I want to be a mommy someday" and "C-56 makes me sick."[30] These tactics made some of their middle-class allies uncomfortable, and the women's concern for their children's health and willingness to speak up also ran them up against more male-dominated local groups who feared the economic consequences of setting off health alarms in their community.

After the health commissioner eventually ordered the closing of the school and the temporary evacuation of pregnant women and young children from the most contaminated areas, the state agreed to purchase the most affected homes. President Jimmy Carter appropriated federal emergency funds. Love Canal set a national precedent that would help similarly affected communities in the future via Superfund legislations, which regulated and set terms for clean-up from toxic polluters.

Not long afterward, in Texarkana, Texas, a less publicized "Black Love Canal" drew African American mothers into a similar battle. For women of color, it was not such a big leap to become public mothers on community issues. But government responsiveness was harder to obtain. In the late 1970s, Patsy Ruth Oliver, an African American mother of five, began to understand why she and her neighbors were experiencing disrupted menstrual cycles for girls, liver, kidney, and thyroid problems, and high rates of cancer. In response to Love Canal, Congress forced large chemical companies to identify their hazardous waste, and in 1979 one of those companies listed Oliver's community as a dangerous site. Beginning in 1980, a series of state and federal investigations began, yet more studies always seemed to be needed—of the soil and water, not the people. For more than ten years, Oliver and her neighbors fought for a buyout of a community that by every official account was thoroughly contaminated with creosote toxins and was generally unfit for human habitation.

Like Lois Gibbs, Oliver knocked on her neighbors' doors, worked with fellow mothers to document their children's health conditions, led marches, headed to the state capitol and the Dallas office of the Environmental Protection Agency, and spoke to the press. She also gained nationally influential allies, including the Reverend Jessie Jackson, and a visit to her community from the still active Lois Gibbs. Finally, by 1993, the fight had been won. Congress had set aside Superfund monies to purchase the community's properties and relocate residents. Oliver continued her environmental activism throughout the Southwest.[31]

In other communities, too, people of color began to identify and publicize the impact of environmental racism, a concept that emerged in the early 1980s. Juana Guthierez, for example, mobilized four hundred women in the "Mothers of East Los Angeles" to stop a toxic waste incinerator from coming to their mostly Hispanic community.[32] In working-class communities generally, women became increasingly proactive on environmental concerns affecting their families. In the late 1980s, the Kenosha, Wisconsin, wives of laid-off Chrysler auto workers led the opposition to the development of a medical waste incinerator in their community and even initiated a successful recall effort of elected officials who had supported the incinerator.[33]

Winona La Duke has pointed out that "nationally, a lot of the leadership for grassroots native environmental organizations comes from women." From her

Ojibwe perspective, considering issues of education, tribal sovereignty, and environmental protection, "whether it's opposing cultural destruction or opposing clear-cutting, it's the same. Opposing clear-cutting is opposing cultural destruction. It would be wrong for me to talk about cultural preservation to my children and not oppose clear-cutting because they won't have forests if I don't . . . I get called a Native American activist, which I think is kind of ludicrous. I mostly consider myself a responsible parent." From the 1960s forward, across cultures, mothers' leadership in movements against community toxins and the destruction of land and safe spaces to rear children broadened, adding new urgency and vital new perspectives to the environmental movement as a whole.[34]

While maternalism in the 1960s and 1970s drew on ideas of participatory democracy, mothers' activism did not always lead in progressive directions. Mothers' activism played an important, though less studied role, in the antibusing movement in Boston in the mid-1970s, when white parents attempted to shield their children from racial integration. Here, and in other cases in history, such as women's involvement in the Ku Klux Klan in the 1920s and in race hatred movements of the 1990s, some mothers drew a tight circle of protection. They defined the interests of "our children" in opposition to "other" community groups. Historian Kathleen Blee, who has written cogently about both the 1920s Klan and more recent race-hate movements, noted, "Such efforts to normalize racism rest largely on the absorption of ordinary social roles (like motherhood) . . . and the use of ordinary networks (like those of family and neighborhood) to build a culture of racial supremacy."[35] Still, between the 1960s and the 1980s, as in the past, maternalist activism largely moved in progressive directions by providing expansive concepts of a society that valued the care work of mothers.

Second Wave Feminism and the Mother Question

By the middle of the 1960s, feminism's Second Wave had enlivened the perspectives of maternalists, while also developing an unprecedented critique of the institution of motherhood itself. For the first time, feminists portrayed motherhood as a very problematic piece of the pedestal on which the unliberated American woman was placed. Second Wave feminism, an uneasy yet influential set of coalitions, evolved as rapidly and evoked as many reactions and reformations of consciousness as any social movement ever has.

The origins of feminism's postsuffrage revival are perhaps as multifaceted as those of 1960s and 1970s maternalism. As early as World War II, union women were active on issues of the social provisioning for wage-earning mothers, with a feminist perspective. Demanding equal pay for equal work, initiating calls for paid maternity leave and child care, and fighting racial and gender injustice at the same time, union activists in the United Auto Workers and United Packinghouse Workers and other unions began challenging these gender structures. Also important to the revival of interest in discrimination against women was an early 1960s coalition of professional, union, religious, academic, and political women who worked on

President John F. Kennedy's Commission on the Status of Women. The commission released its report documenting massive gender discrimination in 1962. Then in 1963 Betty Friedan's best-selling manifesto, *The Feminine Mystique*, offered the most sweeping analysis to date that criticized the myopic focus on domesticity that had shaped her postwar generation of middle-class suburban women.[36]

In 1966, Betty Friedan and like-minded activists launched the National Organization for Women (NOW). Its mission was to "take action to bring women into full participation in the mainstream of American society now, exercising all the privileges and responsibilities thereof in truly equal partnership with men." These activists developed NOW as a pressure group, modeled on the NAACP. The initial focus was on forcing the government to enforce the Civil Rights Act's provisions regarding sex discrimination at work and helping the nation to think about retraining housewives for meaningful work. NOW's early stance on motherhood and marriage was tame, compared to the disruptive cultural questioning that was coming. In 1966, the most visible feminist organization suggested that the United States should "innovate new social institutions which will enable women to enjoy true equality of opportunity and responsibility in society without conflict with their responsibilities as mothers and homemakers."[37]

For younger women in the civil rights, New Left, and counterculture movements, women's roles as wives, mothers, and sex objects were at least as problematic as their lack of advancement in the workplace. They pushed feminism beyond equal opportunity and toward women's liberation from cultural oppression. Only a few years after NOW's modest assertion, radical feminists in Cleveland encouraged Americans to "Bury Mother's Day": "Today, one day of the year, America is celebrating Motherhood. . . . The other 364 days she preserves the apple pie of family life and togetherness and protects the sanctity of male ego and profit. She lives through her husband and children . . . she is sacrificed on the altar of reproduction. . . . She is damned to the world of dreary domesticity by day, and legal rape by night." Another feminist group declared, "Renounce your martyrdom! Become a *liberated* mother A woman, not a 'mom.'"[38] Caregiving of home, family, and men's egos and sexual needs and many other similar issues were linked in this analysis. Gender roles so punitively enforced in the 1950s and early 1960s were about to explode. Between the late 1960s and mid-1970s, women's liberation forced Americans to think critically, en masse, about whether all women should be assigned the roles of wife and mother simply by virtue of being born female.

More traditional feminists, often older women who had already encountered the concrete ceiling of the postwar workplace, continued to work to broaden the possibilities of women's public lives. They pushed for the elimination of restrictions on women's education, employment, athletic opportunities, and political participation. Feminist activists also addressed the ways women suffered financially and in their careers because of domestic obligations and low wages. Labor union feminists continued to fight for improved minimum wage provisions and equal pay for women. Coalitions of feminists pushed for economic fairness in divorce laws and child care options, and they successfully advocated both the decriminilization of abortion (in *Roe v. Wade*, 1973) and the banning of employment discrimination against pregnant women (in the Pregnancy Anti-Discrimination Act), to name a few examples.

Over the course of the 1960s, 1970s, and 1980s, these older and younger cohorts often formed coalitions. The women attempted to create and live out new social theories and new cultural ideals and behaviors while also changing the laws and economic practices that had been predicated on women's confinement to familial roles. In feminism's broadest moments, its strategists, theorists, and activists linked the causes of racial, economic, and gender justice. They reimagined a world without patriarchy, a world in which women's need for autonomy might be reconciled with an appreciation of the caregiving labor traditionally assigned to them.

In practice, feminism often foundered, as did all social movements, on difference. The old differences of race and class, as well as newly visible questions of sexual orientation, appeared. Criticism of motherhood and marriage also provoked complicated emotional reactions among women who had invested their identities in those roles. And the portrayal of feminism by the national media often did not help. Aging male news anchors perpetually knit their brows about "what women wanted," and in frustration the newsmen often reduced the movement to a bunch of "braless bubbleheads" (in the words of a politician quoted on the subject) and shrill man-haters who wanted to destroy the family. Reporters also frequently drew attention to divisions within the movement and among women generally.[39]

Nevertheless, the legacy of feminist thought and action on questions relating to motherhood changed the cultural, legal, and economic landscape in ways that powerfully benefit women to this day. Above all, Second Wave feminism, as both a social movement and a growing body of published social theory, questioned the motherhood mandate more thoroughly than ever before. Feminists radically suggested that women could be fulfilled without being mothers and that they could combine motherhood, if they chose it, with meaningful public work and more equitable partnerships with men. They also opened the possibility for the decoupling of heterosexual marriage and motherhood. Feminists were not alone in critiquing the confines of the nuclear family, but they explored the possibilities and the complexities of assigned gender roles with unparalleled passion and sophistication.

For starters, in *The Feminine Mystique*, Betty Friedan did what previous critics of middle-class motherhood, like the venerable Philip Wylie, had failed to do. She criticized the suffocating gender roles of postwar America while offering an actual solution: provide women opportunities for meaningful work beyond their homes. Like Wylie, she noted that "the more a woman is deprived of function in society at the level of her own ability, the more her housework, mother-work, wife-work, will expand. . . . Without any outside interests, a woman is virtually forced to devote her every moment to the trivia of keeping house." But Friedan insisted that women needed useful work and social supports, like educational opportunities and child care and real professional opportunities, not to supplant marriage and motherhood, but to complement it. She asked, "Who knows of the possibilities of love when men and women share not only children, home, and garden, not only fulfillment of their biological roles, but the responsibilities and passions of the work that creates the human future and the full human knowledge of who they are?" Her question was visionary, although her solutions were not particularly radical and her critique not as broad as it needed to be. Her commentary has since been roundly criticized for its class myopia. Friedan tended to speak of women's "problem with no name" as if all women were middle-class suburban wives and mothers, and she generally failed to criticize the antimother sentiment of her era. She even sometimes veered into mother blame herself. Nevertheless, Friedan struck a chord, and her path-breaking appraisal of privatized motherhood from a feminist perspective proved instrumental in sparking the broader social movement.[40]

Early Second Wave feminists simultaneously debunked motherhood as false consciousness and tried to uplift mothers' labors. In 1966, British psychoanalyst Juliet Mitchell articulated a sort of bridge between the New Left's criticism of capitalism and a reemerging feminist consciousness. Like Charlotte Perkins Gilman had done fifty years earlier, Mitchell spoke of the real value of women's reproductive labor in the home and argued that society should share the work of child-rearing. In an age when the family had fewer economic functions than before, "the need for permanent, intelligent care of children in the initial three or four years of their lives can (and has been) exploited ideologically to perpetuate the family as a total unit," Mitchell argued.[41] For everyone's sake, reproductive labor should be a shared task for which society, not just individual women, was responsible. As a socialist, Mitchell probed the issues of women's invisible labor in the home by drawing attention to both the privatization of that work and women's lack of power in defining its terms. These conditions turned mothers and housewives into a special class of alienated labor.

For Mitchell, women's liberation also needed to happen in the productive realm of wage-earning where women were concentrated in care-giving roles "analogous to the wife-mother role in the family," like nurse, teacher, and secretary. Women's limitations in the workforce combined with restrictions on their sexual autonomy in their oppression. Hoping that society would continue to move toward sexual expression free from the worries of pregnancy, Mitchell considered women's access to birth control and "the legalization of homosexuality" to be central pieces of women's liberation, along with changes in child-rearing. A liberated society would see a wider range of forms for love and care than the mother-child focused socialization within marriage: "Couples living together or not living together, long-term unions with children, single parents bringing up children, children socialized by conventional rather than biological parents, extended kin groups, etc." This vision would be part of the "liberation of women under socialism," itself "a human achievement, the long passage from Nature to Culture which is the definition of history and society."[42]

For a few feminist thinkers on the topic of women and motherhood, nature itself was the problem. As some radical branches of feminism focused on gender as the original form of human oppression, extreme proposals emerged. Just four years after NOW envisioned a way forward for women "without conflict" with their maternal roles, Shulamith Firestone published *The Dialectic of Sex: The Case for Feminist Revolution* (1970) in which she claimed that the capacity for child-bearing constituted women's oppression:

> Nature produced the fundamental inequality—half the human race must bear and rear the children of all of them—which was later consolidated, institutionalized, in the interests of men. Reproduction of the species cost women dearly, not only emotionally, psychologically, culturally but even in strictly material (physical) terms: before recent methods of contraception, continuous childbirth led to constant "female trouble," early aging, and death. Women were the slave class that maintained the species in order to free the other half for the business of the world—admittedly often its drudge aspects, but certainly all its creative aspects.

Because of this, "men and women developed only half of themselves, at the expense of the other half." Firestone advocated the development of extrauterine gestation options for babies, thereby "freeing women from the tyranny of their reproductive biology by every means available." Firestone's suggestions could not have been more perfect to alarm the American mainstream about feminists' assault on all that the culture held sacred. Firestone was influential in the feminist movement, yet her ideas on motherhood were criticized by feminists as well. She not only failed to explain how biology and culture could be linked in women's oppression, but she also singled out female biology in an especially negative way.[43]

Part of the chaotic mix of ideas was the kinetic intellectual energy of feminism itself, unfolding faster than anyone could keep up. It also mattered that feminism's two main points of organizing energy came from older women whose challenges combining motherhood and public roles were now behind them and from younger women whose generation often delayed childbearing. In between were women like Jane Lazarre, who struggled with her generation's preoccupation with autonomy and authenticity. Angst about motherhood figured prominently in this struggle. Lazarre wrote achingly of her early days as a mother and a feminist in her 1976 book, *The Mother Knot.* When her son was only a few days old, she said, "We both felt that the breast was his. As he drew the milk out of me, my inner self seemed to shrink into a very small knot, gathering intensity under a protective shell, moving away, further and further away, from the changes being wrought by this child who was at once separate and a part of me. Frightened that he would claim my life completely, I desperately tried to cling to my boundaries. Yet I held him very close, stroked his skin, imagined that we were still one person."[44]

A committed feminist, Lazarre was nonetheless often uncomfortable with her motherhood in feminist settings. Even as her emotions were inextricably bound up with her young family, she worried that she was a bore to those who were not mothers. "Only the act of giving birth seemed interesting, I knew, to the intelligent, independent young women facing me," Lazarre lamented. "Once that dramatic moment of creation was over, however, the image of motherhood took on, in their minds, hues of graying diapers and red-and-white gingham; they thought of unattractive housedresses, disorderly homes, interrupted careers, diminishing sexuality—with these miserable consequences wrapped in the most unobjective, uncritical, sentimental and enervating kind of love. They thought of lives which were uninteresting, conventional, over. And so did I."[45]

Writing through her raging ambivalence—an emotion previously taboo for mothers to express—Lazarre gave honest voice to the emotionally torn mother. More typical of the era was the unleashed voice of the daughter, including some widely read prose that rhetorically allied itself with feminism. Nancy Friday's best-selling book, *My Mother/My Self: The Daughter's Search for Identity*, for example, also explored maternal ambivalence, but here the daughter's ambivalent, often even hostile voice, was privileged. Friday's psychoanalytic study of mothers and daughters, published in 1977, is replete with vestigial postwar images of the psychologically pathologized middle-class mother. According to Friday, "mother's antisexual rules" and her faulty teachings of the ways of intimacy stymied the daughter's ability to participate in the more liberating aspects of the 1970s sexual revolution. Mothers especially thwarted daughters' sexual selves by keeping their own sexuality secret and by denying their own ambivalence about motherhood. Friday wanted to let the cat out of the bag: "Mothers may love their children, but they sometimes do not like them," she insisted.[46]

As a feminist, Friday tried to take the idea of maternal perfection to task. American culture's notion of the maternal instinct, she claimed, "idealizes motherhood beyond human capacity." When mothers and daughters "pretend that the maternal instinct conquers all, both will be stuck ever after with mechanisms of denial and defense which cut them off from the reality of their mutual feelings; gone is any hope of a true relationship between them. The daughter will repeat this relationship with men and other women." But Friday's intensely psychological concentration and her exclusive focus on mothers as the familial socializing agents led her back to mother blame. Nearly everything that happened in a daughter's life seemed to arise from the faults, however culturally constructed, of mothers cleaving to their time-worn, unliberating scripts. Daughters should acknowledge their anger toward their mothers, and mothers should acknowledge their ambivalence and develop lives of their own, even though daughters were likely to resent them for doing so. Friday quoted a male doctor who said that a woman "must not define herself as 'a mother,' she's got to see herself as a person, a person with work to do, a sexual person, a woman. . . . It isn't necessary to have a profession. She doesn't have to have a high IQ or be president of the PTA to have this added life. So long as she isn't just sitting home, chauffeuring the kids, and baking cookies, giving her children and herself the feeling that their life is hers."[47] Much like Lazarre's book, the whole argument felt like a knot.

These confusing new prescriptions no doubt left many mothers, who were seldom interviewed about their motherhood, more than little bit ambivalent about the general feminist messages.[48] Who was being liberated from whom? Moreover, if mothers developed fascinating work lives and became sexual dynamos, who then would chauffer the kids and bake the cookies? For basic child-care tasks for young children, feminists had an answer: father involvement. Although it seems commonsense today, the idea of insisting on men taking an equal share in the care of infants and young children was a feminist revelation of the Second Wave. Few feminist foremothers, not to mention nonfeminist foremothers and fathers, had dreamed of such a thing. For previous generations, if child care was to be shared, such sharing would be a communal thing, among women. Motherhood was too sacred a calling, too essential to women's dignity and personhood, to share with what most mother admirers claimed was the more selfish and authoritarian sex.

But in the 1970s, after years of mother blame and isolation in the increasingly nuclear-focused families of the postwar era, young women waxed less romantic about child care and more hopeful about the malleability of gender socialization and gender-assigned tasks. In a significant shift, the percentage of college women who said they saw themselves as housewives fifteen years in the future dropped from 65 percent in 1964 to 31 percent in 1970; and by 1973, careers were appearing more important to young women than traditional marriage.[49] Women's increased labor force participation, discussed more fully in chapter 10, would challenge their capacity to handle all the child care in more and more families.

Young women who hoped for more equitable marital arrangements were inspired by feminist claims that housework and child care were real work, often menial, and that men should share in such work. In 1972, *Life* magazine and later *Redbook* and *U.S. News and World Report* featured stories on a "marriage agreement" created by feminist Alix Kates Shulman and her husband. The Shulmans advocated the fifty-fifty sharing of all domestic labor, regardless of work situations. Their agreement enumerated the work of child care in meticulous detail, from waking children up in the morning, to making sure they had their homework done, their paperwork for school, their babysitters arranged, their doctors consulted, their prescriptions filled, and so on. The nation was fascinated; even *Glamour* published an article telling women how to write their own marriage contracts in 1978.[50]

Advocates for shared child care claimed women, men, and children would benefit. In a book that exemplified feminism's movement into serious engagement with academic knowledge, psychologist Nancy Chodorow challenged what she called "The Reproduction of Mothering." Claiming that gender roles were reproduced by the ways girls formed their identity, Chodorow took aim at heteronormative family parenting patterns. In traditional child-rearing arrangements, girls remained continuously connected to their generally available, nurturing mothers. Boys, however, needed to separate from their usually more distant fathers; in this way, detached man and nurturing woman became reproduced. "Because women are themselves mothered by women, they grow up with the relational capacities and needs, and psychological definition of self-in-relationship which commits them to mothering. Men, because they are mothered by women, do not." This dichotomy needed to change to produce more well-rounded human beings.[51]

Unlike previous generations of feminist thinkers on the topic of motherhood (or any other topic), feminists of the 1960s and 1970s had unprecedented access to the tools of academic thinking and distribution of ideas. Women could become experts themselves. They talked with one another, in consciousness-raising groups and in an enormous underground "publication" network of mimeographed broad-sides. They also earned degrees and published research, cultural criticism, poetry, and fiction. They made documentaries and produced art. Moreover, the larger culture engaged with their ideas. In this context, feminist thinkers did more than question, critique, and attempt to liberate women from the most onerous aspects of child care and confinement to the home. They also reimagined and sought to encourage the value of motherhood.

Lauri Umansky has shown that, even by the 1970s, feminist thought on the topic of motherhood helped push the emphasis of the movement away from a sharp focus on emulating men's autonomy and toward a "cultural feminism," which val-ued both caregiving and female autonomy. Cultural feminism also explored the potential of women's biology and their connections with children to rejuvenate and renaturalize American culture, while empowering women. In 1973, in a widely circulated paper called "Mother Right," activist Judith Alpert asserted that "female biology is the basis of women's power" and that women should reclaim their bio-logical capacity for childbearing. "Feminist culture is based on what is best and strongest in women," she argued, "and as we begin to define ourselves as women, the qualities coming to the fore are the same ones a mother projects in the best kind of nurturing relationship to a child: empathy, intuitiveness, adaptability, awareness of growth as a process rather than as goal-ended, inventiveness, protective feel-ings toward others, and a capacity to respond emotionally as well as rationally."[52] After all, as Alpert and other social critics from Women Strike for Peace back to Progressive-era social critic Charlotte Perkins Gilman had claimed, male-defined rationality had made a pretty fine mess of things.

Reviving another idea from the Progressive era, Alpert claimed that mother-hood could unite women: "Because motherhood cuts across economic class, race, and sexual preference, a society in which women were powerful by virtue of being mothers would not be divided along any of these lines. Nor would any new division between women, such as between mothers and childless women arise, because the root of motherhood and the root of female consciousness are, I believe, one and the same." Alpert imagined a matriarchal past in which women in various cultures had held real power, politically and culturally, on the basis of their motherhood. Meanwhile, feminist religious thinkers also reimagined matriarchal societies and female-centered ideas of God. Engaging deeply with philosophy and developing new maternal theories, Sara Ruddick argued in the 1980s that the perspectives mothers developed in doing their day-to-day work of caring for children equipped them (or anyone who engaged in mother-work) with special insights and ways of thinking that could resist a militaristic culture.[53]

As a social movement, feminism in its ever-exploding forms of the 1970s and 1980s was not always as nuanced as Ruddick's and Chodorow's carefully detailed arguments. Because feminist ideas mixed somewhat uncritically with antimater-nalism, ancient matriarchs proved easier to idealize than the actual mothers in women's lives. Still, some feminist theorists engaged in sophisticated and even visionary ways with questions of motherhood and patriarchy. In her pivotal book,

Of Woman Born: Motherhood as Experience and Institution, Adrienne Rich suggested that the ambivalence of mothers about their roles—and perhaps views of daughters about their mothers—stemmed in part from the fact that patriarchy had hijacked motherhood itself. Motherhood was an "institution" not of women's own making, one which "revives and renews all other institutions." To be specific,

> Motherhood—unmentioned in the histories . . . has a history, it has an ideology, it is more fundamental than tribalism or nationalism. My individual, seemingly private pains as a mother, the individual, seemingly private pains of the mothers around me and before me, whatever our class or color, the regulation of women's reproductive power by men in every totalitarian system and every socialist revolution, the legal and technical control by men of contraception, fertility, abortion, obstetrics, gynecology, and extrauterine reproductive experiments—all are essential to the patriarchal system, as is the negative or suspect status of women who are not mothers.

In a related essay, "Motherhood in Bondage," Rich pointed out that motherhood was valorized only when mothers conformed to patriarchal ideals: "Motherhood is admirable, however, only so long as mother and child are attached to a legal father. Mothers out of wedlock, or under the welfare system, or lesbian motherhood, are harassed, humiliated, or neglected."[54]

In addition to illuminating important institutional and economic constraints on mothers, Rich argued that motherhood as ideology and institution confined women emotionally: "Mother-love is supposed to be continuous, unconditional. Love and anger cannot coexist. Female anger threatens the institution of motherhood." But that was partly because authentic mothering—as opposed to participation in the institution of motherhood—was often denied women. Rich wanted to distinguish between "the *potential relationship* of any woman to her powers of reproduction and to children; and the *institution*, which aims at ensuring that the potential—and all women—shall remain under male control." Women were trapped by motherhood, by their exclusion from creating ideas, and by the devaluation of maternal labor, but they could also be empowered as mothers. "To destroy the institution is not to abolish motherhood," Rich insisted. "It is to release the creation and sustenance of life into the same realm of decision, struggle, surprise, imagination, and conscious intelligence, as any other difficult, but freely chosen work."[55] Motherhood could be a choice and a form of self-expression, but women had to repossess it.

Indeed, Rich was right to point to a compelling example of women who were doing just that. Beginning in the 1960s and 1970s, some women who felt they could no longer deny that they were lesbians began to reclaim their own motherhood. When Ellen Nadler went to court to sue her former husband for custody of her five-year-old child, the courts' long tradition of maternal preference in awarding custody did not apply to her. The judge declared her, by virtue of her sexual orientation, "not a fit or proper person to have the care, custody, and control" of a minor child. Nadler appealed, and in the appeal the court skirted the declaration of an unfit mother by claiming that it was in the "best interests" of the child to be in a heterosexual environment. Other courts followed this example. In 1977, the court order for one woman who lost custody of her daughters read: "The active practice of a homosexual life style is so antithetical to a heterosexual one that the introduction of the children into its actual practice will inevitably cause severe conflicts and turmoil within the children."

Even from the few published custody cases available to historians (those that wound up in appellate court), we know that between 1967 and 1985, lesbian mothers and gay fathers lost most of the battles they undertook. In most cases these were women and men who had left heterosexual relationships. They often lost their custody battles in humiliating ways. A psychologist for Mary Jo Rischer's former husband condemned Rischer because she allowed her son to wear a "unisex t-shirt" and to take classes at the YWCA: "It would have been much better for the mother to encourage . . . masculine identifications." This role assigned to mothers, of promoting gender-conforming behavior, was one that lesbian parents presumably might be unable or unwilling to perform.[56] Lesbian mothers were also frequently denied or limited in their visitation rights.

Up until 1973, being gay or lesbian was considered by the American Psychiatric Association to be a mental illness, and this designation figured into many custody decisions. Historian Daniel Rivers notes that "in case after case, gay and lesbian parents were ordered to sign affidavits agreeing never to have their partners and children in their homes at the same time, to undergo regular psychiatric examination testifying to their repudiation of their sexual orientation, and to halt all pro-gay rights activist work in order to maintain parental rights." To claim rights to their children at all, lesbian mothers were challenging notions that virtuous mothers always subsumed personal needs that might challenge their children's needs. When confronting the legal system, they had to prove their maternal fitness because by claiming their sexuality, they had forfeited the assumption that they naturally were good mothers.[57] Indeed, as fathers began to challenge maternal custody preferences of the courts in the 1960s, the "best interest of the child" doctrine was strengthened, while automatic preference for mothers lessened.[58]

Over time, lesbians, feminists, gay male activists, and attorneys chipped away at courtroom biases, on both custody rights and other civil rights issues. Advocacy groups sprang up around the country in support of the custody rights of lesbian mothers. NOW expressed its support of lesbian mothers as early as 1971.[59] Activist Barbara Gittings worked tirelessly to educate the American Psychiatric Association about lesbian and gay people, asserting the then revolutionary point that lesbian and gay people could live well-adjusted happy lives. They were not, by definition, mentally ill. Sympathetic psychologists and psychiatrists worked to combat prejudice within their professional organizations, and they sometimes testified in court cases that lesbians and gay men could be good parents.[60]

As with welfare rights, people who understood the issues published self-help manuals for embattled lesbian mothers. Lawyers like Donna Hitchins used their skills and knowledge to great effect. Hitchins founded the Lesbian Rights project, which took on custody issues as well as lesbian rights in adoption, and developed the Lesbian Mothers Litigation Manual. Psychotherapist Bernice Goodman conducted her own study of lesbian parents, published in 1977, and offered the first evidence that lesbian mothers could have some advantages over heterosexual parents in the way they reared their children. Indeed, the cultural feminism of the 1970s, to which lesbians contributed a great deal, articulated this idea in many ways. Lesbians could raise nonsexist children, outside the heterosexual, patriarchal family. Jeanne Vaughn explained the notion in her anthology of lesbian parenting: "We have an opportunity for radical social change beginning in our homes, change that requires rethinking our views of family, of kinship, of work, of social organization. We need to develop some specifically lesbian-feminist theories of family. How would/did/could we mother our children without the institution of compulsory heterosexuality?"[61]

By the late 1970s, increasing numbers of women wanted to have children openly as lesbians, via adoption, artificial insemination, surrogacy, or agreed upon arrangements with men who could donate sperm. These women were choosing lesbian motherhood on purpose, not just because they had been mothers and now understood themselves to be lesbians. Being a mother was a valued aspect of many women's lives that many lesbian women felt they should not be denied. As one woman put it, "I've always wanted to have a child. In terms of being real tied up with being gay, it was one of the reasons I was hesitant to call myself a lesbian. I thought it automatically assumed you had nothing to do with children." By 2000, the Census showed 34 percent of lesbian couples (and 22 percent of gay couples) residing with a child under age eighteen.[62]

By 2014, lesbians and gay men, along with bisexual and transgendered persons, still lacked full civil rights, including marriage equality in most states. There are often medical and financial barriers to becoming parents via insemination and surrogacy. Custody discrimination continues in the absence of adequate legal protections, and rights vary considerably by state. In states without marriage equality, lesbian parents often exist in unclear legal territory; nonbiological partners are often not legally recognized. Still, the constant fear of losing their children faced by a previous generation of lesbians has subsided somewhat, thanks to previous and continuing work by activists. In a remarkable transformation of expert views, the American Psychiatric Association not only declassified the "condition" of being lesbian or gay as a mental illness, but many expert organizations—including the American Academy of Pediatrics, the American Psychological Association, the National Association of Social Workers, and the American Psychoanalytic Association— now openly state that there is no detriment to children in being reared by lesbian or gay parents.[63]

Indeed, decades of research have now confirmed Bernice Goodman's idea that there are some special advantages to children of lesbian parents. Certainly not all lesbian mothers rear their children in the overtly political way advocated in the heyday of feminist idealism. Some research into lesbian advice literature suggests that it is often not so different from advice to heterosexual mothers. "Your heart and soul have been forever changed," noted one manual. "You will probably never be so challenged or so rewarded by any other job." For women having chosen parenting very deliberately, maternal ambivalence can be even harder to express. Still, when scholars Judith Stacey and Timothy Biublarz reviewed nearly three decades of published research on children of lesbian and gay parents in 2001, they found that these children were less likely to adhere to traditional gender roles and that many of the children developed resilience and strength in asserting their own differences.[64]

Feminism, Race, and Motherhood

Lesbian mothers were not the only ones complicating feminist discussions of motherhood during feminism's Second Wave. Feminists of color generally proved less conflicted about motherhood and more willing than white feminists to articulate a conceptual bridge between motherhood as institution and mothering as practice. Women of color developed some of the most important rethinking of motherhood from perspectives more appreciative than ambivalent.[65] Although there was far too much diversity in the reactions to and reformations of feminism to discuss at length here, some discernible patterns emerge in their ideas. In the 1960s and 1970s, new attention to women's roles enriched ideas of racial justice. At the same time, women of color were well represented among the activists working on equality for women in the public sphere, both in union feminism and in the cross class mobilization that led to the formation of NOW.

Both familial and cultural critiques made by white women's liberationists tended to resonate less with women of color. For example, for some American Indian women, tribal identities made feminist notions of women's roles in families seem distant and irrelevant. Paula Gunn Allen, who wrote on American Indian women's traditions in 1986, insisted that "the tribes see women variously, but they do not question the power of femininity. Sometimes they see women as fearful, sometimes peaceful, sometimes omnipotent and omniscient, but they never portray women as mindless, helpless, simple, or oppressed. And while the women in a given tribe, clan, or band may be all these things, the individual woman is provided with a variety of images of women from the interconnected supernatural, natural, and social worlds in which she lives." Moreover, Allen did not envision a distant matriarchy; instead, she saw her life situation as continuous with and strengthened by visible, if sometimes embattled, maternal tribal traditions: "My ideas of womanhood, passed on largely by my mother and grandmothers, Laguna Pueblo women, are about practicality, strength, reasonableness, intelligence, wit, and competence," Allen said.[66] Whether or not most Indian women shared such views of their mothers, Allen was still able to articulate a description of motherhood that could not have been more at odds with the postwar ideals articulated by the dominant culture, ideas that continued to ensnare white feminists of her era.

Amid growing feminist energy, women of color illuminated the conditions under which their mothers had helped families, communities, and cultures survive. Black feminists, challenging their own communities on issues like the right to contraception, insisted that claims of genocide of African-Americans did not negate the need for black women to control their reproductive destiny. On the issue of motherhood as false consciousness or utter oppression, however, they tended to part company with white feminists. Historian Rivka Polatnick compared a 1960s white middle-class feminist to an African American working-class feminist and found that for the latter group, "being a mother was a major source of positive identity."[67]

Women of color were underrepresented in academia, but those who had the resources to write and research did so in scholarly and creative veins on traditions of motherhood in their communities. Those traditions involved both strength and victimization. Cherrie L. Moraga, for example, recounted, "I remember stories of my mother lying about her age in order to get a job as a hat-check girl at Agua Caliente Racetrack in Tijuana. At fourteen, she was the main support of the family. I can still see her walking home alone at 3 A.M., only to turn all of her salary and tips over to her mother, who was pregnant again."[68]

Feminists of color tended to embrace the complexity of their mothers' choices, even those that seemed to set up later struggles for their daughters. Moraga said that "it was through my mother's desire to protect her children from poverty and illiteracy that we became 'anglocized'; the more effectively we could pass in the white world, the better guaranteed our future." Similarly, Maya Angelou, in her famous memoir, *I Know Why the Caged Bird Sings*, acknowledged how painful it was to see her grandmother beg a white dentist for help with young Angelou's toothache. But Angelou understood that such compromises were a necessary part of fulfilling the complicated care work of mothers and grandmothers.[69]

African American women also used maternal imagination to inform their creativity and their reconstructions of a meaningful past. In her landmark work, "In Search of Our Mothers' Gardens," Alice Walker reclaimed maternal creativity. In her pivotal book, *Black Feminist Thought*, Patricia Hill Collins brought together and developed an intellectual framework of othermothering to make visible the maternal traditions of African American women. Collins not only gave voice to generations of maternal activists and to community traditions of care, but she also challenged African American glorification of black motherhood: "The controlling image of the 'superstrong Black mother' praises Black women's resilience in a society that routinely paints us as bad mothers. . . . Yet, in order to remain on their pedestal, these same superstrong Black mothers must continue to place their needs behind those of everyone else, especially their sons."[70]

Collins insisted that not only white culture assumed the availability of the free emotional labor of mothers. She called for new images of black mothers to inform the struggles for racial and gender justice: "African-American women need a revitalized Black feminist analysis of motherhood that debunks the image of 'happy slave,' whether the White-male created 'matriarch' or the Black-male-perpetuated 'superstrong Black mother.'" From her black feminist tradition, she knew that motherhood could be a "catalyst for social activism," "a base for self-actualization," and "a source of status in the Black community," as well as a source of oppression and pain.[71] Feminism was one lens through which women of color searched for a way forward as they came to understand motherhood as an underresourced job, a site of oppression, and a site of resistance and cultural preservation. Their own traditions of maternal activism and maternal resilience led them to see white feminists' frameworks around motherhood as often too limiting.

Meanwhile, grassroots activist women of color, like Ruby Duncan and Johnnie Tillmon, continued to work to provide more resources for the work of mothering. Feminist antiracist political leaders like Eleanor Holmes Norton, June Jordan, and Shirley Chisholm focused attention of the multifaceted burdens of wage-earning mothers of color. For their part, organized white feminists or white-dominated feminist groups often made common cause with those focused on racial and economic justice as means to empower mothers. Even in 1966, NOW had argued that "the most serious victims of sex discrimination in this country are women at the bottom, including those who, unsupported, head a great percentage of the families in poverty. . . . No adequate attention is being given to those women by any of the existing poverty programs." But, as historian Martha F. Davis has observed, NOW followed rather than led on these issues. "Many NOW members were ambivalent about NWRO's opposition to mandatory job-training programs and its position that women should have a right to stay home with their children."[72] NOW's middle-class dominated membership often did not dwell on poverty issues, and many saw staying at home with children as most decidedly not a path toward women's liberation. Political sisterhood could not always be sustained in the context of a broad organization like NOW, whose political initiatives ranged from supporting divorced women's rights to their husbands' earnings to confronting domestic violence to equalizing athletic opportunities for girls.

For their part, NWRO leaders questioned liberal feminists' fixation on the passage of the Equal Rights Amendment. Equal opportunity legislation, in and of itself, they believed, would not address the multifaceted causes of women's lack of economic power. Yet, here again, important coalitions did emerge. NOW developed a poverty task force, and, under its African American president, Aileen Hernandez, the organization allocated significant resources to women's poverty issues. NOW joined with Tillmon to oppose the heavy-handed work requirements in welfare-to-work federal programs, and feminism's premier magazine, Ms., brought Tillmon's complex and pointed analysis of motherhood and welfare to a wide audience. "Welfare's like a traffic accident," Tillmon claimed. "It can happen to anybody, but especially it happens to women." Poor women bore primary responsibility for their children but were themselves "regarded by everybody as dependents."[73]

At a time when divorce rates were rising and even middle-class women were financially vulnerable as a result, Tillmon's ideas resonated: "Society needs women on welfare as 'examples' to let every woman, factory workers and housewife workers alike, know what will happen if she lets up, if she's laid off, if she tries to go it alone without a man." Tillmon compared welfare to marriage: "Welfare is like a super-sexist marriage. You trade in a man for the man. But you can't divorce him if he treats you bad. He can divorce you, of course, cut you off anytime he wants. But in that case, he keeps the kids, not you." The parallels in women's experiences were clear: Tillmon reminded feminists that economic dependency on a man might still be acceptable for middle-class mothers, but poor mothers' economic dependency on welfare was not.[74]

Despite many missed connections in the first decades of a feminist and racial justice revival, there was also much creative tension and many fruitful conversations. As the insightful writer Letty Cottin Pogrebin argued, in *Ms.* magazine's special 1973 issue "Up with Motherhood," there were some feminists who saw motherhood as integral to women's oppression, but, "the rest of us, scores of feminists of every age, race, marital status, and sexual persuasion are talking seriously, thoughtfully, and candidly about motherhood."[75] Indeed, feminism dramatically changed attitudes among a wide swath of the population. Moreover, policy changes enacted through feminist activism helped women access public roles and the economic and reproductive autonomy long denied them through patriarchal law and custom.

By the end of the 1970s, employers could no longer discriminate against women as women, and they could not fire women for being pregnant. Parents who needed child care received a tax credit for these expenses. Women needing public assistance would no longer have their homes invaded or be questioned about their sexual histories as a condition for receiving funds. Poor women had access to programs like WIC and school lunches for their children. Women had new rights to employment advancement and freedom from various forms of discrimination in higher education. More and more women could command their own economic resource base when and if they needed to be the sole economic support of their children. Women could claim their children as dependents, apply for credit in their own name, and, in many areas of the country, find refuge from violent relationships for both themselves and their children.

Feminism was especially important in emboldening women to claim new rights with respect to their bodies. Echoing, however unconsciously, their nineteenth-century radical antecedents, women of the 1960s and 1970s demanded a new level of autonomy around their bodies with respect to reproduction, sexuality, and medical care. The countercultural movement of the 1960s fueled a strong interest in the "natural" body. Taking matters further, feminists mounted organized challenges to the laws and medical practices that structured women's access to reproductive decision making. In all these areas, women continued to challenge the experts.

A Right to Choose: Challenging Abortion and Sterilization Policy and Practice

As chapter 8 showed, postwar women's often tragic attempts to control their reproduction in the face of massive repression were creating a crisis that the medical profession could no longer ignore. In the early 1960s, birth control was still largely unavailable to single women, abortion had become extremely dangerous, and more women suffered complications of botched abortions, about which they were encouraged to suffer in silence and shame. Even early efforts to claim access to the Pill, approved by the Food and Drug Administration in 1960, usually did not come from women, who feared for their sexual reputations. Instead, they came from physicians and outspoken men who embraced either the sexual revolution or fears about population growth, or some combination of both, who championed women's right to birth control. Similarly, physicians, psychiatrists, nurses, attorneys, social workers, and liberal clergy were in the forefront of demanding abortion reform. A 1955 Planned Parenthood conference provided the first major forum for psychiatrists and physicians to critically consider the issue. By 1968, the American College of Obstetricians and Gynecologists actually approved an agenda of reforming abortion laws. Organized psychiatrists and African American medical societies supported repeal of abortion laws, and the American Public Health Association supported public funding to make abortion more widely available to women who needed it.[76]

Also fueling conversation about abortion were worries about birth defects from the effects of thalidomide, a drug prescribed to pregnant women in the late 1950s and early 1960s, and from a 1963 German measles outbreak. These concerns added to the already growing list of exceptions to abortion restrictions that physician committees were making for women in cases of rape, incest, and psychiatric problems. As the counterculture movement and the sexual revolution unfolded and more people than ever before equated restrictions on sexual freedom with a repressive past, the Supreme Court moved the cause along as well. In 1965, the Court decriminalized contraception nationwide in its *Griswold v. Connecticut* decision. This decision established a "right to privacy" in marital decisions regarding birth control.[77] In 1972 the Court went further, barring states from restricting access to contraception to unmarried people.

On abortion, initial reform proposals at the state level generally involved expanding abortion rights with the consent of husbands and, very importantly, the approval of doctors. Active psychiatrists and physicians believed that abortion laws should be reformed to allow greater leeway for professionals' medical judgments.[78] These kinds of changes to state laws did occur in some states; indeed, four states had legalized some form of abortion before 1973, but they were of very limited to help to women. In reality, owing to economic constraints or simply to shame, most women simply avoided hospital abortion committees.

When feminists jumped into the fray, they challenged the medical framework and pushed for genuine female autonomy, insisting that abortion become a woman's choice, not a woman's negotiation with a physician. "The only real experts on abortion are women," read a leaflet at a 1969 public forum about an abortion bill pending in the New York legislature. The New York Redstockings held the first of many abortion speak-outs. They touched on all facets of the humiliation of restrictive abortion, and they began to reframe the respectable position of "family planning," which very much sounded like it was about married women, to a broader idea of sexual self-determination that involved single women as well.[79] In this way they echoed the early, revolutionary activism of Margaret Sanger, rather than her more eugenically influenced notion of planned reproduction. Advancing the feminist notion that "the personal is political," women who spoke out on abortion took long-private conversations into the public realm.

Some feminists took the cause further. As early as the mid-1960s, Patricia Magginis, founder of the Society for Humane Abortion, sought to make abortion more

available to more women. She offered classes on the topic and distributed refer-
ral information about physician abortion providers abroad, while encouraging
women who had received abortions to write to their legislators on the topic. The
Jane collective of women in Chicago sought out reputable medical abortion providers to protect women from the abuses of an abortion underground. Initially,
the Jane activists spent more than a year assisting abortion procedures with a man
whom they believed was a doctor. When they discovered he was not actually a physician, some Jane members decided they could perform abortions themselves, in a
way that contested a medical model they disliked. Between 1969 and 1973, Jane provided between 11,000 and 12,000 abortions, mostly to poor and desperate women,
from all backgrounds, at a cost of about $100, compared to the going rate in Chi-
cago, which was between $500 and $1000. Jane activist Laura Kaplan recalled that
"we asked ourselves: How do we want to be treated? How can we design a service
through which women can become empowered?" After all, abortion was not just a
medical procedure, but a situation in which women faced a life decision of major
consequence, one in which they needed emotional support from other women.
And for Jane members, as well as for a growing segment of American society, the
right to abortion was part of female citizenship: "The ability to decide when and if
we wanted to have children was integral to our freedom and full participation in
society. We had to take that control."[80]

On this long incendiary issue, there was surprising movement in public opinion. During the *Roe* deliberations, polling data showed 65 percent of Americans in
support of legalizing abortion. Though the Catholic Church spearheaded opposition, by 1969 the majority of American Catholics supported the repeal of laws
that criminalized abortion.[81] Many Protestant congregations came out in favor of
abortion reform. Liberal clergy had in some communities been leaders in helping
troubled women obtain safe abortions. Meanwhile, younger physicians were moving quickly toward the idea of women's self-determination in the matter of abortion. Immediately following the 1973 *Roe v. Wade* decision, one survey found that
75 percent of physicians aged thirty-five or younger supported women's choice.[82]

On the political front, feminist attorneys challenged state laws, and NOW advocated openly for abortion "on demand" and ideally at no cost. Feminist lawyers
took the case of Norma McCorvey to the Supreme Court, challenging an extremely
restrictive Texas law that would not allow abortion even in cases of rape or incest.
Their arguments eventually made the case for the court's historic *Roe v. Wade* ruling on a woman's "right to privacy" in reproductive decisions and pregnant wom-
en's rights to equal protection under the law via the Fourteenth Amendment.

The arguments in favor of legalizing abortion in the 1973 *Roe* case showed the
power of feminist jurisprudence. For example, an important amicus brief submit-
ted by Nancy Stearns, in conjunction with the American Civil Liberties Union,
insisted that women needed to control their reproduction to participate fully in
the public world, just as they had needed the vote and more recent civil rights
protections. Stearns, pointing to the reality of limited social support for mothers,
also referenced "statutes that denied them their jobs and unemployment insurance,

expelled them from school, and gave them no help in getting child support from fathers."[83] This was an indictment of the limited citizenship rights and economic and social provisioning of mothers and mothers-to-be, an argument showing how women's biological difference made them less empowered than men in the public world. At the same time, it was an argument for gender equality and bodily autonomy.

As Laura Kaplan of the Jane collective remembered, the *Roe* victory was an enormous relief for prochoice activists. Disappointing for many, the decision fell short of hopes for free abortion on demand. The Court also rejected a feminist antipoverty argument that the laws preventing abortion were discriminatory against poor women. And with the Hyde Amendment of 1976, abortions for poor women and girls provided by Medicare were discontinued, except in cases of threats to a woman's life. Still, *Roe v. Wade* was clearly a revolutionary step toward female autonomy in reproductive decisions, on a scale never seen before in American history. Even as the United States lagged behind industrialized nations in the provision for the actual babies that women bore, it now had a freer abortion policy than most other countries. Abortions became safe and legal, if not always affordable or widely available geographically. As Leslie Reagan points out, the resulting improvements in maternal health were truly dramatic, on par with "the invention of antiseptics and antibiotics." Access to abortion also moved women closer to partnership in their own medical care and farther from excessive surveillance of their bodies.[84]

For women of color, the meaning of reproductive rights was particularly broad and complex. Although they supported abortion rights in proportions comparable to white women, the reproductive rights of women of color were not easily resolved by the *Roe v. Wade* decision. As we have seen, economic empowerment, educational advocacy, and struggles against racism absorbed a great deal of the political energy of activists. Moreover, women of color in the reproductive rights movement 1970s heyday wanted to make sure that the right not to reproduce was paired with the freedom from reproductive coercion. They needed an end to sterilization abuse and an expansion of available health care in their communities. Women of color, notes historian Rebecca Kluchin, "experienced higher maternal mortality rates, higher rates of poverty-related diseases that complicated their ability to become pregnant and carry a pregnancy to term, and higher rates of death from illegal abortion than white women."[85]

At the same time, population reduction, linked to notions of genocide, was a hot button political issue within communities of color in the late 1960s and early 1970s. The language in the larger political arena reinforced eugenic fears. Stereotypes of African American mothers using the welfare system fueled notions that black women were producing babies for money. Meanwhile, in places like California, pregnant Mexican women were cast as "pregnant pilgrims," seeking citizenship for their children and provoking backlash by white citizens.[86] At a time when physicians often refused sterilization to middle-class white women, the U.S. Department of Health, Education and Welfare freely provided sterilization services for poor women.

Eugenic sterilization had become thoroughly racialized by this time, and congressional testimony revealed that more than two thousand women had been involuntarily sterilized with government antipoverty funds just during the 1972–1973 fiscal year. Further investigation revealed that teaching hospitals often required women of color to consent to sterilization as a condition of receiving an abortion. A dozen Mexican women involuntarily sterilized at a southern California medical center in the mid-1970s brought forth a lawsuit, the records of which showed "that none of the women entered the hospital with an intent to be sterilized; persistent attempts to persuade the women to accept sterilization were made while they were in full labor and/or drugged; consent forms were in English, even though all the women had limited fluency in that language; and the medical staff failed to adequately inform the women of the consequences of the surgery." In the 1970s, the fastest growing form of birth control was sterilization. On Indian reservations, the Indian Health Services hospitals and their affiliates sterilized between 25 and 42 percent of Native American women of childbearing age, often with very questionable consent.[87] Between 1974 and 1979, HEW adopted increasingly stringent standards to prevent sterilization abuse, after a broad coalition of reproductive rights activists provoked much publicity on the issue.

Grassroots organizing by groups like the Black Women's Liberation Group, the Third World Women's Alliance, and the Committee for Abortion Rights and Against Sterilization abuse seeded the building of larger coalitions. In a high-watermark era for feminist and antiracist coalition building, reproductive rights ideas broadened by the late 1970s. White feminists, along with many prominent multicultural organizations actively fighting the issue for some time, helped publicize sterilization abuse. The National Council of Negro Women was especially involved in exposing and protesting sterilization abuse. They were joined by Christian and Jewish women's groups, the Nation of Islam, the Black Panther party, the National Organization for Women, Zero Population Growth, the National Women's Political Caucus, the Women's Equity Action League, and an increasingly feminist-oriented National Welfare Rights Organization. Articulating a broad idea of reproductive rights, Johnnie Tillmon declared, "Nobody realizes more than poor women that all women should have the right to control their reproduction. . . . Ain't no white man going to tell me how many babies I can have. . . . And ain't nobody in the world going to tell me what to do with my body, 'cause this is mine." By the late 1970s and early 1980s, historian Jennifer Nelson has shown that problems of sterilization abuse, pre- and postnatal health care, and child care became mainstays of a new feminist reproductive rights movement.[88]

Meanwhile, the *Roe v. Wade* victory itself was fragile. The year 1973 was also a peak of mobilization for a right-to-life movement. This included not only socially conservative groups like the Catholic Church but also many women, some of whom were sympathetic to aspects of feminism, who became politicized on the issue. Some women who opposed abortion had a visceral reaction. One mother of "a large family," also a nurse, became reluctantly involved in the issue after the 1973 decision, which "just kind of hit many of us . . . we couldn't believe it would go that far."[89] Many women opposed to abortion remained active on the issue, but women by no means maintained control of the burgeoning right-to-life movement. After all, few of them were represented in state and federal governmental bodies.

As we have seen, distrustful attitudes toward women's reproductive autonomy and religious opposition to abortion had deep roots in American society, and a backlash to feminist gains now fueled the fire. By the end of the 1980s, the pro-life movement was successfully using state legislatures and additional Supreme Court cases to restrict access to abortion, not only through the curtailment of federal funding to poor women but also via waiting periods, mandatory abortion counseling, the barring of abortion procedures on state property, and notification requirements to parents or spouses.[90]

The medical community, with the exception of the American Public Health Association, had also resisted incorporating abortion care into hospitals and medical training. By the early 1990s, only 12 percent of residencies in obstetrics and gynecology required training in the provision of first-trimester abortions. Private health insurers often did not cover abortion services. Race and class continued to restrict women's access to abortion, and this was compounded by the geographic unavailability of abortion. More than 80 percent of counties in the U.S. did not provide any abortion services by the early 1990s.[91]

In the aftermath of the Supreme Court decision *Webster v. Reproductive Health Services*, in which the court allowed for some state regulation, the movement to oppose abortion rights mobilized even further: Between 1989 and 1992, activists introduced more than seven hundred bills into state legislatures to restrict abortion access, and violent acts against abortion clinics escalated significantly.[92] The battle only intensified between the 1990s and the present. *Roe v. Wade* was a reproductive rights victory and a turning point for an as-yet unrelenting cultural warfare around the politics of female reproduction.

Challenging Medicalized Birth: The Alternative Birth Movement

Like abortion reform, demands for greater female control of childbirth emerged before feminism's Second Wave but expanded in scope through feminist activism. The La Leche League, founded in 1957 by eight suburban Catholic women, set the stage for legitimizing a return to more natural birthing methods by claiming first that women' bodies were perfectly capable of feeding infants without formula. The innovations of Grantly Dick-Read and later the French physician Ferdinand Lamaze had a limited impact by the early 1960s. Historian Jacqueline Wolf notes that Lamaze, Dick-Read, and his lesser known collaborator Helen Heardman, who supported the new methods with research, provided both "vocabulary and vision" around alternatives to highly medicalized birth and a foundation upon which feminism would build.[93]

Later in the 1960s, as feminist critiques of physicians' control of women's bodies dovetailed with countercultural glorification of the natural body, midwifery reemerged as a woman-centered alternative to medicalized birth. Ina May Gaskin, formerly Ina May Middleton, whose story was mentioned in chapter 8, started

"The Farm" with her husband. In this spiritual community women could give birth outside of hospital settings, via trained midwives. Gaskin published a book, *Spiritual Midwifery* in 1975, advocating midwifery as an alternative to the medical establishment: "We feel that returning the major responsibility for normal childbirth to well-trained midwives rather than have it rest with a predominantly male and profit-oriented medical establishment is a major advance in self-determination for women." Gaskin advanced a feminist agenda via the maternal body, and she got results. Her home-birth midwifery practice had better maternal and child health outcomes than childbirth in hospitals, a comparison that held up in studies of other home birth and midwifery-assisted centers.[94]

The dominance of hospitals and obstetricians, however, was not so easily dislodged. Hospitals continued to account for 99 percent of women's birth experiences over the decades following the midwifery revival, even as late as the 2010s. The American College of Obstetricians and Gynecologists adopted a policy of discouraging home births in 1982, and many obstetricians refused to make themselves available for emergency back-up, thus adding significant barriers to the home birth option. Accordingly, birth activists put significant energy into reforming hospital protocol. Some reform came from within. Certified nurse midwives (CNMs) had gained some access to hospitals and to maternal-infant health programs, especially under the Johnson administration. Along with nurses, CNM's used their professional observations of women's needs to push for changes like rooming-in with babies.[95]

Meanwhile, radical tactics from outside pressure groups pushed physicians to accommodate birthing women. In addition to inspecting maternity practices in hospitals, Mothers Of the wHole Earth Revolt (MOTHER) invited women to speak out about birth experiences, similar to abortion speak-outs, and to let problem physicians know "we know who they are and what they do to women and babies."[96] Activists created birth reform organizations around the country. They educated themselves and other women about supportive physicians and birthing options, including home birth.[97] They insisted on the revision of obstetrics textbooks that infantilized female patients and pushed for laws like the one first created in Massachusetts, requiring hospitals to make public their rates of Cesarean section births.[98] They targeted practices such as pubic shaving, routine enemas, episiotomies, separation of mothers and babies after birth, and the general paternalism of physicians, who often made medical decisions without even consulting, much less obtaining consent, from women in labor.

The birth reform movement also sought to change cultural attitudes toward women's bodies. Books like Suzanne Arms's *Immaculate Deception* (1975) reached wide audiences with critiques of medicalized birth and a certain romanticization of "primitive" childbirth. Sheila Kitzinger's *Women as Mothers* (1978) and Brigitte Jordan's *Birth in Four Cultures*, both published in 1978, amplified Margaret Mead's point that birthing rituals varied by culture, and American medicalized birth was but one of many models. Feminist birth activists distributed the woman-authored feminist manual, *Our Bodies, Ourselves*, promoting bodily self-knowledge and reclamation.

Birth activists also sought to recreate the community aspect of traditional birth. While some had advocated fathers' presence in labor and delivery since the 1950s, trying to bring the togetherness ideal of the nuclear family into the birthing room, feminists went further in the 1960s and 1970s. They wanted woman-centered, rather than simply "family-centered" birth. Women friends, children, and lesbian partners should ideally all be welcomed into the birth experience, as well as male partners. Some birth reform activists also tried to promote a positive view of childbirth's essentially sexual nature. One woman, quoted by Gaskin in her book, spoke of her contractions as "rushes": "As the contractions got stronger, it felt like I was making love to the rushes and I could wiggle my body and push into them and it was really fine."[99] Positive images of birth also found their way into art in Judy Chicago's land-mark *Birth Project* work (1980–1985), needlework-embellished images of a largely taboo subject in Western art, which toured throughout North America.

By the end of the 1970s, particularly for women privileged by race and class, childbirth in the United States had become much more humane. Women were usually awake and were often given fewer drugs. Physicians recognized that these practices generally meant greater safety for babies as well.[100] Birthing mothers also experienced improved continuity of care, less separation from their babies, and more encouragement for breastfeeding. They could room in with their newborns. Many gave birth in the presence of husbands or other loved ones, and routine pubic shaving and other ostensibly sterilizing routines, held over from an era of infectious disease anxiety, were less common. Some women worked with physicians on birth plans, and, very importantly, physicians could not perform procedures on women in labor without their consent. Younger physicians, including more and more women, as well as nurses and certified nurse midwives who practiced in hospitals, created more consultative standards of care in this new environment. Though home birth options remained circumscribed, some women used the nation's new freestanding birthing centers to enjoy a less medicalized and interventionist approach.

At the same time, hospitals proved adept at coopting the idea of natural birth. Women might do Lamaze breathing and refuse pain medication during the first stage of labor, but then they might be encouraged to accept medication for second stage labor. The advance of technologies and procedures in the birthing room, the increasing attention to cost-cutting efficiency in time in labor and hospital stays, along with fears of lawsuits for less than ideal birth outcomes continued to push childbirth medical care toward the "cascade of interventions," recently documented for a wide audience in the film *The Business of Being Born*. The rate of Cesarean section, which was about 4 percent in the mid-1960s, would skyrocket, even during the alternative birth movement years. Obstetricians and gynecologists as a pro-fession have become alarmed by their own results: according to statistics, by the 2010s nearly one-third of births in the United States involve Cesarean sections, and Cesarean sections are the most common surgical procedures in the nation.[101]

Within hospital settings, technology and the ever-expanding possibilities of pharmaceuticals proved too captivating to ignore. Drugs administered during labor remained common, with about 80 percent of mothers still receiving medication of some form for delivery in the late 1980s, and about 90 percent of first-time vaginal birth delivery mothers receiving episiotomies, though the rate did go down over time. Electronic Fetal Monitoring (EFM), introduced in the mid-1960s, was initially intended for women whose health conditions warranted special monitoring, but by the 1980s it became routine. While useful for detecting fetal distress in some situations, EFM limited a laboring woman's mobility and autonomy and sometimes directed attendants' focus toward medical equipment rather than the laboring mother. EFM also contributed greatly to the increase in Cesarean sections, often unnecessary ones. With the baby being increasingly defined as potentially at risk, and an ever-growing expectation that childbirth is a situation in which there can only be one, perfect outcome, the risks of Cesarean sections to mothers have often been ignored. Indeed, maternal mortality is four times higher in sectioned birth than in vaginal deliveries. Evidence continues to be widely available about the high maternal mortality and morbidity rates resulting from Cesarean sections.[102]

As historian Jacqueline Wolf has shown, by the 1990s, home birth was still marginalized, and the alternative birth movement was on the wane, often vilified in mainstream culture. Busy, usually employed women were more often willing to accept medical interventions, including Cesarean sections. Increasingly, young mothers' attentions turned toward the often rocky transition to motherhood after the birth rather than to the birth experience itself. In addition, inadequate access to basic health care and nutrition had created a large population of medically high-risk mothers, a set of problems exacerbated by a highly medicalized, technology-focused model of care. In recent decades attention has often gone to routinizing highly interventionist birth practices rather than to reducing maternal and child health risk factors before or during pregnancy. The interventionist practices themselves, from X-rays back in the 1930s to largely untested ultrasound techniques and very high rates of Cesarean section and induction of labor, have often imperiled both babies and mothers. Since 1913, the United States has had a poor standing among industrial nations in neonatal and maternal death rates. As Wolf has observed, "choice in relation to birth had come to mean acceptance or rejection of three routine treatments—labor induction, epidural anesthesia, and caesarean section—and even in the case of these few treatments, a patient's refusal was not always a realistic possibility."[103]

Physicians, insurance companies who increasingly circumscribed physicians' control, and women themselves, who have tended to see their birth experience as private and isolated choices, all contributed to this trend. As midwifery practices and stand-alone birthing centers closed in the late 1990s and 2000s, family physicians also limited their birthing practices, in part due to fears of malpractice suits. In some parts of the country, however, women have been active in advocating for broader access to midwifery care and postpartum doula care since the late 2000s, and home birth has seen a revival large enough to attract notice, accounting for 0.56 percent of births in 2004 to 0.72 in 2009, when some 29,650 women gave birth at home.[104]

What counts as safe and low-risk childbirth has changed considerably over the course of the twentieth century and into the twenty-first. Since the age of medicalized birth began, women's efforts to regain control of a process that always involved risk have gone in paradoxical directions. When women began to try to reclaim birth as a natural process that had been coopted by male science, they did so at a time when they could anticipate unprecedented safety in the birthing process because of the advancements of science itself.[105] If anything, expectations for "perfect" babies and zero tolerance for the vagaries of biology and human error have only increased, in spite of birth reform activists' unquestioned successes in rehumanizing the birthing process and returning some voice and options to birthing mothers. The situation at present is rife for repoliticization. A revived women's health movement could continue to create linkages between women's reproductive choices, ranging from contraception and abortion to childbirth. Ultimately, women's health activism needs to look more broadly at the necessary social and economic conditions that foster healthy mothers and babies, by hopefully taking the notions of Progressive-era Children's Bureau activists further, thanks to the broad insights of feminism. The combined social vision and energy of maternalists and feminists continues to hold great potential.

Conclusion

The social movements that began in the 1960s and 1970s helped women define their own needs, whether to opt out of motherhood altogether or, more relevantly for the purposes of this study, to demand the resources they needed to mother well and to combine mothering with other human needs and pursuits. Feminism, mixed with both maternalist politics and antimaternalist cultural legacies, was complicated by racial and class tensions. On issues of motherhood, the notion of choice proved both provocative and somewhat limiting. Creating opportunity was essential to empowering mothers and women generally. But so too was a fuller provisioning of the work of women as caregivers and workers in their own right. Progressive-era ideas of government assistance to keep mothers with their children expanded in the 1960s and 1970s, before contracting and becoming vilified. This aspect of the modernization of motherhood, provisioning and regulation by the state, continued to be stunted by racism, cultural ambivalence about single mothers, and a conservative insistence that problems of economic insecurity belonged ultimately to families, not to government. Second Wave feminism and the social movements of the Left as a whole left much unfinished business, even as this generation's ideas expanded and created new possibilities for mothers. The idea of unmooring motherhood from the tight nuclear family and gender role prescriptions would find new and unexpected forms toward the end of the twentieth century and in the early years of the twenty-first.

CHAPTER 10

Mothers' Changing Lives and Continuous Caregiving

In 1992, Vice President Dan Quayle famously criticized a popular sitcom character for choosing to be a single mother. Murphy Brown, he claimed, was "mocking the importance of fathers." Quayle's tirade against a fictional character proved a bit embarrassing. It made headlines and fueled countercritique that, at a time of waning support for the first Bush administration, made sense to many Americans. Diane English, creator of *Murphy Brown*, quipped, "If the Vice President thinks it's disgraceful for an unmarried woman to bear a child, and if he believes that a woman cannot adequately raise a child without a father, then he'd better make sure abortion remains safe and legal."[1]

Quayle's moralizing and English's defense of women's autonomy, though a short-lived scuffle, resonated both forward and backward in time. Two important features of motherhood have been logical extensions of modern life: women's control of reproduction and women's lagging opportunities to financially support their children; these were controversial in 1992, and they are still controversial today. Cultural anxiety about working mothers peaked in the 1980s, thereafter becoming so increasingly commonplace as to provoke fewer and fewer apocalyptic predictions about the future of the country. But public debates about abortion became more heated and polarizing over time, especially with the rise of a well-financed anti-abortion movement and its coordinated legal strategy aimed at dismantling the provisions of in *Roe v. Wade*. Debates about women's reproductive bodies have echoed nineteenth-century struggles, with new technological and partisan political twists and possibilities for surveillance and commercialization of women's wombs unknown to previous generations. Meanwhile, for all the zealous defense of the sanctity of marriage, a dramatic trend toward mothering outside marriage would flummox Americans right down to the present. The very diversity and disruptions of maternal experiences continue to challenge expert prescriptions. New forms of maternal politics have emerged, but mothers have persisted in taking considerable individual responsibility for a fraying social support system as they rear their children.

CHANGING FAMILIES AND FEMALE LIFE PATTERNS

In 1975, Americans saw a marked departure from the monotonously middle-class white family that the postwar purveyors of culture had projected onto their television sets. Divorced single mother Ann Romano appeared in *One Day at a Time*, which aired for nine seasons and enjoyed great popularity. In movies such as *Alice Doesn't Live Here Anymore* (1974) and *An Unmarried Woman* (1978), Americans watched the fictional journeys of single mothers surviving and thriving.[2] The mold was cracking open much more emphatically in the real world. The changes in American family life, and therefore motherhood, in the past half-century, especially since the 1970s, have been more rapid and for many more bewildering than in any other period.

The social movements described in chapter 9 challenged expectations and fueled changes in the family. So too did a growing need for women's income, men's declining income potential as breadwinners, economic contraction, and changes in reproductive possibilities and technologies. Divorce rates increased significantly, more than doubling between 1960 and 1980.[3] Feminism certainly influenced women's willingness to leave relationships that ranged from unsatisfying to abusive, while the individualist ethos of the 1970s contributed to men's departures as well. Furthermore, Americans no longer rushed into marriage; the average age of marriage rose from 20.3 in 1960 to 22 in 1980, and by the 1980s, one in six women were choosing not to marry. By 2010, the average age of marriage for women was 26, and for men, 28.[4]

From the 1960s forward, motherhood became less tightly scripted and confined within heterosexual marriage and male-breadwinning/female-caregiving dichotomies. On the whole, women have long modified their child-rearing practices, in keeping with the challenges posed by each era's economy, the prescriptions of the culture, and personal preferences; women were having on average fewer children. The birth rate had fallen markedly in the 1930s and picked up to historic proportions in the affluent baby boom era, peaking at 3.8 live births per woman, a twentieth-century record. Expanded access to contraception and abortion and a contracted American economy in the 1970s contributed to another falling birth rate, as did concerns about population growth, cultural questioning of the hyperdomesticity of the baby boom era, and women's increased participation in education and the labor force. The birth rate bottomed out at 1.8 children in the mid-1970s. It edged up again to more than 2.0 in the late 1980s and has stayed in that range since, never to return to the baby boom heights. Women also began to defer childbearing, sometimes into their thirties, though this pattern varied a great deal by class and educational level. By the late 2000s, 20 percent of women aged forty to forty-four had never had a child, double the percentage during the late 1970s. In a trend that would have perhaps vindicated nineteenth-century moralists' predictions, women with more education were more likely to delay or even forego childbearing. In 2010, the birth rate hit its lowest point in recorded history, falling sharply in response to the 2008 recession; immigrant women experienced the sharpest decline in the number of children they bore.[5]

Women's control in these decisions has been made possible in large part by the expanded availability of contraception, as well as legal abortion. A recent study by the Guttenmacher Institute reminds us that women continue to use contraception for some of the same reasons their great-grandmothers did: 63 percent of survey respondents said they used contraception in order to take better care of themselves or their families, and 56 percent cited the need to support themselves financially. By the mid 2010s, however, women are planning their labor force participation and their childbearing, often with much greater control than in previous generations; 51 percent and 50 percent of respondents, respectively, said they were using contraceptive in order to complete their education or to keep or get a job. Women's everyday decisions reflected broader realities: putting control of reproduction in women's hands pays off. Scholars have found strong positive correlations between widespread availability of contraceptives and familial health, women's average earnings, and even a narrowing of the wage gap.[6]

Between the 1970s and the present, the rise in mothers' labor-force participation represented an enormous shift in women's generational experiences. The percentage of families with a breadwinner father and a non-wage-earning mother at home fell from 62 percent in 1960 to about 10 percent in the mid-1980s.[7] Despite charges of neglected children and the media's declaration of "mommy wars" and of educated women "opting out" of the workplace, the pattern was here to stay. Women still experienced gaps in their employment histories for caregiving, but their lifetime participation in the labor force became the norm.

Feminism broadened the opportunities available to women, but the twentieth-century trend of greater labor force participation definitely predated Second Wave feminism. The increase in the 1950s, discussed in chapter 8, was less visible because mothers typically worked when their children were between the ages of six and seventeen. Since the 1960s, the age of the youngest child when a woman returned to work grew lower. By 1991, nearly 60 percent of mothers of children under age six were working outside the home, while the figure had been just 20 percent in 1960. Today, more than 70 percent of mothers of children under age eighteen are in the workforce, and the most remarkable change in the past three decades has been the rise of labor-force participation rates of mothers with children under the age of one year: nearly 56 percent of these mothers are currently employed. Even with women's persistently lower earnings on average than men, women have contributed increasingly important proportions of family income. Among married couples, in 1970, women's earnings contributed an average of 26.6 percent to family earnings, and that percentage, climbing steadily every year, reached 35.6 percent in 2007.[8] The family patterns of most mothers now more closely approximated those pioneered by African American mothers and other mothers of color.

By the 1970s, fewer mothers were getting married. In 1950, a mere 5 percent of children had been reared by single mothers. As we have seen, those mothers and their children faced intense discrimination. Not until the 1960s and early 1970s did the Supreme Court rule that children born to single mothers are entitled to equal protection under the law, including the right to child support from their fathers. The rate of out-of-wedlock births climbed in the 1970s and especially increased among poorer women as the Reagan recession of the 1980s set in, making marriage less financially attainable. By the late 1990s, one-third of all children were born to single mothers. By 2012, more than half of the children born to women under age thirty had mothers who were not married, a remarkable 59 percent. This was a truly dramatic shift since the postwar era.[9]

An especially important facet of this trend has been its class dimensions. College-educated women are much more likely to combine marriage and mothering, as are women who earn more. In other words, it is not, as some commentators have suggested, women's economic independence that has caused a trend in the decoupling of marriage and motherhood. Instead, women with less education and fewer resources tend to bear children outside of marriage. Race and ethnicity have continued to be significant variables as well. Conservatives used to argue that poor single women had babies because welfare benefits came too easily, allowing them to rely on government and avoid marriage. The argument does not hold water, especially because the real value of AFDC declined in the 1980s and 1990s, and public assistance has been shredded to within an inch of its life since the welfare reform measures of 1996, which ended the AFDC program in favor of the more restricted TANF. Though the nation experienced a kind of panic around the issue of teen pregnancy between the mid-1970s and 1990s, rates of teen pregnancy have since also declined.[10]

There is no one cause for the decoupling of marriage and motherhood, but an important piece of the explanation lies in the changed prospects of men, especially men without college education. Women continue to earn less than men in all categories of educational achievement, but men's earnings have fallen. The *New York Times* reported in 2012 that "among men with some college but no degrees, earnings have fallen 8 percent in the past thirty years, while the earnings of their female counterparts have risen by 8 percent." Poor mothers in national surveys say that people should marry before they have children, and are even more likely than those in the middle class to say they believe that a child raised by two parents is better off than a child reared by one.[11]

An important study by sociologists Kathryn Edin and Maria Kefalas revealed that, in their actual lives, impoverished women saw marriage as a luxury they can hope for when they have some economic autonomy, in case they needed to leave a relationship. Motherhood, however, was a given for these poor women, a marker of hope and accomplishment and something that often brought order to their lives. One young woman explained, "The way I was raised, [with] so much violence and confusion going on around me, I just wanted to love somebody. And . . . then [my child] filled me up with a lot of stuff that was needed." Edin and Kefalas found that women's relationships with children's fathers often began full of hope. But the men in their lives ultimately did not seem stable enough to be considered marriageable.

Indeed, men had very limited access to living wages, and the urban poverty crisis was keenly felt in these parents' lives: drugs, violence, and incarceration thwarted relationship stability time and again. In Edin and Kefalas's interviews, poor women, whether white, African American, or Hispanic, often said they would rather wait to marry to than go through the messiness of divorce. Motherhood, meanwhile, was not an enormous opportunity cost, as it was for middle-class women: with or without motherhood, the lifetime earnings of severely economically disadvantaged girls and women would be about the same.[12]

Still, it is not just impoverished women and men who have questioned the necessary combination of marriage and motherhood. In the early 1960s half of Americans believed that unhappy married couples should stay together for the sake of the children; but that figure has plummeted to 20 percent in the early twenty-first century. Moreover, some mothers are single by choice even when their social worlds involve men with better economic prospects or potential female partners. One poll in 1989 found 36 percent of single women saying they had given serious consideration to rearing a child on their own.[13] Beginning in the 1970s, the stigmas on being single and on choosing not to have children also began to recede, thanks in part to feminist activism.

Americans in general still highly value both parenthood and the institution of marriage, as evidenced in part by the efforts of lesbian and gay Americans to achieve full marriage rights, and those of a vocal conservative contingent to defend hetero-sexual marriage as the basis of the social order. Nevertheless, there is an enormous divergence between Americans' attitudes toward marriage and their behavior. Since record-keeping on the topic began in the 1910s, the United States has had the high-est divorce rate in the industrialized world; even heterosexual couples who live together and have children in marriagelike relationships are far more likely than their European counterparts to see those relationships end. Edin and Kefalas point out, "The fragility of both marriage and cohabitation means that by age fifteen, only half of American children live with both biological parents, whereas roughly two thirds of Swedish, Austrian, German, and French children do so, as do nearly nine in ten children in Spain and Italy."[14]

The implications of this trend are neither as straightforward nor as alarming as many denunciators of the "decline of the American family" claim. Some children suffer in these situations; others thrive. Their families are only one factor in their development. Moreover, the continuity of maternal caregiving usually provides an anchor for children even when parents' relationships are unstable, and smaller families mean that children often receive more attention. A widely cited psycho-logical study, published in 1999 by Louise Silverstein and Carl Auerbach, found that a stable adult in a child's life mattered much more to children's well-being than the gender of a parent.[15] The many reinventions of American families in recent decades remind us that family is not only a biological construction but also a social one. The growing number and visibility of lesbian and gay families and heightened divorce rates have complicated and enriched the possibilities of family life. In the wake of divorce, men remarried at higher rates than women. This meant that many single mothers also shared care with nonresident former husbands and often step-mothers as well.

The cultural revolutions wrought by the 1960s expanded the possibilities for mothering in other ways. Beginning in the 1960s, parents began to adopt across racial lines with greater frequency, thereby creating families that visibly defied the secret adoption culture of the postwar period. As the stigma on single mother-hood for white women shrunk by the 1970s, most women began to exercise their rights to keep their children conceived out of wedlock or to seek a legal abortion. The old criteria of most white adopters, a healthy white baby, became unrealistic. Historian Barbara Melosh notes that many parents seeking adoption would now "reach out to older children, or those challenged by illness, disability, or psycholog-ical problems. Still others would relinquish the 'as if begotten' family by extending their searches across racial and national boundaries." Adoption became rarer alto-gether after 1970, but it also became less secretive, a trend that created complicated ties among birth mothers and adoptive parents. Indeed, by the 1990s, some of the women who had surrendered their children for adoption between the 1950s and 1970s managed to find and sometimes reunite with their long estranged biologi-cal children.[16] Between 1968 and 1971 there was a threefold increase in transracial adoption. The peak year was 1971, with 2,574 transracial adoptions, but this was still only about 2 percent of all adoptions by nonrelatives. Though small in number, families who adopted domestically across racial lines embodied hope for a society that would one day overcome its racial past.[17]

However, broad, historically rooted same-race preferences in adoption com-bined with a backlash from African Americans and Native Americans to further limit transracial domestic adoptions by the mid-1970s. African Americans cri-tiqued adoption practices that privileged white couples and argued that black children's racial identities could not be well formed within white families. Many American Indians claimed that white adoption of Native American children was a new form of assimilation and elimination of American Indian populations. Native American advocates effectively used claims of tribal autonomy to thwart interracial adoption into white families. Nevertheless, transracial adoption continued on an international scale. By the 1990s, international adoptions by Americans accounted for more than half of all adoptions worldwide and 15 to 20 percent of all adoptions formalized in the United States.[18]

Couples who produced children biologically across the age-old American barrier of race also claimed new rights to rear children. In the postwar period, white moth-ers who had children with African American men had often lost custody of their children just as lesbian mothers did.[19] If white people and people of color married, many states did not recognize their unions as legal. But in 1967 the Supreme Court struck down approximately three hundred years of the "anti-miscegenation" laws that had banned interracial marriage and thereby opened the possibility for legal recognition of interracial families. Meanwhile, the nation continued to diversify racially and ethnically, adding to Americans' awareness that the nation no longer looked like the *Leave It to Beaver* families of the postwar era. Indeed, after a lifting of immigration restrictions in 1965, the nation experienced its largest influx in the whole twentieth century of new immigrants. In contrast to the earlier period, only 10 percent of these new Americans originated in Europe. Asia and Latin America accounted for very significant portions of the new immigrant and refugee populations. By the early 1980s, there were actually growing numbers of mothers from Mexico, El Salvador, Guatemala, and other Latin American countries whose children remained in the mothers' home countries. These transnational mothers tended to their distant children as best they could via phone, letters, and later the Internet, often while caring for the children of middle- and upper-class women who worked outside their homes.[20]

As the above example suggests, while some re-formations of American families were breaking boundaries and expanding possibilities, other trends moved in the opposite direction. Increased racial profiling in states with harsh anti-immigrant policies has meant that Latin American immigrant mothers have been separated from their American-born children in increasing numbers if they themselves lack citizenship. Many risk deportation and separation from their children when they try to access health care or drive a car. Meanwhile, since the 1980s, the U.S. prison population quadrupled, solidifying the nation's dubious distinction of having the world's highest per capita imprisoned population. Since the 1990s, women have been the fastest growing component within an enormous incarcerated population, often imprisoned for nonviolent drug offenses. Consequently, the period between 1991 and 2007 saw a near doubling of the number of children with a mother in prison. Racism in the criminal justice system results in hugely disproportionate convictions for drug sentencing for African Americans compared to whites with similar drug use patterns. As a result, African American children were eight times more likely to have an incarcerated parent than were white children in 2007.[21]

Most incarcerated women are mothers, and they are usually nonviolent offenders overwhelmed by the challenges of poverty and violence in their own lives. More than half of women prisoners have experienced physical or sexual abuse, and nearly three-quarters struggle with mental health diagnoses. Typically these mothers lose custody of their children, often permanently. This loss of custody is encouraged by stiff sentencing for drug offenses, large geographic separations between incarcerated mothers and their children, federal law that encourages termination of rights, and an onerous obstacle course for mothers getting out of prison. State laws allow for refusal of housing, employment, and public assistance to persons convicted of felonies. Between the shrinking of government assistance since welfare reform in 1996 and the renewed policy emphasis on adopting out children in impoverished areas rather than providing financial resources (a provision of the Adoption and Safe Families Act of 1997), mothers disadvantaged by racism and poverty have once again become increasingly vulnerable to losing their children. As legal scholar Dorothy Roberts has cogently explained, the loss to African American communities and the strain on community resources have been especially devastating.[22]

All in all, the old American family ideal—heterosexual, white, middle-class, and defined by gendered dichotomies of breadwinning and caregiving—bore less and less resemblance to reality, even as it continued to be held up as a national icon. Many Americans were anxious and even downright alarmed about these dramatic changes. The primary focal points of anxiety about social change were the topics of working mothers, the female reproductive body, and "bad" mothers who embodied threats to the American family as an institution. As in the past, the "bad" mothers identified were disproportionately nonwhite and often not married.

All these debates underscore a continuing American fixation on the individual mother as a potential superhero. She might still need advice, but in the view of many, she needed no social provisions, such as quality, regulated, and subsidized child care or cash emergency funds for job losses or relationship break-ups. By the 1980s and 1990s, the idea that mothers needed equally invested partners in child care and family management was also fading from the national discussion. To succeed, to make up for the shortcomings of the American social policy structure and traditional gender norms, the American mother primarily needed to be a self-sacrificing and resourceful "mom."

Working Mothers: Cultural Representations and Social Policy

In the 1970s, as more and more mothers were entering the labor force, many people expressed optimism about this shift. But certainly not everyone embraced the idea of the working mother. As noted in chapter 9, one reaction to feminism was a strong defense of traditional marriage and motherhood. Phyllis Schlafley, for example, led a Stop ERA campaign and warned American women in 1977, "If you think diapers and dishes are a never-ending, repetitive routine, just remember that most of the jobs outside the home are just as repetitive." Indeed, most jobs outside the home held by women were just that, a fact that feminists were trying to change. Schlafley insisted that motherhood was the real prize: "After twenty years of diapers and dishes, a mother can see the results of her own handiwork in the good citizen she has produced and trained. After twenty years of faithful work in the business world, you are lucky if you have a good watch to show for your efforts."[23] Her words and her charisma helped fuel a growing backlash to feminism.

Still, there is no question that feminist ideas were combining with a heady individualism and making people rethink the traditional sacrifices of both motherhood and fatherhood. In opinion polls, most Americans supported the goals of the women's movement in the 1970s; in 1972, both major political parties supported the ERA, and landmark social legislation helped remove barriers to women's education and employment prospects. Meanwhile, mainstream women's magazines like *McCall's* ran articles like "How to Go to Work When Your Husband Is against It, Your Children Aren't Old Enough, and There's Nothing You Can Do Anyhow." *Ladies' Home Journal* began featuring a "Working Woman" column by feminist activist Letty Cottin Pogrebin, which ran for ten years. In interviews with children of working mothers, Pogebrin noted, "None of the children said they resent their mothers' jobs, and none feel envious of kids whose mothers are at home."[24]

Such articles, though certainly balanced by more conservative ones elsewhere in the women's magazine and child care advice universe, did provide inspiration.

They encouraged working mothers to see themselves as positive role models for their children, touted labor force participation as an avenue to more egalitarian marriages, and sometimes advocated policy changes for working mothers, like equal pay and quality child care. More than ever before in women's advice literature, there were alternative perspectives, and the magazines' new willingness to hear from actual mothers facilitated this trend. Magazines like *McCall's* began featuring forums and letters of actual mothers, who shared struggles such as guilt, time crunches, and day care challenges. Rather than always hearing from an expert, women often advised one another, and they sometimes exchanged ideas on how to develop collective solutions to their shared challenges.[25]

Even Hollywood flirted with solutions that went beyond the individual. In the film *Nine to Five* (1979), which was based on the stories of actual clerical workers, three put-upon but enterprising women depose their sexist boss and temporarily create a new office work space. They institute flextime, job sharing, and on-site child care. Productivity and employee satisfaction go up, and the women (eventually) get the credit. In the end, the only thing the generously paternalistic CEO does not like about the women's initiatives is the equal pay for their work. For the triumphant characters in the conclusion of *Nine to Five*, this is just another hurdle to jump. But more and more working women in the real world found that workplace flexibility to accommodate caregiving, if flexibility appeared at all, was often at the expense of pay and promotion opportunities Meanwhile, union-affiliated or union-driven activism on the rights of working mothers would founder as unions lost strength and numbers and were forced to defend basic collective bargaining rights, beginning in the 1980s.

By the Reagan era, the nation's optimism about working mothers faded, along with a popular commitment to providing policy solutions to women's changing roles as mothers. Women continued to flood into the labor force. In 1971, President Richard Nixon had vetoed the Comprehensive Child Development Act, a bill with bipartisan support, which would have dramatically increased the availability of child care via an extension of the Economic Opportunity Act. By 1984, 68 percent of working mothers returned to work when their babies were four months old or less. Yet, under Ronald Reagan, federal funding for child-care programs fell by 18 percent. The federal government eliminated its programs to train child-care workers and cut funding for the Child Care food program. Reagan's policies helped the small percentage of American families, usually in the secure middle class, whose employers provided child-care services by offering a tax deduction, which spurred growth in employer-sponsored child care. But the Reagan administration ignored the problem of regulation in an increasingly for-profit child-care market and demonstrated its disapproval of working mothers in a variety of ways, in both policy and rhetoric. Government refusals to create meaningful child-care legislation left a patchwork of centers and in-home providers, largely unregulated, staffed by an overwhelmingly female labor force that was grossly underpaid and therefore experienced highly transient turnover.[26]

Some lucky women could afford quality child care, through nannies or quality in-home care, or through the growing number of employer-sponsored child-care facilities. Some also had maternity leaves, and a few even received some compensation. Such arrangements, however, were rare and largely available only to professional women. Indeed, the Bureau of Labor Statistics reported in 1987 that only 2 percent of American workplaces provided child care for their employees, and about 3 percent subsidized off-site child care. For the most part, the interruption of a baby was a working woman's problem to solve. Employers could legally fire women for not returning to work on the employer's schedule. While the media tended to paint employed mothers as "yuppie" strivers who put their individual needs ahead of their children, growing numbers of mothers actually desperately needed their jobs, if only to work year-round and full-time for a less-than-poverty income level, as a significant number of women did in the 1980s.[27] In fact, much social policy of the era pushed back against and deliberately attempted to forestall the normalization of maternal labor force participation. Federal budget cuts and inaction simply made things harder for the ever-growing numbers of working women.

Meanwhile, the yuppie mother idea made great fodder for the media's claim, beginning in 1990, that there were "mommy wars" raging between stay-at-home mothers and working mothers. In reality, many women did not fit neatly into either category or did not fit for any length of time. To hear the media tell it, as Susan Douglas and Meredith Michaels note, "the working mother supposedly saw her opponent as a boring, limited woman who had just said 'uncle' to patriarchy, spent too much time fondling Tupperware, and because she didn't work was a poor role model for her kids, especially her daughters. The stay-at-home mom supposedly saw her opponent as a selfish careerist who neglected her kids, was too stressed out when she *was* with them, and deserved whatever guilt she felt."[28]

At a time when many mothers really did see either full-time work or full-time motherhood as choices they had to defend, the mommy wars idea hit a nerve. Stay-at-home mothers sometimes rationalized their own life choices by emphasizing the negative impact of temporary caregivers on children and family lives or by judging other mothers. "My sister works full-time—she's a lawyer," one mother observed in the early 1990s. "And her kids are the most obnoxious, whiny kids. . . . She thinks she's doing okay by them because they're in an expensive private school and they have expensive music lessons. . . . But I can't believe they're not going to have some insecurities."[29]

Working mothers sometimes resented the economic privilege of women who could stay home and described their labor force participation as progressive. Hillary Clinton touched off a firestorm on the 1992 presidential campaign trail with her husband when she said, "I suppose I could have stayed home and baked cookies and had teas, but what I decided to do was fulfill my profession, which I entered before my husband was in public life."[30] Clinton was forced to qualify her remarks. *Family Circle* magazine actually challenged both potential first ladies, Clinton and Barbara Bush, to a cookie-baking contest.

Rarely quoted by the media were mothers who tried to resist categorizing other women, even as they claimed their own choices. Liz Davenport, a mother interviewed by sociologist Linda M. Blum in the 1990s, said, "I did love my job . . . it was a conflict the whole time I was pregnant." In the end, she quit her job after her baby was born, in part to nurse her baby. "So, yes, I guess I am very strongly opinionated about [using other caregivers]! But you know, I have friends that do it, and I think their daycare arrangements are great, and I think their children are nice. I'm not trying to condemn people who do it differently . . . I'm not for martyring women and making them stay home and be miserable!"[31] Clearly, nuanced language was required to express the complexity of women's varying life situations, but the sensational catfight approach made better news stories.

Guilt was a common, but also prescribed, emotion among working mothers. If these women did not feel guilty on their own, the mass media was there to help them along. As Douglas and Michaels have chronicled in lucid and nuanced detail, media panics about children's well-being reflected the raging ambivalence Americans experienced regarding mothers' growing labor force participation and related cultural changes. One of the most stunning in its scope and hysteria was the mid-1980s day care scandal involving alleged sexual abuse of children. It was later learned that the accusations relied on grossly manipulated testimony by children. But the story quickly grew legs. More than one hundred cases of satanic child abuse cases actually went to court in the wake of the McMartin case, which involved a California day-care center. California received hundreds of thousands of reports of child abuse, but 84 percent of them were found to be baseless.[32]

Of course, in the context of an American public newly willing to talk about child sexual abuse, it was vital that those situations be uncovered. But the hysteria was out of all proportion to the actual crimes. The media fanned the flames with lurid details, escalating the number of stories about day-care abuse. Vulnerable children, more than a million of them, were in day-care centers and nursery schools, CBS reported in 1984, "enrolled, in most cases, because their mothers must work." Even though most received good care, CBS acknowledged, "elsewhere, in alarming numbers, preschoolers have been exploited, *sexually.*" ABC interviewed a mother, her face hidden, who said her three-year-old had been raped at her child care. "And I never knew it and I feel as though I neglected her, I feel as though I should have known. . . . I don't know how I could have known but you're still responsible for your children." The message was chilling. Combined with grossly exaggerated reports of abducted children, the media suggested that new levels of parental (usually maternal) surveillance of children were required. The reality was that children were more likely to be abused at home, but a viewer would not have known this from the media coverage.[33]

As had happened in the transition to scientific motherhood, the pitch of anxiety-mongering was intensified by an exploding consumer culture. Like their early twentieth-century counterparts, the mothers of the 1980s and 1990s were on the defensive, particularly if they were working outside the home. Marketers were ready to capitalize or, put another way, offer "solutions" in the form of new products and new advice. Throughout the 1980s and forward, stories on safety sold parenting magazines to ever-vigilant mothers, who also consumed articles on potty training, marriage advice, and recipes.

To be fair, the magazines said a lot less about marriage than they did in the 1950s. Motherhood was now to be women's primary occupation. Men, it was assumed, could take a bit more care of themselves. It must be noted, however, that, though *Parents* magazine's title sounds gender neutral, it has been and continues to be marketed to women, not men, just as parenting advice literature has long been. In this respect, little had changed. A cursory visit to a local bookstore's magazine rack today makes the point. The "Men's Interest" section would have us believe that men's realms are sports, sex, cars, and, for a few, fashion. Relationship advice and parenting? See the "Women's Interest" section, along with advice on cleaning your home. Indeed, beginning in the 1980s even cleaning products became advertised as ways to show maternal love. And the books kept up with the magazines. Douglas and Michaels noted that more than eight hundred books were published on motherhood between 1970 and 2000, but only twenty-seven of these appeared in the 1970s. Little surprise, then, that in a poll in the early 2000s, 81 percent of mothers thought it was harder to be a mother than it had been twenty or thirty years earlier, and 56 percent did not think they were doing as good a job as previous generations had done.[34]

Working Mother magazine thankfully offered mothers personal solutions and inspiring ideas and action plans for collective ones. Beginning in 1978, it reassured women that they could be good mothers while they worked and that they could ask more of their employers for things like flexibility, promotions, sick days, and childcare centers. To this day, *Working Mother* continues to profile progressive companies, large and small, that are using the strengths of working mothers to reinvent the workplace and the innovative human resources professionals and working mother entrepreneurs who are making it happen. The mostly private sector innovations the magazine publicizes include mentoring and leadership programs for ambitious mothers, the provision of financial aid for adoptive parents, policies that allow for extended leaves with guarantee of one's job, and paid maternity leaves. At Lego Systems, for example, employees can retain health insurance as part-time workers, mothers can phase back into their work schedules after having a baby, and the company provides coverage for in vitro fertilization and fertility treatments. The magazine also continues to inform working mothers about policies to help them address work-life balance on a larger scale and lauds the contributions of working mothers to the workplace and the economy. Though clearly slanted to mothers with better-than-average career prospects in professional jobs, *Working Mother* has been consistently upbeat: "We understand your challenges, show your options and support your choices. Working Mother: making your impossible dream possible."[35]

But even *Working Mother* has promoted what sociologist Sharon Hays appropriately called "intensive mothering," an updated version of moral motherhood with heightened attention to surveillance, consumer spending, and hypervigilance about enrichment opportunities. Hays points out that, whether mothers are working or not, the intensive mothering ideology implies that motherhood is still a full-time job. Mothers need to be the primary emotional connection point in their children's lives, and they must invest most of their own emotional and financial resources in their children, more or less relentlessly. Accordingly, *Working Mother's* annual "Working Mother of the Year" mothers are not only successful at work, but they are also self-sacrificing. The magazine's "quintessential working mother" says women's studies scholar Jillian M. Duquaine-Watson, "was professional, successful in both work and family life, and selfless in her devotion to her children." At the same time, the magazine tended to ignore "maternal emotions such as anger, jealousy, resentment, hostility, and frustration."[36]

Women in recent decades have continued to report high use of child-care advice literature. Especially in more traditional venues, the experts have continued to tell them that child-rearing is "more worthwhile than any job" and that intensive child care methods are required. As in the 1950s, expert advice in the late twentieth century suggested that children would guide mothers in activating their "instinctive" responses. Young children required a great deal of watching, stimulation, communication, and frequent interactions with a primary caregiver. Mothers, who unfortunately had to work outside the home, were charged with finding ideal child-care arrangements with low adult-child ratios and well-paid employees and low turnover. Also very similarly to the 1950s, child-care experts like the still-active Spock, British author Penelope Leach, and subsidiary advice outlets, such as *What to Expect When You're Expecting* and *What to Expect in the First Year*, continued to portray child-rearing as a separate realm from providing materially for children.[37]

With the growing consensus around intensive mothering ideas, Americans eased up on the old "Momism" worries about over-involved mothers. Also less visible in popular discourse were feminist assertions that mothers were complex people with their own needs and appropriate ambivalence about the underappreciated role of motherhood. Never mind the need for marriage contracts to encourage fathers to do their share. The new mothers of the 1980s and 1990s needed to be deeply involved with their children as primary caregivers and happy about it. While often working more, they also needed to be ever vigilant, continuously emotionally available, creative, and even fun. Douglas and Michaels's extensive review of parenting advice literature led them to this conclusion: "Childhood is filled with peril, but motherhood is fun, fun, fun." Symbolic of the era, in the 1990s, Dr. William Sears and his wife, Martha, a registered nurse and mother of the couple's eight children, popularized what they called "attachment parenting." For the Sears, their millions of readers, and those influenced by them, proper bonding required first "Creating a Peaceful Womb Experience," followed by lengthy breastfeeding, the wearing of babies in a child sling, and "co-sleeping" with baby, all toward the aim of intense mother-child bonding.[38]

Attachment parenting for early childhood prescribed intensive mothering practices, which were supposed to continue throughout childhood and perhaps into early adulthood. These ideas were promoted throughout the culture, even in children's books. In my research on the image of Mama Bear in the popular *Berenstain Bears* children's books, I found a growing micromanaging presence for Mama over time. While she was in the background in the 1960s and 1970s, by the 1980s and 1990s, Mama Bear was ever present, applying sun screen, keeping the cubs from watching too much TV and eating too much junk food, and lying awake at night while Papa slept, worrying about children's troubles, from bullies to stranger danger. Simultaneously, kids in the movies in the 1980s and beyond were cast in soft glow, rarely misbehaved, and were both more ubiquitous and generally cuter than the movie kids of the 1970s.[39]

Drawn to the joys of domesticity, the "new traditionalist" mothers of the 1980s were now "cocooning," choosing to stay home, at least according to the media. Others were seeking, or perhaps should have been seeking a "mommy track," a special career path for women that would allow them flexibility and thus make their lives easier while their children were young. Those not on the mommy track could quickly climb the corporate ladder, as they were "career primary" as opposed to "career and family" women. The "career and family" women could join the fast track later, the argument went. Felice Schwartz, who wrote the article in *Harvard Business Review* that prompted the media to coin the phrase "mommy track," was interested in revealing how difficult companies made life for working mothers of young children, and companies did make it difficult. The "mommy track" solution, though, rubbed many women the wrong way.[40]

Even in the early 2000s, the media was not done telling working women that the grass was greener off the fast track. Many highly educated women, Americans were told in 2003, were now "opting out" of career in favor of staying home with their young children. The media promoted the idea that good mothers knew what was best for their children and would even sacrifice high-powered careers and their own educational investments to do right by them. In truth, mothers were continuing to enter the labor force in droves, but high-profile stories of highly educated women choosing to stay home and celebrity moms too enthralled with their babies to work made compelling examples. Receiving less coverage were the counterclaims of feminist economists who jumped on the story. The data to prove there was "opting out" was very problematic, they noted, and it would be more apt to describe women who jumped off the fast track as being pushed out of workplaces that did so little to accommodate caregiving.[41]

A related debate concerned whether women "chose" jobs that involved shorter work hours to accommodate caregiving, for example, in order to be home when the school bus arrived. Part-time clerical and retail jobs and even some teaching jobs could be "flexed" around children, but they were also lower paid. Did this explain why women still earned less than men? Was it because of their choices? The question remains the subject of much debate. Just under half of mothers continue to report in surveys that they would prefer part-time work to full-time, given their family responsibilities, though lower-income women disproportionately prefer full-time work, and the proportion of women preferring full-time work increased as a result of the recession.[42] Like so many debates about maternal employment, this one is framed in terms of choices mothers make within circumscribed situations, rather than on choices employers or policymakers can make about providing meaningful, well-paid work with room for advancement for people, not just mothers, who embrace both caregiving and breadwinning roles.

WORKING MOTHERS: SOME REALITIES

Innovative companies, and those whose accountants and human resources professionals have managed to convey how critical working mothers are to maintaining a talented labor force, have sometimes shown great imagination and flexibility for working mothers. By bringing into the American workforce the half of the population long deemed responsible for caring for others, most workers—including fathers, people who do elder care, and anyone who wants a life—stand to benefit. The American workplace is capable of change and it has changed a little, usually for the most privileged workers. But, as a nation, we have refused to put a floor underneath working mothers and failed to set basic standards.

In terms of social policy at the federal level, the Family Medical Leave Act (FMLA) of 1993, a signature Clinton presidency accomplishment, stands out. The passage of FMLA was a breakthrough, considering sustained opposition from the first Bush administration, which had continually refused a hearing to the bipartisan Congressional Women's Caucus on the issue.[43] In the end, FMLA mandated by federal law a minimum twelve weeks of unpaid leave during which time the employer would hold a person's job after a birth, adoption, or illness of a child, spouse, or parents. The law does not apply to domestic partners or other family members, such as siblings. Moreover, it is only available to employees who have worked for a company with fifty or more employees for one year at more than twenty-five hours a week. Sociologist Ellen Bravo, who participated in the bipartisan Commission on Leave to evaluate the law's impact, observed in 2007 that about 40 percent of private sector employees were ineligible for the leave based on these criteria. Among those eligible, significant numbers did not take leave that they needed because they felt they could not afford to do so. Of employees, 80 percent take FMLA for less than forty days, about one-third of their eligible time, and many also fear long-term consequences for taking the leave.[44]

The lack of a mandatory right to leave, paid or unpaid, for routine illness is very significant for families. While 178 countries have paid parental leave, the United States is the only industrialized country in the world without it. At the other end are Norway and Sweden, where both parents can take a full year of leave at 80 percent pay. Human Rights Watch recently studied the consequences of unpaid leave in the United States and found these disturbing patterns: "Parents said that having scarce or no paid leave contributed to delaying babies' immunizations, postpartum depression and other health problems, and caused mothers to give up breastfeeding early. Many who took unpaid leave went into debt, and some were forced to seek public assistance. Some women said employer bias against working mothers derailed their careers. Same-sex parents were often denied even unpaid leave." More than two-thirds of low-wage workers are women, and three-quarters of low-wage workers have no paid sick days, a practice that forces mothers to go to work and children to go to school when sick. One-half of low-wage workers also have nonstandard schedules, making scheduling for family time extremely challenging. Meanwhile, closer to the top of the employment scale, rigid workplace cultures combined with intensive mothering make feminist hopes of women's advancement in the workplace less than what was dreamed in the 1970s. More than one half of female executives do not have children, while 80 percent of male executives have children and full-time at-home wives.[45]

Nevertheless, FMLA has had an important impact and may provide the basis for future expansion of social policy. Since 1993, during major family crises and transitions, people have been able to care for some family members and themselves without fear of losing their jobs. Approximately two-thirds of employers to whom the law applied had to make changes in order to comply with the law. Before FMLA, many employers who had policies in place had not allowed time off for adoption, covered men's leaves, or granted time away from work for the care of very sick children. Despite this, the Department of Labor's survey research found little to no cost for employers in implementing the law, and more than 90 percent of businesses reported minimal challenges in doing so.

Essentially, putting working mothers' needs on the policy table was the first step toward making the workplace more humane for those balancing multiple responsibilities. FMLA somewhat resembled maximum hours laws and protective labor legislation of the Progressive era, but with FMLA both women and men became eligible. (Although the law is often associated with working mothers, in fact the most common reason researchers found for taking FMLA in the 1996 report was to care for their own personal health, followed by the need to care for aging parents, a growing issue for the population as a whole.[46]) Currently, only 33 percent of women and 29 percent of men take FMLA to care for an infant, and care of one's own personal health remains the most common use of FMLA. Men are slightly more likely to take time off to care for their own health, and women are slightly more likely to take time off to care for family members, but the gender gap in use of FMLA is not very large.[47]

But without paid leave, taking time away from work for family obligations costs employees in the longer term. Ann Crittenden's insightful book *The Price of Motherhood* (2001), pointed out in great detail just how much we as a society make caregivers, usually women, pay for time out of the labor force to care for children. In addition to the wage gap between women and men, Crittenden showed a growing gap between women who had children and those who did not. "By 1991, thirty-year-old American women without children were making 90 percent of men's wages, while comparable women with children were making only 70 percent." In another survey of nearly two hundred female MBAs, women who had taken an average of 8.8 months out the labor force earned 17 percent less than women in comparable situations without children. Not just professional women but also women in blue-collar jobs lost ground via slower accrual of seniority and fewer opportunities for after-hours training for advancement. Switching to part-time jobs, a pattern more common among women than men, often failed to reduce workload, but the shift did reduce pay and accrual of retirement pensions and Social Security benefits. Crittenden called it the "mommy tax," and she noted that in other countries both governments and men made mothers' jobs easier.[48]

The issues were all connected, too. In the absence of employer incentives to encourage men's time away from work for caregiving, the continuing and exacerbated gender wage gap, and in some states laws that do not prevent discrimination in employment against parents, heterosexual families often continued to structure their lives around male breadwinning and female caregiving. Especially among young people, large majorities agree that the best marriages are those in which both partners participate equally in child care, but workplace circumstances, wage structures, and the costs of child care often prevent them from putting these values into practice. As Stephanie Coontz has cogently argued, the failure of social policy to keep pace with changing family needs and desires bears great responsibility for the stalled revolution in gender roles within families.[49]

In every era, women have patched together caregiving and income earning, despite the confines of cultural prescriptions, gender discrimination in pay, and a dearth of social policy. Working mothers of the recent past are no exception. Many women have found satisfaction and fulfillment working in two roles, even while harried. "Work-life balance," a buzzword of recent decades, has often been elusive, but, for many women, it has been a goal worth striving for. LaShun Lawson, for example, the first African American woman in a professional position with the Atlanta Braves, said, "I'm proud to be a pioneer. . . . My son has told every little boy in his class what I do." In a recent survey by *Working Mother* magazine, money was the number one reason women said they worked, but more than 70 percent of women cited aspects such as satisfaction in the work and the use of their talent and training, while 62 percent said they aspired to serve as role models for their children. With these enormous changes, there has been much angst but also much new energy and innovation in American mothering norms. Indeed, psychological studies have shown that balancing work and family lives is not all about the conflict between the two. Having more than one arena of effectiveness for women has often meant that one area can enrich another and that having an outlet at work can relieve family stress or vice versa.[50]

Many working mothers in recent decades have felt keenly the difference between motherhood ideals of constant availability, sometimes represented in their memories of their own mothers, and the new trade-offs required by extensive labor force participation. As one woman interviewed by sociologist Sharon Hays remarked on the pressures and the guilt, "I felt really torn between what I wanted to do. Like a gut-wrenching decision . . . of course your kids are important, but you know, there's so many outside pressures for women to work. Every ad you see in magazines or on television shows this working woman who's coming home with a briefcase and the kids are all dressed and clean. It's such a lie. I don't know of anybody who lives like that."[51]

While working what Arlie Hochschild famously called the "second shift" of child care and housework, working women have often adapted by ratcheting up the intensity of their mothering in their available hours, participating in a "speed up" of family labor. "I pay a lot of attention to my daughter," one woman noted. "I make it very clear to her that she's very important." Americans have lost leisure time as employers expect more working hours and more mothers work outside the home. Studies have found that working women have scaled back significantly on housework but often have not reduced the hours they devote to children. Many have reduced work hours for the sake of child-care demands, and, if they have flexible careers, many have altered their work hours or arrangements over different stages of family life. Mothers report feeling "always rushed" and constantly "multi-tasking," but in general they have remained committed to focusing time and energy on childrearing.[52]

A major study of diary evidence over several decades showed that mothers spend more time directly interacting with and meeting children's needs today than they did five decades ago. "Time spent in interactive childcare activities, such as playing with children, reading to them, or helping with homework almost tripled, from 1.5 hours per week in 1965 to 4.0 hours [in 2005]," Suzanne M. Bianchi reported. Employed mothers do spend fewer hours in such interaction with their children than nonemployed mothers, but Bianchi's study found that employed mothers spent about as much time as stay-at-home mothers of the 1960s. Considering that fathers have also increased the time spent with children, especially married fathers, children tend to receive significant parental interaction time in families where this is possible.[53]

Increased time spent with children or organizing their lives has also corresponded to changes in American childhood norms. In recent decades, middle-class children's lives have become scheduled to an unprecedented level, with sports, lessons, and other enrichment activities, as well as part-time jobs for teenagers. For children ages three to eleven, time spent in unstructured play and outdoor activity fell almost 40 percent between the early 1980s and late 1990s. While middle-class parents and many struggling to be in the middle class tried to fill children's times with enrichment activities, parents with less resources found that children had fewer safe spaces in which to play. As urban neighborhoods experienced enormous disintegration through drugs and crime in the 1980s, cities often neglected to maintain playgrounds, and safety concerns in a variety of neighborhoods added to the decline of public play spaces.[54]

For mothers, this has meant an additional need for surveillance when their children are in public spaces. Mothers whose neighborhoods and schools are not safe, disproportionately mothers of color and immigrant or refugee mothers, have had to usher children through difficult transitions into adolescence and adulthood with a decreased support system. For more economically secure mothers, changes in childhood have also meant transportation, coordination, and managerial/scheduling responsibilities for after-school time. Children's labor at home—caring for younger children or doing household chores—has become less available to mothers than it was in previous generations. Furthermore, parents have had less help from female relatives as more women, including grandmothers, are at work during the day.

For those mothers with nonstandard work shifts, or in single-parent-headed families, intensive mother-child interactions have become difficult to sustain. The dismantling of the welfare system since 1996 has sent an unprecedented number of low-wage single mothers into the workforce full time. Many have found that trying to keep their children safe and supervised in dangerous neighborhoods while working full time has compromised their parenting standards. Monica, a white single mother who was twenty-nine years old when interviewed by Edin and Kefalas, needed to be away from home six A.M. to six P.M. She reported that before she had this job, "I always did his homework with him. Now . . . he goes to an after-school program where he's supposed to do it," but she was convinced the staff did not enforce homework standards.[55]

With these changes, mothers' juggling acts have been greatly alleviated when fathers participate more in child care. On average, fathers, especially married fathers, have increased the time they spend caring for children and home. Typically, heterosexual men have done more than their fathers' generation, but less than their female partners. Feminism opened up more possibilities for envisioning shared care. Women's increased labor force participation, especially when parents work different shifts, nudged families toward change, and the joys of fatherhood became more widely touted in the larger culture. The amount of time fathers reported spending on housework more than doubled between 1965 and 1985, increasing from four to ten hours per week on average; it leveled off thereafter. Fathers' time doing "primary child care" remained at about two and a half hours per week between 1965 and 1985, but has increased since then, rising to an average of eight hours per week.[56]

Regardless of whether or how much women work, on average wives do about 70 to 80 percent of housework. Children increase mothers' housework by three times the rate that they increase it for fathers. In a recent survey by *Working Mother* magazine, "only one out of three of the working moms said their partner takes an equal role in parenting. Another third said they spend 'somewhat more time' parenting than Dad, while one out of four spend 'much more time.'" It also becomes difficult to measure child-care time in a situation in which women tend to serve as family managers. Bravo reports that "in households where men and women share the work, women still tend to provide most of the arranging for childcare, appointments, and the like, most of the juggling, and most of the care for sick kids. They also do most of the remembering—what size shoes each kid wears, who has which laundry, who needs a clean shirt or signed permission slip." Women also tend to manage and serve as "anchors" in what sociologist Karen V. Hansen has called "networks of care" to help families juggle work and children's schedules.[57]

Scholars and critics continue to debate how much of this pattern has to do with men's habits of claiming leisure time for themselves and how much is mothers' investment in the work of mothering as crucial to their own identities, even when men want to do more. Many of the women interviewed by Sharon Hays in the early 1990s shared the view that "women are just better at raising kids than men. A mom is really inclined to detail, detail, and really watching the kids closely, and dads don't. . . . I think a woman is more able to balance all these things at once. We can think about many things at once: missing tennis shoe over here, what are you going to cook for dinner, now we do this. He's more easy-going." Also, some women felt that fathers did not pay enough attention to children's safety. Women sometimes rationalized gender inequality in household labor by accepting that they were just always going to feel guilt or worry or by suggesting that their male partners simply had a different, more relaxed approach to rearing children.[58] Clearly, women's sense of their own self-worth and effectiveness as mothers has been everywhere reinforced for them in the culture and often in their socialization, while fathers have tended to be less targeted by judgments from outsiders about things like the close supervision of young children.

Cultural and family patterns, however, have continued to change, and many couples negotiate relationship duties differently from previous generations. One mother, for example, reported the good results of an early shared decision: "When we decided to have children, we realized that we were both going to be involved with our work," she said. "So it was part of the plan from the very beginning. As a matter of fact, I thought that we only could have the one [child] and he convinced me that we could handle two and promised to really help, which he really has." Couples often, but not always, fell into gender-traditional patterns over the course of their relationship. One woman, whose husband generally took on laundry duties, explained the way their relationship worked: "Periodically I get fed up, like with the mess, or with something, so I say, 'We've got to do this.' But other than that, it pretty much just gets done whenever. I guess we both kind of feel like the other one's doing the best they can 'cuz I'm working and he's working . . . so we both support each other's work and support what we're doing with our lives and our family." Some shared work became an increasing necessity with mothers' labor force participation. In her study of the logistical arrangements of caregiving, Hansen found fathers as well as uncles and grandfathers to be "indispensable to the operational success of the [care] networks in which they participate."[59] Their duties included transporting kids, caring for them when they were sick, running errands, grocery shopping, and attending children's important events.

Survey research has also revealed men to be more interested in spending time with children than in generations past. Ellen Bravo's husband put it succinctly in a television appearance on the topic of women's work outside the home. "Men should be so grateful to the women's movement," he said, "because they've given us parenting. It's a lot of work, but it's such a joy—we should just say, 'Thanks.'" For their part, women are happier in those heterosexual partnerships that involve shared parenting and housework. And children, when asked, "If you were granted one wish that could change the way your mother's or your father's work affects your life, what would it be?" gave as their most typical answer that they just wanted their parents to be "less stressed and tired." Only 2 percent of children wanted one of their parents to "Stay home," and mothers' employment made no difference in how children assessed their parenting skills. Now that employed motherhood was becoming the norm in the middle class, the children interviewed by researchers reflected what had long been true in working-class families. The sociologist Lillian Rubin, for example, had found in the 1970s that working-class white adults remembered their (1950s era) mothers' work as something that had to be done, for which mothers need not be blamed. "My mother worked on and off all the years we were growing up. It was a hard life for her having to work and take care of all of us at the same time."[60]

Culturally speaking, it may be too soon to tell whether the nation has wrung itself out on the debate about whether women who have careers can still be good mothers, but recent developments suggest a broader acceptance of mothers' work, even full-time work. The Pew Research Center reported in 2009 that 75 percent of Americans "reject the idea that women should return to their traditional roles in society, and most believe that both husband and wife should contribute to the family income." While Dr. Laura Schlessinger continued to tell her vast radio audience into the 2000s that good mothers quit their jobs and stay home, the message became harder to stomach with the recession that began in 2008 and the subsequent revelations of the massive economic insecurity of the middle class, the working class, and the poor.[61] Even though much of America's New Right had found its voice on social issues that included opposing mothers' labor force participation, massive popular support on the right for Republican vice-presidential candidate Sarah Palin in 2008 suggested that things were changing. Unlike previous political mothers, Palin brooked fewer questions about how she would manage her large family, including a very young child with special needs, than had her political predecessors. Regardless, the debates themselves have tended to pit women against women and to suggest that mothers have far more choice than most actually do.

Motherhood, Choice, and Cultural Confusion

In recent decades, both intensive mothering and the idea of motherhood as a difficult choice have deeply shaped the way women talk about their experiences. Mothers continue to tell researchers that their children and their choices as mothers anchor their identities. This is generally true across lines of class and race and mothers' employment status. "My kids are my world," one mother told Sharon Hays in the early 1990s. "I would not do anything without thinking of them first." Women who see themselves as good mothers say they are intensely involved with their children, available to them, and self-sacrificing. It is clear that they invest themselves deeply in maternal identities. As one woman noted, "I've always wanted to be a mother and I don't think the thought has ever crossed my mind of not having children. And I think, if I didn't, something would be missing." In fact, researchers found that women with the hardest mothering situations, in neighborhoods broken by crime and drugs, valued motherhood more than any other relationship and even felt that their children "saved" them. Without children, many said, "I'd be dead or in jail" or "I'd be nowhere at all." One Puerto Rican mother said simply, "My son gives me all the love I need."[62]

As they define good and bad mothering, mothers of all backgrounds have also embraced the idea of the unique impact that mothers must have on children. For example, Eva, a working-class woman whose parents emigrated from Mexico, said, "I think I'm a good mother because I sacrifice a lot for my daughter. I try to think of her future. And a lot of the things I see other people do, like for instance, they'll go out to parties, get drunk, take drugs, and all that. My mom never did that, and I really appreciate that. . . . There are a lot of kids, like for instance, those gangs out there, whose moms are involved in drug dealing too, so they're one-hundred percent at fault for how their kids turn out." Eva's "one-hundred percent at fault" comments resonate with the findings of the impoverished women interviewed by Edin and Kefalas, who believed both the children of drug-using mothers and the children of mothers who did not "do for them" would end up selling drugs on the street. "They are not getting what they want at home," said one mother. "So they go out on the corner, and then they get locked up, get out, and that's not a life for them." [63]

These mothers often recognized that the neighborhoods in which they lived created the greatest challenge to their mothering. One woman described the situation: "It seems like everything I've tried to do from when they were babies up to this point is being totally erased since the change in the neighborhood." But they still expressed a deep personal responsibility as mothers to fend off negative influences by availability and constant presence, what they called "being there." For example, Dominique Watkins, an African American mother interviewed by Edin and Kaflas, said, "When people see me and I'm by myself, they wonder where the children are, because everywhere I go, my children go." Mothers expressed great confidence in their ability to be a buffer and a mediator in a harsh world, putting enormous hope into their relationships with their children. [64]

For these women, good mothers instilled good values, protected their children from violence, whether at home or on the street, sacrificed their own needs for their children's, and supported their children's education and future, while helping their children look presentable, if not fashionably up to date. As one mother said, "I work my butt off to give 'em clothes—and new clothes at that. That's why I always make sure that they have nice clean clothes on [with] no holes. They may not be the best clothes, but they look fair." For many of these mothers, these kinds of sacrifices would help them either replicate or avoid the situations of their own childhoods. "Bad" mothers, however, neglected their kids' needs and sometimes lost their children to protective custody in the process; "bad" mothers put their boyfriends or their own desires for luxuries ahead of their children. [65]

For middle-class women and those in more stable working-class situations, the dangers may have been different, but the definitions of good mothering have remained quite similar. In her research, Hays found a striking commitment to intensive mothering across class lines. Like working-class and poor mothers, Hays's middle-class mothers reported a lot of listening to kids and respecting their individuality, making themselves available to their kids, and practicing self-sacrifice. [66] The "bad" middle-class mothers in their worlds also failed to be there for children: letting children play too many video games, leaving them with nannies so they could go out to lunch, and putting their social lives ahead of their children's needs.

Class differences still continue to shape definitions of good mothering. Hays found, for example, that "although all these mothers want to spare their children future financial hardship, for working-class and poor mothers this leads to a tendency to stress their children's formal education, whereas middle-class mothers are more likely to be engaged in promoting their children's 'self-esteem.'" Hays rightly pointed out that middle-class mothers tended to take for granted that their children would receive and pursue a good education. Also notable is her finding that, "working-class and poor mothers tend to emphasize giving children rules while middle-class mothers are busy providing their children with choices." Working-class and poor mothers felt they protected their children best by teaching them obedience, which they often assumed to be a desirable trait at school and at work. Middle-class women, who understood the worlds of work and education differently, emphasized producing children who could negotiate their way forward in life. One professional middle-class mother commented, "I'd like them to have a really good sense of self; I'd like them to feel really comfortable in the fact that they are who they are, they're independent. I'd like them to see that there's a lot of choices you can make in life."[67]

For some mothers, what they see as their personal employment choices are parts of their notion of good mothering. Many mothers who stayed home with children or "chose" (however that is defined) to work part-time often staked their identities on those choices, just as did women who worked full-time. They saw being a stay-at-home mother as a kind of emotional challenge and achievement, in part because it required sacrifice. In recent decades stay-at-home mothers have often reported isolation and a loss of purpose, much like the feminine mystique situation described by Betty Friedan back in the early 1960s; yet their notions of self-sacrifice and living out their values have often sustained them. A stay-at-home mother interviewed by Hays noted: "My life right now is just all theirs. Sometimes it's a depressing thought because I think, 'Where am I? I want my life back.' . . . I had them, and I want them to be good people. So I've dedicated myself to them right now. Later on I get my life back. They won't always be these little sponges. . . . I want to be comfortable in myself to know that I did everything that I could." Similarly, some employed mothers felt they were better mothers for having some time away from children. One mother, for example, said that she had less patience when she was at home all day. "Whereas when I go to work and come home, I'm glad to see him. You know, you hear people say that they're better parents when they work because they spend more quality time, all those clichés, or whatever. For me that happens to be true."[68]

As these examples suggest, it has been difficult to talk about motherhood in recent decades without expressing ambivalence and a sense that mothers must make and then live with difficult choices. Class and race differences continue to inform the way women think about these issues. But since the 1980s, the notion of choice has also deeply informed tensions among women whose backgrounds may be very similar but who invest themselves in mothering in different ways or choose to exercise their option not to be a mother. For example, women providing in-home child-care services so that they can be with their own young children often find themselves conflicted about providing a service that allows other women to mother in ways they do not support. In one study in which class differences were not large, an in-home provider expressed the view of many other respondents: good care for the children in her charge meant "most of the time . . . just making sure that they are taken care of showing the love that they should be getting at home."[69]

Moreover, a vastly expanded mass media has contributed to the characterization of "good" and "bad" mothers. For example, polls showed that most Americans believed media distortions of the lives and choices of women on public assistance, further distorting the welfare debate. Almost half of Americans opposed welfare spending in 1994, compared to about 18 percent just three years earlier.[70] Some of the "bad" mothers that evoked fear and fascination in turbulent times could be called "the usual suspects"—women who didn't fit the standard white heterosexual norms. Adrienne Rich, in 1976, described the culture's ideas of "bad" mothers, who still exist in contemporary discourse: "Bad" mothers flaunted marriage and capitalism through their singleness, their lesbian identities, their poverty, or their choice to exercise reproductive or economic control. Since the 1980s, the categories also include mothers of "crack babies," "welfare mothers," and mothers who fail to protect their children from unsafe spaces like abusive day-care centers, or from dangerous products. Also targeted have been a growing cadre of "extreme" contemporary mothers whose maternal choices seemed made for reality television. An increasingly multifaceted mass media, exponentially expanded by the Internet, has shown Americans mothers nursing their infants into the kindergarten years, turning them into "Toddlers in Tiaras," and knowingly using drugs while pregnant, to name a few examples. As in previous eras, many of the tensions are played out on the terrain of the maternal body.

THE MATERNAL BODY AND QUESTIONS OF CHOICE

In the postwar period, Americans' maternal angst had focused on women's psyches. In the 1960s and 1970s, women revolted, asserting their rights to both their bodies and their psyches. Since the late 1970s, a renewed politics of the maternal body has revealed and exacerbated deep schisms in American society around the issues of caregiving, sacrifice, and gender, with added layers of concerns about the ethics of technology and new arrangements of reproduction. The idea of the endangered fetus, increasingly identified via new technologies like ultrasound and electronic fetal monitoring, informs these debates, as does the notion of the vulnerable infant, at risk from irresponsible parents, especially mothers. As women made gains in the professional world and many deferred childbearing, the media warned of an "infertility epidemic." The alarm harkened back to the late nineteenth-century censure of women who pursued higher education at the risk of the future maternity. Meanwhile, already vulnerable women have been especially imperiled in their bodily and maternal rights, and the reproductive rights gained in the 1970s have come under increasingly fierce attack. Increasing demands for government involvement with and surveillance of pregnant female bodies have once again suggested that women are essentially defined by their uteri, to go back to a nineteenth-century characterization. But now they are also especially endowed with dangerous impulses that could threaten their children.

In 1986, Mary Beth Whitehead, a working-class woman who had agreed to serve as a surrogate mother to an upper-middle-class couple, engaged in a highly visible custody battle after she changed her mind about relinquishing the baby and wanted to return the couple's money instead. Whitehead's womb and William Stern's sperm had created a baby of uncertain legal standing. Mr. and Mrs. Stern got a court order to remove baby Sara, increasingly known via an avalanche of media stories as "Baby M." Whitehead and her husband hid with the baby in another state. The Sterns then froze the Whiteheads' assets, hired a private detective to find the baby, and ultimately prevailed in the courtroom, in part by casting Whitehead as an "unstable" woman and an unfit mother. Class privilege ultimately seems to have won the day for a couple who wanted a baby but feared the health risks of a pregnancy because Elizabeth Stern had multiple sclerosis. In the process, the idea of renting wombs entered the American discourse, and the story became symbolic of anxieties around new reproductive arrangements.

Part of the issue was the role of biology in framing the right of either biological parent to a child. Not coincidentally, this issue became more emotional at a time of enormous familial change. Corresponding changes in medical technology meant, for example, that "test tube" babies emerged, that fathers' biological relationships to children could be scientifically proven through DNA, and that mothers' wombs increasingly occupied ambiguous legal, cultural, and medical territory. In today's gestational surrogacy, surrogate mothers can carry embryos to which they share no genetic material. Even today, few states regulate surrogacy arrangements in the United States, and the legal status of this commodification of women's uteruses is uncertain. Mary Beth Whitehead's saga has taken on new dimensions in a surrogacy market that has gone increasingly international. Impoverished women in struggling areas of the world are now part of major surrogacy industries, as their gestational fees are remarkably less expensive than those of women in the United States. In India, married mothers of other children agree to live for nine months in confinement similar to the old American maternity home system; they then relinquish the babies they bear and use the money for purposes such as paying off debts and funding their children's education.[71]

While some women's wombs are for sale in an unregulated market, other women's reproductive bodies have been subject to increasing scrutiny. Since the 1980s, we have seen new forms of surveillance of the bodies of the disproportionately poor and nonwhite women in the United States who have tested positive for HIV or whose drug addictions while pregnant have been criminalized. Mandatory prenatal or newborn testing for HIV has not yet taken hold, but medical breakthroughs have shown that it is possible to reduce the risk of HIV infection of a fetus through drug treatment, and this a development has kept the debate alive. Meanwhile, the courts have prosecuted women whose babies tested positive for drugs, sometimes telling such mothers point blank, "You don't deserve to be a mother."[72]

A rural Alabama white woman, Amanda Kimbrough, was arrested when her third child was born prematurely in 2008 and tested positive for Oxycodone. Her two older daughters were temporarily removed from her custody as well. She was charged with chemical endangerment of a child and sentenced to ten years, though later freed on appeal bond. In most states, mothers of newborns who test positive for drugs face child protective services rather than a criminal court, but Kimbrough's case represents one of hundreds since 1973, in which pregnant women have faced criminal charges for endangering a fetus. These are women like Bei Bei Shuai of Indiana, who is serving a prison sentence for a suicide attempt that resulted in the death of her fetus. Fetal homicide laws were originally meant to add extra penalties to people who murdered pregnant women, but in recent decades states have applied them to pregnant women themselves. Emma Ketteringham, the director of legal advocacy at the National Advocates for Pregnant Women, expressed the dawning awareness of what defining personhood at some stage of fetal development might mean for the rights of pregnant women: "It starts with cocaine, and then it's cigarettes and alcohol. How much alcohol? And when? It's only a matter of time until it comes to refusing a bed-rest order because you need to work and take care of your other children and then you have a miscarriage. What if you stay at a job where you're exposed to toxic chemicals, as at a dry cleaner? What if you keep taking your S.S.R.I.'s during pregnancy? If a woman is told that sex during her pregnancy could be a risk to the fetus, and the woman has sex anyway and miscarries, are you going to prosecute the woman—and the man too?"[73]

Attacks on both abortion rights and rights to contraception that had been accepted for generations have posed threats to women's reproductive autonomy that often cannot be avoided even for somewhat privileged women. In 2007, in *Gonzalez v. Carhart*, the Supreme Court banned late-term abortions without any allowance for a woman's health, a decision that many considered the deepest threat to reproductive rights since the pre-*Roe* era. In 2008, Keith Meyer formed Personhood USA, the goal of which is to "establish that a fully rights-endowed person is created when sperm meets egg."[74] By 2013, the organization had attempted to influence state law in twenty-two states. In the new millennium, especially in the early 2010s, the right-to-life movement has surged, attempting to revive surveillance of all female bodies. In the 2010s, state legislators' attempts to use government power to force upon pregnant women new ultrasound and fetal examination technologies have rivaled anything seen in the past, and abortion rights are in more danger than at any time since *Roe v. Wade*.

In the 1980s, at a time when ultrasounds in early pregnancy were increasing but still not the norm, a common view among pro-life activists was, "If there were a window on a pregnant women's stomach, there would be no more abortions." Billboard-sized imaginings of such a window, with portrayals of fully formed fetuses on women whose heads are not even pictured, have since become commonplace. Even by the 1980s women's bodies were taking up less visual space in obstetrics textbooks, and an emphasis on fetal development began to edge out the process of pregnancy.[75] As the interests of pregnant women and babies became pitted against one another in political debates, female bodies became objectified in ways that have bumped hard against the rights that women's health advocates struggled to achieve in the 1970s.

In Mississippi in 2012, a proposed "Personhood" amendment "would have outlawed abortion, embryonic-stem-cell research, cancer treatments that might hurt a fetus, and some popular methods of birth control," according to the *New York Times*. The initiative failed, but strikingly invasive measures directed at pregnant women or potentially pregnant women convulsed their way through state legislatures in 2012 and 2013. A number of state legislatures attempted, sometimes successfully, to require women seeking an abortion to undergo a transvaginal ultrasound, an invasive procedure, labeled "medical rape" by some. Numerous state legislatures banned abortion after twenty weeks of gestation. In 2012, Arizona passed a law banning abortions after twenty weeks of conception; the law requires state officials to host a website with images of fetuses at various stages of development for women to view. Many states also enacted requirements and regulations of abortion providers and clinics designed to force the closure of clinics. By the middle of 2013, conservative legislators and governors had approved more than forty restrictions on abortion in state governments around the country.[76]

Less understood is the fact that the gains made in women's choices surrounding childbirth have also become greatly endangered by the fetal personhood movement. In 1994 an Illinois hospital sought custody of a woman's fetus when she refused a Caesarean section on religious grounds, but the court refused. In 1999, however, the U.S. District Court of Northern Florida ruled in favor of "fetal rights" in a forced Caesarean section situation. A Ms. Pemberton planned to have her second baby at home with a midwife because her doctors refused to perform a vaginal birth. The hospital sought a court order, and a judge ordered Pemberton to the hospital. When she refused, law enforcement came to her home and took her there. Pemberton sued the hospital "for violating her constitutional rights of bodily integrity, the right to refuse treatment, and the right to make important decisions about bearing children 'without undue governmental interference.'" But she lost. According to legal scholar Erin P. Davenport, "The court acknowledged Ms. Pemberton's constitutional rights but determined that the state's interest 'in preserving the life of the unborn child' outweighed her rights. The court actually based its conclusions on *Roe v. Wade*, in which the Supreme Court 'recognized the state's interest in preserving a fetus as it progresses toward viability.'" There is still no legal consensus on this issue, though the American College of Obstetricians and Gynecologists and the American Medical Association have taken the position that women should have the final say in whether to undergo a Cesarean section.[77]

Alongside the drama in the state legislatures, and occasionally hospitals and courtrooms, the cultural politics of abortion are staggeringly complex in their connection to motherhood. The focus on the imperiled fetus, threatened by the mother, connects directly to notions of good and bad mothering. The pro-life movement argues vehemently that women should accept accidental pregnancies no matter what the emotional or financial cost and, increasingly for some, regardless of the health outcomes of either the mother or the fetus. A vocal and long overdue disability rights movement sometimes (though certainly not always) overlaps with the pro-life movement. For some disability rights activists, including those who favor abortion rights, pro-choice activists sometimes miss a larger picture when they emphasize women's ability to distance themselves from the realities of vulnerable bodies. For others, it is only selfish parents who would make the choice to abort a fetus that is not "perfect" or "normal."[78] That notion resonates with more and more people and represents an important counterdiscourse to the eugenic ethos and mother blaming that have shaped attitudes toward children with disabilities in the past.

Making the choice to accept the vagaries of unplanned pregnancies and of continuing pregnancies with unplanned factors such as disability or severe health impairments feels to many diverse Americans like an honorable, ethical, and even heroic route, a reassertion of what Sharon Hays calls the "non-market" values represented by our notions of mothering and maternal sacrifice. One pro-life activist affirmed the position: "You know, the picture painted these days is how much kids cost. These are the reasons given for most abortions. How much work kids are, how much they can change your lifestyle, how they interrupt the timing of your goals. What is ten years out of a seventy-year life span?"[79] For those defending abortion rights, finding a way to claim women's rights and hold onto the notion of intensive motherhood—that updated version of moral motherhood—has become more, not less challenging, since the *Roe v. Wade* decision.

The anthropologist Faye Ginsburg found fascinating examples in the 1980s of how women in one community in North Dakota navigated some of these issues. She interviewed women activists on both sides of the abortion divide in a community that housed the only abortion provider clinic for hundreds of miles in any direction. Ginsburg found striking commonality among those who identified as "pro-choice" or "pro-life." Both drew on maternal ideology in explaining their views, and both saw their work as nurturing and family oriented. For pro-choice women, abortion rights were part of broader efforts to create better conditions in society for women and children. Pro-choice activists saw their work as part of compassionate care for women in a medical system that sometimes demeaned them and as part of strengthening families. Kay Bellevue, who founded the Fargo clinic in 1981, said, "In my experience, people who have made the choice to have an abortion made it because they want a strong family."[80] For these pro-choice activists, abortion was not an easy solution to a complicated problem. It was a right for women who needed it, one of many rights and resources women and children needed to strengthen their families and their opportunities as whole people. In their small community, these women expressed fairly commonplace values around motherhood.

Meanwhile, many pro-life women activists valued feminist ideas but drew the line at abortion. Some felt defensive of the homemaker role, but others advocated flexible work arrangements "that will allow mothers and fathers to take care of their children." As Sally Norddsen, a social worker who had left her job to be home with her children, said, "To me, yes, it is your freedom to choose to reproduce or not to reproduce. But once that's done, you've already made that choice. So when those things get lumped together with women's rights, like equal pay, I get really upset. There are some things, such as abortion, that can actually be destructive to other people."[81] Like pro-choice women, pro-life activists saw themselves as defending nurture and caregiving. They recognized that the larger society devalued these tasks, and they saw their opposition to abortion as an act of resistance. For them, overcoming the challenges and ambivalence of accidental pregnancies was part of an embattled achievement of motherhood and often of traditional marriage.

The changing and uncertain pattern of the female life course, Ginsburg argued, lent enormous emotional weight to the "problem pregnancy," and women of similar backgrounds interpreted the notion of choice in very divergent ways. (Ginsburg did find a bit of a generational difference, with pro-life activists being on average younger than pro-choice activists.) As the stigma of unwed motherhood was reduced and women gained the right to legal abortion, the social consequences of unplanned pregnancies were different for single women than they had been in the postwar period. In Fargo, the main maternity home closed in that pivotal year of 1973, signaling a sea change in women's choices and prompting pro-life women to form new organizations to counsel young women and steer them away from abortion.

Problematic pregnancies, however, could occur at any life stage. According to the Guttmacher Institute, an unintended pregnancy will be faced by at least half of all American women by age forty-five, and each year, about 2 percent of women aged fifteen to forty-four have an abortion, though the rate of abortion among women of child-bearing age has been a mostly steady downward trend since the mid-1980s. The issue of unintended pregnancy has remained so emotional in part because the work of caregiving is so undersupported in American social policy and in the workplace. Nearly every activist Ginsburg interviewed, on either side of the issue, had experienced the transition to motherhood, she says, "as an event surrounded by ambivalence." Kay Bellevue, for example, described her experience as a young mother and leader in La Leche League in the early 1970s, at a time when her own parents were divorcing and one of her children was struggling: "Then I ended up having an abortion myself. My youngest was eighteen months old and I accidentally got pregnant. We had four small kids at the time and we decided if we were going to make it a family unit, we had all the stress we could tolerate if we were going to survive."[82] Pro-life women also told stories of unplanned pregnancies and maternal life transitions as pivotal to the formation of their views on abortion. A number of them had struggled with decisions to leave the workforce or had changed their views on sexuality, marriage, and the centrality of motherhood during their own transition to caring for babies. For pro-life women, abortion became an issue that served as a proxy or symbol of motherhood as a beleaguered choice.

Because the women Ginsburg interviewed were activists on the abortion issue, by definition, they found the issue emotional and compelling. Yet even these women, her research revealed, found common ground. In the context of a community, they

showed considerable respect for one another's views. As pro-choice activist Bellevue said, "I think pro-choice people have a strong basis in theology for the caring, loving perspective they have on abortion as do the antiabortion people have
a basis in theology for their, strong, loving caring perspective about the fetus." On
the other side, pro-life women often saw themselves as educating other women on
both fetal development and women's emotional consequences of having an abortion. For example, the North Dakota chapter of Women Exploited by Abortion
said they were a group "for women who have had an abortion, now realize it was
the wrong decision and want to educate other women on the trauma of abortion."
These civil approaches explored and documented by Ginsburg, to the extent that
they do still exist, have become harder to find. Since the mid-1970s a slight majority
Americans have told the Gallup poll that they support keeping abortion legal, at
least under certain circumstances, while minorities of Americans have opposed it
under all circumstances or thought it should be available under all circumstances.
Throughout the years of polling, those stating they believe abortion should be legal
under all circumstances have almost always outnumbered those who oppose abortion in any circumstance. Moreover, the proportions of people in those categories
have shifted very little over nearly four decades. Still, the debate has continued to
rage on a national level, even if it does not appear to be changing most people's
minds. Abortion has become increasingly used as political fodder and has served as
a critical marker of the nation's partisan divide."[83]

Abortion and contraception have not been the only charged issue surrounding
the maternal female body in recent decades. Often existing in conjunction with the
alternative birth movement discussed in chapter 9 has been a push for women's
right to breastfeed in public and to have more opportunities to breastfeed their
babies in the workplace. Influenced in part by the advocacy of the La Leche League,
physicians and public health authorities have more vociferously advocated for
breastfeeding as the best nutrition for virtually all young babies in recent decades.
In 1978, the American Academy of Pediatrics unequivocally stated that "human
milk is superior to infant formulas" and advised only breast milk for babies for the
first four to six months.[84] Exceptions to these recommendations include mothers
who are HIV positive or for whom drugs, medically managed or illegally used,
might be passed on to babies through the mother's milk, and adoptive mothers.

In Linda Blum's compelling and important anthropological study of breastfeeding ideologies, she found that many women, especially white women, saw breastfeeding as an important measure of their success as mothers. Typically for white
women, breastfeeding embodied "natural" mothering and the value of maternal
labor: "Only a mother can give what a child needs," as one woman said, "nobody
else can, not even a father." Taken from another angle, another woman Blum interviewed said, "I thought I *had* to breastfeed. Everybody was pushing me." Many
women of color were also sensitive to these cultural prescriptions. But race and
class made a big difference in how women thought about the breastfeeding mandate. Popular publications directed at African American audiences promoted
breastfeeding. But African American working-class women were often ambivalent,

and they nursed at lower rates than white women. One woman's stepmother had told her that it was too animal-like to "nurse our kids like that." Others pointed to the struggles of combining working and breastfeeding. "I didn't want that hassle," said one woman, "especially with me going back to work. I want my babies to be attached, but not *that* attached."[85] Like generations before them, African American working-class mothers defied expert advice in part because they did not define child-rearing with such singular attention to exclusive mother-child relationships.

Establishing breastfeeding routines was easier said than done, given the economic and social contexts of mothering. White working-class women told Blum stories of bodies that they felt had failed them because they had been unable to nurse their babies. The problems were generally related to health issues or to lack of space, privacy, or workplace flexibility. Typically, these women worked in service industries. One mother said she got conflicting medical advice about nursing her son because of his projectile vomiting during the first two weeks of his life; although she said her baby was healthy, she also felt "useless, if I couldn't nurse my baby I was a flop as a mother."[86]

Many of these women also expressed frustration with their generation of men. The context here was Flint, Michigan, where the women's fathers, they said, were able and/or willing to provide materially for their families, especially through General Motors, or "Mother Motors, the breast that feeds Flint," as it was sometimes known. "My dad was a good provider," said Melody Jenksman. Stories of breastfeeding for these younger women led to descriptions of younger men who would not "settle down," commit to marriage and breadwinning, and support their female partners by providing the stability they needed to mother their children as they saw fit. "Despite the lack of male breadwinning jobs," notes Blum, these women "clung to their marriage, or to their hopes of being married in the future, rather than moving to more autonomous or woman-centered family strategies." Faye Ginsburg said virtually the same thing about the midwestern, mostly white, pro-life activists she interviewed: "They, along with other right-to-life activists, are well aware of the fragility of traditional marriage arrangements and recognize the lack of other social forms that might ensure the emotional and material support of women with children or other dependents."[87] Like abortion, breastfeeding has been connected in many women's minds with a distressing unraveling of traditional marriage and breadwinning arrangements.

The La Leche League chapter where Blum did another part of her research in the 1990s was almost exclusively white, which is not uncommon for LLL chapters. The group encompassed women who were solidly middle-class and those who were struggling to attain middle-class status. For many, breastfeeding was a marker of middle-class status and a particular kind of maternal and familial achievement: a good mother nursed her babies and made economic sacrifices to do so. "I think in the League there's a deep commitment to putting the child first," said a woman whose family was going into debt so that she could stay home and breastfeed, "and I need to go back [to the League] and be reminded and supported. [League meetings] are like a shot in the arm." For the less economically secure women, breastfeeding often involved enormous and risky financial sacrifices. Conversely, it is telling that among the white working-class women Blum interviewed outside of the League, 70 percent had never even heard of the organization.[88]

For women who found support within it, the League provided a women-centered approach to their bodies and an alternative to impersonal medicalized approaches. As one League mother said, "I really enjoy looking at my breasts as having *a use*. I like that a lot. . . . I would change the whole way a society views a woman's body!" The League mother was so embodied though that her constant physical presence was deemed necessary to the well-being of babies and children. Both nationally and locally, League members expressed significant ambivalence about maternal employment and tended to assume that women could only accomplish breastfeeding via traditional caregiver/breadwinner gender arrangements, a situation less representative than ever before of American family life. While the League's single-issue focus has preserved its mission, it has also prevented its role in coalition building around a maternal politics of social provisions for mothers. Resisting the temptation to expand into the politics of the environment (where toxins can threaten breast milk), home schooling, and abortion, the League even declined to take a public stand on the 1990s boycott of Nestlé products when maternal health and environmental activists pointed to the company's unprincipled marketing of infant formula in impoverished areas of the world. Although the League has been an advocate for breastfeeding rights for mothers in situations of divorce and shared custody, it has been less vocal about breastfeeding rights in the workplace.[89]

Similar to abortion, breastfeeding choice has become identified as a marker of women's devotion to "good" mothering. Here again, the nineteenth-century notions of the maternal body have reemerged, not simply on the basis of scientific evidence. In the larger picture, health research has shown that breastfeeding is just one dimension of infant health, and there is legitimate dispute about how much impact breast versus bottle might have on infant health. Most important, breastfeeding does not balance out factors of poor health or lack of access to quality health care, unsafe environments, or dietary deficiencies. And a health education model alone cannot address women's problems of inflexible workplaces and lack of access to quality health care for themselves and their babies. Maternal overwork, long ago identified by Progressive era health reformers, remains another obstacle to nursing mothers.

Health professionals can and should provide incentives and education around breastfeeding, but singling out the practice can become a way of avoiding larger public responsibility for both infant and maternal health. As Blum says, health education models can sometimes be "part of the attack on social provision and make infant death and disease, like other health problems, appear to be the result of ignorant or bad individual choices, in this case by mothers." The United States has a high infant mortality rate compared to other parts of the industrialized world, and African American babies still die at a rate of *twice* that of white babies, a pattern as evident today as it was a century ago. Meanwhile low-income white babies also face higher risk of disease and death than do class-privileged infants. This difference cannot by any stretch of the imagination be explained by lower rates of breastfeeding. Just as banning abortion will not resolve the difficulties of being a mother in a society with a fraying safety net, promoting breastfeeding in itself will not fix today's infant health problems, especially since many of the diseases prevented by breastfeeding are no longer the major health risks to infants. It is unfortunate, then, that there has been a bifurcation of medical recommendations—that breast is best—and social policy. Blum has argued that if the American Academy of Pediatrics or the American Medical Association were to successfully advocate for the expansion of the Family Medical Leave Act or workplace child care, women's ability to sustain breastfeeding would be greatly increased.[90] Here again, the approach of educating mothers without providing them with new resources to accommodate their changing lives can only go so far. In women's access to health care and reproductive rights, as elsewhere, the continuity of stingy social provisioning coexisted with very rapid economic and demographic changes of the past several decades.

CONCLUSION

In roughly the past forty years, Americans debated women's roles as caregivers and workers and became anxious in ways both old and new about women's maternal bodies. The resurgence of old, privatized "moral mother" ideas, in the form of intensive motherhood, deepened the commitments and raised the stakes of individual mothers' efforts, even as declining economic prospects and stalled social policy limited their prospects. In the wake of the cultural challenges of the 1960s and 1970s, motherhood became less tightly scripted, more culturally expansive and rich with the potential for women to define mothering on their own terms. At the same time, mothers' prospects shrunk in economic terms. Both women and men faced declining real wages; feminist labor activists lost momentum in their efforts to set new family-friendly and equitable standards for all workers while women continued to flood into the labor force. And with the many changes in the American economy and public policy, dramatically rising income inequality put the middle-class and all its idealism about motherhood on the defensive, while shattering the familial hopes of many of the most economically vulnerable Americans. In the new millennium, emerging political advocacy in the name of motherhood will have to reflect these realities—economic, cultural, and technological—while hopefully harnessing the still growing political voice of American women.

Conclusion

Reflecting the focus of current historical research, this book has necessarily been preoccupied with mothers' relationships to the experts, political ideologies, social policies, and the labor force. Seen through this lens, the modernization of motherhood has been about control, rationality, science, psychology, an expanded role for the state, and a social policy structure that leaves much to be desired for caregivers. This plethora of public forces deeply impacted what the culture defined as a private role. Meanwhile, government has been willing to take on new regulatory roles in educational, health, and family law, and even to provide some small subsidies for poor mothers. Gradually, American law has reduced the patriarchal rights of fathers, sometimes assisting mothers and children in the process. This development, too, has been a piece of the modernization of both motherhood and family life as a whole.

As men lost some legal prerogatives within the home, however, they maintained a near monopoly on public power, from politics to the professions. Meanwhile, women gradually gained some rights, particularly in the public sphere as voters and workers and increasingly literate and educated members of society. All this has been part of the backdrop for Americans' many expressions of anxiety about maternal power. Since the mid-nineteenth century, with challenges to the old idea of quickening as the beginning of life and increased anxiety about breastfeeding, disquiet about the maternal body has been one important expression of this anxiety. As allopathic modern medicine consolidated, medical practices and values became deeply enmeshed with ideas about appropriate maternal bodies and appropriately maternal women. Since about the beginning of the twentieth century, the state has also demonstrated an increased willingness either to provide incentives or to establish control mechanisms related to pregnancy, prenatal care, infant feeding, protective labor legislation, and medical interventions for women and infants. These measures have ranged from coerced sterilization to state-required immunizations for babies.

Indeed, the most apparently progressive governmental interventions have been linked in bizarre ways with the most coercive or problematic. In the early twentieth century, Justice Oliver Wendell Holmes justified the involuntary sterilization of the "unfit" with a reference to government's mandate to immunize infants for public health. He argued that "the principle that sustains compulsory vaccination is broad enough to cover cutting the fallopian tubes." In that same era, Justice David M. Brewer linked the provision of protective labor legislation, such as maximum hours just for women, with government's interest in regulating mothers' bodies. "As healthy mothers are essential to vigorous offspring, the physical well-being of woman becomes an object of public interest and care in order to preserve the strength and vigor of the race." This argument justified placing the woman worker in "a class by herself."[1] And in 1999, when her Cesarean-section delivery was mandated, Ms. Pemeberton in Florida had her rights to medical decision making and reproductive freedom in choice of birthing situations abrogated through legal arguments based on *Roe v. Wade*.

Discomfort with women's sexuality has also informed modern motherhood and reproductive debates, especially in the twentieth century. Particularly for poor women and women of color, charges of sexual promiscuity made women vulnerable to involuntary sterilization procedures. In the mid-twentieth century and early twenty-first century, middle-class mothers were especially targeted with accusations of channeling frustrated psychosexual desires into their child-rearing practices. In the later twentieth-century, as the debate over abortion and a renewed opposition to contraception roiled their ways through American culture and politics, the sexual freedoms that had gradually expanded for women became pitted against their motherhood.

Male-dominated governmental bodies and medical traditions shaped by men's authority have not been uniformly harsh toward women. Indeed, there have always been dissenters and feminists. An all-male Supreme Court upheld *Roe v. Wade*, and brave male physicians risked censure to provide a range of reproductive health care to women, to name just two examples. Still, the problem of defining reproductive justice and economic empowerment, or any other form of maternal liberation, remains complicated by women's underrepresentation in public decision making. Women's political voices on issues of reproductive justice were certainly heard in the reelection of Barack Obama in 2012, at a time of intense attacks on women's reproductive rights, but a long-standing ambivalence about trusting women with pregnancy and even infant care continues nonetheless.

Similar problems complicate the creation of a broad safety net for the work of caregiving. American public policy has shown a strong preference for educating mothers instead of providing resources—such as publicly funded child care, generous cash assistance, and universal health care—to help all caregivers do the work of looking after those who cannot care for themselves. Because Americans vested mothers with unique character building and sanctified relationships with their children in the early nineteenth century, they have expressed extraordinary hope for the mother-child relationship. Mothers, essentially, were supposed to do what social policy in a minimally regulated capitalist economy could not or would not: create safe spaces for each of the nation's new generations of children and manage familial resources through self-sacrifice.

Again and again, mothers have done their best to rise to the occasion. In the parts of this book that address the history of mothering practices, we start to see the often-hidden histories of women's patterns of resilience and their creation of familial strategies. Consider two long-term examples: women have defied and even redefined cultural ideals by serving as breadwinners in their families and by insisting on controlling their reproduction. Much more needs to be written about the strategies and lived experiences of mothers. We also need to know more about mothers' multifaceted relationships with their children, their partners, and familial or neighborhood networks of caregivers, whether in resistance, in compliance, or in indifferent regard to the prescriptions of the larger culture.

Contemporary cultural discussions on motherhood must be informed by both history and a richer awareness of cultural diversity. Alternatives to privatized cultural ideals of motherhood have existed throughout U.S. history, especially in the cultural practices of women of color. With the growing diversity of the country, there are yet more opportunities to learn about the rich abundance of approaches to mothering, fathering, and community-based childrearing practices. We need both more contemporary studies of this diversity and more historical studies. And those studies need to address the powerful roles of economic inequality and racism in determining mothers' access to resources.

In some ways, the high visibility and tenacity of moral motherhood ideals have prevented us from seeing this diversity. Moral motherhood has also made less visible the critical economic contributions and breadwinning roles of mothers. This invisibility has been partially responsible for a continuing gender wage gap, which threatens the financial stability of American families. Our cultural ideals of motherhood have not caught up with the realities of mothers' labor-force participation. When we peel back the layers of motherhood as institution, we see mothering realities. In both past and present, we can hear the voices of mothers, asking for common sense solutions to the challenges of raising families and making other diverse contributions to society.

The tensions between American motherhood and mothers' actual lives stem in part from the fact that particular models of motherhood continue to be privileged. The republican mother idea, with its symbolic civic components, has resurfaced in certain eras of American history to inform politics, such as during the Progressive era and during the social protests of the 1960s and 1970s. But the nineteenth-century moral motherhood ideal has been more continuous: in this intensely privatized ideal a mother is enveloped, emotionally and physically, in the "sphere" of childrearing, and she is vested with unique responsibility for children's moral development. This ideal has never been attainable for the majority of Americans; yet it has had a tenacious hold on American culture.

Moral motherhood conflicted somewhat with scientific motherhood, in that mothers' "maternal instincts" were questioned. But scientific motherhood and moral motherhood also intertwined. Scientific mothers had all the more reason to be vigilant about and invested in what was deemed their primary purpose in life: rearing children, now in concert with the experts. In the mid-twentieth century, mother blame dealt a blow to moral motherhood. So too did the cultural questioning of the 1960s and 1970s. Critique of a myopic maternal focus for women obviously had enormously liberating aspects by facilitating greater opportunity for richer lives for women and men, a more gender-equitable society, a tempering of deference to scientific expertise, and some additional resources for maternal work. Yet as Americans critiqued the sentimentalism of maternal ideals, maternalist politics—a political idealism that elevated the special perspective of mothers—also struggled to survive. Women rose up to critique motherhood as institution and to ask for more from a society that asked so much of mothers. Before they got the job done, conservative forces reasserted themselves. A new intensive mothering ideal emerged—an updated version of moral motherhood that coexisted uneasily with women's greatly expanded roles in the workforce and fostered a continued ambivalence in women about their maternal identities.

The reassertion of essentially private mothering ideals seemed distant from the realm of politics, where mothers still desperately needed better representation. Vestiges of a civic motherhood seemed hard to find. In the new millennium, our dominant discourses of motherhood are psychological and privatized. Even the two women who came closest to achieving the nation's highest offices in 2008, Hillary Clinton and Sarah Palin, campaigned in ways that did not embody civic motherhood. Clinton ran for the Democratic nomination for president on a tough-as-a-man approach, while Republican vice presidential nominee Palin's entire policy platform opposed the provisions and rights for mothers for which feminists had long struggled.

Over the course of American history, scientific discourses of motherhood gradually supplanted the primacy of the religious views that had helped develop moral motherhood ideals. Both ways of looking at motherhood lost some hold in the last several decades of the twentieth century. Moral motherhood, initially based in Protestant religious notions of maternal self-denial, lost many of its religious overtones and instead remained in place through the more psychological and secular notion of intensive motherhood: By the late twentieth century, women's maternal sacrifices were not sacred per se, at least for most Americans, as they were in the nineteenth century; but they were deemed necessary for families. Furthermore, female sacrifices served a cultural function through an insistence on the moral power of making the hard choice in a society beset by individualism and market values. In this way, moral motherhood found continuing resonance up to the present.

Yet the very weakness of moral motherhood ideology has also proven to be the flipside of its strength. The energy of mothers' investment in their special roles in children's lives has led to new political formations and new potential for the politics of motherhood in the past, and there are signs of a resurgence. There is good news for mothers, and for women generally, in the new millennium. Research-based and policy-oriented books, websites, and advocacy organizations reach wide audiences and promote a broader safety net and opportunity structures for those doing the work of caregiving. *The Motherhood Manifesto*, a book-length project connected to the advocacy organization, Momsrising, spells out maternal provisioning in a multipronged yet consistent way: expanded maternity and paternity leave, open and flexible workplaces, increased power for parents to choose after school programs and to prevent children's exposure to both environmental and cultural toxins, health care for all children, excellent childcare, and realistic and fair wages.

Ellen Bravo's *Taking on the Big Boys: Why Feminism Is Good for Families, Business, and the Nation*, argues for union rights, living wages for all caregivers, including child-care workers, the expansion of Family Medical Leave and the Earned Income Tax Credit, and mandated paid sick days, to name just a few examples of her visionary investigation of the needs of families. The Motherhood Initiative for Research and Community Involvement in Toronto, Canada, offers international, multidisciplinary, and community-focused research and advocacy on issues of maternal justice, informed by cultural critiques. In *The Twentieth-First Century Motherhood Movement*, motherhood scholar Andrea O'Reilly makes visible an enormous range of organizations and social theorists advancing new maternal feminist agendas to empower mothers.[2] Other advocacy organizations abound, from the Institute for Work and Families in New York City to Catalyst, which assesses women's advancement in workplaces, to the Family Violence Prevention Fund and the still active, outspoken National Organization for Women and Planned Parenthood. Conversations about provisioning mothers increasingly have international dimensions, as more and more development experts recognize that economic investments in mothers benefit families' well-being and that the strong correlation between women's education and lower birth rates and better familial health can drive investments in women's empowerment worldwide.

Meanwhile, working women's reshaping of the workplace and development of new "family friendly" business models provides reason to hope. Women lead in the start-up of new businesses and now form roughly half of the U.S. workforce. Most of these women are mothers. In a multitasking, highly networked world in which people juggle multiple projects, women's leadership strengths in their family roles are increasingly recognized as assets in the workplace as well. Ann Crittenden, who contributed so much to our understanding of the price tag of caregiving, has also made the case for an integrated idea of women's leadership strengths: "Anyone who has learned how to comfort a troublesome toddler, soothe the feelings of a sullen teenager, or managed the complex challenges of a fractious household can just as readily smooth the boss's ruffled feathers, handle crises, juggle several urgent matters at once, motivate the team, and survive the byzantine office intrigues. Leadership begins at home."[3] Crittenden's notion of mothers' special talents is skill-based, rather than essentially about God-given or biologically determined gender roles. Her ideas echo other leadership studies and find expression, too, in the fact that a mother can now calculate her would-be paycheck for maternal and household manager work at salary.com.

Maternal coalition building is enhanced by these developments but remains endangered by vastly expanding income inequality, an intense partisan divide, and continuing disparities based on race, class, and sexual orientation. The challenges of mothers raising children as sole income earners on a paltry minimum wage are poorly represented in discussions of work-life balance. Even less is said of mothers who are losing parental rights to their children through shrinking social provisions and mass incarceration. The thorny politics of reproductive justice have also thus far inhibited coalition building. Recent threats to reproductive rights could change this. Activists for abortion rights and childbirth rights have not always overlapped, but they are more likely to do so in response to the fetal rights movement. Only by having honest conversations about what our society does and does not do for mothers and families—all mothers and families, including the most vulnerable—can we hope to bridge the worldview chasm that appears to have widened between those on the "pro-choice" and "pro-life" ends of the abortion debate. The debate serves as a focal point, perhaps even a proxy, for what are even more complex political questions about the place of women, mothers and caregiving in society.

The confusion about maternal identities has also opened a space for innovation. The social movements and demographic changes of the 1960s and 1970s helped decenter the traditional gender-defined nuclear family as a social script and an ideal. We may cling to the ideology, but there are too many alternatives in people's experiences. Women are inventing new maternal scripts, advising one another, and finding new ways to share the work of caregiving and child-rearing. There are now countless communities, online and in person, of mothers (and fathers) with special challenges, situations, or sets of values who can find strength in other parents. Divorced mothers, single mothers, stepmothers, disabled mothers, lesbian mothers, mothers of transgendered youth, mothers of multiples, mothers of children with mental illness, working mothers, stay-at-home mothers, mothers with literary aspirations, mothers who aspire to evangelical Christian parenting, or mothers who seek feminist and antiracist parenting—there is a point of connection for anyone with access to the internet.

In an era when many alternatives exist, the experts have likewise been decentered. The heavy-handed syndicated advice of psychologist John Rosemund continues to represent a one-size-fits-all expert approach. But he and other experts writing in the old detached, rule-oriented style have significant competition, from both popular literature and the more flexible approaches adopted by many physicians. Historian Rima Apple has argued that physicians have taken a more positive view of "the inquiring and educated patient." This is partly because physicians' authority has waned since the era when scientific advances revolutionized the control of infectious diseases. The influx of women into medicine has also changed physician-patient relationships. Well-child and well-woman care and consultations on chronic conditions are more often the subjects of doctor visits. In the age of the Internet, many patients have become discerning consumers of medical care and advice. Some mothers continue to embrace and promote the idea of "talking back to the experts," though, for many others, the issue has been side-stepping those experts, seeking alternatives, and, as has long been the case, using advice selectively. Women have continued to show great interest in scientific and medical information.[4] But the skepticism of the 1960s and 1970s has remained and been augmented by a growing uncertainty about sources of truthful information in the information age. The hypermodernity of the early decades of the twentieth century, in which science and its purveyors were godlike figures, has faded significantly, and likewise some of mothers' subservience to expertise has diminished.

Medical science has developed less blaming relationships with mothers in some interesting ways. Biological perspectives on mothers, so long associated with problematic patriarchal cultural baggage, have developed an unusually neutral tone on some key issues. For example, medical thinking today often attributes children's mental illnesses or neurologically atypical brains not to mothers' psychological pathology but to biological factors. No respected physician today claims that mothers cause autism in their children by failing to love them properly. Similarly, postpartum depression is widely considered to be a medical condition caused by chemical and hormonal changes, not by women's ambivalence about being a mother. Many people legitimately question the role of promoting pharmaceutical products as a panacea for these problems. But, taking the long view, there is also a refreshing diminution of the mother blame in scientific medicine compared to the past century and a half.[5] Perhaps not coincidentally, mothers and daughters of today's generation express a great sense of closeness and see modeled for them a bit less of Disney's frightening, jealous middle-aged woman, vengeful against youthful beauty and a bit more of friendly and honest relationships à la *Gilmore Girls*. It is as if the disrupted female intergenerational bonds inherent in modernization and American's incessant mobility are finding new space to re-form.

Today, Americans are worried and hopeful about mothering, in ways both old and new. It remains to be seen how and whether the various dimensions of modern motherhood will wind their way into the new millennium's notions of good mothering and whether the country will return to and reinvent a broader view of how children can be nurtured, protected, and socialized into civil society in a way that values caregiving work. This history of motherhood and mothering is, I hope, a starting point for broader conversations. Quite literally, we are all here because of our mothers, and maternal labors have provided the backbone of each generation. We need to see, understand, appreciate, learn from, and elevate into our public discourse the rich legacies of mothers—their work, their skills, and their social imagination—so that the hand that rocks the cradle can at the very least have an equal say in the rule of the world.

Notes

INTRODUCTION

1. *New York Magazine* quoted in Linda K. Kerber, "The Republican Mother and the Woman Citizen: Contradictions and Choices in Revolutionary America," in *Women's America: Refocusing the Past*, ed. Linda K. Kerber and Jane Sherron DeHart, 6th ed. (New York: Oxford University Press, 2004), 121; Abbott quoted in Jan Lewis, "Mother's Love: The Construction of an Emotion in Nineteenth-Century America," in *Mothers and Motherhood: Readings in American History*, ed. Rima Apple and Janet Golden (Columbus: Ohio State University Press, 1997), 54; Halle quoted in Michael Goldberg, "Breaking New Ground: 1800–1848," in *No Small Courage: A History of Women in the United States*, ed. Nancy F. Cott (New York: Oxford University Press, 2000), 195.

2. Quoted in Mary P. Ryan, *Cradle of the Middle Class: The Family in Oneida County, New York, 1790–1856* (New York: Cambridge University Press, 1981), 159, 158.

3. See Adrienne Rich, *Of Woman Born: Motherhood as Experience and Institution* (New York: W. W. Norton, 1976). See also Andrea O'Reilly, *From Motherhood to Mothering: The Legacy of Adrienne Rich's "Of Woman Born"* (Albany: SUNY Press, 2004), and Andrea O'Reilly, *Rocking the Cradle: Thoughts on Feminism, Motherhood, and the Possibility of Empowered Mothering* (Toronto: Demeter Press, 2006).

4. There are certainly some good studies of fatherhood already available, and I am indebted to these perspectives as well. See, for example, Robert L. Griswold, *Fatherhood in America: A History* (New York: Basic Books, 1993); Ralph La Rossa, *The Modernization of Fatherhood: A Social and Political History* (Chicago: University of Chicago Press, 1997); Shawn Johansen, *Family Man: Middle-Class Fatherhood in Industrializing America* (New York: Routledge, 2001); Ralph La Rossa, *Of War and Men: World War II in the Lives of Fathers and Their Families* (Chicago: University of Chicago Press, 2011); and Barbara Hobson, *Making Men into Fathers: Men, Masculinities, and the Social Politics of Fatherhood* (Cambridge: Cambridge University Press, 2002).

CHAPTER 1 — INVENTING A NEW ROLE FOR MOTHERS

1. Laurel Thatcher Ulrich, *Good Wives: Image and Reality in the Lives of Women in Northern New England: 1650–1750* (New York: Oxford University Press, 1982), 154, 156.

2. Quoted in Carl N. Degler, "Introducing Children to the Social Order," in *Childhood in America*, ed. Paula S. Fass and Mary Ann Mason (New York: New York University Press, 2000),

211; reprinted in *Early American Women: A Documentary History, 1600–1900*, ed. Nancy Woloch (New York: McGraw-Hill, 1997), 34. On Puritan childhood, see Karen Calvert, "The Material Culture of Early Childhood," in *Childhood in America*, 619–624; John Demos, "Family Life in Plymouth Colony," in *Childhood in America*, 203–205; Phillippe Ariès, "Education and the Concept of Childhood," in *Childhood in America*, 283–285; Steven Mintz, *Huck's Raft: A History of American Childhood* (Cambridge, MA: Harvard University Press, 2006), 7–31.

3. Anne Bradstreet, "In Reference to Her Children, 23 June, 1659" Quoted in Paula S. Fass and Marry Ann Mason, eds., *Childhood in America* (New York: New York University Press, 2000), 80; quoted in Mintz, *Huck's Raft*, 15.

4. In 1619, the Virginia Company asked the mayor of London to furnish them with one hundred children "for the strength and increasing of the Colony," especially for children ages twelve and upward. The children were to be apprenticed until age twenty-one if male and until married if female, and then placed on public lands. "Request by Virginia Company to Mayor of London, 1619," in *Childhood in America*, 241.

5. Ulrich, *Good Wives*, 148; see Mary Ryan, *Mysteries of Sex: Tracing Women and Men through American History* (Chapel Hill: University of North Carolina Press, 2006), 71.

6. Mintz, *Huck's Raft*, 17, 13, 27.

7. "Massachusetts Statute, 1642," in *Childhood in America*, 537; Ulrich, *Good Wives*, 54–58 passim.

8. Catherine M. Scholten, "Women as Childbearers," in *Childhood in America*, 14; quoted in Ulrich, *Good Wives*, 146; Marilyn Salmon, "The Cultural Significance of Breast-Feeding and Infant Care in Early Modern England and America," in *Mothers and Motherhood: Readings in American History*, ed. Rima Apple and Janet Golden (Columbus: Ohio State University Press, 1997), 25.

9. Anne Bradstreet, "In Reference to Her Children, 23, June, 1659," in *Childhood in America*, 81; Mintz, *Huck's Raft*, 15; quoted in Ulrich, *Good Wives*, 144–145.

10. Salmon, "Cultural Significance," in *Mothers and Motherhood*, 12, 6–9; Jennifer L. Morgan, *Laboring Women: Reproduction and Gender in New World Slavery* (Philadelphia: University of Pennsylvania Press, 2004), 65.

11. Ulrich, *Good Wives*, 23. For a detailed example of eastern Native American women's labor contributions, see Theda Perdue, *Cherokee Women: Gender and Culture Change, 1700–1835* (Lincoln: University of Nebraska Press, 1998). See also Sharlene Hesse-Biber and Gregg Lee Carter, *Working Women in America: Split Dreams* (New York: Oxford University Press, 2000), 23–24.

12. Quoted in Mary Frances Berry, *The Politics of Parenthood: Child Care, Women's Rights, and the Myth of the Good Mother* (New York: Viking, 1993), 47. For more on enslaved women in the colonial era, see Carol Berkin, *First Generations: Women in Colonial America* (New York: Hill and Wang, 1996); Morgan, *Laboring Women*; Deborah Gray White, *Aren't I a Woman? Female Slaves in the Plantation South* (New York: W. W. Norton, 1985).

13. Historical research that contextualizes English marriage and its emphasis on economic dependence for women includes Berkin, *First Generations*; Kathleen M. Brown, *Good Wives, Nasty Wenches, and Anxious Patriarchs: Gender, Race, and Power in Colonial Virginia* (Chapel Hill: Institute of Early American History and Culture, University of North Carolina Press, 1996); Ann Marie Plane, *Colonial Intimacies: Indian Marriage in Early New England* (Ithaca, NY: Cornell University Press, 2000); White, *Aren't I a Woman?*; Perdue, *Cherokee Women*. Quoted in Ulrich, *Good Wives*, 146; Sonya Michel, *Children's Interests/Mothers' Rights: The Shaping of America's Child Care Policy* (New Haven: Yale University Press, 1999), 19.

14. On intercultural encounters and the impact of disease, see Paul V. Adams et al., *Experiencing World History* (New York: New York University Press, 2000), 260; Colin G. Calloway,

New Worlds for All: Indians, Europeans, and the Remaking of Early America (Baltimore: Johns Hopkins University Press, 1997); James H. Merrell, *The Indians' New World: Catawbas and Their Neighbors from European Contact through the Era of Removal* (Chapel Hill: Institute of Early American History and Culture, University of North Carolina Press, 1989). For the colonial era, research on mothering, especially outside New England, is limited, but family and marriage information can be found in White, *Aren't I a Woman*; Perdue, *Cherokee Women*; Berkin, *First Generations*; Brown, *Good Wives, Nasty Wenches*; Plane, *Colonial Intimacies*. For non-English colonial interactions, Jennifer M. Spear, *Race, Sex, and Social Order in Early New Orleans* (Baltimore: Johns Hopkins University Press, 2009); James F. Brooks, "'This Evil Extends Especially to the Feminine Sex': Negotiating Captivity in the New Mexico Borderlands," in *Women's America: Refocusing the Past*, ed. Linda K. Kerber and Jane Sherron DeHart 6th ed. (New York: Oxford University Press, 2004), 38–44.

15. Sara M. Evans, *Born for Liberty: A History of Women in the America* (New York: Free Press, 1989), 26, 30. Laurel Thatcher Ulrich, *A Midwife's Tale: The Life of Martha Ballard, Based on Her Diary, 1785–1812* (New York: Vintage Books, 1990), 156–157.

16. Quoted in Peter Bardaglio, "'Shameful Matches': The Regulation of Interracial Sex and Marriage in the South before 1900," in *Sex, Love, Race: Crossing Boundaries in North America*, ed. Martha Hodes (New York: New York University Press, 1999), 14. Quoted in *Women's America*, 67.

17. Margaret Marsh and Wanda Ronner, *The Empty Cradle: Infertility in America from Colonial Times to the Present* (Baltimore: Johns Hopkins University Press, 1996); Margaret Marsh, "Motherhood Denied: Women and Infertility in Historical Perspective," in *Mothers and Motherhood*, 217.

18. Quoted in *Major Problems in American Women's History*, 2nd ed., ed. Mary Beth Norton and Ruth M. Alexander, 77; quoted in Linda K. Kerber, *No Constitutional Right to Be Ladies: Women and the Obligations of Citizenship* (New York: Hill and Wang, 1998), 10.

19. Linda K. Kerber, *Women of the Republic: Intellect and Ideology in Revolutionary America* (Chapel Hill: University of North Carolina Press, 1980); reprinted in Woloch, *Early American Women*, 136.

20. Mintz, *Huck's Raft*, 28.

21. Ibid., 26–27; Evans, *Born for Liberty*, 67–97 passim.

22. Evans, *Born for Liberty*, 73; quoted in Mary P. Ryan, *Cradle of the Middle Class: The Family in Oneida County, New York, 1790–1856* (New York: Cambridge University Press, 1981), 190.

23. For further discussion of the private/public dichotomy and citizenship, see Stephanie Coontz, *The Way We Never Were: American Families and the Nostalgia Trap* (New York: Basic Books, 2000), 53; quoted in Welter, "The Cult of True Womanhood, 1820–1860," in *Major Problems in American Women's History*, ed. Norton and Alexander, 120.

24. For an excellent discussion of this cultural shift, see Christine Stansell, *City of Women: Sex and Class in New York, 1789–1860* (Urbana: University of Illinois Press, 1987), 25. Quoted in Linda K. Kerber, "The Republican Mother and the Woman Citizen: Contradictions and Choices in Revolutionary America," in *Women's America*, 125; quoted in *Early American Women*, 139.

25. Jan Lewis, "Mother's Love: The Construction of an Emotion in Nineteenth-Century America," in *Mothers and Motherhood*, 54, 59.

26. Quoted in Kathleen Brown, "The Maternal Physician: Teaching American Mothers to Put the Baby in the Bathwater," in *Right Living: An Anglo-American Tradition of Self-Help Medicine and Hygiene*, ed. Charles E. Rosenberg (Baltimore: Johns Hopkins University Press, 2003), 105–106; quoted in Sylvia D. Hoffert, *Private Matters: American Attitudes toward Childbearing and Infant Nurture in the Urban North, 1800–1860* (Urbana: University of Illinois Press, 1989), 147; Ryan, *Cradle*, 160, 199.

27. Lewis, "Mother's Love," 61; Lydia Maria Child, *The Mother's Book* (Boston, 1831), 22; Catharine E. Beecher, *A Treatise on Domestic Economy: Young Ladies at Home and at School* (1841; repr., New York: Source Books Press, 1970), 140.

28. Quoted in Lewis, "Mother's Love," 65, 55; Julia Grant, *Raising Baby by the Book: The Education of American Mothers* (New Haven: Yale University Press, 1998), 28.

29. Beecher, *Treatise*, 142; Michael Goldberg, "Breaking New Ground: 1800–1848," in *No Small Courage: A History of Women in the United States*, ed. Nancy F. Cott (New York: Oxford University Press, 2000), 194–195.

30. Mintz, *Huck's Raft*, 47, 76.

31. Ibid., 76, 77, 80.

32. Hoffert, *Private Matters*, 176–177, 184; Lewis, "Mother's Love," 54; quoted in Mintz, *Huck's Raft*, 81.

33. Beecher, *Treatise*, 230, 225; Heman Humphrey, *Domestic Education* (Amherst, MA, 1840), 16; Lewis, "Mother's Love," 66.

34. Mintz, *Huck's Raft*, 164; Stansell, *City of Women*, 214; Coontz, *The Way We Never Were*, 128.

35. Coontz, *The Way We Never Were*, 129; see Linda Gordon, *Heroes of Their Own Lives: The Politics and History of Family Violence* (New York: Penguin, 1988), 95–99.

36. Quoted in Hoffert, *Private Matters*, 143, 142.

37. Quoted in ibid., 154, 155, 157.

38. Ryan, *Cradle*, 197; Hoffert, *Private Matters*, 158, 157, 147, 159.

39. Hoffert, *Private Matters*, 176.

40. Carroll Smith-Rosenberg, "The Female World of Love and Ritual: Relations between Women in Nineteenth-Century America," in *Women's America*, 168–182; Ryan, *Cradle*, 192.

41. Ryan, *Cradle*, 192, 193; Smith-Rosenberg, "Female World," 172, 174.

42. Ryan, *Cradle*, 175.

43. Quoted in ibid., 175.

44. Marilyn S. Blackwell, "The Republican Vision of Mary Palmer Tyler," in *Mothers and Motherhood*, 36.

45. Ibid., 39, 41.

46. Beecher, *Treatise*, 3, 5, 4.

47. Quoted in Evans, *Born for Liberty*, 71.

48. Ryan, *Cradle*, 147.

49. Ibid., 147, 148, 142.

50. Coontz, *The Way We Never Were*, 11.

51. Janet Golden, "The New Motherhood and the New View of Wet Nurses, 1780–1865," in *Mothers and Motherhood*, 78

52. Ibid., 73, 74, 76, 84; Hoffert, *Private Matters*, 148.

53. Quoted in Sally G. McMillen, *Motherhood in the Old South: Pregnancy, Childbirth, and Infant Rearing* (Baton Rouge: Louisiana State University Press, 1990), 187. See, for example, Jaqueline Jones, *Labor of Love, Labor of Sorrow: Black Women, Work and the Family, From Slavery to the Present* (New York: Vintage Books, 1985), 9–42 passim.

54. See, for example, Elliott West, "Beyond Baby Doe: Child Rearing on the Mining Frontier," in *The Women's West*, ed. Susan Armitage and Elizabeth Jameson (Norman: University of Oklahoma Press, 1987), 179–192.

CHAPTER 2 — CONTRADICTIONS OF MORAL
MOTHERHOOD: SLAVERY, RACE, AND REFORM

1. Harriet Jacobs, *Incidents in the Life of a Slave Girl* (New York: Oxford University Press, 1988), 96.

2. Quoted in Sara Evans, *Born for Liberty: A History of Women in America* (New York: Free Press, 1989), 110; quoted in Nancy Woloch, *Women and the American Experience*, 3rd ed. (Boston: McGraw Hill, 2000), 184.

3. Micki McElya, *Clinging to Mammy: The Faithful Slave in Twentieth-Century America* (Cambridge, MA: Harvard University Press, 2007), 6.

4. Quoted in *Black Women in White America: A Documentary History*, ed. Gerda Lerner (New York: Vintage Books, 1973), 51–52; Harriet Jacobs, *Incidents*, 57.

5. Quoted in Lerner, *Black Women*, 10–12.

6. Claire Robertson, "Africa into the Americas? Slavery and Women, the Family, and the Gender Division of Labor," in *More Than Chattel: Black Women and Slavery in the Americas*, ed. David Barry Gaspar and Darlene Clark Hine (Bloomington: Indiana University Press, 1996), 13.

7. Wilma King, "'Suffer with Them Till Death': Slave Women and Their Children in Nineteenth-Century America," in *More Than Chattel*, 152, 157, 156; Deborah Gray White, *Ar'n't I a Woman? Female Slaves in the Plantation South* (New York: W. W. Norton, 1985), 96; quoted in Lerner, *Black Women*, 53.

8. King, "'Suffer with Them Till Death,'" 153; Jacobs, *Incidents*, 17

9. Quoted in Lerner, *Black Women*, 35, 37, 38.

10. Quoted in King, "'Suffer with Them Till Death,'" 156.

11. Ibid., 156.

12. Quoted in ibid., 151; Robertson, "Africa into the Americas," 22.

13. Robertson, "Africa into the Americas," 21; Evans, *Born for Liberty*, 110; Stephanie Shaw, "Mothering Under Slavery in the Antebellum South," in *Mothers and Motherhood: Readings in American History*, ed. Rima Apple and Janet Golden (Columbus: Ohio State University Press, 1997), 299, 300.

14. Quoted in Lerner, *Black Women*, 33, 40.

15. See Patricia Hill Collins, *Black Feminist Thought: Knowledge, Consciousness, and the Politics of Empowerment* (New York: Routledge, 2000), 187–215 passim; White, *Ar'n't I a Woman?*, 127; quoted in Mary Frances Berry, *The Politics of Parenthood: Child Care, Women's Rights, and the Myth of the Good Mother* (New York: Viking, 1993), 62.

16. Ellen Carol DuBois and Lynn Dumenil, *Through Women's Eyes: An American History with Documents* (Boston: Bedford/St. Martin's, 2005), 157; Maria W. Stewart, "Religion and the Pure Principles of Morality, The Sure Foundation on Which We Must Build" (Boston, 1831).

17. See, for example, Mary P. Ryan's tallies of occupational categories in Utica, New York, between 1817 and 1865, and Stuart M. Blumin's explication of class structure in midcentury Philadelphia. Mary P. Ryan, *Cradle of the Middle Class: The Family in Oneida County, New York* (Cambridge: Cambridge University Press, 1981), 253; Stuart M. Blumin, *The Emergence of the Middle Class: Social Experience in the American City, 1760–1900* (Cambridge: Cambridge University Press, 1989), 73.

18. Quoted in Jacqueline Jones, *Labor of Love, Labor of Sorrow: Black Women, Work and the Family, from Slavery to the Present* (New York: Basic Books, 2010), 49, 77.

19. Jones, *Labor of Love*, 62. I have also borrowed the term "American apartheid" from Jones, *Labor of Love*, 78.

20. Ibid., 62–63, 78.

21. Ibid., 46, 59, 58, 75.

22. Ibid., 129, 126. To name just one prominent example, after Senator Strom Thurmond died in 2003, news finally emerged of his impregnation of a fifteen-year-old family servant in 1924, when he was twenty-two years old.

23. Reproduced advertisement and quotation in McElya, *Clinging to Mammy*, 61, 57.

24. Jones, *Labor of Love*, 137; quoted in McElya, *Clinging to Mammy*, 173.

25. McElya, *Clinging to Mammy*, 183.

26. Ibid., 183, 193, 163; Jacobs, *Incidents*, 34; Kimberly Wallace-Sanders, *Mammy: A Century of Race, Gender, and Southern Memory* (Ann Arbor: University of Michigan Press, 2008), 36. For further discussion of this statue and other artistic and literary examples of the mammy debate, see Wallace-Sanders, *Mammy: A Century*, especially 93–117 passim.

27. See Wallace-Sanders, *Mammy: A Century*; McElya, *Clinging to Mammy*; *Global Woman: Nannies, Maids, and Sex Workers in the New Economy*, ed. Barbara Ehrenreich and Arlie Russell Hochschild (New York: Henry Holt, 2002), and Grace Chang, "Undocumented Latinas: The New 'Employable Mothers,'" in *Mothering: Ideology, Experience, and Agency*, ed. Evelyn Nakano Glenn, Grace Chang, and Linda Rennie Forcey (New York: Routledge, 1994), 259–286.

28. Quoted in Lori D. Ginzberg, *Women in Antebellum Reform* (Wheeling, IL: Harlan Davison, 2000), 9; quoted in *Major Problems in American Women's History: Documents and Essays*, ed. Mary Beth Norton and Ruth M. Alexander, 2nd ed. (Lexington, MA: D. C. Heath, 1996), 110.

29. For further detail, see Christine Stansell, *City of Women: Sex and Class in New York 1789–1860* (Urbana: University of Illinois Press, 1987), and Peggy Pascoe, *Relations of Rescue: The Search for Female Moral Authority in the American West, 1874–1939* (New York: Oxford University Press, 1990).

30. Quoted in Marlene LeGates, *In Their Time: A History of Feminism in Western Society* (New York: Routledge, 2001), 178, 180; quoted in Evans, *Born for Liberty*, 104. There is some controversy among historians about whether the accounts of observers accurately recounted Truth's testimony.

31. Harriet Beecher Stowe, *Uncle Tom's Cabin; or, Life Among the Lowly* (Bedford, MA: Applewood Books, 1851), 316.

32. Ibid.

33. LeGates, *In Their Time*, 180.

34. Ginzberg, *Women in Antebellum Reform*, 216; Evans, *Born for Liberty*, 103.

35. Quoted in Janet Zollinger Giele, *Two Paths to Women's Equality: Temperance, Suffrage, and the Origins of Modern Feminism* (New York: Twayne, 1995), 117.

36. Stansell, *City of Women*, 210. For details on female aspects of the CAS work, see Stansell, *City of Women*, 212–214.

37. Evans, *Born for Liberty*, 130; quoted in Mary E. Odem, "Delinquent Daughters: The Age-of-Consent Campaign," in *Childhood in America*, ed. Paula S. Fass and Mary Ann Mason, (New York: New York University Press, 2000), 495; Giele, *Two Paths*, 100.

38. Quoted in Giele, *Two Paths*, 46.

39. Quoted in Evans, *Born for Liberty*, 127, and see 119–144 passim.

CHAPTER 3 — MEDICALIZING THE MATERNAL BODY

1. Quoted in Eleanor Lewis and Kenneth Lockridge, "'Sally has been Sick': Pregnancy and Family Limitation among Virginia Gentry Women, 1780–1830," in *Mothers and Motherhood: Readings in American History*, ed. Rima Apple and Janet Golden (Columbus: Ohio State University Press, 1997), 203; quoted in Janet Farrell Brodie, *Contraception and Abortion in Nineteenth-Century America* (Ithaca, NY: Cornell University Press, 1994), 41.

2. Susan E. Klepp, *Revolutionary Conceptions: Women, Fertility, and Family Limitation in America, 1760–1820* (Chapel Hill: University of North Carolina Press, 2009), 9, 7; Linda Gordon, *Woman's Body, Woman's Right: Birth Control in America* (New York: Penguin, 1990), 150; Jacqueline Jones, *Labor of Love, Labor of Sorrow: Black Women, Work, and the Family from Slavery to the Present* (New York: Vintage Books, 1985), 61, 91.

3. Gordon, *Woman's Body*, 38.

4. Klepp, *Revolutionary Conceptions*, 116, 214.

5. Ibid., 64, 107, 109.

6. Ibid., 15, 261–262.

7. Quoted in Lewis and Lockridge, "Sally has been Sick,'" 199, 200.

8. Ibid., 199, 200, 201, 206; Brodie, *Contraception and Abortion*, 21, 35. See also Judith Walzer Leavitt, "Under the Shadow of Maternity: American Women's Responses to Death and Debility Fears in Nineteenth-Century Childbirth," in *Women and Health in America: Historical Readings*, ed. Judith Walzer Leavitt, 2nd ed. (Madison: University of Wisconsin Press, 1999), 328–346.

9. Klepp, *Revolutionary Conceptions*, 61; quoted in Leavitt, "Under the Shadow of Maternity," 331.

10. Klepp, *Revolutionary Conceptions*, 195; Regina Morantz, "Making Women Modern: Middle Class Women and Health Reform in 19th Century America," *Journal of Social History* 10:4 (Summer 1977): 490–507; Brodie, *Contraception and Abortion*, 87. See also James H. Cassedy, *Medicine in America: A Short History* (Baltimore: Johns Hopkins University Press, 1991), 33–39 passim.

11. Quoted in Morantz, "Making Women Modern," 350; quoted in Brodie, *Contraception and Abortion*, 127.

12. Quoted in Mortantz, "Making Women Modern," 351. Historians continue to struggle to understand the varying meanings of the term "race" in the social imagination of nineteenth-century and early twentieth-century writers. Meanings ran the gamut, from notions of racial difference—and hierarchy—to utopian ideas about perfection of the human race. Wright seems to fall closer to this second end of the continuum. Perfecting American racial "stock" assumed more racist and classist overtones as modern eugenic thought took hold.

13. Quoted in Morantz, "Making Women Modern," 347.

14. Brodie, *Contraception and Abortion*, 91, 92.

15. Ibid., 97–99.

16. Sylvia D. Hoffert, *Private Matters: American Attitudes toward Childbearing and Infant Nurture in the Urban North, 1800–1860* (Urbana: University of Illinois Press, 1989), 68–69.

17. See Jennifer L. Morgan, *Laboring Women: Reproduction and Gender in New World Slavery* (Philadelphia: University of Pennsylvania Press, 2004), 12–49; Marie Jenkins Schwartz, *Birthing a Slave: Motherhood and Medicine in the Antebellum South* (Cambridge, MA: Harvard University Press, 2006), 15, 78. See also Diana Price Herndl, "The Invisible (Invalid) Woman: African American Women, Illness, and Nineteenth-Century Narrative," in *Women and Health*, 131–145.

18. Schwartz, *Birthing a Slave*, 19, 37. Elite southern women did sometimes hire physicians as backup in case of birth complications. See V. Lynn Weiner, *Born Southern: Childbirth, Motherhood, and Social Networks in the Old South* (Baltimore: Johns Hopkins University Press, 2010), 145.

19. Schwartz, *Birthing a Slave*, 238.

20. Ibid., 238, 239, 240.

21. Ibid., 138, 234–235, 111–112, 113, 141; Weiner, *Born Southern*, 143.

22. Schwartz, *Birthing a Slave*, 312, 295–301; Herndl, "The Invisible (Invalid) Woman," 132, 133.

23. Deborah Kuhn McGregor, *From Midwives to Medicine: The Birth of American Gynecology* (New Brunswick, NJ: Rutgers University Press, 1998), 197, 66; Judith Walzer Leavitt, *Brought to Bed: Childbearing in America, 1750–1950* (New York: Oxford University Press, 1986), 77, 76.

24. Andrea Tone, *Devices and Desires: A History of Contraceptives in America* (New York: Hill and Wang, 2001), 8. See, for example, Cornelia Hughes Dayton, "Taking the Trade:

Abortion and Gender Relations in an Eighteenth-Century New England Village," in *Women's America: Refocusing the Past*, ed. Linda K. Kerber and Sherron DeHart, 6th ed. (New York: Oxford University Press, 2004), 97–113. Klepp, *Revolutionary Conceptions*, 229–230, 69; Leslie J. Reagan, *When Abortion Was a Crime: Women, Medicine, and the Law in the United States, 1867–1973* (Berkeley: University of California Press, 1997), 9–10.

25. Susan E. Klepp, "Lost, Hidden, Obstructed, Repressed: Contraceptive and Abortive Technology in the Early Delaware Valley," in *Early American Technology: Making and Doing Things from the Colonial Era to 1850*, ed. Judith A. McGaw (Chapel Hill: University of North Carolina Press, 1994), 77.

26. Klepp, *Revolutionary Conceptions*, 166, 189–192, 183.

27. Tone, *Devices and Desires*, 69; Brodie, *Contraception and Abortion*, 85.

28. Klepp, *Revolutionary Conceptions*, 96–99, 104–105.

29. James C. Mohr, *Abortion in America: The Origins and Evolution of National Policy, 1800–1900* (New York: Oxford University Press, 1978), 101–102, 50; Gordon, *Woman's Body*, 51.

30. Brodie, *Contraception and Abortion*, 224–225.

31. On the efforts of regular physicians to establish credibility and influence state licensing laws in the antebellum period, and the consolidation of their authority after the Civil War, see Cassedy, *Medicine in America*, 25–33 and 86–96 passim.

32. Quoted in Carroll Smith-Rosenberg and Charles Rosenberg, "The Female Animal: Medical and Biological Views of Woman and Her Role in Nineteenth-Century America," in *Women and Health* (Madison: University of Wisconsin Press, 1984), 13.

33. Sarah Blaffer Hrdy, *Mother Nature: Maternal Instincts and How They Shape the Human Species* (New York: Ballantine Books, 1999), 3, 14; Hoffert, *Private Matters*, 147. See also Janet Golden, *A Social History of Wet Nursing in America: From Breast to Bottle* (Cambridge: Cambridge University Press, 1996.)

34. Quoted in Mohr, *Abortion in America*, 151.

35. Quoted in Smith-Rosenberg and Rosenberg, "The Female Animal," 19; Gordon, *Woman's Body*, 59, 52.

36. Mohr, *Abortion in America*, 165–166.

37. Quoted in Smith-Rosenberg and Rosenberg, "The Female Animal," 18.

38. Quoted in Mohr, *Abortion in America*, 111.

39. Linda Gordon, "Voluntary Motherhood: The Beginnings of Feminist Birth Control Ideas in the United States," in *Mothers and Motherhood*, 429.

40. Quoted in ibid., 430.

41. Ibid., 435, 427.

42. Golden, *A Social History of Wet Nursing* 24; Mohr, *Abortion in America*, 112.

43. Tone, *Devices and Desires*, 35, 37.

44. Brodie, *Contraception and Abortion*, 254, 255, 257; Mohr, *Abortion in America*, 166; Reagan, *When Abortion Was a Crime*, 13, 80.

45. Mohr, *Abortion in America*, 240; Brodie, *Contraception and Abortion*, 281–282, 288, 287.

46. Klepp, *Revolutionary Conceptions*, 280.

47. Quoted in Reagan, *When Abortion Was a Crime*, 11; Kathryn Kish Sklar, "Florence Kelley and Women's Activism in the Progressive Era," in *Women's America*, 328.

48. Smith-Rosenberg and Rosenberg, "The Female Animal," 15; quoted in Vern Bullough and Martha Voght, "Women, Menstruation, and Nineteenth-Century Medicine," in *Women and Health*, 29–30; Ellen Carol DuBois and Lynne Dumenil, *Through Women's Eyes: An American History with Documents* (Boston: Bedford/St. Martin's, 2005), 320.

49. Smith-Rosenberg and Rosenberg, "The Female Animal," 16, 17.

50. Leavitt, *Brought to Bed*, 42, 63, 39; Hoffert, *Private Matters*, 65.

51. Hoffert, *Private Matters*, 65, 66; Leavitt, *Brought to Bed*, 72.

52. Leavitt, *Brought to Bed*, 44.

53. Quoted in Hoffert, *Private Matters*, 43, 70.

54. Ibid., 70, 73, 75.

55. Weiner, *Born Southern*, 146–147.

56. Leavitt, *Brought to Bed*, 116, 117.

57. Ibid., 45; Janet Carlisle Bogdan, "Childbirth in America, 1650–1990," in *Women, Health, and Medicine in America: A Historical Handbook,* ed. Rima D. Apple (New York: Garland Publishing, 1990), 113. Laurel Thatcher Ulrich, "'The Living Mother of a Living Child': Midwifery and Mortality in Post-Revolutionary New England," in *Mothers and Motherhood,* 175; Leavitt, "Under the Shadow of Maternity," 332; Johanna Schoen, *Choice and Coercion: Birth Control, Sterilization, and Abortion in Public Health and Welfare* (Chapel Hill: University of North Carolina Press, 2005), 25; Ulrich, "Living Mother," 185.

58. Joan J. Mathews and Kathleen Zadak, "The Alternative Birth Movement in the United States: History and Current Status," in *Mothers and Motherhood,* 279; Molly Ladd-Taylor, *Mother-Work: Women, Child Welfare, and the State, 1890–1930* (Urbana: University of Illinois Press, 1994), 23

59. Margaret Marsh, "Motherhood Denied: Women and Infertility in Historical Perspective," in *Mothers and Motherhood,* 219–220.

60. Ibid., 227, 225. See also Margaret Marsh, *The Empty Cradle: Infertility in America from Colonial Times to the Present* (Baltimore: Johns Hopkins University Press, 1996).

61. Quoted in Marsh, "Motherhood Denied," 225, 224.

62. Ibid., 227; McGregor, *From Midwives to Medicine*, 153, 157.

63. Marsh, "Motherhood Denied, 230.

64. Klepp, *Revolutionary Conceptions,* 280.

CHAPTER 4 — SCIENCE, EXPERTISE, AND ADVICE TO MOTHERS

1. Quoted in Molly Ladd-Taylor, *Raising a Baby the Government Way: Mothers' Letters to the Children's Bureau 1915–1932* (New Brunswick, NJ: Rutgers University Press, 2001), 118.

2. Quoted in Julia Grant, *Raising Baby by the Book: The Education of American Mothers* (New Haven: Yale University Press, 1998), 39; quoted in Rima D. Apple, *Perfect Motherhood: Science and Childrearing in America* (New Brunswick, NJ: Rutgers University Press, 2006), 53.

3. Quoted in Jacqueline H. Wolf, *Don't Kill Your Baby: Public Health and the Decline of Breastfeeding in the 19th and 20th Centuries* (Columbus: Ohio State University Press, 2001), 33, 27.

4. Quoted in Ann Hulbert, *Raising America: Experts, Parents, and a Century of Advice about Children* (New York: Alfred A. Knopf, 2003), 39.

5. Grant, *Raising Baby*, 25; Apple, *Perfect Motherhood*, 26.

6. Milton Kotelchuck, "Safe Mothers, Healthy Babies: Reproductive Health in the Twentieth Century," in *Silent Victories: The History and Practice of Public Health in Twentieth-Century America,* ed. John W. Ward and Christian Warren (Oxford and New York: Oxford University Press, 2007), 111.

7. See Apple, *Perfect Motherhood.*

8. Sylvia D. Hoffert, *Private Matters: American Attitudes toward Childbearing and Infant Nurture in the Urban North, 1800–1860* (Urbana: University of Illinois Press, 1989), 177; Apple, *Perfect Motherhood,* 8. See also Sally G. McMillen, *Motherhood in the Old South: Pregnancy, Childbearing, and Infant Rearing* (Baton Rouge: Louisiana State University Press, 1990), 159; Wolf, *Don't Kill Your Baby,* 4.

9. Apple, *Perfect Motherhood,* 37, 39.

10. Ward and Warren, *Silent Victories*, viii.

11. Hulbert, *Raising America*, 27; Ladd-Taylor, *Raising a Baby the Government Way*, 14.

12. Molly Ladd-Taylor, *Mother-Work: Women, Child Welfare, and the State, 1890–1930* (Urbana: University of Illinois Press, 1994), 18–19, 82; Ladd-Taylor, *Raising a Baby the Government Way*, 19, 11.

13. Jacquelyn S. Litt, *Medicalized Motherhood: Perspectives from the Lives of African American and Jewish Women* (New Brunswick, NJ: Rutgers University Press, 2000), 26; Michele Mitchell, *Righteous Propagation: African Americans and the Politics of Racial Destiny after Reconstruction* (Chapel Hill: University of North Carolina Press, 2004), 168.

14. Litt, *Medicalized Motherhood*, 72, 117–118; Natalia Molina, *Fit to Be Citizens? Public Health and Race in Los Angeles, 1879–1939* (Berkeley: University of California Press, 2006), 60, 80, 90, 99. On white attitudes toward African Americans and disease, see Mitchell, *Righteous Propagation*.

15. Apple, *Perfect Motherhood*, 35–37.

16. See Apple, *Perfect Motherhood*, especially chapters 1–4.

17. Lifebuoy soap advertisement, *Children: The Magazine for Parents*, February 1928, 51; Borden milk advertisement, "With millions threatened—is your child safe?" *Time*, February 18, 1924, 26–27; Scot Tissue advertisement, *Children: The Magazine for Parents*, October 1926, 13.

18. Lynn Weiner, "Reconstructing Motherhood: The La Leche League in Postwar America," in *Mothers and Motherhood: Readings in American History*, ed. Rima Apple and Janet Golden (Columbus: Ohio State University Press, 1997), 368; Wolf, *Don't Kill Your Baby*, 197.

19. Wolf, *Don't Kill Your Baby*, 42, 1. The United States adopted a standard for milk pasteurization in 1927, but only in the 1940s did pasteurization become the norm nationwide. Robert V. Tauxe and Emilio J. Esteban, "Advances in Food Safety to Prevent Foodborne Diseases in the United States," in *Silent Victories*, ed. Ward and Warren, 25; quoted in Apple, *Perfect Motherhood*, 60.

20. Wolf, *Don't Kill Your Baby*, 3, 4; Jacqueline H. Wolf, "Saving Babies and Mothers: Pioneering Efforts to Decrease Infant and Maternal Mortality," in *Silent Victories*, 143; quoted in Ladd-Taylor, *Raising a Baby the Government Way*, 20.

21. Wolf, *Don't Kill Your Baby*, 4; Hulbert, *Raising America*, 64–65

22. Ladd-Taylor, *Raising a Baby the Government Way*, 38.

23. Apple, *Perfect Motherhood*, 31. Quoted in Wolf, *Don't Kill Your Baby*, 28.

24. Quoted in Ladd-Taylor, *Raising a Baby the Government Way*, 79.

25. See Christine Simmons, *Making Marriage Modern: Women's Sexuality From the Progressive Era to World War II* (New York: Oxford University Press, 2009), 178–217 passim, regarding "sexual adjustment" advice for wives; Wolf, *Don't Kill Your Baby*, 24, 25.

26. Wolf, *Don't Kill Your Baby*, 189–190; Eagle Brand milk advertisement, *Ladies' Home Journal*, September 1930, 133.

27. Judith Walzer Leavitt, "Birthing and Anesthesia: The Debate Over Twilight Sleep," in *Mothers and Motherhood*, 216–241; Apple, *Perfect Motherhood*, 61.

28. Quoted in Apple, *Perfect Motherhood*, 58, 60, 57.

29. Ibid., 59, 60.

30. Quoted in Kotelchuck, "Safe Mothers," 109; quoted in Apple, *Perfect Motherhood*, 50.

31. Ladd-Taylor, *Raising a Baby the Government Way*, 4.

32. Quoted in ibid., 34.

33. Apple, *Perfect Motherhood*, 51–52.

34. Quoted in Ladd-Taylor, *Raising a Baby the Government Way*, 22.

35. Kotelchuck, "Safe Mothers,"109; quoted in Ladd-Taylor, *Raising a Baby the Government Way*, 18.

36. Quoted in Ladd-Taylor, *Raising a Baby the Government Way*, 53, 50.

37. Quoted in ibid., 54, 82.

38. Quoted in ibid., 35, 52, 53.

39. Lynn Curry, "Modernizing the Rural Mother," in *Mothers and Motherhood*, 499, 502, 503.

40. Ibid., 501–502.

41. Ibid., 503, 505.

42. Quoted in ibid., 501.

43. Quoted in Apple, *Perfect Motherhood*, 164; quoted in Ladd-Taylor, *Raising a Baby the Government Way*, 30.

44. Quoted in Litt, *Medicalized Motherhood*, 43, 44.

45. Quoted in Patricia Preciado Martin, *Songs My Mother Sang to Me: An Oral History of Mexican-American Women* (Tucson: University of Arizona Press, 1992), 107.

46. Quoted in Apple, *Perfect Motherhood*, 34.

47. Quoted in Hulbert, *Raising America*, 70; quoted in Litt, *Medicalized Motherhood*, 60–61.

48. Grant, *Raising Baby*, 102–103.

49. Quoted in Mitchell, *Righteous Propagation*, 96, 101.

50. Quoted in ibid., 55.

51. Quoted in ibid., 74.

52. Apple, *Perfect Motherhood*, 90, 91, 92.

53. Ibid., 79–80.

54. Karl Menninger, "Mental Hygiene in the Home," *Ladies' Home Journal*, October 1930, 109.

55. Linda W. Rosenzweig, *The Anchor of My Life: Middle-Class American Mothers and Daughters, 1880–1920* (New York: New York University Press, 1993), 27, 26, 32, 34.

56. Hulbert, *Raising America*, 109.

57. "Inside Tips for Fathers," *Children: The Magazine for Parents*, October 1926, 13.

58. Steven Mintz and Susan Kellogg, *Domestic Revolutions: A Social History of American Family Life* (New York: Free Press, 1988), 107–108, 117.

59. Quoted in Hulbert, *Raising America*, 111; Menninger, "Mental Hygiene," 109.

60. Mintz and Kellogg, *Domestic Revolutions*, 125; Grant, *Raising Baby*, 51.

61. Nancy F. Cott, *The Grounding of Modern Feminism* (New Haven: Yale University Press, 1987), 202–203.

62. Mintz and Kellogg, *Domestic Revolutions*, 124.

63. Quoted in Grant, *Raising Baby*, 50; Robert L. Griswold, *Fatherhood in America: A History* (New York: Basic Books, 1993), 129. Although *Children* (later renamed *Parents*) magazine was initially directed to both parents, it emphasized mother care. Magazines for fathers did not emerge. General interest magazines such as *Time* rarely addressed domestic concerns. Advertising directed at men as fathers was almost exclusively limited to concerns such as life insurance, which emphasized men's breadwinner roles.

64. Quoted in Hulbert, *Raising America*, 42, 123–124, 141.

65. Quoted in Grant, *Raising Baby*, 46.

66. Mintz and Kellogg, *Domestic Revolutions*, 123.

67. Ladd-Taylor, *Raising a Baby the Government Way*, 90–91, 89, 84.

68. Hulbert, *Raising America*, 154, 159, 158

69. Associated Child Guidance Bureau, Inc. advertisement, *Children: The Magazine for Parents*, February 1928, 47; "A Conscientious Director of School Campus: And so to camp for health and fun," *Children: The Magazine for Parents*, February 1928, 4; "Help your children get a good start," Encyclopedia ad, *Ladies' Home Journal*, September 1930, 110; Elizabeth

Cleveland, "If Parents Only Knew: The Co-operative Parent's Catechism," *Children: A Magazine for Parents*, February 1928, 13.

70. Kathleen W. Jones, "'Mother Made Me Do It': Mother-Blaming and the Women of Child Guidance," in *Bad Mothers: The Politics of Blame in Twentieth-Century America*, ed. Molly Ladd-Taylor and Lauri Umansky (New York: New York University Press, 1998), 101, 105, 107.

71. Ibid., 109, 113.

72. Ibid., 112

73. Apple, *Perfect Motherhood*, 90.

74. Hulbert, *Raising America*, 174.

75. Griswold, *Fatherhood in America*, 128.

CHAPTER 5 — GRAND DESIGNS: UPLIFTING AND CONTROLLING THE MOTHERS

1. For more on the history of Mother's Day, see Katharine Lane Anatoli, "Memorializing Motherhood: Anna Jarvis and the Defense of Mother's Day" (PhD diss., West Virginia University, 2010); quoted in Molly Ladd-Taylor, *Mother-Work: Women, Child Welfare, and the State, 1890–1930* (Urbana: University of Illinois Press, 1994), 142.

2. Charlotte Perkins Gilman, "The New Mothers of a New World," in *Charlotte Perkins Gilman: A Nonfiction Reader*, ed. Larry Ceplair (New York: Columbia University Press, 1991), 247–249. Quoted in Ladd-Taylor, *Mother-Work*, 106; Gilman, "New Mothers of a New World," 249.

3. Quoted in Nancy F. Cott, *The Grounding of Modern Feminism* (New Haven: Yale University Press, 1987), 193.

4. Quoted in Elizabeth Ewen, *Immigrant Women in the Land of Dollars: Life and Culture on the Lower East Side, 1890–1925* (New York: Monthly Review Press, 1985), 124.

5. Ellen Carol DuBois and Lynne Dumenil, eds., *Through Women's Eyes: An American History with Documents* (Boston: Bedford/St. Martin's, 2005), Table 2, A-37; Nelson Lichtenstein et al., American Social History Project, *Who Built America? Working People and the Nation's Economy, Politics, Culture, and Society*, Vol. 2: *Since 1877*, 2nd ed. (Boston: Bedford/St. Martin's, 2000), 34.

6. DuBois and Dumenil, *Through Women's Eyes*, Table 3, A-38; Linda Gordon, *Pitied But Not Entitled: Single Mothers and the History of Welfare* (New York: Free Press, 1994), 21, 18, 22.

7. Ladd-Taylor, *Mother-Work*, 28–29; Alice Kessler-Harris, *Out to Work: A History of Wage-Earning Women in the United States* (New York: Oxford University Press, 1982), 111–112.

8. Mary Van Kleeck, *Artificial Flower Makers* (New York: Survey Associates, 1913); quoted in *America's Working Women: A Documentary History, 1600 to the Present*, ed. Rosalyn Baxandall and Linda Gordon (New York: W. W. Norton, 1995), 156. On the transformation of the home and social policy resulting from women's industrial homework see, Eileen Boris, *Home to Work: Motherhood and the Politics of Industrial Homework in the United States* (Cambridge: Cambridge University Press, 1994).

9. Kessler-Harris, *Out to Work*, 376, 249; Ladd-Taylor, *Mother-Work*, 30–31.

10. Quoted in Ladd-Taylor, *Mother-Work*, 25.

11. Ibid., 31; Gordon, *Pitied*, 23.

12. Sonya Michel, *Children's Interests/Mothers' Rights: The Shaping of America's Child Care Policy* (New Haven: Yale University Press, 1999), 54; quoted in Ewen, *Immigrant Women*, 124; Teresa L. Amott and Julie A. Matthaei, *Race, Gender, and Work: A Multicultural Economic History of Women in the United States* (Boston: South End Press, 1991), 305; Vicki L. Ruiz, "'Star Struck': Acculturation, Adolescence, and Mexican American Women, 1920–1950," in *Unequal Sisters: A Multicultural Reader in U.S. Women's History*, 3rd ed., ed. Vicki L. Ruiz and Ellen Carol DuBois (New York: Routledge, 2000), 349.

13. Amott and Matthaei, *Race, Gender, and Work*, 76, 125; "I Live a Treadmill Life," (Anonymous) in Gerda Lerner, ed. *Black Women in White America: A Documentary History* (New York: Vintage Books, 1973), 227–228.

14. Quoted in Ewen, *Immigrant Women*, 81.

15. Michael B. Katz, *In the Shadow of the Poorhouse: A Social History of Welfare in America*, 10th Anniversary ed. (New York: Basic Books, 1996), 159

16. Ewen, *Immigrant Women*, 144.

17. Quoted in ibid., 89, 87.

18. Eric Foner, *The Story of American Freedom* (New York: W. W. Norton, 1998), 187.

19. Quoted in Ewen, *Immigrant Women*, 88, 89.

20. Ibid., 135.

21. Quoted in Vicki L. Ruiz, *From Out of the Shadows: Mexican Women in Twentieth-Century America* (New York: Oxford University Press, 1998), 48.

22. Quoted in Ladd-Taylor, *Mother-Work*, 137.

23. Mimi Abromovitz, *Regulating the Lives of Women: Social Welfare Policy from Colonial Times to the Present* (Boston: South End Press, 1988), 166, 168, 169. Single mothers remained disproportionately vulnerable to the removal of their children into the Progressive era. See Linda Gordon, *Heroes of Their Own Lives: The Politics and History of Family Violence, 1860–1960* (New York: Penguin Books, 1988), 82–115 passim.

24. Gordon, *Pitied*, 60.

25. Quoted in Ladd-Taylor, *Mother-Work*, 116, 125.

26. Ibid., 136.

27. Gwendolyn Mink, *The Wages of Motherhood: Inequality in the Welfare State, 1917–1942* (Ithaca, NY: Cornell University Press, 1995), 43, 49; Steven Mintz, *Huck's Raft: A History of American Childhood* (Cambridge, MA: Harvard University Press, 2004), 174.

28. Mink, *Wages of Motherhood*, 50.

29. Gordon, *Pitied*, 50.

30. Barbara J. Nelson, "The Origins of the Two-Channel Welfare State: Workmen's Compensation and Mothers' Aid," in *Women, the State and Welfare*, ed. Linda Gordon (Madison: University of Wisconsin Press, 1990), 142; Gordon, *Pitied*, 50.

31. George J. Sanchez, "'Go After the Women': Americanization and the Mexican Immigrant Woman, 1915–1929," in *Mothers and Motherhood: Readings in American History*, ed. Rima D. Apple and Janet Golden (Columbus: Ohio State University Press, 1997), 485.

32. Gordon, *Pitied*, 46.

33. K. Tsianina Lomawaima, *They Called It Prairie Light: The Story of Chliocco Indian School* (Lincoln: University of Nebraska Press, 1994), 4, 6; Mintz, *Huck's Raft*, 171.

34. David Wallace Adams, *Education for Extinction: American Indians and the Boarding School Experience, 1875–1928* (Lawrence: University of Kansas Press, 1995), 213; Lomawaima, *They Called It Prairie Light*, 24; quoted in Margaret D. Jacobs, *White Mother to a Dark Race: Settler Colonialism, Maternalism, and the Removal of Indigenous Children in the American West and Australia, 1880–1940* (Lincoln: University of Nebraska Press, 2009), 66.

35. Jacobs, *White Mother*, 133.

36. Quoted in ibid., 133, 199.

37. Quoted in ibid., 322.

38. Ibid., 406, 204.

39. Quoted in ibid., 205–206.

40. Quoted in Karen W. Tice, "Mending Rosa's 'Working Ways': A Case Study of an African American Mother and Breadwinner," in *"Bad" Mothers: The Politics of Blame in*

Twentieth-Century America, ed. Molly Ladd-Taylor and Lauri Umansky (New York: New York University Press, 1998), 32, 33.

41. Quoted in ibid., 35, 36.

42. Ibid., 34.

43. Emily K. Abel, "Hospitalizing Maria Germani," in *"Bad" Mothers*, 63, 64.

44. Gordon, *Pitied*, 276, 196.

45. Mink, *Wages of Motherhood*, 29.

46. Gordon, *Pitied*, 280.

47. Michel, *Children's Interests*, 54.

48. Ibid., 35, 54–55.

49. Elizabeth Rose, *A Mother's Job: The History of Day Care, 1890–1960* (New York: Oxford University Press, 1999), 81, 82.

50. Ibid., 57–58, 61; Michel, *Children's Interests*, 40.

51. Quoted in Rose, *A Mother's Job*, 70.

52. Ibid., 65.

53. Ibid., 71, 29.

54. Ibid., 49.

55. Michel, *Children's Interests*, 53, 100.

56. Michel, *Children's Interests*, 9, 3.

57. *Muller v. State of Oregon*, 208 U.S. (1908).

58. Linda K. Kerber and Jane Sherron De Hart, *Women's America: Refocusing the Past*, 6th ed. (New York: Oxford University Press, 2004), 340.

59. Quoted in Kessler-Harris, *Out to Work*, 202.

60. Quoted in ibid., 187.

61. Ibid., 192, 194.

62. Ibid., 189, 192.

63. *Muller v. State of Oregon*, 208 U.S. 412 (1908).

64. Quoted in Kessler-Harris, *Out to Work*, 212.

65. I am indebted to Michele Mitchell for the "aspiring" terminology to describe some of these activists. Information on the range of activities comes from Michele Mitchell, *Righteous Propagation: African Americans and the Politics of Racial Destiny After Reconstruction* (Chapel Hill: University of North Carolina Press, 2004), 149.

66. Quoted in Gordon, *Pitied*, 126, 127; Anna Julia Cooper, *A Voice From the South by a Black Woman of the South*, Xenioa O. (N.p.: Aldine Printing House, 1892), reprinted in *The Responsibility and Opportunity of the Twentieth Century Woman* (Blackwell, Mrs. A.W. n.p., n.d.,), 22.

67. Quoted in Gordon, *Pitied*, 118.

68. Ibid., 124–125; quoted in Mitchell, *Righteous Propagation*, 101.

69. Gordon, *Pitied*, 136, 137.

70. Ibid., 142.

71. Mink, *Wages of Motherhood*, 8.

CHAPTER 6 — MODERN REPRODUCTION: THE FIT AND UNFIT MOTHER

1. Andrea Tone, *Devices and Desires: A History of Contraceptives in America* (New York: Hill and Wang, 2001), 170.

2. Quoted in Molly Ladd-Taylor, *Raising a Baby the Government Way: Mothers' Letters to the Children's Bureau, 1915–1932* (New Brunswick, NJ: Rutgers University Press, 1986), 183; quoted in Tone, *Devices and Desires*, 108.

3. Ladd-Taylor, *Raising a Baby the Government Way*, 180.

4. Johanna Schoen, *Choice and Coercion: Birth Control, Sterilization and Abortion in Public Health and Welfare* (Chapel Hill: University of North Carolina Press, 2005), 27.

5. Ellen Chesler, *Woman of Valor: Margaret Sanger and the Birth Control Movement in America* (New York: Simon and Schuster, 1992), 329. Sanger quoted in Chesler, *Woman of Valor*, 196–197.

6. Ibid., 330; Halliday G. Sutherland, *Birth Control: A Statement of Christian Doctrine Against the Neo-Malthusians by Halliday G. Sutherland M.D. (Edin.)* (London: Harding & More Ltd, 1922), ix, 83–84; Carol McCann, *Birth Control Politics in the United States, 1916–1945* (Ithaca, NY: Cornell University Press, 1994), 44–45.

7. Linda Gordon, *The Moral Property of Women: A History of Birth Control Politics in America* (Urbana: University of Illinois Press, 2002), 86. The term "race suicide" was not invented by Roosevelt but was coined by economist and sociologist Edward Alsworth Ross. See Lovett, Laura L. Lovett, *Conceiving the Future: Pronatalism, Reproduction, and the Family in the United States, 1890–1938* (Chapel Hill: University of North Carolina Press, 2007), 79; quoted in Paul A. Lombardo, *Three Generations, No Imbeciles: Eugenics, the Supreme Court, and Buck v. Bell* (Baltimore: Johns Hopkins University Press, 2008), 32.

8. Quoted in Schoen, *Choice and Coercion*, 52.

9. Quoted in Leslie J. Reagan, *When Abortion Was a Crime: Women, Medicine, and Law in the United States, 1867–1973* (Berkeley: University of California Press, 1997), 38–39; quoted in Gordon, *Moral Property*, 227–228.

10. Tone, *Devices and Desires*, 152; Chesler, *Woman of Valor*, 300, 303–305.

11. Tone, *Devices and Desires*, 125, 134, 138, 135, 136.

12. Schoen, *Choice and Coercion*, 250; Tone, *Devices and Desires*, 154, 155.

13. Quoted in Schoen, *Choice and Coercion*, 28.

14. Ibid., 31, 35, 57.

15. Ibid., 34, 47–48, 44–45.

16. Tone, *Devices and Desires*, 152, 151, 163.

17. Quoted in ibid., 160, 159.

18. Schoen, *Choice and Coercion*, 29; Tone, *Devices and Desires*, 152.

19. Reagan, *When Abortion*, 36–37.

20. Quoted in Ladd-Taylor, *Raising a Baby the Government Way*, 66, 62–63.

21. Quoted in Reagan, *When Abortion*, 109.

22. Ruth Milkman and Vanessa V. Tinsley, "A Statistical Portrait," in *Women, Families, and Communities: Readings in American History*, ed. Nancy Hewitt and Kirsten Delegard, 2nd ed. (New York: Pearson Longman, 2008), 306; Reagan, *When Abortion*, 40.

23. Reagan, *When Abortion*, 104, 114.

24. Ibid., 134, 139, 143, 158, 143.

25. Schoen, *Choice and Coercion*, 95.

26. Quoted in Lombardo, *Three Generations*, 47. The practice of selective breeding certainly had premodern roots. See Martin S. Pernick, *The Black Stork: Eugenics and the Death of "Defective" Babies in American Medicine and Motion Pictures Since 1915* (New York: Oxford University Press, 1996), 21. The modern version involved professional expertise, a belief in science, and a much broader concept of social engineering connected to nationalism and to race, ethnicity, gender, and class.

27. Quoted in Wendy Kline, *Building a Better Race: Gender, Sexuality, and Eugenics from the Turn of the Century to the Baby Boom* (Berkeley: University of California Press, 2001), 65; quoted in Mark A. Largent, *Breeding Contempt: The History of Coerced Sterilization in the United States* (New Brunswick, NJ: Rutgers University Press, 2008), 7.

28. Pernick, *The Black Stork*, 17–18; Lombardo, *Three Generations*, 56.

29. Kline, *Building a Better Race*, 41; Lombardo, *Three Generations*, 25–27 passim. The surgery itself advanced, though it was always more complicated to sterilize women than men. Salpingectomy, a relatively new procedure, involved the removal of one or both fallopian tubes.

30. Lombardo, *Three Generations*, 43.

31. Dorothy Roberts, *Killing the Black Body: Race, Reproduction, and the Meaning of Liberty* (New York: Pantheon, 1997), 71.

32. Lombardo, *Three Generations*, 117.

33. Quoted in Kline, *Building a Better Race*, 50; Largent, *Breeding Contempt*, 77, 92.

34. Quoted in Pernick, *The Black Stork*, 55, 56; Schoen, *Choice and Coercion*, 108.

35. Largent, *Breeding Contempt*, 81; quoted in Lombardo, *Three Generations*, 134; Kline, *Building a Better Race*, 59.

36. Schoen, *Choice and Coercion*, 95, 76.

37. Kline, *Building a Better Race*, 54, 56; Lombardo, *Three Generations*, 39, 4.

38. Quoted in Lombardo, *Three Generations*, 61, 62.

39. Quoted in Kline, *Building a Better Race*, 43, 93; quoted in Schoen, *Choice and Coercion*, 93.

40. Kline, *Building a Better Race*, 19

41. Quoted in ibid., 27.

42. Quoted in Steven Noll, "The Sterilization of Willie Mallory," in *"Bad Mothers": The Politics of Blame in Twentieth-Century America*, ed. Molly Ladd-Taylor and Lauri Umansky (New York: New York University Press, 1998), 49.

43. Quoted in ibid., 50.

44. Kline, *Building a Better Race*, 107, 119, 100.

45. Ibid., 100, 121.

46. Schoen, *Choice and Coercion*, 88, 126; Largent, *Breeding Contempt*, 83, 96.

47. Schoen, *Choice and Coercion*, 84, 125; Lombardo, *Three Generations*, 62.

48. Quoted in Schoen, *Choice and Coercion*, 95.

49. Ibid., 113, 114; Kline, *Building a Better Race*, 114, 113.

50. Kline, *Building a Better Race*, 79, 80.

51. Schoen, *Choice and Coercion*, 92; Kline, *Building a Better Race*, 30, 122.

52. Margaret Sanger Papers Project, "No Healthy Race Without Birth Control," March 1921, http://www.nyu.edu/projects/sanger/secure/documents/speech_no_healthy_race _without_bc.html.

53. Chesler, *Woman of Valor*, 216; McCann, *Birth Control Politics*, 125, 126. On "fitter families," see Lovett, *Conceiving the Future*, 132–161 passim; quoted in Kline, *Building a Better Race*, 64; quoted in Robert, *Killing the Black Body*, 73; quoted in Lombardo, *Three Generations*, 156.

54. Chesler, *Woman of Valor*, 215; McCann, *Birth Control Politics*, 17; Margaret Sanger, "The Civilizing Force of Birth Control," in *Sex in Civilization*, ed. V. F. Calverton and S. D. Schmalhausen (Garden City, NY: Doubleday, 1939), 525–537. History Matters Website: http:// historymatters.gmu.edu/d/5082/.

55. Quoted in Ladd-Taylor, *Raising a Baby the Government Way*, 181; quoted in Kline, *Building a Better Race*, 90, 91.

56. Pernick, *The Black Stork*, 31.

57. Ibid., 10.

58. Quoted in ibid., 82, 74.

59. Kline, *Building a Better Race*, 104.

60. Steven Mintz and Susan Kellogg, *Domestic Revolutions: A Social History of American Family Life* (New York: Free Press, 1988), 110.

CHAPTER 7 — MOTHERS' RESILIENCE AND ADAPTATION IN MODERN AMERICA

1. Quoted in Evelyn Nakano Glenn, *Issei, Nisei, War Bride: Three Generations of Japanese American Women in Domestic Service* (Philadelphia: Temple University Press, 1986), 217. Quoted in Bonnie Thornton Dill, "'The Means to Put My Children Through,' Child-Rearing Goals and Strategies among Black Female Domestic Servants," in *The Black Woman*, ed. La Frances Rodgers-Rose (Beverly Hills, CA: Sage Publications, 1980), 113 (article 107–124).

2. Quoted in Linda W. Rosenzweig, *The Anchor of My Life: Middle-Class American Mothers and Daughters, 1880–1920* (New York: New York University Press, 1993), 119, 113. Quoted in Dill, "The Means," 117.

3. Quoted in Tillie Olsen, ed., *Mother to Daughter, Daughter to Mother: A Feminist Press Daybook and Reader* (New York: Feminist Press, 1984), 80.

4. Quoted in Patrician Preciado Martin, *Songs My Mother Sang to Me: An Oral History of Mexican American Women* (Tucson: University of Arizona Press, 1982), 59, 104, 106. Interview with Ruth Cloud, from the documentary *Her Mother Before Her: Winnebago Women's Stories of Their Mothers & Grandmothers* by Jocelyn Riley (Madison: Wisconsin Historical Society, 1992).

5. Quoted in Elizabeth Ewen, *Immigrant Women in the Land of Dollars: Life and Culture on the Lower East Side, 1890–1925* (New York: Monthly Review Press, 1985), 303, 236.

6. Interview with Irene Thundercloud, *Her Mother Before Her*; quoted in Vicki L. Ruiz, "'Star Struck': Acculturation, Adolescence, and Mexican American Women, 1920–1950," in *Unequal Sisters: A Multicultural Reader in U.S. Women's History*, ed. Vicki L. Ruiz and Ellen Carol DuBois, 3rd ed. (New York: Routledge, 2000), 351.

7. Quoted in Olsen, *Mother to Daughter*, 245; quoted in Sydney Stahl Weinberg, "Jewish Mothers and Daughters: Positive and Negative Role Models," in *Mothers and Motherhood: Readings in American History*, ed. Rima D. Apple, and Janet Golden (Columbus: Ohio University Press, 1997), 336–337.

8. Ewen, *Immigrant Women*, 154; Glenn, *Issei, Nisei*, 217.

9. Quoted in Sarah Deutsch, *No Separate Refuge: Culture, Class, and Gender on an Anglo-Hispanic Frontier in the American Southwest, 1880–1940* (New York: Oxford University Press, 1987), 45.

10. Stephanie Coontz, "Working-Class Families, 1870–1890," in *American Families: A Multicultural Reader*, ed. Stephanie Coontz, Maya Parson, and Gabrielle Raley (New York: Routledge, 1999), 94–127.

11. Ibid., 111. Evelyn Nakano Glen made this argument very persuasively in her study of Japanese American families. See Glenn, *Issei, Nisei*, 191–200.

12. See Bart Landry, *Black Working Wives: Pioneers of the American Family Revolution* (Berkeley: University of California Press, 2000.) See, for example, Katherine M. B. Osburn, "'Dear Friend and Ex-Husband': Marriage, Divorce, and Women's Property Rights on the Southern Ute Reservation, 1887–1930," , and Harry A. Kersey Jr. and Helen M. Bannan, "Patchwork and Politics: The Evolving Roles of Florida Seminole Women in the Twentieth Century," both in *Negotiators of Change: Historical Perspectives on Native American Women*, ed. Nancy Shoemaker (New York: Routledge, 1995), 157–175, 193–212; Eileen Boris, *Home to Work: Motherhood and the Politics of Industrial Homework in the United States* (Cambridge: Cambridge University Press, 1994), 104.

13. See Deutsch, *No Separate Refuge*, 48–49; Glenn, *Issesi, Nisei*, 210; quoted in Patricia Hill Collins, *Black Feminist Thought* (New York: Routledge, 2000), 193.

14. Glenn, *Issei, Nisei*, 217.

15. Susan Porter Benson, *Household Accounts: Working-Class Family Economies in the Interwar United States* (Ithaca, NY: Cornell University Press, 2007), 124.

16. Quoted in Weinberg, "Jewish Mothers and Daughters," 335, 336; Mary Frances Berry, *The Politics of Parenthood: Child Care, Women's Rights, and the Myth of the Good Mother* (New York: Viking, 1993), 73.

17. Weinberg, "Jewish Mothers and Daughters," 335.

18. Miriam Cohen, *Workshop to Office: Two Generations of Italian Women in New York City, 1900–1950* (Ithaca, NY: Cornell University Press, 1992), 124, 123; quoted in Richard A. Garcia, *Rise of the Mexican American Middle Class: San Antonio, 1929–1941* (College Station: Texas A&M University Press, 1991), 144.

19. Deborah Fink, *Agrarian Women: Wives and Mothers in Rural Nebraska, 1880–1940* (Chapel Hill: University of North Carolina Press, 1992), 143, 149, 150.

20. Elizabeth Rose, *A Mother's Job: The History of Day Care, 1890–1960* (New York: Oxford University Press, 1999), 52; quoted in Julia Kirk Blackwelder, "Women of the Depression: Anglo, Black, and Hispanic Families in San Antonio," in *Women, Families and Communities: Readings in American History*, ed. Nancy Hewitt and Kirsten Delegard, 2nd ed. (New York: Pearson Longman, 2008), 134.

21. Benson, *Household Accounts*, 61.

22. Ibid., 45; Ewen, *Immigrant Women*, 125; Robert L. Griswold, *Fatherhood in America: A History* (New York: Basic Books, 1993), 103.

23. Quoted in Elna C. Green, ed., *Looking for the New Deal: Florida Women's Letters during the Great Depression* (Columbia: University of South Carolina Press, 2007), 13 (letter dated 1929).

24. Quoted in Molly Ladd-Taylor, ed., *Raising a Baby the Government Way: Mothers' Letters to the Children's Bureau, 1915–1932* (New Brunswick, NJ: Rutgers University Press, 1986), 135.

25. Robert S. McElvaine, ed., *Down and Out in the Great Depression: Letters from the Forgotten Man* (Chapel Hill: University of North Carolina Press, 1983), 62–63.

26. Quoted in Annelise Orleck, *Common Sense and a Little Fire: Women and Working-Class Politics in the United States, 1900–1965* (Chapel Hill: University of North Carolina Press, 1995), 218; quoted in Ewen, *Immigrant Women*, 126.

27. Orleck, *Common Sense*, 220, 228, 227.

28. Quoted in ibid., 235, 237.

29. Ibid., 238, 239, 249.

30. Quoted in ibid., 243, 219, 217.

31. Linda Gordon, "Black and White Visions of Welfare: Women's Welfare Activism, 1890–1945," in *Unequal Sisters*, ed. Ruiz and DuBois, 214–241.

32. Blackwelder, "Women of the Depression," 134; Green, ed., *Looking for the New Deal: Florida Women's Letters during the Great Depression*, 44; Fink, *Agrarian Women*, 155, 185.

33. Deutsch, *No Separate Refuge*, 146, 147.

34. Dill, "The Means to Put My Children Through," 109, 110.

35. Quoted in Ladd-Taylor, *Raising a Baby the Government Way*, 149, 151, 158.

36. Blackwelder, "Women of the Depression," 134; quoted in Green, *Looking for the New Deal*, 28.

37. Quoted in George J. Sanchez, *Becoming Mexican American: Ethnicity, Culture, and Identity in Chicano Los Angeles, 1900–1945* (New York: Oxford University Press, 1993), 149.

38. Linda Gordon, *Heroes of Their Own Lives: The Politics and History of Family Violence* (New York: Penguin Books, 1988), 258, 260, 264.

39. Quoted in Ewen, *Immigrant Women*, 234.

40. Quoted in Glenn, *Issei, Nisei*, 211; quoted in Sanchez, *Becoming Mexican American*, 146.

41. Lillian B. Rubin, *Worlds of Pain: Life in the Working Class* (New York: Basic Books, 1976), 93.

42. Fink, *Agrarian Women*, 165–168.

43. Quoted in ibid., 165.

44. Ibid., 165, 167, 189–191.

45. Quoted in Olsen, *Mother to Daughter*, 115.

46. Rosenzweig, *The Anchor*, 86, 87, 95.

47. Ewen, *Immigrant Women*, 208, 212, 209; Ruiz, "'Star Struck,'" in *Unequal Sisters*, 353.

48. Ruiz, "'Star Struck,'" 352, 354.

49. Quoted in Sanchez, *Becoming Mexican American*, 263; Garcia, *Rise of the Mexican American Middle Class*, 114, 134.

50. Rosenzweig, *The Anchor*, 171, 172.

51. Quoted in Vicki L. Ruiz, *From Out of the Shadows: Mexican Women in Twentieth-Century America* (New York: Oxford University Press, 1998, 2008), 56; quoted in Paula Giddings, *When and Where I Enter: The Impact of Black Women on Race and Sex in America* (New York: Bantam Books, 1984), 86–87; quoted in Paula Giddings, "Afterword," in *Double Stitch: Black Women Write About Mothers and Daughters*, ed. Patricia Bell-Scott (New York: HarperPerennial, 1993), 254.

52. Rosenzweig, *The Anchor*, 104, 91, 93.

53. Quoted in ibid., 105, 108.

54. Ibid., 184, 175.

55. For a thoughtful discussion of maternal neglect and abuse in historical context, see Gordon, *Heroes of Their Own Lives*.

CHAPTER 8 — THE MIDDLE-CLASS WIFE-AND-MOTHER BOX

1. For more on women's roles during World War II, see Emily Yellin, *Our Mothers' War: American Women at Home and at the Front during World War II* (New York: Free Press, 2004). On honoring maternal sacrifice in both world wars, see Holly S. Fenelon, *That Knock at the Door: A History of Gold Star Mothers in America* (Bloomington, IN: iUniverse, 2012). See also Rebecca Jo Plant, *Mom: The Transformation of Motherhood in Modern America* (Chicago: University of Chicago Press, 2010), 77–85 passim.

2. Jennifer Colton, "Why I Quit Working," *Good Housekeeping*, September 1951, reprinted in *Women's Magazines 1940–1960: Gender Roles and the Popular Press*, ed. Nancy A. Walker, 83–84.

3. Quoted in Nina C. Leibman, *Living Room Lectures: The Fifties Family in Film and Television* (Austin: University of Texas Press, 1995), 205. See also Leibman, *Living Room Lectures*, 187–218 passim.

4. Stephanie Coontz, *The Way We Never Were: American Families and the Nostalgia Trap* (New York: Basic Books, 1992), 27. For more detail and argument on the transfer of significant work back to mothers, away from commercial agencies, which offset some benefits of modern conveniences, see Ruth Schwarz Cowan, *More Work for Mother: The Ironies of Household Technology from the Open Hearth to the Microwave* (New York: Basic Books, 1983), 94–99 passim.

5. Coontz, *The Way*, 24, 77.

6. Ibid., 62, 76.

7. Ibid., 29, 30, 25, 26–27.

8. Jessica Weiss, *To Have and to Hold: Marriage, the Baby Boom, and Social Change* (Chicago: University of Chicago Press, 2000), 122, 92, 101–102.

9. Coontz, *The Way*, 38; Lynn Spigel, *Make Room for TV: Television and the Family Ideal in Postwar America* (Chicago: University of Chicago Press, 1992), 51.

10. Elaine Tyler May, *Homeward Bound: American Families in the Cold War Era* (New York: Basic Books, 1998); 121; Elaine Tyler May, *Barren in the Promised Land: Childless Americans and the Pursuit of Happiness* (Cambridge, MA: Harvard University Press, 1997), 128; Weiss, *To Have*, 4.

11. May, *Homeward Bound*, 69–70; May, *Barren*, 135; Coontz, *The Way*, 33.

12. Quoted in Brett Harvey, *The Fifties: A Women's Oral History* (New York: HarperCollins, 1993), 89–90; quoted in Wendy Kline, *Building A Better Race: Gender, Sexuality, and Eugenics from the Turn of the Century to the Baby Boom* (Berkeley: University of California Press, 2001), 149; quoted in May, *Homeward Bound*, 123; May, *Barren*, 132.

13. Wainwright Evans, "Are Good Mothers 'Unfaithful Wives'?" *Better Homes and Gardens*, July 1941, reprinted in Walker, *Women's Magazines*, 102–103; Weiss, *To Have*, 206; Coontz, *A Strange Stirring: The Feminine Mystique and American Women at the Dawn of the 1960s* (New York: Basic Books, 2011), 4.

14. Philip Wylie, *Generation of Vipers*, 2nd ed. (New York: Holt, Rinehart and Winston, 1955), 198, 207.

15. Quoted in Plant, *Mom*, 21.

16. Edward A. Strecker, *Their Mothers' Sons: The Psychiatrist Examines an American Problem* (Philadelphia: J. B. Lippincott, 1946); Ferdinand Lundberg and Marynia F. Farnham, M.D., *Modern Woman: The Lost Sex* (New York: Grosset and Dunlap, 1947); May, *Barren*, 153.

17. Plant, *Mom*, 13; Leslie J. Reagan, *Dangerous Pregnancies: Mothers, Disabilities, and Abortion in Modern America* (Berkeley: University of California Press, 2010), 64–66. I am also indebted to Jess Wedeen, whose undergraduate research helped me understand the different messages sent to parents of children with physical disabilities compared to neurological ones.

18. For more detail, see Ann Hulbert, *Raising America: Experts, Parents, and a Century of Advice About Children* (New York: Alfred A. Knopf, 2003), 278–279; Reagan, *Dangerous Pregnancies*, 66; quoted in David E. Simpson, J. J. Hanley, and Gordon Quinn, *Refrigerator Mothers*, KTQ Films, 2002. See, for example, Jane Taylor McDonnell, "On Being the 'Bad' Mother of an Autistic Child," in *"Bad" Mothers: The Politics of Blame in Twentieth-Century America*, ed. Molly Ladd-Taylor and Lauri Umansky (New York: New York University Press, 1998), 220–229.

19. Ruth Feldstein, *Motherhood in Black and White: Race and Sex in American Liberalism, 1930–1965* (Ithaca, NY: Cornell University Press, 2000), 53–60 passim; quotes, 57, 100.

20. Plant, *Mom*, 8, 91.

21. Strecker, *Their Mothers' Sons*, 160; Plant, *Mom*, 118–145 passim.

22. Wylie, *Generation of Vipers*, 203; Strecker, *Their Mothers' Sons*, 133; Sara M. Evans, *Born for Liberty: A History of Women in America* (New York: The Free Press, 1989), 247; Annelise Orleck, *Common Sense and a Little Fire: Women and Working-Class Politics in the United States, 1900–1965* (Chapel Hill: University of North Carolina Press, 1995), 271–276 passim.

23. Lundberg and Farnham, *Modern Woman: The Lost Sex*, 304–305, 228, 229; J. Edgar Hoover, "Mothers . . . Our Only Hope," *Woman's Home Companion*, 1944, reprinted in *Women's Magazines*, ed. Walker, 45.

24. Quoted in Hulbert, *Raising America*, 205; "You Can't Have a Career and Be a Good Wife," *Ladies' Home Journal*, 1944, reprinted in *Women's Magazines*, ed. Walker, 74, 72.

25. Lundberg and Farnham, *Modern Woman*, 319; quoted in May, *Homeward Bound*, 119.

26. Quoted in Plant, *Mom*, 113.

27. Lundberg and Farnham, *Modern Woman*, 320; Strecker, *Their Mothers' Sons*, 31.

28. Rima D. Apple, *Perfect Motherhood: Science and Childrearing in America* (New Brunswick, NJ: Rutgers University Press, 2006), 117; Benjamin Spock, *Baby and Child Care*, 2nd ed. (New York: Pocket Books, 1957), 3.

29. Spock, *Baby and Child Care*, 2d ed., 2, 3; quoted in Hulbert, *Raising America*, 246.

30. Quoted in Julia Grant, *Raising Baby by the Book: The Education of American Mothers* (New Haven: Yale University Press, 1998), 220.

31. Apple, *Perfect Motherhood*, 117.

32. Quoted in Grant, *Raising Baby*, 218, 243.

33. Quoted in ibid., 221.

34. Quoted in ibid., 221; quoted in Apple, *Perfect Motherhood*, 133.

35. Quoted in Hulbert, *Raising America*, 257, 205, 247.

36. Spock, *Baby and Child Care*, 2nd ed., 16, 34, 270, 492–503 passim.

37. Ibid., 137–144 passim, 300–303.

38. Quoted in Hulbert, *Raising America*, 228; quoted in Grant, *Raising Baby*, 233.

39. Quoted in Grant, *Raising Baby*, 225.

40. Hulbert, *Raising America*, 205.

41. Apple, *Perfect Motherhood*, 61.

42. Ibid., 112.

43. Quoted in Jacqueline H. Wolf, *Deliver Me from Pain: Anesthesia and Birth in America* (Baltimore: Johns Hopkins University Press, 2009), 111, 136.

44. Ibid., 141, 142, 144, 160.

45. Richard W. Wertz and Dorothy C. Wertz, *Lying-In: A History of Childbirth in America*, expanded ed. (New Haven: Yale University Press, 1989), 181.

46. Quoted in Apple, *Perfect Motherhood*, 130; Wertz and Wertz, *Lying-In*, 183, 185.

47. Wolf, *Deliver Me*, 110; Plant, *Mom*, 140.

48. Spock, *Baby and Child Care*, 2nd ed., 484, 485–486, 487.

49. Quoted in Grant, *Raising Baby*, 230.

50. Quoted in ibid., 235, 236.

51. Quoted in Weiss, *To Have*, 55.

52. Quoted in ibid., 55, 56; "Meet the Berckmans: The Story of a Mother Working on Two Fronts," *Ladies' Home Journal*, October 1942, reprinted in *Women's Magazines*, ed. Walker, 39.

53. Weiss, *To Have*, 52.

54. Dorothy Sue Cobble, *The Other Women's Movement: Workplace Justice and Social Rights in Modern America* (Princeton, NJ: Princeton University Press, 2004), 132–133, 127–130 passim; quoted in Weiss, *To Have*, 58, 67; Michel, *Children's Interests/Mothers' Rights*, 190.

55. Coontz, *A Strange Stirring*, 64.

56. Quoted in Harvey, *The Fifties*, 116, 117.

57. Quoted in ibid., 120, 117–118; May, *Homeward Bound*, 23.

58. Quoted in Harvey, *The Fifties*, 127.

59. May, *Homeward Bound*, 137–138.

60. Elise Denlinger, "Living *The Feminine Mystique*: The Carolyn Teach Denlinger Diaries, 1955–1980," unpublished paper, 2009, in possession of author.

61. Ibid., quoted in May, *Homeward Bound*, 170.

62. Denlinger, "Living *The Feminine Mystique*"

63. Quoted in Harvey, *The Fifties*, 122.

64. Quoted in ibid., 125; Denlinger, "Living *The Feminine Mystique*."

65. Ibid.; Stephanie Coontz makes this argument compellingly throughout her book, *A Strange Stirring*.

66. Weiss, *To Have*, 93–113 passim; May, *Homeward Bound*, 181.

67. Quoted in Harvey, *The Fifties*, 94, 102; Denlinger, "Living *The Feminine Mystique*."

68. Ann Fessler, The *Girls Who Went: The Hidden History of Women Who Surrendered Children for Adoption in the Decades before Roe v. Wade* (New York: Penguin Press, 2006), 67, 29, 30, 29; Rickie Solinger, *Wake Up Little Susie: Single Pregnancy and Race before Roe v. Wade* (New York: Routledge, 1992), 13.

69. Quoted in Harvey, *The Fifties*, 1; Beth L. Bailey, "Prescribing the Pill: The Coming of the Sexual Revolution to America's Heartland," in *Women's America: Refocusing the Past*, ed. Linda K. Kerber and Sherron de Hart 6th ed. (New York: Oxford University Press, 2004), 565.

70. Quoted in Fessler, *Girls Who Went*, 41, 42, 43, 44.

71. Barbara Melosh, *Strangers and Kin: The American Way of Adoption* (Cambridge, MA: Harvard University Press, 2002), 137; May, *Barren*, 142.

72. Quoted in ibid., 11, 12, 119, 53.

73. Quoted in ibid., 15.

74. Quoted in ibid., 16, 17, 19, 20.

75. Quoted in ibid., 22, 23.

76. Solinger, *Wake Up*, 21.

77. Ibid., 150, 33. For more on the prewar background, see Regina G. Kuntzel, *Fallen Women, Problem Girls: Unmarried Mothers and the Professionalization of Social Work, 1890–1945* (New Haven: Yale University Press, 1993).

78. Quoted in Solinger, 87, 88–90, 80.

79. Quoted in ibid., 93.

80. Solinger, *Wake Up*, 97, 145.

81. Fessler, *The Girls Who Went*, 68, 75. Single fathers did not have legal claims on children until the 1970s. See Melosh, *Strangers and Kin*, 14; see also Solinger, *Wake Up*, 36.

82. Fessler, *The Girls Who Went*, 101, 112.

83. Ibid., 71.

84. Solinger, *Wake Up*, 193, 36, 37, 47, 51.

85. *Buck v. Bell* was not overturned, but legal precedents made state-ordered sterilization more difficult after the mid-1940s. See Johanna Schoen, *Choice and Coercion: Birth Control, Sterilization, and Abortion in Public Health and Welfare* (Chapel Hill: University of North Carolina Press, 2005), 105; Solinger, *Wake Up*, 41, 55.

86. Solinger, *Wake Up*, 7, 6, 67.

87. Julie Berbitsky, *Like Our Very Own: Adoption and the Changing Culture of Motherhood, 1851–1950* (Lawrence: University of Kansas Press, 2000), 167–168; Melosh, *Strangers and Kin*, 171–172.

88. Quoted in Solinger, *Wake Up*, 79; Kunzel, *Fallen Women*, 319.

89. Quoted in Harvey, *The Fifties*, 27.

90. Coontz, *The Way*, 32.

91. Leslie Reagan, *When Abortion Was A Crime: Women, Medicine, and the Law in the United States, 1967–1973* (Berkeley: University of California Press, 1997), 162–163, 166, 169, 170.

92. Ibid., 173, 178, 180.

93. Ibid., 202.

94. Ibid., 201.

95. Ibid., 207, 205.

96. Ibid., 197, 198, 199.

97. Quoted in ibid., 197.

98. Ibid., 192.

99. Schoen, *Choice and Coercion*, 145; Reagan, *When Abortion*, 214, 209.

100. Reagan, *When Abortion*, 202.

101. Berbitsky, *Like Our Very Own*, 163; Melosh, *Strangers and Kin*, 105; Margaret Marsh and Wanda Ronner, *The Empty Cradle: Infertility in America from Colonial Times to the Present* (Baltimore, MD: Johns Hopkins University Press, 1996), 182.

102. Quoted in Marsh, "Motherhood Denied: Women and Infertility in Historical Perspective," in *Mothers and Motherhood: Readings in American History*, ed. Rima Apple and Janet Golden (Columbus: Ohio State University Press, 1997), 225; May, *Barren*, 131, 140, 141.

103. See Marsh and Ronner, *The Empty Cradle*, 131–209 passim; May, *Barren*, 148, 141, 154; May, *Homeward Bound*, 132.

104. May, *Barren*, 171.

105. Ibid., 172, 173, 170.

106. Ibid., 173, 159; quoted in Berbitsky, *Like Our Very Own*, 93.

107. Quoted in May, *Barren*, 158, 160.

108. Quoted in Berbitsky, *Like Our Very Own*, 148; Melosh, *Strangers and Kin*, 113, 112.

109. Quoted in Melosh, *Strangers and Kin*, 116, 117. Melosh notes that exceptions were sometimes made for African American working mothers (118.)

110. Quoted in Berbitsky, *Like Our Very Own*, 103.

111. Quoted in May, *Barren*, 144.

112. Berbitsky, *Like Our Very Own*, 77.

CHAPTER 9 — MOTHER POWER AND MOTHER ANGST

1. Paula Giddings, *When and Where I Enter: The Impact of Black Women on Race and Sex in America* (New York: William Morrow, 1984), 325–330; quoted in Nancy A. Naples, *Grassroots Warriors: Activist Mothering, Community Work, and the War on Poverty* (New York: Routledge, 1998), 14

2. Quoted in Jacqueline H. Wolf, *Deliver Me from Pain: Anesthesia and Birth in America* (Baltimore: Johns Hopkins University Press, 2009), 147–148.

3. Susan J. Douglas and Meredith W. Michaels, *The Mommy Myth: The Idealization of Motherhood and How It Has Undermined All Women* (New York: Free Press, 2004), 44; quoted in Ann Hulbert, *Raising America: Experts, Parents, and a Century of Advice about Children* (New York: Alfred A. Knopf, 2003), 269, 271.

4. Quoted in Gail Collins, *When Everything Changed: The Amazing Journey of American Women from 1960 to the Present* (New York: Little, Brown and Company, 2009), 197; quoted in Douglas and Michaels, *The Mommy Myth*, 39.

5. Quoted in Naples, *Grassroots Warriors*, 19.

6. Ibid., 44, 2.

7. Quoted in ibid., 150, 118.

8. Quoted in ibid., 22, 23, 24.

9. Quoted in ibid., 25

10. Ibid., 110, 17.

11. Ibid., 119, 120, 119, 39.

12. Annelise Orleck, *Storming Caesars Palace: How Black Mothers Fought Their Own War on Poverty* (Boston: Beacon Press, 2005), 9, 102–103. Note: ADC (Aid to Dependent Children) became AFDC (Aid to Families with Dependent Children) in 1962, so I use both abbreviations in the 1960s.

13. Ibid., 219–220, 177, 145.

14. Quoted in ibid., 119, 107.

15. Quoted in ibid., 222.

16. Ibid., 226, 225, 220.

17. Ibid., 117.

18. Ibid., 124, 113.

19. Ibid., 171, 269; Douglas and Michaels, *The Mommy Myth*, 173–202.

20. Demetrios James Caraley, "Ending Welfare as We Know It: A Reform Still in Progress," *Political Science Quarterly* 116, 4 (Winter 2001/2002): 525–561. Michael E. Fix and Karen C. Tumlin, "Welfare Reform and the Devolution of Immigrant Policy," *Urban Institute Research of Record*, October 1, 1997. Available at: http://www.urban.org/publications/307045.html. See also, Lynn Fujiwara, *Mothers Without Citizenship: Asian Immigrant Families and the Consequences of Welfare Reform* (Minneapolis: University of Minnesota Press, 2008), 154–178.

21. Quoted in Orleck, *Storming*, 112.

22. Swerdlow, *Women Strike for Peace: Traditional Motherhood and Radical Politics in the 1960s* (Chicago: University of Chicago Press, 1993), 20.

23. Julia Ward Howe, Mother's Day Proclamation, 1870. http://www.wagingpeace.org/articles/0000/1870_howe_mothers-day.htm.

24. Quoted in Swerdlow, *Women Strike for Peace*, 19, 16.

25. Quoted in ibid., 101, 117.

26. Swerdlow, *Women Strike for Peace*, 135, 132.

27. James Longhurst, *Citizen Environmentalists* (Hanover, NH: University Press of New England, 2010), 101, 100, 97–98.

28. Quoted in ibid., 106.

29. Quoted in Alexis Jetter, Interview with Lois Gibbs, "'What Is Your Wife Trying to Do—Shut Down the Chemical Industry?': The Housewives of Love Canal," in *The Politics of Motherhood: Activist Voices from Left to Right*, ed. Alexis Jetter, Annelise Orleck, and Diana Taylor (Hanover, NH: University Press of New England: 1997), 32, 33.

30. Quoted in Jetter interview with Gibbs, "'What Is Your Wife Trying to Do,'" 40; Elizabeth D. Blum, *Love Canal Revisited: Race, Class, and Gender in Environmental Activism* (Lawrence: University Press of Kansas, 2008), 97–99.

31. Alexis Jetter, "A Mother's Battle for Environmental Justice," in *The Politics of Motherhood*, 44–52.

32. Dollie Burwell, "Sometimes the Road Gets Lonely," in *The Politics of Motherhood*, 68.

33. Robert Gottlieb, *Forcing the Spring: The Transformation of the American Environmental Movement* (Washington, DC, and Covelo, CA: Island Press, 1993), 211.

34. Annelise Orleck and Alexis Jetter, Interview with Winona LaDuke, "Reclaiming Culture and the Land: Motherhood and the Politics of Sustaining Community," in *The Politics of Motherhood*, 80, 78. Gottlieb, *Forcing the Spring*, 212.

35. Kathleen Blee, "Mothers in Race-Hate Movements," in *The Politics of Motherhood*, 255. See also Kathleen M. Blee, *Women of the Klan: Racism and Gender in the 1920s* (Berkeley: University of California Press, 1991).

36. Dorothy Sue Cobble, *The Other Women's Movement: Workplace Justice and Social Rights in Modern America* (Princeton, NJ: Princeton University Press, 2004); Daniel Horowitz, "Rethinking Betty Friedan and The Feminine Mystique: Labor Union Radicalism in Cold War America," in *Unequal Sisters: A Multicultural Reader in U.S. Women's History*, ed. Vicki L. Ruiz and Ellen Carol DuBois, 3rd ed. (New York: Routledge, 2000), 492–518; Stephanie Coontz, *A Strange Stirring: The Feminine Mystique and American Women at the Dawn of the 1960s* (New York: Basic Books, 2011).

37. Quoted in Miriam Schneir, ed., *Feminism In Our Time: The Essential Writings, World War II to the Present* (New York: Vintage, 1994), 96, 100.

38. Quoted in Lauri Umansky, *Motherhood Reconceived: Feminism and the Legacies of the Sixties* (New York: New York University Press, 1996), 38; quoted in Douglas and Michaels, *The Mommy Myth*, 37.

39. ABC News coverage of Women Strike for Equality in 1970 ended with a quote from West Virginia Senator Jennings Randolph, who referred to the women's movement as "a small band of braless bubbleheads." Quoted in Susan J. Douglas, *Where the Girls Are: Growing Up Female with the Mass Media* (New York: Random House, 1994), 164; on media's emphasis of divisions in the movement, see 165.

40. For an excellent detailed study of Friedan's work in context, see Coontz, *A Strange Stirring*. On Friedan's antimaternalism, see Plant, *Mom: The Transformation of Motherhood in Modern America* (Chicago: University of Chicago Press, 2010).

41. Juliet Mitchell, "Women: The Longest Revolution," reprinted in *Feminism*, ed. Schneir, 206.

42. Ibid., 205, 210, 211, 212;

43. Firestone, quoted in Schneir, *Feminism*, 246, 247; Umansky, *Motherhood Reconceived*, 32.

44. Sara M. Evans, *Tidal Wave: How Women Changed America at Century's End* (New York: The Free Press, 2003), 55; Jane Lazarre, *The Mother Knot* (Durham, NC: Duke University Press, 1997), 28.

45. Lazarre, *The Mother Knot*, 43.

46. Nancy Friday, *My Mother/My Self: The Daughter's Search for Identity* (New York: Dell Publishing, 1977, 1987), 21–24.

47. Ibid., 35, 27, 43.

48. Most of Friday's interviewees were mothers themselves, but their status as daughters by far dominated the book.

49. K. Patricia Cross, *Beyond the Open Door: New Students to Higher Education* (San Francisco: Jossey-Bass, 1974), 147. William Chafe, *The Unfinished Journey: America Since World War II*, 2nd ed. (New York: Oxford University Press, 1991), 436.

50. Douglas and Michael, *The Mommy Myth*, 42, 43.

51. Quoted in Umansky, *Motherhood Reconceived*, 138–139. Dorothy Dinnerstein also critiqued hetero-normative parenting in her 1976 book, *Mermaid and the Minotaur: Sexual Arrangements and Human Malaise (New York: Harper and Row, 1976).* For further analysis of Dinnerstien's impact, see Umansky, *Motherhood Reconceived*, 140–146.

52. Quoted in Umansky, *Motherhood Reconceived*, 110.

53. Quoted in ibid., 110–111. See, for example, Mary Daly, *Beyond God the Father: Toward a Philosophy of Women's Liberation* (Boston: Beacon Press, 1973), and Riane Eisler, *Chalice and the Blade: Our History, Our Future* (San Francisco: Harper and Row, 1987); Sara Ruddick, *Maternal Politics: Toward A Politics of Peace* (Boston: Beacon Press, 1989.)

54. Umansky, *Motherhood Reconceived*, 103; Adrienne Rich, *Of Woman Born: Motherhood as Experience and Institution* (New York: W. W. Norton, 1976), 45, 28, 15; Adrienne Rich, *On Lies, Secrets, and Silence: Selected Prose, 1966–1978* (New York: W. W. Norton, 1979), 196.

55. Rich, *Of Woman Born*, 29, 286.

56. Quoted in Christine J. Allison, "The Making of a 'Bad' Mother: A Lesbian Mother and Her Daughters," in *"Bad" Mothers: The Politics of Blame in the Twentieth Century*, ed. Molly Ladd-Taylor and Lauri Umansky (New York: New York University Press, 1998), 252; Dani Rivers, "In the Best Interests of the Child: Lesbian and Gay Parenting Custody Cases, 196 1985," *Journal of Social History* 43, 4 (Summer 2010): 917, 922, 927.

57. Ellen Lewin, "Negotiating Lesbian Motherhood: The Dialectics of Resistance Accommodation," in *Mothering: Ideology, Experience, Agency*, ed. Evelyn Nakano (Grace Chang, and Linda Rennie Forcey (New York: Routledge, 1994), 334.

58. Rivers, "In the Best Interests," 924, 919; Ellen Lewin, "Negotiating Lesbian hood," 334. The film *Kramer versus Kramer* (1979) also gave popular expression t

of fathers' rights. For an insightful discussion of the film, see Douglas and Michaels, *The Mommy Myth*, 81–83.

59. Umansky, *Motherhood Reconceived*, 42.

60. Ibid., 42; Rivers, "In the Best Interests," 919, 927–928.

61. Ibid., 929; quoted in Lewin, "Negotiating Lesbian Motherhood," 334.

62. Quoted in Lewin, "Negotiating Lesbian Motherhood," 338; Geoffrey W. Bateman, "Children of LGBTQ Parents," *GLBTQ Social Sciences* (2007): 1.

63. See Allison, "The Making of a 'Bad' Mother," 252–256; "Lesbian and Gay Parenting," American Psychological Association. Available at: http://www.apa.org/pi/lgbt/resources/parenting.aspx.

64. Quoted in Kristen G. Esterberg, "Planned Parenthood: The Construction of Motherhood in Lesbian Mother Advice Books," in *Feminist Mothering*, ed. Andrea O'Reilly (Albany: State University of New York Press, 2008), 81; Bateman, "Children of LGBTQ Parents," 4.

65. See Umansky, *Motherhood Reconceived*, 77–102 passim.

66. Paula Gunn Allen, *The Sacred Hoop: Recovering the Feminine in American Indian Traditions* (Boston: Beacon Press, 1986), 44

67. M. Rivka Polatnick, "Diversity in Women's Liberation Ideology: How a Black and a White Group of the 1960s Viewed Motherhood," in *Mothers and Motherhood: Readings in American History*, ed. Rima Apple and Janet Golden (Columbus: Ohio State University Press, 1997), 393.

68. Quoted in Cherrie L. Moraga and Gloria E. Anzaldúa, eds., *This Bridge Called My Back: Writings by Radical Women of Color*, 3rd ed. (Berkeley, CA: Third Woman Press, 2002), 24.

69. Quoted in ibid., 25; Maya Angelou, *I Know Why the Caged Bird Sings* (New York: Random House, 1969).

70. Patricia Hill Collins, *Black Feminist Thought: Knowledge, Consciousness, and the Politics of Empowerment* (New York: Routledge, 1990, 2000), 188.

71. Ibid., 190, 191.

72. Martha F. Davis, "Welfare Rights and Women's Rights in the 1960s," in *Major Problems in American History Since 1945*, ed. Robert Griffith and Paula Baker (Boston: Houghton Mifflin, 2001), 393, 394.

73. Ibid., 396, 397, 399.

74. Johnnie Tillmon, "Welfare is a Women's Issue," *Ms.*, 1972. Available at: http://www.msmagazine.com/spring2002/tillmon.asp.

75. Quoted in Douglas and Michaels, *The Mommy Myth*, 41.

76. Beth Bailey, "Prescribing the Pill: The Coming of the Sexual Revolution in America's Heartland," in *Women's America: Refocusing the Past*, ed. Linda Kerber and Sherron de Hart, 6th ed. (New York: Oxford University Press, 2004), 560–568. For further detail, see Elaine Tyler May, *America and the Pill: A History of Promise, Peril, and Liberation* (New York: Basic Books, 2010); Leslie J. Reagan, *When Abortion Was a Crime: Women, Medicine, and the Law in the United States, 1867–1973* (Berkeley: University of California Press, 1997), 234.

77. Leslie Reagan, *Dangerous Pregnancies: Mothers, Disabilities, and Abortion in Modern America* (Berkeley: University of California Press, 2010); Reagan, *When Abortion*, 237.

78. Reagan, *When Abortion*, 220.

79. Christine Stansell, *The Feminist Promise: 1792 to the Present* (New York: The Modern Library, 2010), 324.

80. Laura Kaplan, "Beyond Safe and Legal: The Lessons of Jane," in *Abortion Wars: A Half Century of Struggle, 1950–2000*, ed. Rickie Solinger (Berkeley: University of California Press, 1998), 33–35, 38.

81. Reagan, *When Abortion*, 234.

82. Stansell, *The Feminist Promise*, 337, 327; Reagan, *When Abortion*, 234. See David P. Cline, *Creating Choice: A Community Responds to the Need for Abortion and Birth Control, 1961–1973* (New York: Palgrave Macmillan, 2006).

83. Quoted in Stansell, *The Feminist Promise*, 334.

84. Kaplan, "Beyond Safe and Legal," 33; Reagan, *When Abortion*, 236, 245, 246, 249; Stansell, *The Feminist Promise*, 337.

85. Rebecca M. Kluchin, *Fit to Be Tied: Sterilization and Reproductive Rights in America, 1850–1950* (New Brunswick, NJ: Rutgers University Press, 2009), 149.

86. Ibid., 84–85.

87. Loretta J. Ross, "African-American Women and Abortion," in *Abortion Wars*, ed. Solinger, 181; Angela Pattatucci-Aragon, "Hispanic/Latina Women and Reproductive Rights," in *Historical and Multicultural Encyclopedia of Women's Reproductive Rights in the United States*, ed. Judith A. Baer (Westport, CT: Greenwood Press, 2002), 105; Margaret M. Russell, "African-American Women and Reproductive Rights," in *Multicultural Encyclopedia*, ed. Baer, 25; Kluchin, *Fit to Be Tied*, 108.

88. Quoted in Kluchin, *Fit to Be Tied*, 75; Jennifer Nelson, *Women of Color and the Reproductive Rights Movement* (New York: New York University Press, 2003).

89. Quoted in Kristin Luker, *Abortion and the Politics of Motherhood* (Berkeley: University of California Press, 1984), 150.

90. For more information on important Supreme Court cases, see Reagan, *When Abortion Was a Crime*, 251. Most notable were *Webster v. Reproductive Health Services* (1989) and *Planned Parenthood v. Casey* (1992), in which the court upheld *Roe* but allowed for barring of state property for abortions.

91. Carole Joffe, Patricia Anderson, and Jody Steinauer, "The Crisis in Abortion Provision and Pro-Choice Medical Activism in the 1990s," in *Abortion Wars*, ed. Solinger, 321; Reagan, When Abortion, 252.

92. Rickie Solinger, "Chronology of Abortion Politics," in Abortion Wars, ed. Solinger, xiv.

93. Wolf, *Deliver Me from Pain*, 139, 151. See also Lynn Y. Weiner, "Reconstructing Motherhood: The La Leche League in Postwar America," in *Mothers and Motherhood: Readings in American History*, ed. Rima D. Apple and Janet Golden (Columbus: Ohio State University Press, 1997), 362–388; Solinger, "Chronology of Abortion Politics," xiv. Richard W. Wertz and Dorothy C. Wertz, *Lying-In: A History of Childbirth in America* (New Haven: Yale University Press, 1989), 195.

94. Quoted in Umansky, *Motherhood Reconceived*, 72; Wolf, *Deliver Me*, 144; Joan J. Mathews and Kathleen Zadak, "The Alternative Birth Movement in the United States: History and Current Status," in *Mothers and Motherhood*, ed. Apple and Golden, 283.

95. Matthews and Zadak, "The Alternative Birth Movement," 285, 286, 280–281; http://www.cdc.gov/nchs/data/databriefs/db84.pdf.

96. Quoted in Wolf, *Deliver Me*, 148.

97. Ibid., 146.

98. Ibid., 148, Wertz and Wertz, *Lying-In*, 263.

99. See Judith Walzer Leavitt, Make Room for Daddy: The Journey from Waiting Room to Birthing Room (Chapel Hill, N.C.: University of North Carolina Press, 2009); Christa Craven, *Pushing for Midwives: Homebirth Mothers and the Reproductive Rights Movement* (Philadelphia: Temple University Press, 2010), 52, 43, 49; quoted in Umanksy, *Motherhood Reconceived*, 72.

100. Jacqueline Wolf points out that the environmental movement's attention to toxics also led to greater attention to the issues of pain medication. The 1950s findings of Virginia

Apgar, who discovered that pain medication for birthing mothers crossed the placenta, were taken more seriously by the 1970s. Wolf, *Deliver Me*, 160.

101. Wertz and Wertz, *Lying-In*, 195; Ricki Lake, Executive Producer and Abby Epstein, Director, *The Business of Being Born* (2008); Wolf, *Deliver Me*, 178; Denise Grady, "Majority of Caesareans are Done Before Labor," *New York Times*, August 31, 2010. http://query .nytimes.com/gst/fullpage.html?res=9901EEDF113DF932A0575BC0A9669D8B63.

102. Wertz and Wertz, *Lying-In*, 178.

103. Wolf, *Deliver Me*, 165–171, 264, 217, 192; Wertz and Wertz, *Lying-In*, 271.

104. Wolf, *Deliver Me*, 192, 193; on the revival of advocacy for midwifery, see Craven, *Pushing for Midwives*; "Home Births in the United States, 1990–2009," http://www.cdc.gov/nchs/ data/databriefs/db84.pdf.

105. Wertz and Wertz, *Lying-In*, 178.

CHAPTER 10 — MOTHERS' CHANGING LIVES AND CONTINUOUS CAREGIVING

1. Susan J. Douglas and Meredith W. Michaels, *The Mommy Myth: The Idealization of Motherhood and How It Has Undermined All Women* (New York: Free Press, 2004), 232–233.

2. See ibid., 76–79.

3. See ibid., 76–79; Nancy Woloch, *Women and the American Experience*, 4th ed. (Boston: McGraw-Hill, 2006), 168.

4. Sara M. Evans, *Born for Liberty: A History of Women in America* (New York: Free Press, 1989, 1997), 302; Suzanne M. Bianchi, "Family Change and Time Allocation in American Families," *The ANNALS of the American Academy of Political and Social Science* 658, 21 (2011): 22.

5. Carl Haub, "The U.S. Recession and the Birth Rate," Population Reference Bureau, 2012. Available at: http://www.prb.org/articles/2009/usrecessionandbirthrate.aspx; Gail Collins, *When Everything Changed: The Amazing Journey of American Women From 1960 to the Present* (New York: Little, Brown and Company), 311; Bianchi, "Family Change and Time Allocation," 23; http://www.pewsocialtrends.org/2012/11/29/u-s-birth-rate-falls-to-a-record -low-decline-is-greatest-among-immigrants/.

6. http://www.guttmacher.org/pubs/journals/j.contraception.2012.08.012.pdf.

7. Collins, *When Everything Changed*, 271.

8. Woloch, *Women and the American Experience*, 4th ed., 563; "Employment Characteristics of Families," Bureau of Labor Statistics, April 26, 2012. Available at: http://www.bls .gov/news.release/famee.nr0.htm; "Contribution of Wives' Earnings to Family Income, 1970– 2006," Table 24, Bureau of Labor Statistics, December 2008. Available at: http://www.bls.gov/ cps/wlf-table24–2008.pdf.

9. In *Levy v. Louisiana* (1968), the Court extended equal protection rights of the Fourteenth Amendment to children born out of wedlock, and in *Gomez v. Perez* (1973), the Court ruled that such children could not be denied child support and inheritance. Steven Mintz, *Huck's Raft: A History of American Childhood* (Cambridge, MA: Harvard University Press, 2004). 333; Kathryn Edin and Maria Kefalas, *Promises I Can Keep: Why Poor Women Put Motherhood Before Marriage* (Berkeley: University of California Press, 2005, 2011), 2, x, vii; Jason DeParle and Sabrina Tavernise, "For Women Under 30, Most Births Occur Outside Marriage," *New York Times*, February 17, 2012.

10. http://www.cdc.gov/nchs/data/databriefs/db18.pdf; Edin and Kefalas, *Promises*, 197– 199; Stephanie A. Ventura, "Changing Patterns in Nonmarital Childbearing in the U.S.," NCHS Data Brief No. 18, May 2009. Available at: http://www.cdc.gov/nchs/data/databriefs/ db18.pdf.

11. DeParle and Tavernise, "For Women Under 30"; Edin and Kefalas, *Promises*, 208.

12. Edin and Kefalas, *Promises*, 175, 205.

13. Ibid., 200; Stephanie Coontz, *The Way We Never Were: American Families and the Nostalgia Trap* (New York: Basic Books, 1992, 2000), 186.

14. Edin and Kefalas, *Promises*, 213.

15. For good discussion, see Coontz, *The Way We Never Were*, 221–225, and Mintz, *Huck's Raft*, 341–342; Louise B. Silverstein and Carl F. Auerbach, "Deconstructing the Essential Father," *American Psychologist* 54, 6 (1999): 397–407.

16. Ann Fessler, *The Girls Who Went Away: The Hidden History of Women Who Surrendered Children for Adoption in the Decades Before Roe v. Wade* (New York: Penguin, 2006).

17. Barbara Melosh, *Strangers and Kin: The American Way of Adoption* (Cambridge, MA: Harvard University Press, 2002), 174–175, 159.

18. Ibid., 175, 177, 166. See also Barbara Katz Rothman, *Weaving a Family: Untangling Race and Adoption* (Boston: Beacon Press, 2005.)

19. See Renee Romano, "'Immoral Conduct': White Women, Racial Transgressions, and Custody Disputes," in *"Bad" Mothers: The Politics of Blame in Twentieth-Century America*, ed. Molly Ladd-Taylor and Lauri Umansky (New York: New York University Press, 1998), 230–251.

20. Evans, *Born for* Liberty, 311. See Pierette Hondagneu-Sotelo and Ernestine Avila, "'I'm Here, But I'm There': The Meanings of Latina Transnational Motherhood," *Gender and Society* 11, 5 (October 1997): 548–571. See also Barbara Ehrenreich and Arlie Russell Hochschild, *Global Woman: Nannies, Maids, and Sex Workers in the New Economy* (New York: Henry Holt and Company, 2002).

21. Dorothy E. Roberts, "Prison, Foster Care, and the Systematic Punishment of Black Mothers," *UCLA Law Review* 59, 6 (August 2012):1474–1500.

22. http://www.sentencingproject.org/doc/publications/womenincj_total.pdf; Roberts, "Prison, Foster Care."

23. Phyllis Schlafley, *The Power of the Positive Woman*, excerpted in *Second to None: A Documentary History of American Women*, Vol. 2: *From 1865 to the Present*, ed. Ruth Barnes Moynihan, Cynthia Russett, and Lauri Crumpacker (Lincoln: University of Nebraska Press, 1993), 286, 287.

24. Quoted in Douglas and Michaels, *The Mommy Myth*, 70–71.

25. Ibid., 71–73.

26. For example, in 1958 children of full-time employed mothers were typically cared for at home; 56.6 percent of children of full-time mothers met that profile, most often being cared for by a relative besides the father. By 1982, the most common arrangement was care in another person's home, for 46.3 percent of children, with just a little over half of those children being cared for by nonrelatives. Care for children of full-time working mothers in child care centers rose in the same period from 4.5 percent to 19.9 percent. Sonya Michel, *Children's Interests/Mothers' Rights The Shaping of America's Child Care Policy* (New Haven: Yale University Press, 1999), 258.

27. For further discussion, see Michel, *Children's Interests/Mothers' Rights*, 255–274 passim; Collins, *When Everything Changed*, 304–305; Douglas and Michaels, *The Mommy Myth*, 86–87.

28. Douglas and Michaels, *The Mommy Myth*, 204.

29. Arguably, they still do. See, for example, the debate about Democratic strategist Hilary Rosen's comment on Ann Romney's lack of employment outside the home in *USA Today:* http://www.usatoday.com/news/opinion/forum/story/2012–04–17/mom-wars-hilary-rosen -ann-romney-work-home/54357842/1; quoted in Sharon Hays, *The Cultural Contradictions of Motherhood* (New Haven: Yale University Press, 1996), 140.

30. Amy Walter and Z. Byron Wolf, "Working Moms, First Ladies, and Recalling Hillary Clinton's 'Baking Cookies' Comment," ABC News, April 12, 2012. Available at: http://abcnews.go.com/blogs/politics/2012/04/working-moms-first-ladies-and-recalling-hillary-clintons-cookies/.

31. Quoted in Linda M. Blum, *At the Breast: Ideologies of Breastfeeding and Motherhood in the United States* (Boston: Beacon Press, 1999), 77–78.

32. Douglas and Michaels, *The Mommy Myth*, 96, 102.

33. Ibid., 93, 103.

34. Ibid., 231, 8–9, 3.

35. 2011 *Working Mother* Best Companies, Available at: http://www.workingmother.com/best-company-list/116542; Jillian M. Duquaine-Watson, "All You Need Is Love: Representations of Maternal Emotion in *Working Mother* Magazine, 1995–1999," in *Mother Matters: Motherhood as Discourse and Practice*, ed. Andrea O'Reilly (Toronto: Association for Research on Mothering, 2004), 128.

36. See Hays, *Cultural Contradictions;* Duquaine-Watson, "All You Need Is Love," 128, 131, 125.

37. Hays, *Cultural Contradictions*, 57, 51–70 passim.

38. Douglas and Michaels, *The Mommy Myth*, 320, 319.

39. Jodi Vandenberg-Daves, "Mama Bear as Domestic Micro Manager: The Evolution of Cultural Ideas of Motherhood in the Berenstain Bears Book Series, 1960–2000," in *Mother Matters*, ed. O'Reilly, 111–124; Douglas and Michaels, *The Mommy Myth*, 205.

40. Douglas and Michaels, *The Mommy Myth*, 204, 207–208. Schwartz did not herself coin the phrase "mommy track."

41. Ibid., 206; Collins, *When Everything Changed*, 362–366. See Bernie D. Jones, ed., *Women Who Opt Out: The Debate Over Working Mothers and Work-Family Balance* (New York: New York University Press, 2012).

42. See Ellen Bravo, *Taking On the Big Boys: Or Why Feminism Is Good for Families, Business, and the Nation* (New York: The Feminist Press, 2007), 149–173; Pew Research Center, August 19, 2013. Available at: http://www.pewresearch.org/fact-tank/2013/08/19/mothers-and-work-whats-ideal/

43. Patricia Schroeder, *Congressional Record*, 101st Congress, May 8, 1990, reprinted in *Second to None*, ed. Moynihan et al., 352.

44. Bravo, *Taking On the Big Boys*, 47; "FMLA: Fact and Statistics," American Association of University Women. Available at: http://www.aauw.org/act/laf/library/fmlastatistics.cfm.

45. Bravo, *Taking On the Big Boys*, 52, 48, 51; "Failing Its Families: Lack of Paid Leave and Work-Family Supports in the US," Human Rights Watch, February 23, 2011. Available at: http://www.hrw.org/reports/2011/02/23/failing-its-families-0; Liz Watson and Jennifer E. Swanberg, "Flexible Workplace Solutions for Low-Wage Workers: A Framework for a National Conversation," Workplace Flexibility, Georgetown Law, and the Institute for Workplace Innovation, May 2011. Available at: http://www.uky.edu/Centers/iwin/LWPolicyFinal.pdf.

46. Bravo, *Taking On the Big Boys*, 58; "A Workable Balance: Report to Congress on Family and Medical Leave Policies." Available at: http://www.dol.gov/whd/fmla/chapter1.htm.

47. "A Workable Balance." "FMLA: Fact and Statistics," American Association of University Women. Available at: http://www.aauw.org/act/laf/library/fmlastatistics.cfm.

48. Ann Crittenden, *The Price of Motherhood: Why the Most Important Job in the World Is Still the Least Valued* (New York: Henry Holt and Company, 2001), 95, 96–97, 103–109 passim.

49. Stephanie Coontz, "Why Gender Equality Stalled," *New York Times*, Feb. 16, 2013.

50. Quoted in Carol Evans, *This Is How We Do It: The Working Mothers' Manifesto* (New York: Hudson Street Press, 2006), 18; see Laurel A. McNall, Jessica M. Nicklin, and Aline D. Masuda, "A Meta-Analytic Review of the Consequences Associated with Work-Family enrichment," *Journal of Business Psychology* 25 (2010): 381–396; http://www/nytimes.com/2013/02/17/opinion/sunday/why-gender-equality-stalled.html?pagewanted=all&_r=0.

51. Quoted in Hays, *Cultural Contradictions*, 144.

52. Arlie Hochschild, *The Second Shift* (New York: Penguin Books, 1989, 2003); quoted in Hays, *Cultural Contradictions*, 112; Bianchi, "Family Change and time Allocations"; Evans, *This Is How*, 31–32.

53. Bianchi, "Family Change and Time Allocation," 26, 28.

54. Mintz, *Huck's Raft*, 347, 348.

55. Edin and Kefalas, *Promises*, 154–155.

56. Bianchi, "Family Change and Time Allocation," 28.

57. Bravo, *Taking On the Big Boys*, 211–212, Evans, *This Is How*, 183; Karen V. Hansen, *Not-So-Nuclear Families: Class, Gender, and Networks of Care* (New Brunswick, NJ: Rutgers University Press, 2005).

58. Hays, *Cultural Contradictions*, 80, 101, 104–107.

59. Quoted in Scott Coltrane, *Family Man: Fatherhood, Housework, and Gender Equity* (New York: Oxford University Press, 1996), 57, 67; Hansen, *Not-So-Nuclear Families*, 21.

60. Quoted in Bravo, *Taking On the Big Boys*, 218, 219; Evans, *This Is How*, 183; quoted in Lillian B. Rubin, *Worlds of Pain: Life in the Working-Class Family* (New York: Basic Books, 1976, 1992), 27.

61. Kim Parker, "The Harried Life of the Working Mother," Pew Research Center Publications, October 1, 2009. Available at: http://pewresearch.org/pubs/1360/working-women-conflicted-but-few-favor-return-to-traditional-roles. For a cogent discussion of Dr. Laura Schlessinger, see Douglas and Michaels, *The Mommy Myth*, 308–311.

62. Quoted in Hays, *Cultural Contradictions*, 104, 109; quoted in Edean and Kefalas, *Promises*, 11, 175.

63. Quoted in Hays, *Cultural Contradictions*, 87; Edin and Kefalas, *Promises*, 148, 150.

64. Edin and Kefalas, *Promises*, 139, 9.

65. Ibid., 146, 143–162 passim.

66. Hays, *Cultural Contradictions*, 112–114.

67. Ibid., 86, 91.

68. Ibid., 137, 147.

69. Quoted in Margaret K. Nelson, "Family Day Care Providers: Dilemmas of Daily Practice," in *Mothering: Ideology, Experience, Agency*, ed. Evelyn Nakano Glenn, Grace Chang, and Linda Rennie Forcey (New York: Routledge, 1994), 192. See also Jennifer A. Butler and Daniel P. Modaff, "When Work Is Home: Agency, Structure, and Contradictions," *Management Communication Quarterly* 20 (August 2008). There were and are, of course, additional class tensions between some women who care for the children of those who are more financially secure than they are.

70. Douglas, *The Mommy Myth*, 197.

71. See Bree Kessler, "Recruiting Wombs: Surrogates as the New Security Moms," *Women's Studies Quarterly* 37, 1/2, Technologies (Spring-Summer 2009): 167–182; Rafia Zakaria, "The Cheapest Womb: India's Surrogate Mothers," *Ms.* Blog, June 25, 2010. Available at: http://msmagazine.com/blog/blog/2010/06/25/the-cheapest-womb-indias-surrogate-mothers.

72. See Karen Zivi, "Contesting Motherhood in the Age of AIDS: Maternal Ideology in the Debate Over Mandatory HIV Testing," *Feminist Studies* 31, 2 (Summer 2005): 347–374; quoted in Dorothy E. Roberts, "Punishing Drug Addicts with Babies: Women of Color, Equality, and the Right of Privacy," in *Abortion Wars: A Half Century of Struggle, 1950–2000*, ed. Rickie Solinger (Berkeley: University of California Press, 1998), 134.

73. Quoted in Ada Calhoun, "The Criminalization of Bad Mothers," *New York Times*, April 25, 2012.

74. Ibid.

75. Faye D. Ginsburg, *Contested Lives: The Abortion Debate in an American Community* (Berkeley: University of California Press, 1989), 104; R. A. Moore, et al., "Use of Diagnostic

Imaging in Fetal Monitoring Devices in the Care of Pregnant Women," *Public Health Reports* 105, 5 (September/October 1990): 471–475. Available at: http://www.ncbi.nlm.nih.gov/pmc/articles/PMC1580112/; Blum, *At the Breast*, 60.

76. The Guttmacher Institute summarized the state of state laws as of September 2013 in the following report; Guttmacher Institute, "State Policies in Brief as of September 1, 2013: An Overview of Abortion Laws," Available at: http://www.guttmacher.org/statecenter/spibs/spib_OAL.pdf; Calhoun, "The Criminalization of Bad Mothers"; John M. Glionna, "Arizona Passes Law Restricting Abortion," *Los Angeles Times*, April 13, 2012; Manny Fernandez, "Abortion Restrictions Become Law in Texas, but Opponents Will Press Fight," *New York Times*, July 18, 2013, available at: http://www.nytimes.com/2013/07/19/us/perry-signs-texas-abortion-restrictions-into-law.html; Juliet Eilperin,"Abortion limits at state level return issue to the national stage," *Washington Post*, July 5, 2013, Available at: http://www.washingtonpost.com/politics/abortion-limits-at-state-level-return-issue-to-the-national-stage/2013/07/05/f86dd76c-e3f1–11e2-aef3–339619eab080_story.html.

77. Erin P. Davenport, "Court-Ordered Cesarean Sections: Why Courts Should Not Be Allowed to Use a Balancing Test," *Duke Journal of Gender Law and Policy* 18, 79 (2010): 83–85, 96.

78. See, for example, Marsha Saxton, "Disability Rights and Selective Abortion," in *Abortion Wars*, ed. Solinger, 374–393, and Gail Landsman, "'Too Bad You Got a Lemon': Peter Singer, Mothers of Children with Disabilities, and the Critique of Consumer Culture," in *Consuming Motherhood*, ed. Janelle S. Taylor, Linda L. Layne, and Danielle F. Wozniak (New Brunswick, NJ: Rutgers University Press, 2004), 100–121; Cynthia Lewiecki-Wilson, "Uneasy Subjects: Disability, Feminism, and Abortion," in *Disability and Mothering: Liminal Spaces of Embodied Knowledge*, ed. Cynthia Lewiecki-Wilson and Jen Cellio (Syracuse, NY: Syracuse University Press, 2011), 63–80.

79. Hays, *Cultural Contradictions;* quoted in Ginsburg, *Contested Lives*, 190.

80. Quoted in Ginsburg, *Contested Lives*, 154.

81. Quoted in ibid., 185, 188

82. Guttmacher Institute, "Facts on Induced Abortion in the United States," July 2013. Available at: http://www.guttmacher.org/pubs/fb_induced_abortion.html; Ginsburg, *Contested Lives*, 151, 153.

83. Quoted in Ginsburg, *Contested Lives*, 151, 101; Gallup, "Abortion," Sept. 8, 2013, available at: http://www.gallup.com/poll/1576/abortion.aspx

84. Blum, *At the Breast*, 45.

85. Quoted in ibid., 73, 138, 169, 164.

86. Quoted in ibid., 118.

87. Quoted in ibid., 110, 112, 113; Ginsburg, *Contested Lives*, 191.

88. Blum, *At the Breast*, 83, 123.

89. Ibid., 63, 71, 93, 92–96.

90. Ibid., 48, 47, 53.

CONCLUSION

1. Quoted in Paul A. Lombardo, *Three Generations, No Imbeciles: Eugenics, the Supreme Court, and Buck v. Bell* (Baltimore: Johns Hopkins University Press, 2008), 169; *Muller v. Oregon*, 208 U.S. 412 (1908).

2. Joan Blades and Kristin Rowe-Finkbeiner, *The Motherhood Manifesto: What America's Moms Want—and What to Do About It* (New York: Nation Books, 2006); Andrea O'Reilly, ed., *The Twenty-First Century Motherhood Movement: Mothers Speak Out on Why We Need to Change the World and How to Do It* (Toronto: Demeter Press, 2011).

3. Ann Crittenden, *If You've Raised Kids, You Can Manage Anything* (New York: Gotham Books, 2004), 1.

4. Rima D. Apple, *Perfect Motherhood: Science and Childrearing in America* (New Brunswick, NJ: Rutgers University Press, 2006), 139, 140, 143, 146–149 passim; Jessica Nathanson and Laura Camille Tuley, eds., *Mother Knows Best: Talking Back to the Experts* (Toronto: Demeter Press, 2009).

5. For a thoughtful discussion on this topic, including the historical role of mother blame, see Judith Warner, *We've Got Issues: Children and Parents in the Age of Medication* (New York: Riverhead Books, 2010).

Index

Abel, Emily, 119

abolitionism, 3, 28, 33, 34, 38, 44, 45–46. *See also* antislavery movement; slavery

abortificants, 58, 59, 60, 65

abortion, 50, 56, 246, 273–276, 277, 279; access to, 2, 64, 238, 242, 248, 249; activism, 238–240; advice about, 54; attacks on rights to, 272, 273; and birth control, 136–138; and breastfeeding, 278; complications from, 204–205; and Comstock Law, 62; criminalization of, 58; death from, 133; debates over, 61–62, 247, 281, 285; and decline in birth rate, 66; decriminalization of, 225; definitions of, 58–59, 62; emotional consequences of, 276; and equal protection, 239; and federal funding, 242; and feminism, 205; financial means for, 65; frequency of, 60, 275; funding for, 238; for health reasons, 65; and hospitals, 238, 242; and Jane collective, 239, 240; and Knowlton, 54; late-term, 272; and law, 58, 62, 65, 72, 130, 137, 138, 202–203, 205, 211, 225, 238–240, 272, 273; and marriage, 137, 203; and maternal health, 274; and medicalized body, 55; methods for, 60; mid-nineteenth-century controversy over, 58–63, 65–66, 67; and money, 138; and morality, 133; outside hospital structures, 204; and physicians, 58, 60–63, 72, 137–138, 149, 202, 203, 205, 211, 238, 239, 242; in postwar period, 202–205; and pregnancy outside of marriage, 195; public opinion about, 149, 202–205, 239, 276; and quickening, 58; and rape, 204, 238, 239, 273; rates of, 60, 65, 275; restrictions on, 3, 242, 273; and right to privacy, 239; risks of, 58, 133, 136, 204, 237; and Sanger, 133, 136; secrecy about, 204; self-induced, 137, 138; and sterilization, 145, 241; as termination of life, 58; therapeutic, 138; and unwed mothers, 200, 203, 252; as women's choice, 211; women's opposition to, 241–242. *See also* pregnancy

abortion clinics, 202–203, 242, 273

Adams, Abigail, 17, 18, 49

Adams, John, 17

Addams, Jane, 105, 109, 121, 126

adolescence, 2, 94

adoption, 176, 196–199, 201, 205, 207–209, 233, 252, 253

Adoption and Safe Families Act of 1997, 253

advertising, 79, 82, 84, 93, 95, 99, 129, 135–136, 151

advice, 4, 101; and changing childhood norms, 100; and childhood development, 99; and Children's Bureau, 87; female traditions of, 79; medical and psychological, 79; from medical experts, 188; and mental health, 94, 95; physician-authored, 81; scientific, 81, 101–102; and Spock, 182–183, 184–185, 188. *See also* experts

African American church, 214

African Americans, 31, 48, 117–118, 150, 153; and abortion, 135; activism of, 41–42, 43, 126–127, 161, 162; and adoption, 208; in agricultural work, 40–41, 45, 119; and birth control, 135; birth rates among, 49, 92; and breastfeeding, 276–277; and childbirth, 55–57; and child care, 127; and Child Study Association, 92; and civil rights, 43, 155,

About the Author

Jodi Vandenberg-Daves is a historian and professor of Women's, Gender, and Sexuality Studies at the University of Wisconsin–La Crosse. She is editor and coauthor of *Making History: A Guide to Historical Research Through the National History Day Program*. Her work has appeared in the *Journal of American History*, *Women's Studies Quarterly*, *International Labor and Working-Class History*, the *Journal of the Association for Research on Mothering*, and *History of Education*.